BTEC Level 3 National Sport
Performance & Excellence

Second Edition

endorsed by
edexcel

BTEC Level 3 National Sport
Performance & Excellence

Second Edition

Jennifer Stafford-Brown
and Simon Rea

DYNAMIC LEARNING

HODDER EDUCATION

Orders: please contact Bookpoint Ltd, 130 Milton Park, Abingdon, Oxon OX14 4SB. Telephone: (44) 01235 827720. Fax: (44) 01235 400454. Lines are open from 9.00 – 5.00, Monday to Saturday, with a 24-hour message answering service. You can also order through our website www.hoddereducation.co.uk.

British Library Cataloguing in Publication Data
A catalogue record for this title is available from the British Library

ISBN: 978 1 444 112 009

First Published 2010
Impression number   10 9 8 7 6 5 4 3 2 1
Year   2016 2015 2014 2013 2012 2011 2010

Copyright © 2010 Jennifer Stafford-Brown, Simon Rea

Cover photo © Action Plus Sports Images/Alamy
Typeset by Fakenham Photosetting, Fakenham, Norfolk

Printed in Italy

Contents

If you see this icon next to a unit, you will be able to access it by logging onto Dynamic Learning Student Online.

Acknowledgements

I would like to thank a number of people who have provided me with help in various different ways in researching and writing this textbook.

First of all, my thanks go out to my husband Matt and children Ellie and Alex for their patience and encouragement throughout the writing process, and to my parents, Ann and Brian, for all of their support and help over the years.

A big 'thank you!' to my friend and co-author, Simon, for all of his hard work, expertise and enthusiasm.

I would also like to thank a number of subject specialists including Paul Butler, David Pryce and Ian Gittens, for their contributions in writing or updating two units available within this textbook (**Unit 12** *Current Issues in Sport* and **Unit 24** *Physical Education & the Care of Young Children & Young People*) and a unit that is available via Dynamic Learning—**Unit 20** *Talent Identification and Development in Sport*.

Finally, I would also like to thank Lavinia Porter and Alison Walters and all of the people who have helped with the publication of this text book.

JENNIFER STAFFORD-BROWN

Thank you to all the people who made these books possible: Lavinia Porter and Alison Walters at Hodder; my co-author, Jenny, for her continual support and enthusiasm; and to the additional authors for sharing their expertise.

Thank you to my parents, Tony and Pam, the Sewells and the Samways, for their interest, support and understanding and continuing the family's love of sport.

Above all, to Tanya, who gave me the time and space to get the writing done and who brought love, fun and happiness to my life.

SIMON REA

The authors and publishers wish to thank the following for their permission to reproduce their images:

Unit 1 introduction	Warren Little/Getty Images
1.29	David Rogers/Getty Images
Unit 2 introduction	Wolf/Corbis
2.6	PCN Photography/Corbis
2.7	Ahmad Yusni/AFP/Getty Images
2.8	Colin Hawkins/Photolibrary Group
Unit 3 introduction	Aflo Photo Agency/Photolibrary Group
3.4	Hamish Blair/Getty Images
3.6	© imagebroker/Alamy
3.7	STEVE ALLEN/SCIENCE PHOTOLIBRARY
Unit 4 introduction	Vincent Thian/AP Photo/Press Association Images
4.3	Christof Koepsel/Bongarts/Getty Images
Unit 5 introduction	Agence Zoom/Digital Vision/Getty Images
5.1	Clive Brunskill/Getty Images
Unit 7 introduction	Comstock Images/Getty Images
7.5	Glyn Kirk/Action Plus
7.7	© Shelley Gazin/The Image Works/www.topfoto.co.uk

Unit 8 introduction	Tom Dulat/Getty Images
8.1	Peter Spurrier/Action Plus
8.2	ANTONY DICKSON/AFP/Getty Images
8.3	Neil Tingle/Action Plus
8.4	Heinz Kluetmeier/Sports Illustrated/Getty Images
Unit 11 introduction	© Comstock/Corbis
11.3	Philip Wilkins/Photolibrary Group
11.4	© Comstock Select/Corbis
11.5	Photolibrary.com
11.6	© Maximilian Stock Ltd/Photolibrary Group
11.11	Neil Tingle/Action Plus
11.15	Marcos Welsh/age fotostock/Photolibrary Group
Unit 12 introduction	PATRICK KOVARIK/AFP/Getty Images
Unit 14 introduction	© Roy Morsch/Corbis
14.1	ARTHUR GLAUBERMAN/SCIENCE PHOTOLIBRARY
14.3	MARTIN M. ROTKER/SCIENCE PHOTOLIBRARY
14.4	CNRI/SCIENCE PHOTOLIBRARY
14.6	iStockPhotos.com/Oleg Kozlov
Unit 15 introduction	RAUL ARBOL EDA/AFP/Getty Images
15.11	Glyn Kirk/Action Plus
Unit 17 introduction	Claudio Villa/Getty Images
Unit 18 introduction	Agence Zoom/Digital Vision/Getty Images
18.11	Action Images/Nick Potts
18.12	© Pete Leonard/Corbis
18.13	ALEX BARTEL/SCIENCE PHOTOLIBRARY
18.14	DR M. A. ANSARY/SCIENCE PHOTOLIBRARY
Unit 19 introduction	Sipa Press/Rex Features
Unit 20 introduction	John Giustina/Iconica/Getty Images
20.1	Harry How/Getty Images
20.2	© Pavel Losevsky – Fotolia.com
20.3 (a - ectomarph)	Mike Hewitt/Action Plus
20.3 (b - mesomarph)	Glyn Kirk/Action Plus
20.3 (c - endomarph)	Glyn Kirk/Action Plus
Unit 24 introduction	Sherman Ken/Photolibrary Group
24.1	© ACE STOCK LIMITED/Alamy
24.3	Donna Day/Workbook Stock/Getty Images
Unit 41 introduction	Chris Speedie/Stone/Getty Images

Introduction

BTEC National Sport (Performance & Excellence) for the Edexcel examination boards is a subject that helps to prepare you for work in the sports industry or for higher education within the fields of sport science and sport.

BTEC Level 3 National Sport: Performance & Excellence Second Edition is a comprehensive textbook that covers all mandatory units in the BTEC National Sport (Performance & Excellence) qualifications that include:

- National Certificate in Sport
- National Subsidiary Diploma in Sport
- National Diploma in Sport (Performance and Excellence)
- National Extended Diploma in Sport (Performance and Excellence)

To ensure that you are following the correct pathway for your chosen qualification, please see the table in 'Pathways for BTEC National Sport (Performance and Excellence) Qualifications'.

As well as all mandatory units, *BTEC Level 3 National Sport: Performance & Excellence Second Edition* contains many of the more popular optional units that you can take. Some optional units have been provided as PDFs for you to read online or download via Dynamic Learning. For details of these, look for the Dynamic Learning icon on the Contents page. For details about Dynamic Learning and how to access these online units, see the inside front cover of this book.

The BTEC National Sports and BTEC National Sport (Development, Coaching and Fitness) qualifications are all assessed through coursework. You will be given assignments that cover all of the grading criteria for each unit that you are studying. *BTEC Level 3 National Sport: Performance & Excellence Second Edition* will help to show you where you can find the information related to the grading criteria that you are working on, which will help to ensure that you are including the appropriate subject content in your coursework.

Success in this qualification is a combination of your teacher's expertise, your own motivation and ability as a student, and accessibility to the appropriate resources–including a relevant textbook! Written by senior external verifiers and experienced BTEC National Sport teachers, *BTEC Level 3 National Sport: Performance & Excellence Second Edition* is highly relevant to your qualification and provides you with resources that will not only support and help you prepare for your assessments, but will also stretch and challenge you.

Within *BTEC Level 3 National Sport: Performance & Excellence Second Edition* you will find that each unit offers a wide range of learning resources, including:

- **Activities** related to each of the grading criteria to help you to practice assessment activities for your coursework. Each activity has a suggested time-frame so that you will have an idea of how long you need to spend on each.
- **Clear signposting throughout:** each section is clearly signposted with the relevant grading criteria
- **Quick quizzes:** at the end of each learning outcome are a number of short questions to help consolidate your knowledge before you move on to the next section.
- **Learning goals** are placed at the start of each unit to keep you on track with the requirements of the Edexcel BTEC National Sport and Sport (Development, Coaching and Fitness)
- **Definition boxes** are provided throughout, giving you clear definitions of complex physiological and technical phrases without you having to look these up in a separate glossary section
- **Useful websites** are suggested at the end of each unit so that you can access these directly to top up your knowledge in important areas of unit content
- Lots of sports photographs and clear illustrations to help bring your learning to life.

BTEC Level 3 National Sport: Performance & Excellence Second Edition is written in a clear, highly readable way that will help you to understand and learn about Sport and prepare you and provide information for your assessments in this course.

Pathways for BTEC National Sport (Performance & Excellence) Qualifications

To ensure that you are following the correct pathway for the **Certificate**, **Subsidiary Diploma** or **Diploma** in BTEC Sport (Performance & Excellence), please see the table below.

Unit	Certificate	Subsidiary Diploma	Diploma
1 Principles of Anatomy & Physiology in Sport	✓	✓	✓
2 The Physiology of Fitness	✓	✓	✓
3 Assessing Risk in Sport	✓	✓	✓
		Choose either Unit 7 or Unit 29 plus a selection of the remaining units below	
4 Fitness Training & Programming		✓	✓
7 Fitness Testing for Sport & Exercise	✓	✓	✓
11 Sports Nutrition		✓	✓
17 Psychology for Sports Performance		✓	✓
27 Technical & Tactical Skills in Sport		✓	✓
28 The Athlete's Lifestyle		✓	✓
5 Sports Coaching		✓	✓
6 Sports Development		✓	
8 Practical Team Sports		✓	✓
9 Practical Individual		✓	
10 Outdoor and Adventurous Activities		✓	
12 Current Issues in Sport		✓	✓
13 Leadership in Sport		✓	
14 Exercise, Health & Lifestyle		✓	
15 Instructing Physical Activity & Exercise		✓	✓
18 Sports Injuries			✓
19 Analysis of Sports Performance			✓
20 Talent Identification & Development of Sport			✓

Unit	Certificate	Subsidiary Diploma	Diploma
21 Sport & Exercise Massage			✓
22 Rules, Regulation & Officiating in Sport			✓
23 Organising Sports Events			
24 Physical Education & the Care of Children & Young People		✓	
25 Sport as a Business			
26 Work Experience in Sport		✓	✓
28 The Athlete's Lifestyle			
29 Principles and Practices in Outdoor Adventure	✓	✓	
39 Sports Facilities & Operational Management		✓	✓
41 Profiling Sports Performance			✓
42 Research Investigation in Sport & Exercise Sciences			✓
43 Laboratory & Experimental Methods in Sport & Exercise Sciences			✓

To ensure that you are following the correct pathway for the **Extended Diploma** please use the table below.

Unit	Extended Diploma
1 Principles of Anatomy & Physiology in Sport	✓
2 The Physiology of Fitness	✓
3 Assessing Risk in Sport	✓
4 Fitness Training & Programming	✓
7 Fitness Testing for Sport & Exercise	✓
11 Sports Nutrition	✓
17 Psychology for Sports Performance	✓
27 Technical & Tactical Skills for Sport	✓
28 The Athlete's Lifestyle	✓
	Choose 10 optional units of those units below.
5 Sports Coaching	✓
8 Practical Team Sports	✓
10 Outdoor & Adventurous Activities	
12 Current Issues in Sport	✓
13 Leadership in Sport	

Unit	Extended Diploma
14 Exercise, Health & Lifestyle	✓
15 Instructing Physical Activity & Exercise	✓
18 Sports Injuries	✓
19 Analysis of Sports Performance	✓
20 Talent Identification & Development of Sport	✓
21 Sport & Exercise Massage	✓
22 Rules, Regulation & Officiating in Sport	✓
23 Organising Sports Events	✓
24 Physical Education & the Care of Children & Young People	✓
25 Sport as a Business	✓
26 Work Experience in Sport	✓
29 Principles and Practices in Outdoor Adventure	
39 Sports Facilities & Operational Management	✓
41 Profiling Sports Performance	✓
42 Research Investigation in Sport & Exercise Sciences	✓
43 Laboratory & Experimental Methods in Sport & Exercise Sciences	✓

1: Principles of Anatomy & Physiology in Sport

1.1 Introduction

In order for us to take part in sport and exercise, our body has to be able to produce energy and movement. Our body is made up of many different systems that work together to allow us to take part in physical activity, such as sprinting over a short distance or running continually for many miles.

This unit explores the structure and function of the main body systems involved in human movement – these include the skeletal, the muscular, the cardiovascular, the respiratory and the energy systems. These systems are all very different; however, they all work together to produce movement.

By the end of this unit you should know the:

● structure and function of the skeletal system
● structure and function of the muscular system
● structure and function of the cardiovascular system
● structure and function of the respiratory system
● different types of energy systems.

Assessment and grading criteria		
To achieve a PASS grade the evidence must show that the learner is able to:	To achieve a MERIT grade the evidence must show that, in addition to the pass criteria, the learner is able to:	To achieve a DISTINCTION grade the evidence must show that, in addition to the pass and merit criteria, the learner is able to:
P1 describe the structure and function of the skeletal system		
P2 describe the different classifications of joints		
P3 identify the location of the major muscles in the human body		
P4 describe the function of the muscular system and the different fibre types	**M1** explain the function of the muscular system and the different fibre types	**D1** analyse the function of the muscular system and the different fibre types
P5 describe the structure and function of the cardiovascular system	**M2** explain the function of the cardiovascular system	
P6 describe the structure and function of the respiratory system	**M3** explain the function of the respiratory system	
P7 describe the three different energy systems and their use in sport and exercise activities.	**M4** explain the three different energy systems and their use in sport and exercise activities.	**D2** analyse the three different energy systems and their use in sport and exercise activities.

1.2 The Structure and Function of the Skeletal System

The skeleton is the central structure of the body and provides the framework for all the soft tissue to attach to, giving the body its defined shape. The skeleton is made up of bones, joints and cartilage and enables us to perform simple and complex movements such as walking and running.

Axial and Appendicular Skeleton

The axial skeleton (Fig 1.1) is the central core of the body or its axis. It consists of the skull, the vertebrae, the sternum and the ribs. It provides the core that the limbs hang from.

The appendicular skeleton (Fig 1.2) comprises the parts hanging off the axial skeleton. It consists of the shoulder girdle (scapula and clavicle), the pelvic girdle, upper and lower limbs.

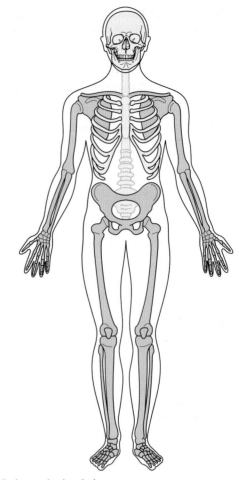

Fig 1.2 Appendicular skeleton

Types of Bone

The bones of the body fall into five general categories based on their shape.

- Long
- Short
- Flat
- Irregular
- Sesamoid.

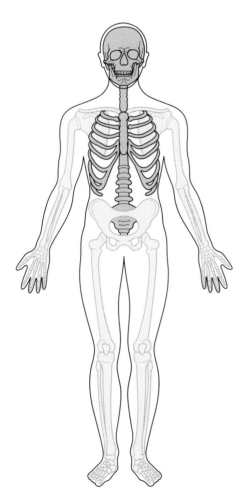

Fig 1.1 Axial skeleton

Type of bone	Example in body	Description
Long	Femur, tibia, humerus	Cylindrical in shape and found in the limbs. Main function is to act as a lever
Short	Carpals, calcaneum	Small and compact, often equal in length and width. Designed for strength and weight bearing
Flat	Sternum, cranium, pelvis	Protection for the internal organs of the body
Irregular bones	Vertebrae, face	Complex individual shapes. Variety of functions, including protection and muscle attachment
Sesamoid	Patella	Found in a tendon. Eases joint movement and resists friction and compression

Table 1.1 Different types of joint

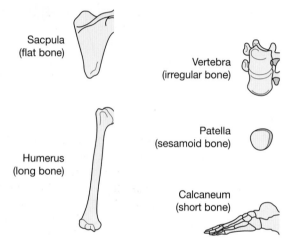

Sacpula (flat bone)

Vertebra (irregular bone)

Patella (sesamoid bone)

Humerus (long bone)

Calcaneum (short bone)

Fig 1.3 Five types of bone

Major Bones of the Body

The skeleton consists of 206 bones, over half of which are in the upper and lower limbs. Babies are born with around 300 bones and over time these fuse together to reduce the number.

Cranium

The cranium consists of eight bones fused together that act to protect your brain. There are 14 other facial bones, which form the face and jaw.

Sternum

This is the flat bone in the middle of the chest that is shaped like a dagger. It protects the heart and gives an attachment point for the ribs and the clavicles.

Ribs or Costals

Adults have 12 pairs of ribs, which run between the sternum and the thoracic vertebrae. The ribs are flat bones that form a protective cage around the heart and lungs. An individual will have seven pairs of ribs that attach to both the sternum and vertebrae

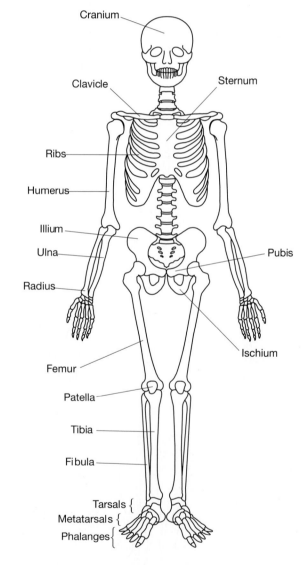

Fig 1.4 Anterior view of a skeleton

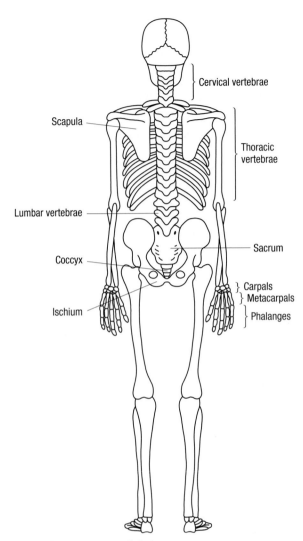

Cervical vertebrae

Scapula

Thoracic vertebrae

Lumbar vertebrae

Coccyx

Sacrum

Ischium

Carpals
Metacarpals

Phalanges

Fig 1.5 Posterior view of skeleton

the elbow joint with the humerus and runs in line with the little finger. The radius is positioned beside the ulna and runs in line with the thumb side. When the hand turns, the radius turns across the ulna.

Hand

The hand has three areas made up of different types of bones. First, the wrist is made up of eight carpals, which are small bones arranged in two rows of four; the five long bones between the wrist and fingers are the metacarpals and the bones of the fingers are called phalanges. There are 14 phalanges altogether with three in each finger and two in the thumb. There are a total of 30 bones in the upper limb.

Pelvis

The pelvis protects and supports the lower internal organs, including the bladder, the reproductive organs and also, in pregnant women, the developing foetus. The pelvis consists of three bones, the ilium, the pubis and the ischium, which have become fused together to form one area.

The Leg

The leg consists of four bones: the femur is the longest bone in the body and forms the knee joint with the tibia, which is the weight-bearing bone of the lower leg; the fibula is the non-weight bearing bone of the lower leg and helps form the ankle; the patella is the bone that floats over the knee, it lies within the patella tendon and smoothes the movement of the tendons over the knee joint.

Foot

Like the hand, the foot has three areas: the seven tarsals, which form the ankle; the five metatarsals, which travel from the ankle to the toes; and the 14 phalanges, which make up the toes. There are three phalanges in each toe, with only two in the big toe. Again, the lower limb has 30 bones; it has one less tarsal but makes up for it with the patella.

Vertebrae

The spine is made up of five areas:

- cervical – 7
- thoracic – 12
- lumbar – 5
- sacrum – 5
- coccyx – 4.

The seven cervical vertebrae make up the neck and run to the shoulders. The twelve thoracic vertebrae make up the chest area, and the five lumbar vertebrae make up the lower back. The sacrum consists of five vertebrae, which are fixed together and form joints

(true ribs), three that attach from the vertebrae to a cartilage attachment on the sternum, and two that attach on the vertebrae but are free as they have no second attachment (floating ribs).

Clavicle

This bone connects the upper arm to the trunk of the body. One end is connected to the sternum and the other is connected to the scapula. The role of the clavicle is to keep the scapula at the correct distance from the sternum.

Scapula

This bone is situated on the back of the body. The scapula provides points of attachment for many muscles of the upper back and arms.

Arm

This consists of three bones: the humerus (upper arm), the radius and the ulna (lower arm). The ulna forms

with the pelvis, and the coccyx, which is four bones joined together – the remnants of when we had a tail.

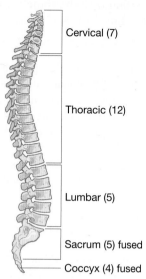

Cervical (7)

Thoracic (12)

Lumbar (5)

Sacrum (5) fused

Coccyx (4) fused

Fig 1.6 Structure of the vertebral column

1.3 Functions of the Skeleton

P1

The skeleton performs the following functions.

- Provides a bony framework for the body – the bones give the body a distinctive shape and a framework to which muscles and other soft tissue can attach. Without bones we would just be a big sac of muscles and fluids.
- Allows movement of the body as a whole and its individual parts – the bones act as levers, and by forming joints they allow muscles to pull on them and produce joint movements. This enables us to move in all directions and perform the functions we need on a daily basis.
- Offers protection to the organs found within the skeleton – the bones support and protect the vital organs they contain. For example, the skull protects the brain; the ribs offer protection to the heart and lungs; the vertebrae protect the spinal cord; and the pelvis offers protection to the sensitive reproductive organs.
- Production of blood cells – certain bones contain red bone marrow, and the bone marrow produces red blood cells, white blood cells and platelets. The bones that contain marrow are the pelvis, sternum, vertebrae, costals, cranial bones and clavicle.
- Storage of minerals and fats – the bones themselves are made of minerals stored within cartilage; therefore, they act as a mineral store for calcium, magnesium and phosphorous, which can

be given up if the body requires the minerals for other functions. The bones also store dietary fats (triglycerides) within the yellow bone marrow.
- Attachment of soft tissue – bones provide surfaces for the attachment of soft tissue such as muscles, tendons and ligaments. This is why they are often irregular shapes and have bony points and grooves to provide attachment points.

Structure of a Long Bone

- Epiphysis – this is the ends of the bone.
- Diaphysis – this is the long shaft of the bone.
- Hyaline cartilage – this is the thin layer of bluish cartilage covering each end of the bone.
- Periosteum – this is the thin outer layer of the bone. It contains nerves and blood vessels that feed the bone.
- Compact bone – this is hard and resistant to bending.
- Cancellous bone – this lies in layers within the compact bone. It has a honeycomb appearance and gives the bones their elastic strength.

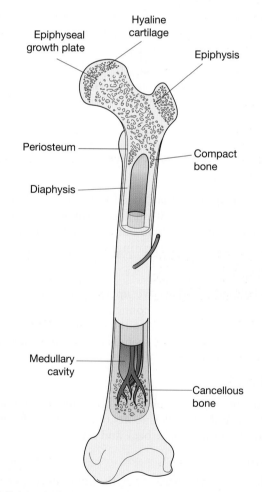

Epiphyseal growth plate

Hyaline cartilage

Epiphysis

Periosteum

Compact bone

Diaphysis

Medullary cavity

Cancellous bone

Fig 1.7 Long bone

● Medullary cavity – this is the hollow space down the middle of the compact bone and contains bone marrow. There are two types of bone marrow: red marrow, which produces blood cells, and yellow marrow, which stores fat.

Bone Growth

In a fetus, most of the skeleton consists of cartilage, which is a tough flexible tissue. As the fetus develops, minerals are laid down in the cartilage and the bones become harder and less flexible. This process is called ossification and it continues until we are adults. Bones keep growing until between the ages of 18 and 30, depending upon the bone and the body part. When a bone grows it occurs at the epiphyseal plate, which is an area just behind the head of the bone at each epiphysis; as a bone grows, its two ends are slowly pushed away from each other.

Bones are very much alive and full of activity. We know bones are living material because they can repair if they are damaged, grow when we are young and they produce blood cells. Bones contain blood vessels and nerves.

Bone is continually being broken down and replaced; this process is done by different cells, osteoblasts and osteoclasts:

● osteoblasts are cells that will build bone
● osteoclasts are cells that destroy or clean away old bone.

Osteoclasts and osteoblasts will replace around 10 per cent of bone every year; this means that no matter how old we are our skeleton is no older than ten years of age!

Key term

Ossification: The process of creating bone from cartilage.

Connective Tissue

There are connective tissues in the body to connect tissue and stabilise joints. There are three types of connective tissue:

● cartilage
● ligament
● tendon.

Cartilage is a dense and tough tissue that cushions joints. It comes in three types:

● hyaline (found at the ends of bones)
● fibro (thick chunks found in the knee and between vertebrae)
● elastic (gives shape to structures such as the ear and the nose).

Ligaments:

● attach bone to bone
● act to give stability to joints
● are tough, white and inelastic.

Tendons:

● attach muscle to bone
● carry the force from muscle contraction to the bone
● are tough, greyish and inelastic.

All these types of connective tissue have a very poor blood supply, hence their whitish colour, and will take a long time to repair if they become damaged.

Student activity 1.1   30 minutes   P1

Structure and function of the skeleton

Our skeleton is made up of 206 bones and has many different functions.

Task 1

Label a diagram of the skeleton to name all of the major bones.

Task 2

Draw a spider diagram that illustrates the different functions of the skeleton.

Task 3

Write a report that describes the structure and function of the different parts of the skeleton, including:

• the axial and appendicular skeletons
• the different types of bones
• the five main functions of the skeleton as a whole.

7

1.4 Joints

P2

The place where two or more bones meet is called a joint or an articulation. A joint is held together by ligaments, which give the joints their stability.

Key term

Joint: Where two or more bones meet

Joints are put into one of three categories depending upon the amount of movement available.

1 Fixed joints/fibrous – these joints allow no movement. These types of joints can be found between the plates in the skull.

Suture in dome of skull

2 Slightly moveable/cartilaginous – these joints allow a small amount of movement and are held in place by ligaments and cushioned by cartilage. These types of joints can be found between the vertebrae in the spine.

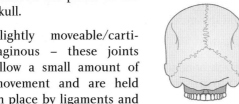

Fig 1.8 A fixed joint

3 Moveable/synovial – these joints allow a wide range of movement and all have a similar joint structure.

Figure 1.10 shows the structure of a synovial joint, which is made up of the following components.

- Synovial capsule – keeps the contents of the synovial joint in place.
- Synovial membrane – releases synovial fluid onto the joint.
- Synovial fluid – a thick 'oil like' solution that lubricates the joint and allows free movement.
- Articular cartilage – a bluish-white covering of cartilage that prevents wear and tear on the bones.

There are six types of synovial joints and all allow varying degrees of movement. The six types of synovial joint are: hinge, ball and socket, pivot, condyloid, sliding, and saddle.

Hinge joint

These can be found in the elbow (ulna and humerus) and knee (femur and tibia). They allow flexion and

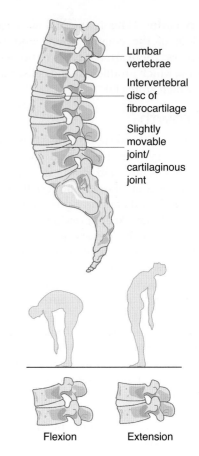

Lumbar vertebrae

Intervertebral disc of fibrocartilage

Slightly movable joint/ cartilaginous joint

Flexion   Extension

Fig 1.9 A cartilaginous joint

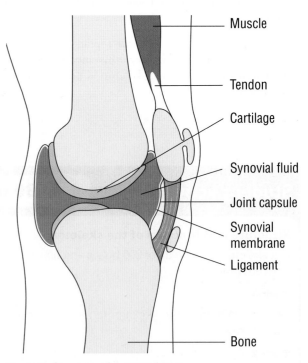

Muscle

Tendon

Cartilage

Synovial fluid

Joint capsule

Synovial membrane

Ligament

Bone

Fig 1.10 Structure of a synovial joint

extension of a joint. Hinge joints are like the hinges on a door, and allow you to move the elbow and knee in only one direction.

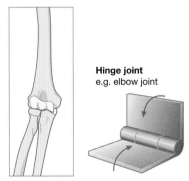

Hinge joint
e.g. elbow joint

Fig 1.11 Hinge joint

Ball and Socket Joint

These types of joint can be found at the shoulder (scapula and humerus) and hip (pelvis and femur) and allow movement in almost every direction. A ball and socket joint is made up of a round end of one bone that fits into a small cup-like area of another bone.

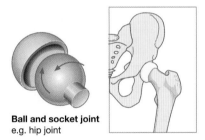

Ball and socket joint
e.g. hip joint

Fig 1.12 Ball and socket joint

Pivot Joint

This joint can be found in the neck between the top two vertebrae (atlas and axis). It allows only rotational movement – for example, it allows you to move your head from side to side as if you were saying 'no'.

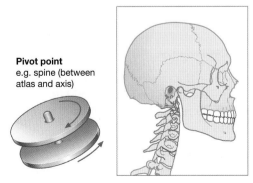

Pivot point
e.g. spine (between atlas and axis)

Fig 1.13 Pivot joint

Condyloid joint

This type of joint is found at the wrist. It allows movement in two planes; this is called biaxial. It allows you to bend and straighten the joint, and move it from side to side. The joints between the metacarpals and phalanges are also condyloid.

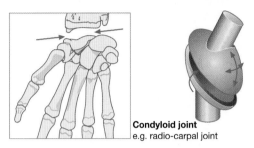

Condyloid joint
e.g. radio-carpal joint

Fig 1.14 Condyloid joint

Saddle Joint

This type of joint is found only in the thumbs. It allows the joint to move in three planes: backwards and forwards, and from side to side, and across. This is a joint specific to primates and gives us 'manual dexterity', enabling us to hold a cup and write, among other skills.

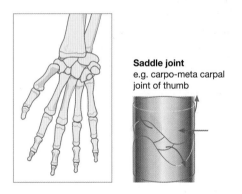

Saddle joint
e.g. carpo-meta carpal joint of thumb

Fig 1.15 Saddle joint

Gliding Joint

This type of joint can be found in the carpal bones of the hand. These types of joint occur between the surfaces of two flat bones. They allow very limited movement in a range of directions.

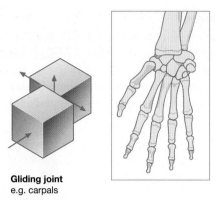

Gliding joint
e.g. carpals

Fig 1.16 Gliding joint

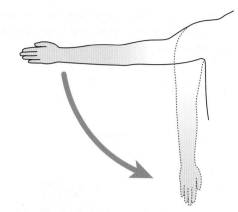

Fig 1.19 Adduction

Types of Joint Movement

To enable us to understand sporting movements we need to be able to describe or label joint movements. Joint movements are given specific terms (see below).

General Movements

General movements apply to more than one joint.

● Flexion – this occurs when the angle of a joint decreases. For example, when you bend the elbow it decreases from 180 degrees to around 30 degrees.

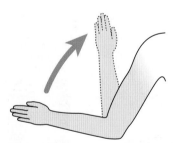

Fig 1.17 Flexion

● Extension – this occurs when the angle of a joint increases. For example, when you straighten the elbow it increases from 30 degrees to 180 degrees.

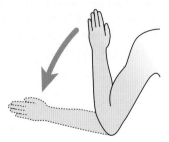

Fig 1.18 Extension

● Adduction – this means movement towards the midline of the body.

● Abduction – this means movement away from the midline of the body. This occurs at the hip during a star jump.

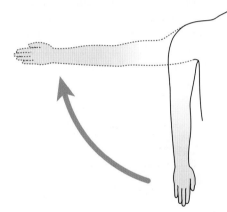

Fig 1.20 Abduction

● Circumduction – this means that the limb moves in a circle. This occurs at the shoulder joint during an overarm bowl in cricket.

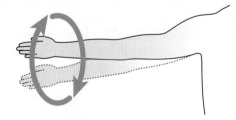

Fig 1.21 Circumduction

● Rotation – this means that the limb moves in a circular movement towards the middle of the body. This occurs in the hip in golf while performing a drive shot.

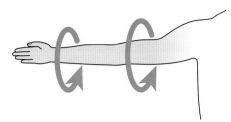

Fig 1.22 Rotation

Specific Movements

Specific movements apply to a specific joint.

- Pronation – this means when the hand is facing down while the elbow is flexed. Pronation occurs as the hand moves from facing up to facing down, and is the result of the movement of the pivot joint between the ulna and radius. This would happen when a spin bowler delivers the ball in cricket.

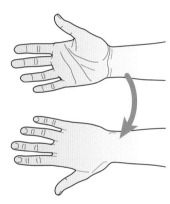

Fig 1.23 Pronation

- Supination – this means when the palm of the hand is facing up. Supination occurs as the hand moves from facing down to facing up, and is the result of the movement of the pivot joint between the ulna and radius. You can remember this by thinking that you carry a bowl of soup in a supinated position. Throwing a dart involves supination of the forearm.

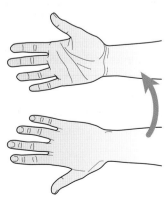

Fig 1.24 Supination

- Plantarflexion – this means that the foot moves away from the shin bone and you will be pointing your toes or raising onto your tiptoes. It is specific to your ankle joint and occurs when you walk.

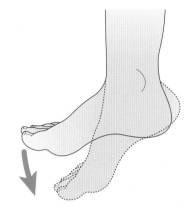

Fig 1.25 Plantarflexion

- Dorsiflexion – this means that the foot moves towards the shin as if you are pulling your toes up. It is specific to the ankle joint and occurs when you walk.

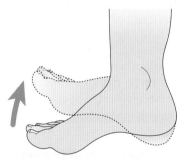

Fig 1.26 Dorsiflexion

- Inversion – this means that the soles of the feet are facing each other. It occurs at the gliding joints between the tarsals rather than at the ankle joint.

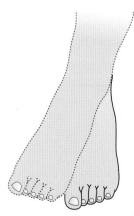

Fig 1.27 Inversion

11

● Eversion – this means that the soles of the feet are facing away from each other. It occurs at the gliding joints between the tarsals rather than at the ankle joint.

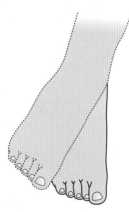

Fig 1.28 Eversion

● Hyperextension – this is the term given to an extreme or abnormal range of motion found within a joint – for example, at the knee or elbow.

Key learning points 1

● The functions of the skeleton are shape, movement, protection, blood production and mineral storage.
● Bones grow at their growth plates.
● There are three types of joint: fixed, slightly moveable and moveable/synovial.

Q Quick quiz 1

Ossification	Calcium	Flexion
Ribs	Abduction	Bone marrow
The leg	Bone marrow	
Immovable	Pivot	

Choose a word from the boxes above to answer each of the following questions.

1   What is the main mineral stored in bones?
2   Where are blood cells produced?
3   Which bones protect the heart and lungs?
4   Which limb consists of four bones?
5   What is the name given to the process of cartilage turning into bone?
6   The hinge joint allows only this type of movement and no other.
7   Which term describes movement away from the body?
8   This type of joint can be found in the neck.
9   This type of joint can be found in the skull.
10   This part of the bones produces new blood cells.

Student activity 1.2   30 minutes   P2

Different types of joints

The different joints in our body allow varying amounts of movement – some allow none, whereas others have a wide range of movement, which allows us to take part in sport and exercise activities.

Task 1

Describe the three different classifications of joints and give examples of each.

Task 2

Describe the six different types of synovial joint and the types of movements that they allow.

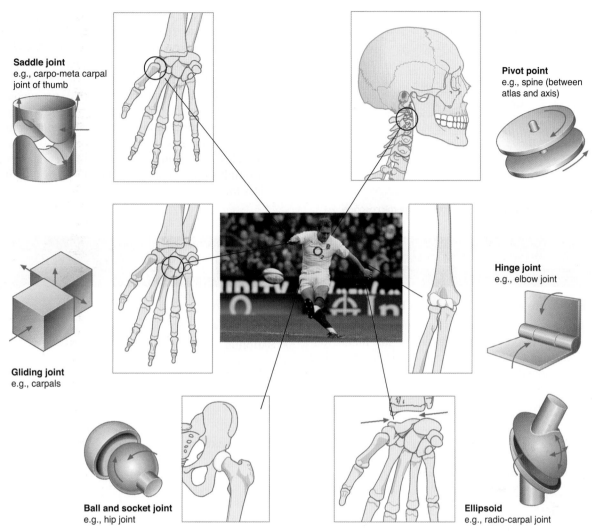

Saddle joint
e.g., carpo-meta carpal joint of thumb

Pivot point
e.g., spine (between atlas and axis)

Gliding joint
e.g., carpals

Hinge joint
e.g., elbow joint

Ball and socket joint
e.g., hip joint

Ellipsoid
e.g., radio-carpal joint

Fig 1.29 Synovial joints in action

1.5 The Structure and Function of the Muscular System

The muscular system will work in conjunction with the skeleton to produce movement of the limbs and body. The muscular system always has to work with the nervous system because it will produce a nervous impulse to initiate movement.

Major Muscles of the Body

There are three types of muscle tissue: smooth, cardiac and skeletal.

1 Smooth muscles – smooth muscles are also called involuntary muscles because they are out of our conscious control. They can be found in the digestive system (large and small intestine), the circulatory system (artery and vein walls) and the urinary system. Smooth muscles contract with a peristaltic action in that the muscle fibres contract consecutively rather than at the same time, and this produces a wavelike effect. For example, when food is passed through the digestive system it is slowly squeezed through the intestines.

2 Cardiac muscle – the heart has its own specialist muscle tissue, which is cardiac muscle. Cardiac muscle is involuntary muscle. The heart has its own nerve supply via the sino-atrial node, and it works by sending a nervous impulse through consecutive cells. The heart will always contract fully – that is, all the fibres will contract – and contracts around 60–80 times a minute. The function of the myocardium is to pump blood around the body.

13

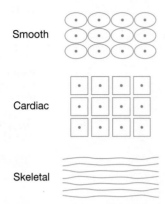

Smooth

Cardiac

Skeletal

Fig 1.30 Types of muscle fibre under the microscope

3 Skeletal muscle – skeletal muscle is muscle that is attached to the skeleton across joints. It is under voluntary control as we decide when to contract muscles and produce movement. Skeletal muscle is arranged in rows of fibres, and it is also called striated, or striped, on account of its appearance. The coordinated contractions of skeletal muscle allow us to move smoothly and produce sports skills. There are over 700 skeletal muscles in the human body, and they make up around 40 per cent of our body weight (slightly less for a female).

 Student activity 1.3   **25 minutes**   **P3**

Major muscles in the human body

There are lots of different muscles in the human body and you will need to know the names and locations of each so that you can go on to understand how they produced movements.

Task 1

Working in pairs, write the following muscle names on to some sticky labels:

- Biceps
- Biceps Brachii
- Biceps Femoris
- Deltoid
- Erector Spinae
- Gastrocnemius
- Gluteus Maximus
- Iliopsoas
- Latissimus Dorsi
- Obliques
- Pectoralis Major
- Rectus Abdominus

- Rectus Femoris
- Rhomboids
- Sartorius
- Semimembranosus
- Semitendinosus
- Soleus
- Teres Major
- Tibialis Anterior
- Trapezius
- Triceps
- Triceps Brachii
- Vastus Intermedius
- Vastus Lateralis
- Vastus Medialis

Task 2

One of you will be the anterior muscles and the other will be the posterior muscle groups. In your pairs, place the appropriate muscle labels over your partner's clothes to indicate where each major muscle is located.

1.6 Function of the Muscular System – Movement

 P4   **M1**   **D1**

Tendons are responsible for joining skeletal muscles to your skeleton. Skeletal muscles are held to the bones with the help of tendons.

Tendons are cords made of tough tissue; they work to connect muscle to bones. When the muscle contracts, it pulls on the tendon, which in turn pulls on the bone and makes the bone move.

When muscles contract they work as a group in that the muscle contracting is dependent on other muscles to enable it to do its job. A muscle can play one of four roles, as outlined below.

1 **Agonist (or prime mover)** – this muscle contracts to produce the desired movement.

2 Antagonist – this muscle relaxes to allow the agonist to contract.

3 Synergist – this muscle assists the agonist in producing the desired movement.

4 Fixator – these muscles will fix joints and the body in position to enable the desired movement to occur.

An antagonistic muscle pair comprises muscle that contracts to produce the movement and muscle that relaxes to produce the movement. For example, when you perform a bicep curl, the biceps brachii will be the agonist as it contracts to produce the movement, while the triceps brachii will be the antagonist as it relaxes to allow the movement to occur.

Types of Muscle Movement

Muscles can contract or develop tension in three different ways.

1 Concentric contraction: this involves the muscle shortening and developing tension. The origin and insertion of the muscle move closer together and the muscle becomes fatter. To produce a concentric contraction, a movement must occur against gravity.

2 Eccentric contraction: an eccentric contraction involves the muscle lengthening to develop tension. The origin and the insertion of the muscle move further away from each other. An eccentric contraction provides the control of a movement on the downward phase, and it works to resist the force of gravity.

If a person is performing a bench press, they will produce a concentric contraction to push the weight away from their body. However, on the downward phase they will produce an eccentric contraction to control the weight on the way down. If they did not, gravity would return their weight to the ground and they would be hurt in the process. The agonist muscle will produce concentric or eccentric contractions, while the antagonist muscle will always stay relaxed to allow the movement to occur.

3 Isometric contraction: if a muscle produces tension but stays the same length, then it will be an isometric contraction. This occurs when the body is fixed in one position; for example a gymnast on the rings in the crucifix position. Also, when we are standing up, our postural muscles produce isometric contractions

Muscle Fibre Types

Within our muscle we have two types of muscle fibre, which are called fast twitch and slow twitch fibres due

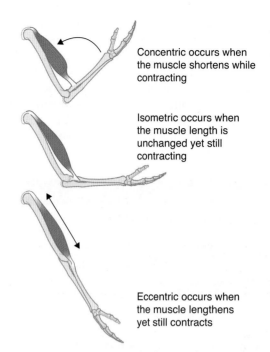

Concentric occurs when the muscle shortens while contracting

Isometric occurs when the muscle length is unchanged yet still contracting

Eccentric occurs when the muscle lengthens yet still contracts

Fig 1.31 Types of muscle contraction at the biceps brachii

to the speed at which they contract (see Table 1.2). If we look at the evolution of humans, we were originally hunters and gatherers; this meant that we had to walk long distances to find animals to eat and then, when we saw one, we would have to chase after it as fast as we could. Therefore, we adapted slow twitch muscle fibres to walk long distances and fast twitch muscle fibres to run quickly after our prey.

Slow Twitch Fibres (Type 1)

These will be red in colour as they have a good blood supply. They have a dense network of blood vessels, making them suited to endurance work and they are slow to fatigue. They also contain many mitochondria to make them more efficient at producing energy using oxygen.

Key term

Mitochondria: the energy-producing organelles within cells.

Fast Twitch Fibres (Type 2)

These contract twice as quickly as slow twitch fibres and are thicker in size. They have a poor blood supply, are whiter in appearance and, due to the lack of oxygen, they will fatigue fairly quickly. Their faster, harder contractions make them suitable for producing fast, powerful actions such as sprinting and lifting heavy weights.

Within the group of fast twitch fibres there are two types: 2A and 2B. The type that is used depends upon the intensity of the chosen activity. Type 2B fibres work when a person is working very close to their maximum intensity, while type 2A work at slightly lower intensities but at higher intensities than slow twitch fibres are capable of. For example, a 100-m runner would be using type 2B fibres, while a 400-m runner would be using type 2A fibres.

Slow twitch (Type I)	Fast twitch (Type 2)
Red	White
Contract slowly	Contract rapidly
Aerobic	Anaerobic
Endurance based	Speed/strength based
Can contract repeatedly	Easily exhausted
Exert less force	Exert great forces

Table 1.2 Basic characteristics of fast twitch and slow twitch

Characteristics	Slow twitch (Type I)	Fast oxidative glycolytic F.O.G. (Type 2A)	Fast twitch glycolytic F.T.G. (Type 2B)
Speed of contraction (ms)	Slow (110)	Fast (50)	Fast (50)
Force of contraction	Low	High	High
Size	Smaller	Large	Large
Mitochondrial density	High	Lower	Low
Myoglobin content	High	Lower	Low
Fatiguability	Fatigue resistant	Less resistant	Easily fatigued
Aerobic capacity	High	Medium	Low
Capillary density	High	High	Low
Anaerobic capacity	Low	Medium	High
Motor neuron size	Small	Large	Large
Fibres/motor neuron	10–180	300–800	300–800
Sarcoplasmic reticulum development	Low	High	High

Table 1.3 Structural characteristics of muscle fibres
Source: (Adapted from Sharkey 'Physiology of Fitness', Human Kinetics 1990).

Key learning points 2

- There are three types of muscle: cardiac, smooth and skeletal.
- Cardiac and smooth muscle are involuntary and skeletal muscle is voluntary.
- Muscles work in antagonistic pairs where one muscle pulls (agonist) and the other muscle relaxes (antagonist).
- There are two types of muscle fibre – slow twitch and fast twitch,
- Slow twitch muscle fibres are used in endurance sports.
- There are two types of fast twitch muscle fibres: 2A and 2B. 2B are used in maximal intensity exercise, 2A during slightly lower intensity. Both are used for fast powerful actions such as sprinting or lifting weights.

Q Quick quiz 2

Answer the following questions about the muscular system.

1 Give three examples of where you may find smooth muscle.
2 Give five examples of skeletal muscles.
3 What is the name of the muscle that produces movement?
4 What is the name of the muscle that helps with the movement?
5 What is the name of the muscle that fixes the joint?
6 Look at the table below, then fill in the gaps:

Sporting action	Type of movement	Joint	Agonist	Antagonist	Fixator
Sit up – upwards phase	Flexion	Spine	Abdominals		
Press up – downwards phase	Flexion	Elbow		Triceps	
Football kick	Extension	Knee			
Chest press – upwards phase	Extension	Elbow			
Rugby conversion kick	Flexion	Hip			

(a) Name three athletes that would have mainly type 1 muscle fibres in their legs.

(b) Name three athletes that would have mainly type 2A muscle fibres in their legs.

Student activity 1.4  60 minutes

The function of the muscular system

Our muscular system works to pull on our skeleton to produce movement.

Task 1

Using hand-drawn illustrations, describe, explain and analyse the function of the muscular system. Include in your answer:

- antagonistic muscle pairs
- fixator
- synergist
- different types of contraction.

Task 2

Describe, explain and analyse the different fibre types that can be found in muscle tissue, and give examples of the different sports in which they may be used.

1.7 The Cardiovascular System

The cardiovascular system is made up of three parts:

- heart
- blood vessels
- blood.

Close your hand into a fist and look at it. Your fist is approximately the same size as your heart, around 12 cm long, 9 cm wide and 6 cm thick. It is located behind the sternum and tilted to the left. The heart is made up mainly of cardiac muscle, which is also known as myocardium. The heart is a muscular pump that pumps the liquid, which is blood, through the pipes, which are the blood vessels.

The cardiovascular system is responsible for the following actions:

- delivering oxygen and nutrients to every part of the body
- carrying hormones to different parts of the body
- removing the waste products of energy production such as carbon dioxide and lactic acid
- maintaining body temperature by re-directing blood to the surface of the skin to dissipate heat.

Structure of the Heart

The heart is a large muscular pump that is made up of thick walls. The heart muscle is called the myocardium and is divided into two halves, which are separated by the septum. The right-hand side of the heart is responsible for pumping deoxygenated blood to the lungs, and the left-hand side pumps oxygenated blood around the body. Each side of the heart consists of two connected chambers. Each side will have an atrium and a ventricle. The top chambers – the atria

(plural of atrium) – are where the blood collects when it enters the heart. The lower chambers are called the ventricles, and are the large pumps which send the blood up to the lungs or around the body. Once the blood has entered the heart from the veins it will be sucked into the ventricles as they relax, and there follows powerful contraction of the ventricles. The left ventricle is the largest and most muscular because it has to send the blood to the furthest destinations and thus has to produce the most pressure.

Blood Flow through the Heart

Blood flows through the heart and around the body in one direction. This one-way 'street' is maintained due to special valves placed within the heart and within the blood vessels leading from the heart.

The heart is sometimes called a 'double pump' because the right-hand side of the heart pumps blood to the lungs and the left-hand side of the heart pumps blood to the body.

Right-hand side

1. When the heart is relaxed, deoxygenated blood from the body enters the heart via the venae cavae.
2. Blood enters the right atrium.
3. The right atrium contracts and pushes blood down through the tricuspid valve and into the right ventricle.
4. The right ventricle contracts, the tricuspid valve closes, and blood is pushed up and out of the heart through the semilunar valve and into the pulmonary artery, which takes the blood to the lungs.
5. The heart relaxes and the semilunar valves close to prevent blood flowing back into the heart.
6. The blood flows to the lungs where it becomes oxygenated and ready to be returned to the heart for distribution around the body.

Left-hand side

1. When the heart is relaxed, oxygenated blood from the lungs enters via the pulmonary vein.
2. Blood enters the left atria.
3. The left atria contracts and pushes blood down through the bicuspid valve and into the left ventricle.
4. The left ventricle contracts; the bicuspid valve closes to prevent blood flowing back into the heart. Blood is then pushed up and out of the heart through the semilunar valve and into the aorta, which is the large artery leaving the heart, taking blood to the rest of the body.
5. The heart relaxes and the semilunar valves close to prevent blood flowing back into the heart.

Pulmonary valve   Aortic valve

Right atrium   Left atrium

RA   **LA**

Septum

Tricuspid valve   Bicuspid valve

RV **LV**

Right ventricle   Left ventricle

Fig 1.32 A simplified cross-section of the heart

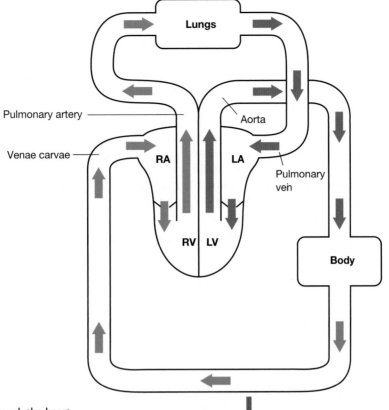

Fig 1.33 Blood flow through the heart

Blood Vessels

In order to make its journey around the body, blood is carried through five different types of blood vessels:

- arteries
- arterioles
- capillaries
- venules
- veins.

Arteries and Arterioles

Arteries are the large blood vessels that leave the heart. They have thick, muscular walls, which contract and relax to send blood to all parts of the body. The main artery leaving the heart is the aorta and it quickly splits up into smaller vessels, which are called the arterioles. Arterioles mean 'little arteries'. Artery walls contain elastic cartilage and smooth muscle. This flexible wall allows the vessels to expand and contract, which helps to push the blood along the length of the arteries. This action is called peristalsis and is how smooth muscle contracts.

Arteries do not contain any valves as they are not required and they predominantly carry oxygenated blood. The exception to this is the pulmonary artery, which carries deoxygenated blood away from the heart.

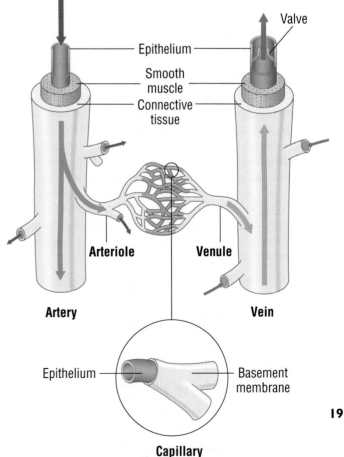

Fig 1.34 The five linked blood vessels

19

- Arteries carry blood away from the heart.
- Arteries have thick, muscular walls.
- Arteries carry predominantly oxygenated blood.
- Arterioles are the small branches of arteries.

Capillaries

Once the arteries and arterioles have divided, they will eventually feed blood into the smallest blood vessels, called capillaries. These are found in all parts of the body, especially the muscles, and are so tiny that their walls are only one cell thick. There are tiny spaces within these thin cell walls, which allow oxygen and other nutrients to pass through (a process called diffusion). The blood flows very slowly through the capillaries to allow for this process. In the capillaries the blood will also pick up the waste products of metabolism: carbon dioxide and lactic acid. There are more capillaries than any other type of blood vessel in the body.

- Capillaries are tiny blood vessels one cell thick.
- Small spaces in the thin walls of capillaries allow for diffusion.
- Oxygen and nutrients will diffuse into the cells.
- Carbon dioxide and lactic acid will flow from the cells into the capillaries.

Veins and Venules

The capillaries will eventually feed back into larger blood vessels called venules, which are the smallest veins, and they eventually become veins. The walls of these veins are thinner and less muscular than arteries, and they carry blood back to the heart. They also contain smooth muscle and contract to send the blood back to the heart. The veins are generally acting against gravity, so they contain non-return valves to prevent the blood flowing back once the smooth muscle has relaxed. These valves prevent the pooling of blood in the lower limbs. Veins predominantly carry deoxygenated blood, with the exception of the pulmonary vein, which carries oxygenated blood to the heart from the lungs.

- Veins always take blood towards the heart.
- Veins have thin, muscular walls.
- Veins have non-return valves to prevent backflow.
- Veins predominantly carry deoxygenated blood.
- Venules are smaller branches, which feed into veins.

Function of the Heart

The cells of the body need a steady and constant supply of oxygen. Blood is responsible for carrying and delivering oxygen to all the body's cells, and this blood is pumped around the body and to the lungs by the heart. The left-hand side of your heart pumps the oxygenated blood to the cells of the muscles, brain, kidneys, liver and all the other organs. The cells then take the oxygen out of the blood and use it to produce energy. This is called metabolism and it produces waste products, such as carbon dioxide. The deoxygenated blood then continues its journey back to the heart, enters the right-hand side and is pumped out of the right ventricle to the lungs. At the lungs, the blood becomes oxygenated and the waste product carbon dioxide is 'unloaded' and breathed out.

Blood

Blood is the medium in which all the cells are carried to transport nutrients and oxygen to the cells of the body. Among other things, blood will transport the following: oxygen, glucose, proteins, fats, vitamins, hormones, enzymes, platelets, carbon dioxide and electrolytes.

Blood is made up of four components:

- red blood cells
- white blood cells
- platelets
- plasma.

Blood can be described as a thick, gloopy substance due to the high concentration of solids it carries. Blood is made up of 55 per cent plasma and 45 per cent solids, which is a very high concentration.

Red Blood Cells

Of the blood cells in the body, around 99 per cent of them are red blood cells or erythrocytes. They are red in colour due to the presence of a red-coloured protein called haemoglobin. Haemoglobin has a massive attraction for oxygen, and thus the main role of the red blood cells is to take on and transport oxygen to the cells. There are many millions of red blood cells in the body; for example, there are 5 million red blood cells for 1 mm^3 volume of blood.

White Blood Cells

White blood cells are colourless or transparent and are far fewer in number (1:700 ratio of white to red blood cells). The role of white blood cells, or leucocytes, is to fight infection; they are part of the body's immune system. They destroy bacteria and other dangerous organisms and thus remove disease from the body.

Platelets

Platelets are not full cells but rather parts of cells; they act by stopping blood loss through clotting. They become sticky when in contact with the air to form the initial stage of repair to damaged tissue. Platelets also need a substance called factor 8 to enable them to clot. A haemophiliac is a person whose blood does not clot; this is not because they are short of platelets but rather factor 8, which enables the platelets to become active.

Plasma

Plasma is the liquid part of the blood, which is straw-coloured in appearance. It is the solution in which all the solids are carried.

Key learning points 3

- The heart has four chambers, two atria and two ventricles.
- The ventricles pump blood to the body and lungs.
- Valves in the heart make sure blood flows in one direction.
- Blood travels through five different types of blood vessesls, arteries, arterioles, capillaries, venules and veins.
- The heart adapts to aerobic training by becoming bigger and stronger.

Q Quick quiz 3

Structure of the heart

Fill in the blanks.

The heart is split into _____ sides and has _____ chambers. The top two chambers are called _____ and the bottom two chambers are called _____. The heart is split into two separate sides by the _____.

There are _____ valves that allow the blood to pass through the heart in one direction. The valve between the atrium and ventricle on the right side of the heart is called the _____ valve. The valve on the left side of the heart between the atrium and the ventricle is called the _____ valve. The valve between the pulmonary artery and right ventricle is called the _____ valve. The valve between the left ventricle and the aorta is called the _____ valve.

Student activity 1.5 60 minutes P5 M2

Structure and function of the cardiovascular system

Our cardiovascular system is responsible for supplying our body with blood, which contain nutrients and oxygen that provide our muscles with energy for movement.

Task 1

By hand, draw:

(a) the structure of the heart

(b) a diagram to illustrate how blood circulates through the heart, to the lungs and to the body.

Task 2

Describe and explain the structure of the cardio-vascular system including:

- the heart
- the blood vessels.

Task 3

Describe and explain the function of the cardiovascular system.

1.8 The Respiratory System

P6 **M3**

The respiratory system is responsible for transporting the oxygen from the air we breathe into our body. Our body then uses this oxygen in combination with the food we have eaten to produce energy. This energy is then used to keep us alive by supplying our heart with energy to keep beating and pumping blood around the body, which in turn allows us to move and take part in sports and many more different types of activities. Each person has two lungs running the length of the ribcage; the right lung is slightly larger than the left lung. The left lung has to make space for the heart in an area called the cardiac notch.

Structure of the Respiratory System

The aim of the respiratory system is to provide contact between the outside and internal environments so that oxygen can be absorbed by the blood and carbon dioxide can be given up. It is made up of a system of tubes and muscles, which deliver the air into two lungs. The average person takes around 26,000 breaths a day to deliver the required amount of oxygen to the cells of the body.

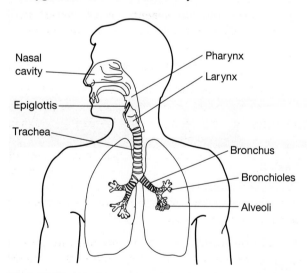

Fig 1.35 The respiratory system

Figure 1.35 shows the respiratory system in which the following processes occur.

1. Air enters the body through the mouth and nose.
2. It passes through the pharynx, which is the back of the throat area.
3. It then passes through the larynx, which is responsible for voice production.
4. Air passes over the epiglottis. The epiglottis closes over the trachea when we swallow food to stop the food going down 'the wrong way' into our trachea and down into our lungs.
5. The air enters the trachea, which is a membranous tube with horseshoe-shaped cartilage that keeps it open and delivers air to the lungs.
6. The trachea will divide into two bronchi, one into each lung.
7. The two main bronchi will divide into bronchioles, which will further subdivide 23 times and result in 8 million terminal bronchioles in each lung.
8. Around the bronchioles are groups of air sacs, called alveoli. There are around 600 million alveoli in each lung, and it is here that the exchange of gases (oxygen and carbon dioxide) occurs. Each alveolus is in contact with a capillary where the blood is present.

Respiratory Muscles

The respiratory system also includes two types of muscles that work to move air into and out of the lungs.

The diaphragm is a large dome-shaped muscle that covers the bottom of the ribcage. At rest it is dome-shaped, but when contracted it flattens and pushes the two sides of the ribcage away from each other.

The intercostal muscles attach between the ribs; when they contract they push the ribs up and out and increase the size of the chest cavity, drawing air in. If you put your hands on your ribs and breathe in, you will feel your ribs push up and out; this is the action of the intercostal muscles.

Mechanisms of Breathing

Breathing is the term given to inhaling air into the lungs and then exhaling air out. The process basically works on the principle of making the thoracic cavity (chest) larger, which decreases the pressure of air within the lungs. The surrounding air is then at a higher pressure, which means that air is forced into the lungs. Then the thoracic cavity is returned to its original size, which forces air out of the lungs.

Breathing In (Inhalation)

At rest

The diaphragm contracts and moves downwards; this results in an increase in the sise of the thoracic cavity and air is forced into the lungs.

Exercise

During exercise, the diaphragm and intercostal muscles contract, which makes the ribs move upwards and outwards, and results in more air being taken into the lungs.

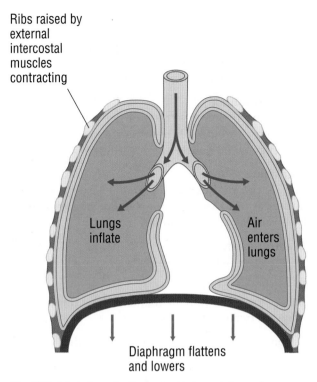

Ribs raised by external intercostal muscles contracting

Lungs inflate

Air enters lungs

Diaphragm flattens and lowers

Fig 1.36 Inhalation, diaphragm and intercostal muscles

Functions of the Respiratory System

The aim of breathing is to get oxygen into the bloodstream where it can be delivered to the cells of the body. At the cells it enters the mitochondria where it combines with fats and carbohydrates to produce energy, with carbon dioxide and water produced as waste products. This energy is used to produce muscular contractions, among other things.

Fats/carbohydrates + oxygen = energy + carbon dioxide + water

It is important to say that when the body produces more energy, the amount of carbon dioxide increases in the body and which dissolves in the water in the body so that it becomes a weak acid. The body does not like the acidity of the blood to increase, so the respiratory centre in the brain speeds up the rate of breathing to get rid of the excess carbon dioxide. Therefore, the breathing rate increases because carbon dioxide levels rise, rather than as a result of the cells demanding more oxygen.

Diffusion of Gases

> **Key term**
>
> **Diffusion:** the movement of gas from an area of high concentration to an area of low concentration.

Gases will move around through a process of diffusion.

Diffusion is how gases move from one place to another. For example, if a person is wearing perfume, it will diffuse around a room so that everyone can smell it. This is because the person is in an area of high concentration of the perfume and the gas moves to areas of low concentration.

In the respiratory system diffusion takes place in the lungs and the muscles.

- Diffusion in the lungs – in the lungs we have a high concentration of oxygen, and in the muscles we have a high concentration of carbon dioxide, and they will diffuse across the semi-permeable membrane. Oxygen is attracted into the blood by the haemoglobin, which is a protein in the red blood cells, and it attaches to this haemoglobin.
- Diffusion in the muscles – in the muscles we have a high concentration of carbon dioxide and a low concentration of oxygen due to the process of energy production. As a result the oxygen diffuses into the muscles and is attracted by the myoglobin in the muscles and the carbon dioxide diffuses

Breathing Out (Exhalation)

At rest

The diaphragm relaxes and returns upwards to a domed position. The thoracic cavity gets smaller, which results in an increase in air pressure within the lungs so that air is breathed out of the lungs.

Exercise

During exercise, the intercostal muscles contract to help decrease the size of the thoracic cavity, which results in a more forcible breath out.

Composition of Air

The air that is inspired is made up of a mixture of gasses; the air exhaled is different in its composition of gases (see Table 1.4).

Inhaled air	Gas	Exhaled air
79.04%	Nitrogen	79%
20.93%	Oxygen	17%
0.03%	Carbon dioxide	4%

Table 1.4 Composition of inhaled and exhaled air

Oxygen is extracted from the air and replaced by carbon dioxide. However, most of the oxygen stays in the air and this is why mouth-to-mouth resuscitation works, because there is still 17 per cent available to the casualty.

into the bloodstream. It is then taken to the lungs to be breathed out.

Respiratory Volumes

In order to assess an individual's lung function, we use a spirometer. An example of the readings given by a spirometer is shown in Fig 1.37.

An individual will have a lung capacity of around 5 litres, which is about the amount of air in a basketball. It will be slightly lower for a female and slightly higher for a male, due to the differing sizes of the male and female ribcages.

Tidal volume

This is the amount of air breathed in with each breath.

Inspiratory reserve volume

This is the amount of space that is available for air to be inhaled. If you breathe in and stop, and then try to breathe in more, this extra air inhaled is the inspiratory volume.

Expiratory reserve volume

This is the amount of air that could be exhaled after you have breathed out. If you exhale and then stop, and then try to exhale more, the air that comes out is the expiratory reserve volume.

Vital capacity

This is the maximum amount of air that can be breathed in and out during one breath. It is the tidal volume, plus the inspiratory reserve volume, plus the expiratory reserve volume.

Residual volume

This is the amount of air left in the lungs after a full exhalation. Around 1 litre will always remain, or else the lungs would deflate and breathing would stop.

Total lung volume

This is the vital capacity plus the residual volume, and measures the maximum amount of air that can be present in the lungs at any moment.

Breathing rate

This is the number of breaths taken per minute.

Respiratory volume

This is the amount of air that is moving through the lungs every minute:

Respiratory volume = breathing rate × tidal volume

For example, at rest a person may have a tidal volume of 0.5 litres per minute and a breathing rate of 12 breaths per minute. But during exercise both of these will rise, and at high exercise intensities tidal volume may rise to 3 litres per minute and breathing rate to 35 breaths per minute.

At rest respiratory volume:

0.5 litres × 12 = 6 litres/minute

During exercise respiratory volume:

3 litres × 35 = 105 litres/minute

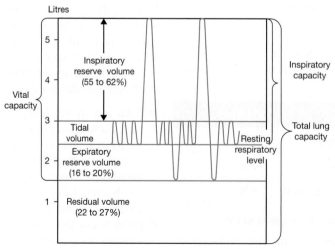

Fig 1.37 Lung volumes as shown on a spirometer trace

Key learning points 4

- Air travels into the body through the mouth and nose, down the trachea and into the bronchus. It then passes into the bronchioles and down into the alveoli. In the alveoli gaseous exchange takes place, which takes oxygen into the body and passes carbon dioxide out of the body.
- The diaphragm and intercostal muscles contract to allow you to breathe in and out.

Q Quick quiz 4

1 Describe which structures air flows through on its way from the mouth to the alveoli.
2 Explain the mechanics of breathing in and out.
3 What happens to tidal volume during exercise? Explain why this occurs.

Epiglottis	Diffusion	Trachea	Flattens	Inhalation
Carbon dioxide	Diaphragm	Oxygen	Gaseous exchange	Alveoli

4 Choose a word from the boxes above to answer the following.
  (a) This gas passes out of the blood stream and into the lungs.
  (b) When a person swallows, this closes over the trachea to prevent food going into the lungs.
  (c) This has horseshoe-shaped cartilage to help to keep it open.
  (d) The diaphragm does this during breathing in.
  (e) This is the process where gases move from a high to a low concentration.
  (f) This is the area in the lungs where gaseous exchange takes place.
  (g) When exhaling, this muscle relaxes and moves upwards into a domed position.
  (h) This is the name of the process in the lungs where oxygen is taken into the blood and carbon dioxide is breathed out.
  (i) All of our body cells need this gas to survive.
  (k) The name of the process for breathing in.

Student activity 1.6   45 minutes   P6   M3

The structure and function of the respiratory system

Task 1

By hand draw the structure of the respiratory system. Include in your diagram the following structures:

- nasal cavity
- epiglottis
- pharynx
- larynx
- trachea
- bronchus
- bronchioles
- lungs
- pleural membrane
- thoracic cavity
- visceral pleura
- pleural fluid
- alveoli
- diaphragm
- intercostals muscle – internal and external.

Task 2

Write a report that:

(a) Describes and explains the structure of each part of the respiratory system.

(b) Describes and explains the function of the respiratory system.

1.9 Energy Systems

 P7   M4   D2

The body needs a steady supply of energy to enable it to perform the functions it needs to stay alive:

- muscular contractions and movement
- circulation
- transmission of nerve impulses
- digestion of foods
- repairing and replacing tissue.

ATP

The only form of energy that the body can use is called ATP, or adenosine triphosphate. In the muscles ATP will provide the energy to enable the muscle fibres to shorten and develop tension. As long as there is a supply of ATP then the muscles will be able to contract. To supply this energy the body has three different energy systems:

- creatine phosphate system
- lactic acid system
- aerobic system.

ATP is produced by breaking down the foods that we eat in our diet. The food types that contain energy in the form of kilocalories (kcals) are:

- carbohydrate   1 g gives 4 kcals
- fat   1 g gives 9 kcals
- protein   1 g gives 4 kcals

ATP is a high-energy compound made up of one adenosine molecule attached to three phosphate molecules. These molecules are bound together by high-energy bonds.

The adenosine and phosphate molecules do not contain any energy; the energy is stored in the high-energy bonds and therefore to liberate energy we need to break down the bonds attaching the molecules. To break one of the bonds we need an enzyme called ATPase. When ATP has been broken down we are left with a second compound called adenosine di phosphate (ADP). A loose phosphate will also be created by the reaction.

Unfortunately, we have very limited stores of ATP in the muscles and ADP cannot be broken down any further. To allow further production of energy we need to remake or resynthesise ATP. We have the ingredients in ADP and the spare phosphate, and what is needed is energy to reattach the phosphate to the ADP. It is the three-energy system that provides the energy for this reaction to happen.

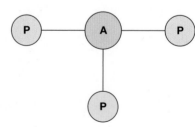

Fig 1.38 ATP

Creatine Phosphate System

If energy is needed for an activity of high intensity and low duration, such as 100-m sprinting, or jumping in basketball, it will be needed very rapidly to produce a muscular contraction. The cells contain a small amount of ATP (about 3 seconds' worth) and a small amount of a second high-energy compound called creatine phosphate (CP). There is enough CP to provide a further 5 to 7 seconds' worth of energy. The CP will be broken down to provide the energy to resynthesise the ATP.

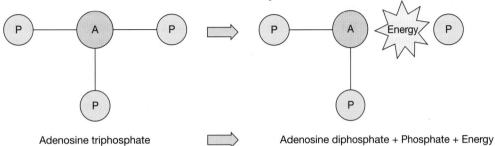

Adenosine triphosphate   Adenosine diphosphate + Phosphate + Energy

Fig 1.39 Breakdown of ATP to ADP

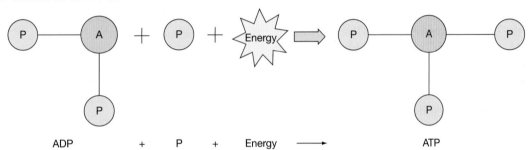

ADP   +   P   +   Energy ⟶   ATP

Fig 1.40 Resynthesis of ATP

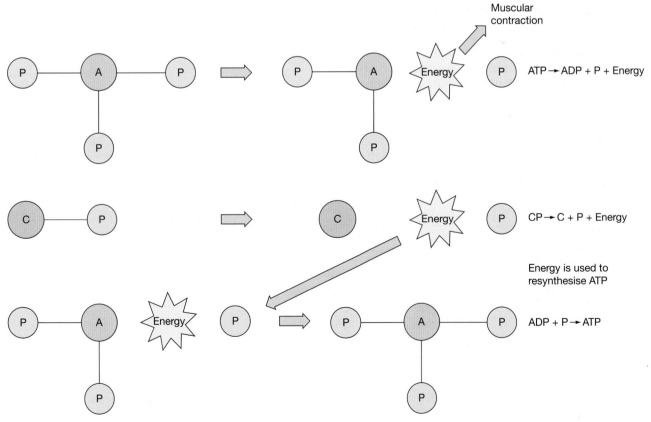

Muscular contraction

ATP → ADP + P + Energy

CP → C + P + Energy

Energy is used to resynthesise ATP

ADP + P → ATP

Fig 1.41 Creatine phosphate resynthesises ATP

This system will last until the stored CP has run out. Along with breaking down the stores of ATP in the muscles this system will last for around 8 to 10 seconds and is used for high-intensity activities.

Lactic Acid System

When stores of ATP and PC have run out, the body has a second way of providing energy quickly. This is used when activity is intense and lasts around 1 to 3 minutes. This system relies upon the breakdown of glucose that has been stored in the muscles (this is called glycogen). Energy for muscular contraction is still needed rapidly and the body does not have time to deliver oxygen to the working muscles; therefore, the glucose has to be broken down without oxygen. This is called anaerobic (absence of oxygen) and is referred to as anaerobic glycolysis.

As glucose is broken down in the muscles to provide the energy to resynthesise ATP, a by-product, lactic acid, is produced. This lactic acid can produce a burning, uncomfortable feeling in the muscles and limit performance. In reality the glucose is first broken down into pyruvic acid and then into lactic acid. This process will produce three ATP per glucose molecule.

$$\text{Glucose} \rightarrow \text{Pyruvic acid} = \text{no oxygen} \rightarrow \text{Energy} = \text{Lactic acid}$$

Aerobic System

This system differs from the other two because it requires oxygen to break down glucose or fat and produce energy for the resynthesis of ATP. It will be used when the intensity of an activity is lower and the duration longer. It tends to be used during rhythmical, repetitive activities such as long-distance running, cycling and swimming.

The aerobic system will produce carbon dioxide, water and heat as waste products of the aerobic breakdown of glucose and fats. Carbon dioxide is breathed out with some of the water, which can also be lost as sweat when the heat is dissipated from the body.

The aerobic system can produce energy by breaking down glucose (from carbohydrates) or fat. Fat is a much richer store of energy for ATP resynthesis, but can be used only in low-intensity exercise because it is a lengthy process. At the higher intensities fuel is needed more quickly and glucose will be used to provide this energy.

The fuel used also depends upon the fitness of the individual because fitter people become more effective at burning fats. The result of this is that their glycogen stores will go further and last longer. For example, Paula Radcliffe can run a marathon without any discernible loss of performance towards the end of the race.

The aerobic system provides the most plentiful supply of oxygen in that if one molecule of glycogen is broken down aerobically it will provide 38 ATP; while one molecule of fat will provide 128 ATP.

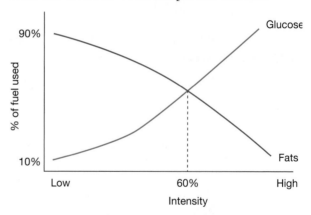

Fig 1.42 Fuel used for the aerobic system depends upon the intensity of the activity

Anaerobic				Aerobic
Creatine phosphate	Lactic acid			Oxygen
Weight lifting	Tennis	800 m run	1500 m run	Marathon
100 m run	Football	200 m swim	400 m swim	Skating 10 k
Shot-put	Rugby	Boxing		50 k walk
Golf swing	400 m run			50 k cycle

Fig 1.43 Energy continuum

Criteria	Creatine phosphate	Lactic acid	Aerobic
Speed of energy production	Very fast	Fast	Slow
Energy source	Creatine phosphate	Glycogen	Glycogen and fat
Amount of ATP produced	Very limited	Limited	Unlimited
Production of waste products	None	Lactic acid is produced as a by-product	Carbon dioxide and water which are eliminated
Duration of energy production	8–10 seconds	1–3 minutes	Up to 2 hours
Intensity used as % of maximum intensity	High intensity (95–100%)	Moderate to high intensity (60–95%)	Low intensity (<60%)
Length of time to recover	30 seconds to 4 minutes	20 minutes to 2 hours	Time to rest and replace glycogen stores

Table 1.5 Summary of energy systems

Application to Sport

Different sports will utilise different energy systems depending upon the demands of the sport and the speed at which energy is required (see Table 1.5 and Fig 1.43).

The sports of football and tennis may appear to use the aerobic system because they last for a long time; however, they predominantly use the anaerobic system due to the fact that they involve bursts of energy followed by periods of recovery, rather than consistent movement.

Key learning points 5

- ATP is used by muscles to produce movement.
- ATP is produced through three energy systems – creatine phosphate, lactic acid and the aerobic energy system.
- The creatine phosphate and lacitc acid energy systems do not use oxygen and are classes as anaerobic energy systems.

Quick quiz 5

Energy requirements of physical activity

In order to take part in sports, our bodies use the food we have eaten to go through the energy systems to produce energy. Different sports have different energy requirements:

Type of exercise	Kilocalories used per hour
Aerobics	450
Aqua aerobics	400
Bicycling	450
Cross-country ski machine	500
Hiking	500
Jogging, 5 mph	500
Rowing	550
Running	700
Skipping with rope	700

29

Type of exercise	Kilocalories used per hour
Spinning	650
Step aerobics	550
Squash	650
Swimming	500
Table tennis	290
Tennis	350
Walking, 3 mph	280

1 Look at the list of energy requirements for different sports in the table above. Note the four that require the most kcalories, and try to explain why you think they require the most energy.

2 Which activities would use the CP energy system?

3 Which activites would use the lactic acid energy system?

4 Which activities would use the aerobic energy system?

Student activity 1.7　　⏱ 60 minutes　P7　M4　D2

Energy Systems and sport and exercise

Task 1

Select different sport or exercise activities that uses the:

(a) the creatine phosphate energy sytem

(b) lactic acid energy sytem

(c) aerobic energy systems.

Task 2

Describe, explain and analyse the three different energy systems and how they are used in your selected sport and exercise activities.

Further reading

Kapit, W. and Elson, L. (2001) *The Anatomy Coloring Book*, Benjamin Cummings.

Useful websites

www.bhf.org.uk/research_health_professionals/resources.aspx

Guidance, statistics and information about research publications from the British Heart Foundation.

www.bhf.org.uk/keeping_your_heart_healthy/Default.aspx

Information for the general public on how to keep your heart healthy.

www.getbodysmart.com

An online examination of human anatomy and physiology that will help you to see the structure of the different body systems.

www.innerbody.com

Good information and diagrams of the different body systems.

www.instantanatomy.net

Useful anatomy pictures and information.

www.medtropolis.com/VBody.asp

A very good interactive website for anatomy with quizzes and tutorials.

2: The Physiology of Fitness

2.1. Introduction

This unit explores the effects of both short- and long-term exercise on the body. The short-term effects of exercise on the musculoskeletal, cardiovascular, respiratory and energy systems will be explored first, followed by the long-term effects of exercise and how the various body systems adapt to training. A range of methods to investigate the physiological effects of exercise on the body systems are also explored.

By the end of this unit you should:

- know the body's response to acute exercise
- know the long-term effects of exercise on the body systems
- be able to investigate the physiological effects of exercise on the body systems.

Assessment and grading criteria

To achieve a PASS grade the evidence must show that the learner is able to:	To achieve a MERIT grade the evidence must show that, in addition to the pass criteria, the learner is able to:	To achieve a DISTINCTION grade the evidence must show that, in addition to the pass and merit criteria, the learner is able to:
P1 describe the musculoskeletal and energy systems' response to acute exercise	**M1** explain the response of the musculoskeletal, cardiovascular and respiratory systems to acute exercise	
P2 describe the cardiovascular and respiratory systems' responses to acute exercise		
P3 describe the long-term effects of exercise on the musculoskeletal system and energy systems		
P4 describe the long-term effects of exercise on the cardiovascular and respiratory systems	**M2** explain the long-term effects of exercise on the musculoskeletal, cardiovascular, respiratory and energy systems	
P5 collect physiological data to investigate the effects of exercise on the musculoskeletal, cardiovascular, respiratory and energy systems, with tutor support	**M3** collect physiological data to investigate the effects of exercise on the musculoskeletal, cardiovascular, respiratory and energy systems, with limited tutor support	**D1** independently investigate the physiological effects of exercise on the musculoskeletal, cardiovascular, respiratory and energy systems
P6 review physiological data collected, describing the effects of exercise on the musculoskeletal, cardiovascular, respiratory and energy systems.	**M4** review physiological data collected, explaining the effects of exercise on the musculoskeletal, cardiovascular, respiratory and energy systems.	**D2** review physiological data collected, analysing the effects of exercise on the musculoskeletal, cardiovascular, respiratory and energy systems.

2.2 The Body's Response to Acute Exercise

The Musculoskeletal System

The musculoskeletal system comprises the skeletal system and the muscular system.

Before taking part in exercise, we all know that we should warm up the body in order to prepare it for the different types of movements and activities that we are about to take part in. This process of warming up helps our musculoskeletal system to get ready for exercise and also makes us less likely to injure this system.

During a warm-up, we usually increase the heart rate and carry out mobilisation activities. By increasing our heart rate, we are pumping our blood round the body at a faster rate, which has the effect of warming up our muscles. When muscles become warmer, they become more pliable.

Key term

Pliable: able to change shape more easily.

Imagine a piece of plasticine. When it is cold and you pull it apart, it is likely to break and split into two pieces. However, if you warm up the plasticine in your hands and then pull it apart, it will start to stretch rather than break – this is because it has become more pliable. This same principle applies to muscles – if a muscle is cold and is suddenly stretched, it is more likely to tear, whereas if it is warmed up, it is more likely to stretch and not tear.

The process of mobilisation is used to increase joint mobility. Joint mobility is used to enable the joints to become lubricated, by releasing more synovial fluid onto the joints and then warming it up so it becomes more efficient. This means moving joints through their full range of movement. The movements will start off small and slowly become larger, until a full range of movement is achieved. The joints that need to be mobilised are shoulders, elbows, spine, hips, knees and ankles.

When taking part in resistance exercises, such as lifting weights, the process is actually designed to break some muscle fibres. These 'breaks' are called micro-tears, as the damage is usually very minimal. However, this 'damage' has to occur in order for the muscle to have the stimulation to rebuild itself, so that over time it will become bigger and stronger (see Section 2.3 for more details on the long-term effects of exercise on the body systems).

Acute Response of the Energy Systems to Exercise

The function of energy systems is to produce adenosine triphosphate (ATP). ATP is used to make our muscles contract and therefore allows us to take part in exercise. It is basically a protein (adenosine) with three (tri) phosphates (phosphate) attached to it.

When chemical bonds are broken, energy is released. Therefore, when a phosphate is broken off the ATP to make ADP (adenosine diphosphate; di = two), energy is released, which is used to make the muscles contract.

Fig 2.1 Adenosine triphosphate (ATP)

ATP is not stored in large amounts in skeletal muscle and therefore has to be made from ADP continually for our muscles to continue contracting. There are three energy systems that the body uses to make ATP. They differ in the rate at which they make ATP. At the onset of exercise, we want ATP supplied very quickly. However, if we are on a long walk, we do not need such a fast production of ATP, so the body uses a different energy system to make it.

Anaerobic Energy Systems

Anaerobic energy systems do not require oxygen. Both the phosphocreatine and lactic acid energy systems are anaerobic.

Phosphocreatine energy system

At the onset of exercise, the energy system that supplies the majority of ATP is the phosphocreatine system (also known as the creatine phosphate system). It supplies ATP much quicker than any other energy system. It produces ATP in the absence of oxygen, and is therefore an anaerobic energy system.

Phosphocreatine (PC) is made up of a phosphate and a creatine molecule. When the bond between the phosphate and the creatine is broken, energy is released which is then used to make the bond between ADP and a phosphate.

PC stores are used for rapid, high-intensity contractions, such as in sprinting or jumping. These stores only last for about ten seconds.

Lactic acid energy system

Once our PC stores have run out, we use the lactic acid system. This is also known as anaerobic glycolysis, which literally means the breakdown of glucose in the absence of oxygen. When glucose is broken down, it is converted into a substance called pyruvate. When there is no oxygen present, the pyruvate is converted into lactic acid. This system produces ATP very quickly, but not as quickly as the PC system.

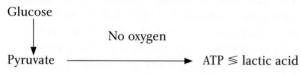

The lactic acid energy system is the one that is producing the majority of the ATP during high-intensity exercise lasting between 30 seconds and three minutes, such as an 800 m race.

Aerobic Energy System

The aerobic energy system requires oxygen. After we have been exercising for a few minutes, we start to use the aerobic energy system. The aerobic energy system provides ATP at a slower rate than the previous two energy systems discussed. It is responsible for producing the majority of our energy while our bodies are at rest or taking part in low-intensity exercise, such as jogging. It uses a series of reactions, the first being aerobic glycolysis, as it occurs when oxygen is available to break down glucose. As in the anaerobic energy system, glucose is broken down into pyruvate. Because oxygen is present, pyruvate is not turned into lactic acid, but continues to be broken down through a series of chemical reactions, which include:

● Krebs cycle
● Electron transport chain.

Both the Krebs cycle and the electron transport chain take place in organelles called mitochondria.

The majority of ATP is produced in these organelles, so they are very important for energy production.

The Energy Continuum

The energy systems all work together to produce energy; however, what we are doing determines which energy system supplies the majority of the ATP.

The energy continuum highlights which energy systems are producing the most amount of energy at different stages of an activity.

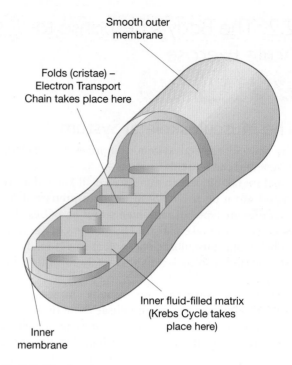

Fig 2.2 Mitochondrion

At rest, nearly all of our energy is provided by the aerobic energy system; then, if we suddenly start to exercise, we need more ATP than the aerobic energy system can supply, so the phosphocreatine and lactic acid energy systems supply the ATP.

In some sport and exercise activities, the energy supply comes from all three energy systems at different points – for example, in football, when you are jogging slowly, the aerobic energy system is used; for a short sprint to get to the ball, the phospho-creatine system is used; then running back down the pitch and running quickly to defend will mainly use the lactic acid energy system.

Energy Requirements of Physical Activity

In order to take part in sports, our body uses the food we have eaten, converted by the energy systems to produce energy. Different sports have different energy requirements (see Table 2.1).

Type of exercise	Kilocalories used per hour
Aerobics	450
Aqua aerobics	400
Bicycling	450
Cross-country ski machine	500
Hiking	500
Jogging, 5 mph	500
Rowing	550
Running	700
Skipping with rope	720
Spinning	650
Step aerobics	550
Squash	650
Swimming	500
Table tennis	290
Tennis	350
Walking, 3 mph	280

Table 2.1 Energy requirements for different sports

Acute Response of the Cardiovascular System to Exercise

The cardiovascular system consists of the heart and the blood vessels, through which the heart pumps blood around the body. During exercise, a number of changes take place to the cardiovascular system to ensure that the muscles receive the required amounts of oxygen and nutrients.

If you take part in one exercise session – for example, a game of basketball, the cardiovascular system responds in a variety of ways, some of which you may well be aware of:

● Increased heart rate
● Increased blood pressure
● Redirection of blood flow
  – Blood vessels close to the skin surface become enlarged – this occurs via a process called vasodilation
  – More blood is pumped to working skeletal muscle
  – Less blood is pumped to organs that are not in need of oxygen (e.g. digestive system); this process is called vasoconstriction.

Heart Rate: Anticipatory Increase and Activity Response

During exercise, the heart rate needs to be increased in order to ensure that the working muscles receive enough nutrients and oxygen, and that waste products are removed. Before you even start exercising, there is an increase in your heart rate, called the anticipatory rise. The anticipatory rise occurs because when you think about exercising your body releases adrenaline, which makes your heart beat faster.

Key term

Adrenaline (also known as epinephrine): a hormone released during times of stress which gets the body ready for action (e.g. increases blood pressure, heart rate, etc.).

Once you start exercising, your body releases more adrenaline, which further increases your heart rate. In a trained athlete, heart rate can increase by up to three times within one minute of starting exercise.

35

Blood Pressure

Blood pressure is necessary in order to force blood to flow around the body. The contraction of the heart produces this blood pressure as it pushes blood into the blood vessels. Two values are given when a person has their blood pressure taken; a typical blood pressure for the average adult male is 120/80. The two values correspond to the systolic value (when the heart is contracting) and the diastolic value (when the heart is relaxing). The higher value is the systolic value and the lower is the diastolic value. Blood pressure is measured in milligrams of mercury, mmHg.

As discussed previously, exercise has the affect of increasing heart rate, which means the heart is contracting more frequently, which then has the effect of increasing a person's blood pressure. A typical blood pressure reading for a person the onset of exercise would be around 140/85.

Redirection of Blood Flow

Blood flows through the body through arteries, arterioles, capillaries, veins and venules. However, not every one of these blood vessels is in use at the same time. Blood is directed to where it is needed, so for example, after we have eaten some food, more blood is directed to the stomach to help us to digest it. When a person is exercising or taking part in a sport, blood is directed to the muscles that are working: if a person is running, more blood will be directed to flow around the leg muscles, so that oxygen and nutrients can be delivered to these muscles so that they can function; if a person is playing tennis, more blood will be directed to the arm that is holding the racket compared to the other arm, as the racket arm is doing more work.

During exercise or sports participation, blood is also directed to flow through blood vessels that are close to the skin surface, to help to cool down the

body. You will no doubt have experienced the colour change in your face when you are taking part in an energetic sport – it will turn from a paler colour to a pink or red colour.

Short-term Effects of Exercise on the Respiratory System

The respiratory system is responsible for getting oxygen into the body and getting carbon dioxide out of the body (described in detail in Unit 1: Principles of Anatomy and Physiology in Sport). Oxygen is utilised to help produce energy so that we can take part in sporting activities. The process of creating energy also produces a waste product called carbon dioxide, which needs to be removed from the body and is breathed out by the lungs.

Pulmonary Ventilation and Breathing Rate

The amount of air we breathe in and out per minute is called pulmonary ventilation and is given the symbol V_E.

Pulmonary ventilation can be worked out using the following equation:

$$V_E = \text{Frequency} \times \text{Tidal volume}$$

Frequency is the number of breaths per minute.

Tidal volume is the volume of air breathed in and out during one breath.

At rest, the average breathing rate is around 12 breaths per minute. The average tidal volume is 0.5 l (this will vary depending on age, gender and a person's size). Therefore, the average pulmonary ventilation at rest is:

$$V_E = 12 \times 0.5$$
$$= 6 \text{ litres}$$

When you start to exercise, you need to take more oxygen into your body in order for it to be used to help produce energy. At the start of exercise, this increased oxygen demand occurs by breathing at a faster rate, and by breathing in and breathing out more air during each breath (i.e. tidal volume increases).

The intercostals muscles are used to aid breathing during exercise.

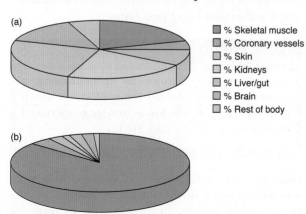

(a)
- ■ % Skeletal muscle
- ■ % Coronary vessels
- □ % Skin
- □ % Kidneys
- □ % Liver/gut
- □ % Brain
- □ % Rest of body

(b)

Fig 2.3 (a) The distribution of cardiac output at rest and (b) the distribution of cardiac output during exercise

Key term

Intercostal muscles: these are located between the ribs. There are two kinds of intercostal muscles: internal and external. They help with inspiration and expiration during exercise.

External intercostal muscles cause the rib cage to pivot on the thoracic vertebrae and move upwards and outwards.

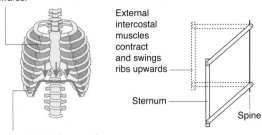

External intercostal muscles contract and swings ribs upwards

Sternum

Spine

Diaphragm contracts downwards, increasing the 'depth' of the thoratic cavity.

Fig 2.4 Action of the ribcage during inspiration

Relaxation of respiratory muscles cause the rib cage to move downwards and inwards.

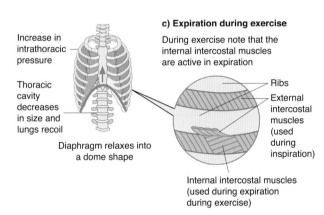

c) Expiration during exercise

Increase in intrathoracic pressure

Thoracic cavity decreases in size and lungs recoil

Diaphragm relaxes into a dome shape

During exercise note that the internal intercostal muscles are active in expiration

Ribs

External intercostal muscles (used during inspiration)

Internal intercostal muscles (used during expiration during exercise)

Fig 2.5 Action of the ribcage during expiration

The external intercostal muscles help with inspiration and the internal intercostal muscles help with expiration. As exercise becomes more strenuous, the abdominal muscles will also help aid expiration.

Key learning points 1

- At the onset of exercise, the various systems respond to try to increase oxygen delivery, energy production and carbon dioxide removal.
- The short-term effects of exercise on the body systems are as follows:
  - **Musculoskeletal system:** increased joint range of movement; micro-tears in muscle fibres from resistance exercises
  - **Energy system:** ATP is produced by anaerobic energy systems – the phosphocreatine energy system, the lactic acid energy system and the aerobic energy system
  - **Cardiovascular system:** increase in heart rate; increase in blood pressure; redirection of blood flow to working skeletal muscles and skin surface
  - **Respiratory system:** increase in breathing rate; increase in tidal volume.

Student activity 2.1   ⏱ 60–90 mins   P1 P2 M1

Task 1

Draw a spider diagram that illustrates the musculoskeletal, cardiovascular, respiratory and energy systems' responses to acute exercise.

Task 2

Using the spider diagram that you have drawn in Task 1, write a report that describe and explains the responses to acute exercise of the:

- Musculoskeletal system
- Energy systems
- Cardiovascular system
- Respiratory system.

(Q) Quick quiz 1

Select the appropriate term from the following list to answer each of the questions below:

- Adrenaline
- Synovial fluid
- Pulmonary ventilation
- 12
- Spirometer
- Micro-tears
- 120/80
- Sit-and-reach test
- Tidal volume
- Skeletal muscle.

1 The average breathing rate for a person at rest.

2 This test can be used to measure the range of movement at joints.

3 This hormone is released before and during exercise, to increase the heart rate.

4 The technical term for breaths per minute.

5 This is released into the joints during a warm-up to help increase their range of movement.

6 An adult's average resting blood pressure.

7 The amount of air breathed in and out in one breath.

8 This can be used to measure tidal volume.

9 These occur in muscle tissue during resistance exercises.

10 Blood is directed here during exercise.

2.3 Long-term Effects of Exercise on the Body Systems

Chronic exercise means that a person has been participating in regular exercise for long periods of time (a minimum of eight weeks). This regular participation affects the body in a number of ways that make it more able to cope with the stresses of the exercise. This results in the person being able to exercise at higher intensities and/or for longer periods of time – this process is called adaptation.

Cardiovascular Adaptations

The main adaptations that occur to the cardio-vascular system through endurance training are concerned with increasing the delivery of oxygen to the working muscles. If you were to dissect the heart of a top endurance athlete, you would find that the size of the walls of the left ventricle are markedly thicker than those of a person who does not perform endurance exercise. This adaptation is called cardiac hypertrophy.

Adaptation occurs in the same way that we increase the size of our skeletal muscles – the more we exercise our muscles, the larger or more toned they become. In the same way, the more we exercise our heart through aerobic training, the larger it will become. This will then have the effect of increasing the stroke volume, which is the amount of blood that the heart can pump out per beat. As the heart wall becomes bigger, it can pump more blood per beat, as the thicker wall can contract more forcibly. As the stroke volume is increased, the heart no longer needs to beat as often to get the same amount of blood around the body. This results in a decrease in heart rate, which is known as bradycardia.

Key terms

Cardiac hypertrophy: the size of the heart wall becomes thicker and stronger.

Bradycardia: decreased resting heart rate.

Fig 2.6 The athlete's body has adapted to strength training

due to an increase in the number of red blood cells (which contain the haemoglobin) further aids the transport of oxygen. Though haemoglobin content rises, the increase in blood plasma is greater, and consequently the blood haematocrit (ratio of red blood cell volume to total blood volume) is reduced, which lowers viscosity (thickness) and enables the blood to flow more easily. Resting blood pressure is also reduced, which puts less strain on a person's heart. Recovery time after exercise is reduced, which means breathing rate and heart rate return to resting values sooner than a person who has not taken part in endurance training. There is also an increase in a person's fitness.

Strength training produces very few adaptations to the cardiovascular system, as this training does not stress the heart or oxygen delivery and extraction systems for sustained periods of time.

Muscular System Adaptations

Resistance Training

If you exercise with some sort of resistance (e.g. weights, resistance bands, body weight as in press-ups), it will stress the skeletal muscle. This actually results in parts of the muscle breaking. The more you stress the muscle with heavier weights, the more the muscle breaks down. After having rested and eaten the right foods, the body then starts to repair itself and will actually mend the muscle tissue and make it bigger and better than before. If you continue this process, the muscle tissue will keep getting bigger, which will result in an increase in your muscle size – this is called hypertrophy.

An average male adult's heart rate is 70 beats per minute (b.p.m.). However, Lance Armstrong, a Tour de France champion, has a recorded resting heart rate of 30 b.p.m.! As stroke volume increases, cardiac output also increases, so an endurance athlete's heart can pump more blood per minute than non-trained people. However, resting values of cardiac output do not change; these are around 5 l per minute.

An endurance athlete has more capillaries, allowing more blood to travel through them. This process, called capillarisation, aids in the extraction of oxygen from the bloodstream. An increase in haemoglobin

Fig 2.7 Muscles get larger through resistance training

Key term

Hypertrophy: an increase in the size of skeletal muscle.

Resistance exercise will also result in increasing the strength of muscle tendons.

Endurance Training

Endurance training results in an increase in the muscular stores of muscle glycogen. There is increased delivery of oxygen to the muscles through an increase in the concentration of myoglobin and increased capillary density through the muscle. The ability of skeletal muscle to consume oxygen is increased as a direct result of an increase in the number and size of the mitochondria and an increase in the activity and concentration of enzymes involved in the aerobic processes that take place in the mitochondria. As a result, there is greater scope to use glycogen and fat as fuels. Slow-twitch fibres can enlarge by up to 22 per cent, which offers greater potential for aerobic energy production. Hypertrophy of slow-twitch fibres means that there is a corresponding increase in the stores of glycogen and triglycerides. This ensures a continuous supply of energy, enabling exercise to be performed for longer.

These adaptations result in an increased maximal oxygen consumption (VO_2max) being obtained before the anaerobic threshold is reached and fatigue begins.

Skeletal adaptations

Our skeleton responds to aerobic weight-bearing exercise or resistance exercise by becoming stronger and more able to withstand impact, which means you are less likely to break a bone if you fall over.

Key term

Weight-bearing exercise: when we are using our body weight as a form of resistance (e.g. walking, running).

This occurs because the stimulation of exercise means the mineral content (calcium, in particular) is increased, which makes bones harder and stronger. Exercise also has an effect on joints by increasing the thickness of cartilage at the ends of the bones and increasing the production of synovial fluid. This will have the effect of making joints stronger and less prone to injury. Strength training increases the strength of muscle tendons, which again makes them less prone to injury. Lastly, the ligaments which hold our bones together are able to stretch to a greater degree, which helps to prevent injuries such as joint strains.

Respiratory System Adaptations

The respiratory system deals with taking oxygen into the body and also with helping to remove waste products associated with muscle metabolism. Training reduces the resting respiratory rate and the breathing rate during sub-maximal exercise. Endurance training can also provide a small increase in lung volumes: vital capacity increases slightly, as does tidal volume, during maximal exercise. The increased strength of the respiratory muscles is partly responsible for this, as it aids lung inflation.

Endurance training also increases the capillarisation around the alveoli in the lungs. This helps to increase the rate of gas exchange in the lungs, and therefore increase the amount of oxygen entering the blood and the amount of carbon dioxide leaving the blood.

Energy System Adaptations

High-intensity training results in hypertrophy of fast-twitch fibres. There are increased levels of ATP and PC in the muscle and an increased capacity to generate ATP by the PC energy system. This is partly due to the increased activity of the enzymes that break down PC. ATP production by anaerobic glycolysis is increased as a result of enhanced activity of the glycolytic enzymes. There is also an increased ability to break down glycogen in the absence of oxygen.

As lactic acid accumulates, it decreases the pH levels of the blood, making it more acidic. This increased level of hydrogen ions will eventually prevent the glycolytic enzyme functioning. However, anaerobic training increases the buffering capacity of the body and enables it to work for longer in periods of high acidity.

Aerobic training will increase the number of mitochondria in slow-twitch muscle fibres. This will allow greater production of ATP through the aerobic energy system. Greater amounts of glycogen can be stored in the liver and skeletal muscle. Aerobic training results in an increase in the number of enzymes required for body fat to be broken down, and more body fat is stored in muscle tissue, which means that more fat can be used as an energy source.

Anaerobic or strength training predominantly uses the PC and lactic acid energy systems. Chronic anaerobic/strength training increases the body's tolerance levels to low pH. This means that more energy can be produced by the lactic acid energy system, and the increased production of lactic acid can be tolerated for longer.

Key learning points 2

- Adaptations to aerobic exercise are:
  - **Cardiovascular system:** cardiac hypertrophy; increased stroke volume; decreased resting heart rate; increased number of capillaries; increased number of red blood cells; decreased haematocrit.
  - **Respiratory system:** decreased resting breathing rate; increased lung volume; increased vital capacity; increased tidal volume (in maximal exercise); increased strength of respiratory muscles; increased capillarisation around alveoli.
  - **Neuromuscular system:** increased myoglobin content; increased number of capillaries; increased number of mitochondria; hypertrophy of slow-twitch muscle fibres; increased stores of glycogen; increased stores of fat.
  - **Energy systems:** increased number of aerobic enzymes; increased breakdown of fat.
- Adaptations to anaerobic exercise are:
  - **Cardiovascular system:** no significant adaptations.
  - **Respiratory system:** no significant adaptations.
  - **Neuromuscular:** hypertrophy of fast-twitch muscle fibres; increased content of ATP; increased content of PC; increased tolerance to lactic acid.
  - **Energy systems:** increased number of anaerobic enzymes.
  - **Skeletal system:** increased strength of bones; increased strength of tendons; increased stretch of ligaments.

Student activity 2.2 60–90 mins

Taking part in long-term exercise programmes – such as four 30-minute jogging sessions per week for eight weeks or a six-week resistance training programme – will stimulate the body adapt to the exercise so that it is able to perform the activity more readily, with less perceived effort.

Task 1

Draw a spider diagram that illustrates how the following energy systems adapt to long-term exercise:

- Cardiovascular
- Respiratory
- Skeletal
- Neuromuscular.

Task 2

Write a report that describes and explains how the cardiovascular, respiratory, skeletal, neuromuscular and energy systems adapt to long-term exercise.

Quick quiz 2

1 Explain what cardiac hypertrophy is and how this can help an endurance athlete.
2 Explain how capillarisation around the lungs can increase the rate of gas exchange.
3 Explain how the skeletal system adapts to weight-bearing exercises.
4 Describe how the cardiovascular and respiratory systems of Paula Radcliffe will have adapted through endurance training.
5 Describe how the muscular and skeletal systems of Usain Bolt will have adapted through resistance training.

2.4 Investigating the Physiological Effects of Exercise on the Body Systems

In order to investigate the effects of exercise on the body systems, you will need to select at least two different types of exercise activities to explore, as different activities produce different effects on the body systems.

Examples of types of exercise that you may like to investigate include:

- Aerobic exercises (e.g. jogging, cycling) – for these activities you may have access to a treadmill or cycle ergometer, which would make it easier to take physiological readings of the participant while exercising
- Resistance exercise (e.g. fixed weights, free weights, resistance bands and body weight)
- Circuit – this type of exercise is called interval training, in which a person will exercise at a high intensity for short periods of time (about one minute) and then have a short rest period before carrying out a different activity at a different circuit station
- Strength training – this type of exercise uses a form of resistance to exercise against (e.g. body weight as in press-ups, fixed or free weights, resistance bands).

Methods of Investigation

Your method of investigation will need to take into account what you are trying to find out.

Fig 2.8 A resistance exercise class

Physiological reading	Pre-exercise	During exercise	After exercise
Heart rate (b.p.m.)			
Blood pressure			
Ventilation rate			
Tidal volume			
Range of movement available at selected joints			

Table 2.2 Recording physiological readings

The investigation design will depend on what you are hoping to examine. For example, if you want to investigate how the body systems adapt to an endurance or resistance training programme, you would need to take pre-training programme measurements of each of the body systems and then record all these measurements again once the training programme is complete, in order to determine if any of the body systems have adapted as a result of the training.

Whatever your research design, you will need to ensure that you take the following measurements in your investigation:

● Pre-exercise results
● During-exercise readings
● Post-exercise readings.

You will therefore need to ensure that you select exercises for your investigation that can be carried out while physiological measurements are taken.

Recording Information

You will need to design a recording sheet onto which you can record your physiological readings. An example of a recording sheet is shown in Table 2.2.

Taking Pre-exercise Physiological Readings

The information in this section provides you with ideas for measuring different physiological variables for each of the different body systems. You will probably have access to most of the equipment used in these examples at your centre; however, if you have access to more advanced pieces of testing equipment, it would be a good idea to use these in your investigation.

Respiratory System

Measuring pre-exercise breathing rate and tidal volume

1   While sitting or lying down, count the number of times you breathe in during one minute – try to breathe as normally as possible.
2   Write down the number of breaths and then work out your pulmonary ventilation, using the equation: V_E = Frequency × Tidal volume.
3   Using a spirometer, work out how much air you breathe in and out (your tidal volume) at rest.

Cardiovascular System

Measuring pre-exercise and anticipatory heart rate

1   If you have a heart-rate monitor, place it around your chest. If not, find your pulse point, either on your neck or at your wrist.
2   Sit quietly for five minutes, then take your resting heart rate. If you have a heart-rate monitor, write down the heart rate that appears on the monitor. If not, feel for your pulse point, then count your heart rate for 60 seconds and write it down.
3   Think about what exercise you are about to perform for one minute.
4   Record your heart rate after having thought about your exercise.

Measuring blood pressure

Blood pressure is taken using a manual sphygmomanometer and a stethoscope or an electronic blood-pressure meter. If you are using a manual sphygmomanometer, follow the guidelines shown below and make sure the process is supervised by a suitably qualified person.

1   Sit quietly and relax for around five minutes.
2   Your left arm should be resting on a chair arm, with the elbow at 45 degrees and the palm of the hand facing up.
3   Find the brachial pulse – it should be on the inner side of the arm, just under the biceps muscle.
4   Place the blood-pressure cuff about 2–3 cm above the elbow.
5   Place the earpieces of the stethoscope in your ears and place the stethoscope over the brachial pulse.
6   Inflate the cuff up to 200 mmHg.
7   Slowly open the valve by turning it anticlockwise and release the pressure.
8   Listen out for the first time you hear the thud of the heartbeat and make a mental note of it; this is the systolic blood pressure reading.
9   Keep deflating the cuff and when the heartbeat becomes muffled or disappears, this is your diastolic reading.
10   Keep deflating the cuff and, if necessary, repeat after around 30 seconds to check your readings.

Musculoskeletal System

Measuring pre-exercise range of movement at joints

For these activities, you will need to compare your joint range of movement before and after exercise. It is important that you remember that your body will not be warmed up before exercise participation;

therefore, during any testing, you must be very careful not to overstretch and risk the possibility of injuring your body.

You should take part in a range of different flexibility tests and make a note of the readings for each test; these might include:

- Sit and reach
- Calf stretch
- Shoulder stretch.

If you have access to a goniometer, use this to measure the range of movement available at selected joints.

Energy Systems

Physiological readings for how energy systems respond to exercise usually require quite sophisticated equipment, such as blood-lactate analysers and online gas analyses to measure the respiratory quotient. If you have access to this type of equipment, you will gain some useful information on which energy systems are being used at different points in the exercise activity, and post-training results will show how the energy systems have adapted to training.

Most centres do not have access to this kind of equipment, so the physiological readings will have to be inferred from the results of the tests shown below. For these activities you will need access to a running track, a stopwatch and a rate of perceived exertion (RPE) chart.

Borg's 15-point Scale

RPE was developed by Gunnar Borg and is a scale that can be used by the participant to rate how hard they feel they are working between two extremes. Rather than monitoring heart rate, the participant is introduced to the scale and then asked during the aerobic session where they feel they are on the scale.

- 6
- 7   Very, very light (rest)
- 8
- 9   Very light – gentle walking
- 10
- 11   Fairly light
- 12
- 13   Somewhat hard – steady pace
- 14
- 15   Hard
- 16
- 17   Very hard
- 18
- 19   Very, very hard
- 20   Exhaustion

Borg's Modified RPE Scale

Borg's scale has been modified to a ten-point scale because some participants have found working between 6 and 20 difficult.

- 0   Nothing at all
- 1   Very light
- 2   Fairly light
- 3   Moderate
- 4   Some what hard
- 5   Hard
- 6
- 7   Very hard
- 8
- 9
- 10   Exhaustion

Phosphocreatine Energy System

To test the phosphocreatine energy system:

1 Measure out 30 m on the running track.
2 With a stopwatch, time how long it takes you to sprint 30 m.
3 Walk quickly back to the start line and repeat the whole process so that you complete a total of six 30 m sprints.
4 Record the times for each 30 m sprint and your perceived exertion for each.
5 Add up the total times for each run.

Lactic Acid Energy System

To test the lactic acid energy system:

1 Measure out 300 m on the running track.
2 With a stopwatch, time how long it takes you to run 300 m.
3 Walk quickly back to the start line and repeat the process twice more, so that you complete a total of three 300 m sprints.
4 Record the times for each run and your perceived exertion for each.
5 Add up the total times for each run.

Aerobic Energy System

To test the aerobic energy system:

1 Work out how many times you need to run round the track to complete an 800 m run.
2 With a stopwatch, time how long it takes you to complete an 800 m run.
3 Record the time taken for this run and your perceived exertion.

Energy System Adaptation

In order to determine how the energy systems have altered as a result of training, you will need to repeat these tests after the training. If the results show a reduction in:

- total time for a specific set of runs
- perceived exertion for a specific set of runs

you can infer that the training has led to adaptations of the main energy system responsible for supplying ATP for that set of runs.

During-exercise Tests

Where possible, each of the pre-test measurements will need to be taken at a certain point while the person is exercising. You may wish to take a number of readings (e.g. at two-minute or five-minute intervals until the exercise has been completed).

Post-exercise Tests

Once the person has stopped exercising, these physiological readings will need to be taken again. You will need to take at least one post-exercise physiological reading of each variable, but if you want to track the recovery of your subject, you would need to take a series of readings (e.g. at two- to five-minute intervals until the readings have returned to pre-exercise levels).

Review of the Effects of Exercise on the Body Systems

You will need to examine all the data that you have obtained from your physiological readings and energy system run tests, in order to review what you have found out.

From this information, try to determine how exercise affected the various body systems during the first round of tests – did they respond how you expected them to in relation to the knowledge you have gained from the first part of this unit? If some body systems did not respond in the way you expected, can you try to describe why this may have happened (maybe you had trouble taking the physiological data while the subject was exercising, so they might have had to slow down or alter their intended exercise intensity)?

Then you will need to determine if the subject's body systems adapted as a result of taking on a specific training programme and how the differences in physiological readings and energy system runs illustrate the adaptations that have taken place.

Lastly, you will need to consider the types of exercise you used in your testing process and the advantages and disadvantages of this choice in terms of ease of taking physiological measurements, and so on.

Key learning points 3

- Methods of investigation include comparison of pre-exercise, during-exercise and post-exercise physiological readings.
- Physiological readings include heart rate, blood pressure, flexibility tests, tidal volume rating of perceived exertion.
- Both acute and long-term adaptations to the body systems need to be examined.

Student activity 2.3 | 3–5 hours | P5 P6 M3 M4 D1

Task 1

Carry out an investigation or investigations so that you can collect physiological data on the effects of exercise on the following body systems:

- Musculoskeletal
- Cardiovascular
- Respiratory
- Energy.

Task 2 | D2

Examine the physiological data you have collected and, using these data, write a review that describes, explains and analyses the effects of exercise on the following body systems:

- Musculoskeletal
- Cardiovascular
- Respiratory
- Energy.

Q Quick quiz 3

1 How and why does heart rate change from resting, during-exercise to post-exercise values?
2 How and why does breathing rate change from resting, during-exercise to post-exercise values?
3 Explain the different methods of measuring how energy systems function and adapt to training.
4 Explain what the rating of perceived exertion means.

Further reading

Adams, G.M. (2001) *Exercise Physiology Laboratory Manual: Health and Human Performance*, McGraw-Hill Higher Education.

American College of Sports Medicine (2005) *ACSM's Guidelines for Exercise Testing and Prescription*, 7th edn, Lippincott Williams and Wilkins.

American College of Sports Medicine (2007) *ACSM's Health-Related Physical Fitness Assessment Manual*, Lippincott Williams and Wilkins.

Coulson, M. (2007) *The Fitness Instructor's Handbook: A Complete Guide to Health and Fitness – Fitness Professionals*, A&C Black.

Heyward, V.H. (2006) *Advanced Fitness Assessment and Exercise Prescription*, Human Kinetics.

National Coaching Foundation (1987) *Physiology and Performance: NCF Coaching Handbook No. 3*, Coachwise.

Powers, S.K. and Howley, E.T. (2006) *Exercise Physiology: Theory and Application to Fitness and Performance*, McGraw Hill Higher Education.

Sharkey, B.J. and Gaskill, S.E. (2006) *Fitness and Health*, Human Kinetics.

Watson, A.W.S. (1996) *Physical Fitness and Athletic Performance: A Guide for Students, Athletes and Coaches*, Longman.

Useful journals

American College of Sport Medicine's Health and Fitness Journal
British Journal of Sports Medicine
Exercise and Sport Sciences Reviews
International Journal of Sports Science and Coaching
Medicine and Science in Sports and Exercise
Research Quarterly for Exercise and Sport

Useful websites

www.getbodysmart.com
Free tutorials and quizzes from an American site that looks at human anatomy and physiology, helping you to see the structure of the different body systems.

www.innerbody.com
Free and informative diagrams of the different body systems, including respiratory, cardiovascular, skeletal and muscular

www.instantanatomy.net
Free useful anatomy pictures and information, mainly from a medical viewpoint

3: Assessing Risk in Sport

3.1 Introduction

Safety is a very important factor to consider when taking part in sports or leading sporting events. If sports leaders fail to ensure that health and safety guidelines are adhered to, this could result in a charge of 'negligence' being brought against them through the civil courts. It is therefore important that learners understand the legislative factors, regulations and legal responsibilities involved while working in sporting situations.

This unit will cover ways in which a sports leader can plan and carry out a sporting activity safely under the overall supervision of a more experienced person. It includes how to carry out risk assessments, preparation of the site and participants for the activity, and maintaining the safety of participants while taking part in the activity. The unit closes with ideas on how to plan a safe sporting activity.

By the end of this unit you should:

- know the key factors that influence health and safety in sport
- be able to carry out risk assessments
- know how to maintain the safety of participants and colleagues in a sports environment
- be able to plan a safe sporting activity.

Assessment and grading criteria

To achieve a PASS grade the evidence must show that the learner is able to:	To achieve a MERIT grade the evidence must show that, in addition to the pass criteria, the learner is able to:	To achieve a DISTINCTION grade the evidence must show that, in addition to the pass and merit criteria, the learner is able to:
P1 describe four legislative factors that influence health and safety in sport	**M1** compare and contrast the influences of legislation, legal factors and regulatory bodies on health and safety in sport	
P2 describe the legal factors and regulatory bodies that influence health and safety in sport		
P3 carry out risk assessments for two different sports activities, with tutor support	**M2** independently carry out risk assessments for two different sports activities	**D1** review the risk assessment controls and evaluate their effectiveness
P4 describe three procedures used to promote and maintain a healthy and safe sporting environment	**M3** explain three procedures used to promote and maintain a healthy and safe sporting environment	**D2** analyse three procedures used to promote and maintain a healthy and safe sporting environment.
P5 produce a plan for the safe delivery of a selected sports activity and review the plan.	**M4** explain the plan for the safe delivery of a selected sports activity and review the plan.	

3.2 Key Factors that Influence Health and Safety in Sport

Legislative Factors

> ### Key terms
>
> **Legislation:** a generic term for laws, which includes acts, regulations, orders and directives.
>
> **Directive:** a legislative act passed by the European Union that member states must adhere to.

A number of laws and acts have been devised to try to ensure that all safety precautions are taken into account while at work and during sports participation. Any person who works should be aware of these acts and make sure they do everything possible to adhere to the legislation.

Health and Safety at Work Act 1974

The Health and Safety at Work Act became law in 1974 in response to thousands of accidents and near misses in the workplace. Its purpose is to ensure that employers take reasonable steps to ensure the health, safety and welfare of their employees while they are at work. These steps include:

● Making sure the working environment and equipment are up to the necessary standard
● Ensuring that regular and appropriate safety checks are carried out
● Ensuring the safe use, handling and storage of equipment and substances
● Providing information, training and supervision to ensure that employees can do their jobs safely
● Regular monitoring of the working environment to ensure it is hygienic and that no toxic contaminants are present.

The Health and Safety at Work Act also requires employees to take reasonable steps to ensure their own safety. They are expected to cooperate with the employer to meet legal obligations and use the equipment provided appropriately.

Both the employer and employees benefit from this Act because:

● Fewer accidents mean better health for employees
● Fewer accidents mean more regular earnings for employees
● Less sickness means money saved by the employer and the NHS.

The majority of accidents that occur in the workplace are due to the following actions and circumstances:

● Lifting and carrying
● Slips, trips and falls
● Being hit by moving objects or vehicles
● Moving machinery
● Harmful substances.

Some illness and diseases can be work-related – for example, occupational deafness, back pain and stress.

The following three factors can affect health and safety in the workplace:

1. **Occupational factors** – people may be at risk from injuries or illnesses because of the work they do.
2. **Environmental factors** – the conditions in which people work may cause problems.
3. **Human factors** – poor attitudes and behaviour can contribute to accidents.

It is the responsibility of both the employer and employees to ensure that health and safety standards are maintained.

After the Health and Safety at Work Act was passed in 1974, RIDDOR was added in 1995. RIDDOR stands for the Reporting of Injuries, Diseases and Dangerous Occurrences Regulations, which came into force on 1 April 1996. It means that all work-related accidents, diseases and dangerous occurrences should be reported to the Incident Contact Centre (ICC). These include:

● Deaths
● Major injuries
● Injuries that last for more than three days
● Injuries to members of the public where they are taken to hospital
● Work-related diseases
● Dangerous occurrences – where something happens that does not result in a reportable injury, but which could have done.

Personal Protective Equipment Regulations 2002

Personal protective equipment should be used when a hazard cannot be sufficiently controlled by other health and safety measures.

A range of PPE exists to protect various parts of the body, such as goggles for the eyes, a helmet for the head, ear plugs for the ears, and so on.

> ### Key term
>
> **Personal protective equipment (PPE):** clothes and other items worn to protect the wearer against hazards.

Control of Substances Hazardous to Health Regulations (COSHH) 2002

Hazardous substances can cause a wide range of health problems, such as dermatitis and asthma; they may also cause other problems, such as explosions or fires.

In the sports industry you may be exposed to a range of hazardous substances, such as cleaning fluids or chlorine, which is used in swimming pools. All hazardous substances should have labels that detail the nature of the hazardous substance (e.g. corrosive, irritant, poison).

You must ensure that you have been trained in how to use the equipment properly and that you wear the appropriate PPE when dealing with these substances. All hazardous substances should be kept in a locked cabinet.

Key term

Hazardous substance: any material or substance with the potential to cause illness or injury to the people who come into contact with it.

Manual Handling Operations Regulations 1992

In the sports industry you will probably find yourself having to lift, move and set up sporting equipment. Therefore it is important that you learn safe lifting techniques. Maintaining a straight back at all times is the proper way to lift items, as shown in Figure 3.1. Typical injuries from incorrect manual handling are back sprains and strains, cuts, bruises, crushing, fractures, hernias and trapped nerves.

Key term

Manual handling: using the body to lift, carry, push or pull a load.

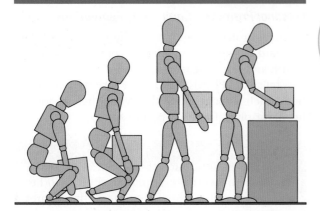

Fig 3.1 Manual handling guide

Health and Safety (First Aid) Regulations 1981

These regulations require companies and organisations to have sufficient first-aid facilities and equipment in case of illness or injury to employees. The number of qualified first-aiders will be related to the number of employees working in the organisation.

Fire Safety and Safety of Places of Sport Act 1987

This act was drawn up after the Bradford City football ground fire tragedy in 1985. It requires that all sports arenas and stadiums have sufficient means of escape in the event of a fire. Venues must also provide adequate equipment for fighting fires.

Adventure Activities Licensing Authority (AALA)

The Adventure Activities Licensing Authority was founded in 1996 and works in conjunction with the Adventure Licensing Service. Both are run by the Health and Safety Executive. Adventure Activities Licensing is responsible for inspecting activity centres and other outdoor and adventurous activity providers. If it is satisfied that a provider meets nationally accepted standards of good practice, it will issue a licence. This helps to provide the public with assurances that the activities are not exposing the participants to unnecessary danger or risks of injury.

Despite all this legislation, there are still fatalities in the workplace: in 2005–06, 220 workers were killed and 361 members of the public were fatally injured. This should remind you to remain vigilant

Fig 3.2 Health and Safety legislation

50

Prohibition
These signs tell you what you are not allowed to do, e.g. No smoking
Shape: Circular
Colour: White with red border and red crossbar running from top left to bottom right

Warning
These signs warn you of a danger
Shape: Triangular
Colour: Yellow with black border and letters

Mandatory
These signs tell you what you *must* do, e.g. wear ear protectors
Shape: Circular
Colour: Blue background with white symbol and letters

Warning
These signs tell you about safe areas or equipment, e.g. fire exit
Shape: Square or oblong
Colour: Green background with white symbol and letters

Fig 3.3 Safety signs

in maintaining your own and your co-workers' health and safety while at work.

Safety Signs

There are four types of safety signs (see Figure 3.3). Each type has a certain shape, colour and meaning.

Legal Factors

The court system within Britain has a structure that all legal cases have to pass through. There are a range of courts that deal with different types of charges:

- **Magistrates' court** – this is the lowest court in England and deals mainly with minor criminal matters
- **Crown court** – this deals with serious criminal charges, such as murders, with a judge and jury
- **Supreme Court** – this is the highest court in England and deals with appeals on important issues from the Court of Appeal
- **European Court of Justice** – this is the supreme law court in Europe. The decisions of this court have to be enforced by all member states.

Statutory Law

These are written laws set down by a governing authority. Any person breaking these laws is liable to be arrested by the police and prosecuted accordingly.

Civil Law

Civil law deals with the rights of private citizens and does not involve the police. An example of civil law would be when a person is suing a company or an individual for some form of negligence, or when a partner in a marriage wishes to divorce the other person.

If a company does not abide by the Health and Safety at Work Act and a person is injured as a result of this negligence, the company can be prosecuted because it has broken a statutory law. Also, the

---

Student activity 3.1   30 minutes   P1

There are a number of different types of legislation in sport today in order to help protect people from injury and ill health.

Task 1

Examine the dates on which each of the Acts came into effect. Carry out research to try to answer the following:

- What significant event occurred in 1985 which may have resulted in the Fire Safety and Safety of Places of Sport Act 1987?

- What event in 1993 may have resulted in the Adventure Activities Licensing Authority being formed?

- Why was RIDDOR added to the Health and Safety at Work Act?

Task 2

Prepare a leaflet describing four legislative factors that influence health and safety in sport.

employee who is injured can take out a civil case and sue the company for compensation.

Case Law

Case law is when a similar case has occurred previously and the accused person is prosecuted and/or sued in a similar manner to the previous case.

In Loco Parentis

In loco parentis basically means 'in place of the parent'. This means that a person or organisation has to take on the functions and responsibilities of a parent. An example of this would be a teacher supervising a student on a school trip. The teacher has overall responsibility for the child's health and safety. A person taking on a role *in loco parentis* is expected to apply the same standard of care as would a 'reasonable parent' acting within a range of reasonable responses.

Negligence

Negligence is the name given to a situation in which a person in a supervisory role basically fails to meet a 'standard' of care. The supervisor may be careless in their actions or lack of actions, such as not carrying out a full risk assessment which then results in a person taking part in the activity suffering from an injury or even death.

If a person is deemed to be negligent they may be held liable for any injuries or damages to the people involved.

Regulatory Bodies

A number of regulatory bodies have been set up to help to police employers and facilities so that they adhere to appropriate legislation. The Health and Safety Commission is in charge of health and safety regulation in the UK. The Health and Safety Executive and local authorities are responsible for enforcing these regulations. Staff from these organisations will inspect facilities and speak to staff to ensure the facility is being run appropriately. If the facility is not being run in accordance with legislation, it will be given actions to address within a set time period, or the facility may even be closed down until it is able to show that it meets health and safety guidelines.

Key learning points

- A range of laws is in place in order to protect the employee and employer in the workplace. These include: Health and Safety at Work Act, Personal Protective Equipment Regulations, Control of Substances Hazardous to Health Regulations, Health and Safety (First Aid) Regulations, Manual Handling Operations Regulations, Fire Safety and Safety of Places of Sport Act, Adventure Activities Licensing Authority.
- Statutory law is where a person is prosecuted, and involves the police.
- Civil law does not involve the police.
- Case law is where a case in the past is referred to.
- The Health and Safety Executive enforces regulations in the workplace.

Student activity 3.2    60 minutes   P2   M1

Task 1

Design a poster with written text that describes the legal factors and regulatory bodies that influence health and safety in sport.

Task 2

Write a report that compares and contrasts the influences on health and safety in sport of the following:

- Legislation
- Legal factors
- Regulatory bodies.

Quick quiz 1

- Health and Safety at Work Act
- Magistrates' court
- *In loco parentis*
- Fire Safety and Safety of Places of Sport Act
- Civil law
- Negligence
- Health and Safety (First Aid) Act
- Crown court
- Statutory law
- Personal protective equipment

  Choose a term from the list above to answer each of the following questions.

1. This means in 'place of the parent'.
2. This is where a person fails to meet a standard of care.
3. This ensures that employers take reasonable steps to ensure the health, safety and welfare of their employees while they are at work.
4. This law requires companies and organisations to have sufficient first-aid facilities and equipment.
5. This is where people who have committed serious criminal offences go to court.
6. This law deals with the rights of private citizens.
7. A shin pad is an example of this.
8. This law requires all sports arenas and stadiums to have sufficient means of escape in the event of a fire.
9. This law deals with written law set down by a governing authority.
10. This is where people who have committed minor criminal offences are tried.

3.3 Risk Assessment

Risk assessment is a technique for preventing accidents and ill health by helping people to think about what could go wrong and devising ways to prevent problems. Risk assessment is good practice and is also a legal requirement. It often enables organisations to reduce the costs associated with accidents and ill health, and to decide on their priorities, highlight training needs and assist with quality assurance programmes. A risk assessment is usually performed by the manager or instructors working in the sports centre. It allows people to take time to consider what could go wrong while taking part in their activity. The risk assessment examines the possible hazards that may occur, the risks involved, the likelihood of them happening and how the hazards could be prevented.

Risk assessments should be logged, kept and reviewed regularly to see if they are up to date and to make sure that none of the details have changed.

Hazard

A hazard is anything with the potential to cause harm. A range of hazards can be found in any workplace. Examples include:

- Fire
- Electricity
- Harmful substances
- Damaged/wet flooring
- Unfastened shoelaces
- Jewellery worn during sports participation
- Water in a swimming pool.

Key term

Hazard: a potential source of danger.

Risk

A risk is linked to the chance of somebody being harmed by the potential hazard. Risks are often categorised into how likely they are to happen. When something is described as low-risk, it means that the likelihood of it happening is low, whereas something that is high-risk is likely to happen. Examples of risks include:

- Slipping on a wet floor and twisting your ankle
- Drowning in a swimming pool
- Tripping over your shoelaces and cutting your knee
- Catching your earring on clothing or an opponent's hand and ripping your ear.

Key term

Risk: the possibility of something bad happening.

Undertaking a Risk Assessment

Once you have highlighted the hazard, the easiest way to assess the potential problems that may arise is to use the following formula: Likelihood χ Severity. Likelihood – is it likely to happen:

1. Unlikely.

Capsizing in a kayak	
Likelihood of it happening	Severity
2 Quite likely	I no injury

Table 3.1 Risk assessment of capsizing in a kayak

Is the risk worth taking?	
Likelihood × Severity	Risk worth taking?
I	Yes
2	Yes, with caution
3	Yes, with extreme caution
4	Possibly, with extreme caution
5 or above	No

Table 3.2 To risk or not?

2. Quite likely.
3. Very likely.

Severity – how badly someone could be injured:

1. No injury/minor incident.
2. Injury requiring medical assistance.
3. Major injury or fatality.

For example, Table 3.1 attempts to assess the risk of capsizing in a kayak.

By multiplying the likelihood by the severity, you will be able to draw up a chart that looks at the potential problems, enabling you to make a decision about whether you want to take the risk or not (see Table 3.2).

In the example in Table 3.1, the likelihood times the severity is $2 \times 1 = 2$.

Control Measures

Hazards in the workplace should be removed whenever possible. Sometimes, however, there is no alternative but to keep a hazard. In such cases, it is important to reduce the risk – the likelihood of an accident – by introducing appropriate control measures. If some flooring is wet or damaged, for example, reducing the risk might include placing a barrier around the damage or putting up warning signs.

Other control measures could include participants wearing/using specialist protective clothing and/or equipment to help minimise the risk of injury.

The Risk Assessment Process

1. Identify the area to be assessed (e.g. resistance equipment in the gym).
2. List the hazards that you can identify (e.g. free weights incorrectly stored, wet floor).
3. Identify the risks and the people who are at risk from the hazards listed (e.g. first-time users, inexperienced users).
4. Assess the likelihood of an accident happening (e.g. if a person comes to the gym for the first time to use free weights, what is the likelihood that they may suffer from a lower back injury through an incorrect lifting technique?). Identify the likelihood, between 1 and 3, of this risk happening.
5. How severe will the outcome of the accident be, on a scale of 1 to 3?
6. Work out the level of risk.
7. Is the risk worth taking? Look at what control measures can be put in place to reduce the risk of injury (e.g. ensure all gym users are given an induction prior to using the equipment).

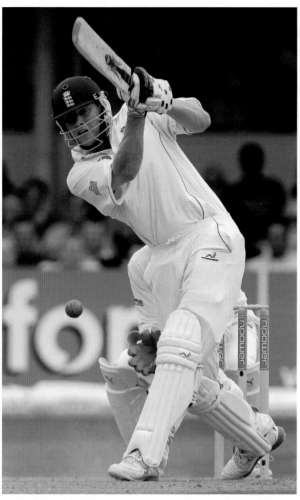

Fig 3.4 Protective clothing worn for playing cricket

Key learning points 2

- A hazard is something that has the potential to cause injury or compromise safety.
- A risk is the likelihood of something unpleasant happening.
- A risk assessment is a list of possible hazards that states the likelihood of them happening, and ways of controlling them.
- Level of risk is worked out by multiplying likelihood of risk by severity. A risk level of five or more means that either more safety precautions should be introduced or the activity should not take place.

Example of a risk assessment form

Location of risk assessment:
Risk assessor's name:
Date:

Hazard	People at risk	Likelihood	Severity	Level of risk	Control measures

Fig 3.5 Example of a risk assessment form

Student activity 3.3   60–90 mins   P1   M2   D1

Task 1

Choose two of your favourite sporting activities. Make a list of:

- All the risks and hazards associated with each of your selected sports
- All the hazards associated with each of your selected sports
- All the safety equipment you need in order to reduce the risk of injury in each of your selected sports.

Task 2

Copy and complete the risk assessment form on page 55 for each of your selected sporting activities.

Task 3

Examine your risk assessments and the control measures that you have put in place and then write a report that evaluates their effectiveness.

Q Quick quiz 2

1. List three hazards and three risks associated with each of the following sports:

    (a) netball

    (b) rugby

    (c) high jump

    (d) shot put

    (e) hurdles

    (f) swimming

    (g) hockey

    (g) badminton.

2. List all the items of personal protective clothing and equipment that a person might wear to help protect them while participating in the following sports:

    (a) football

    (b) cricket

    (c) hockey

    (d) triathlon

    (e) windsurfing

    (f) rock climbing

    (g) mountain biking.

3.4 Maintaining the Safety of Participants and Colleagues in a Sports Environment

P4   M3   D2

The general manager and his team of managers of a sport or leisure facility are responsible for running a safe and secure environment. They will ensure that every member of staff receives training on how the facility operates, as well as two manuals that provide information on how every part of the facility should operate under normal conditions and what to do in an emergency situation – these are usually referred to as Normal Operating Procedures (NOP) and Emergency Operating Procedures (EOP).

The NOP provides instructions on how to deal with everyday situations, whereas the EOP provides instructions on how to deal with minor and major emergency situations, such as disorderly behaviour from customers or dealing with a drowning incident.

Normal Operating Procedures (NOP)

This document contains details of all the services the leisure facility provides (e.g. swimming pool dimensions, squash courts and their dimensions) and is specific to that individual facility.

The manual will indicate any potential risk factors and hazards that staff should be aware of. These may include:

- **Known hazards** (e.g. unruly behaviour by the customer, customers with prior health problems, misuse of equipment)

- **Pool hazards** (e.g. slippery poolside, diving in shallow water, blind spots in the pool)
- **Customers at risk (**e.g. weak swimmers, elderly customers, customers under the influence of alcohol or drugs).

There follow instructions on how to carry out risk assessments so that these hazards and risks can be minimised.

Methods of dealing with the public will be included in the manual, which incorporates forms of communication and rules and regulations that customers must adhere to; an example of this is the poolside rules (e.g. no running on the poolside, no pushing, no ducking).

Staff duties and responsibilities are also covered. The manual will contain details of what is expected from them (e.g. they should wear the uniform provided, lifeguards must always carry a whistle, they must never leave a pool area unattended). There are usually details of staff training requirements too (e.g. a lifeguard will usually be required to attend training sessions at least once a month so that their skills are up to date and have been practised recently).

Details of staffing requirements for a range of situations are usually included within this document (e.g. supervision of diving, the number of lifeguards required on the poolside in relation to the number of swimmers – the more swimmers there are, the more lifeguards need to be on duty).

Pool, sports hall and changing room hygiene is also an area that should be covered in this document, which gives instructions on how to carry out everyday cleaning duties. Details of first-aid supplies and how to locate a first-aider will also be in this document.

All leisure facilities will have some form of alarm system to summon help or warn people of a fire; the NOP will contain details of where these alarms are located and how to use them.

Emergency Operating Procedures (EOP)

This manual details how staff should respond to a range of emergency situations:

- Fire
- Customer suffering from a minor injury (e.g. grazed knee)
- Customer suffering from a major injury (e.g. knocked unconscious with a head injury)
- How to deal with a drowning incident
- Bomb threat
- Emission of a toxic gas
- Structural failure
- Spinal injury
- How to deal with blood, vomit and faeces.

Staff Training

Most centres will ensure their staff are up to date with their role requirements and that their qualifications are up to date, either by running in-house training or by paying for their staff to attend relevant training events elsewhere. Pool lifeguards will often be expected to attend weekly training events to ensure they are able to carry out all the different rescue techniques. In most centres, all staff will be expected to have a basic first-aid award, and will be expected to attend regular training events to ensure their first-aid skills are up to date. Staff meetings are often held on a weekly basis to update staff on any centre changes or staffing changes, and so on.

Checking Facilities

There should be regular inspections to ensure the facility is functioning as it should be. Some checks may be required on a regular basis throughout the day, and others may need to be performed at the start and end of each day. For example, examining the changing facilities to ensure they are clean and tidy, and testing the swimming pool water to assess the chlorine levels, should be carried out once every few hours; checking that all the lights are working inside and outside the building only really needs to be carried out once or twice a day.

All sports and leisure facilities have regular inspections from various authorities to ensure that the organisation is maintaining a high level of health and safety. For example, the fire department will check such things as the number and functioning of fire extinguishers and that the fire exits are easily accessible.

Equipment should be checked regularly. Although there is not a legal requirement to inspect the equipment, a centre could be prosecuted if there

Fig 3.6 A person from the fire department checking equipment

was an accident due to faulty equipment. A typical pro forma for checking equipment should have the following headings:

- Name of equipment
- When equipment was checked
- Name of person checking equipment
- Any action taken
- Signature of the inspector
- Results of check.

Student activity 3.4   **60–90 mins**   **P4**   **M3**   **D2**

Task 1

Go into your local sports facility or leisure centre and ask if you may have a look at its NOP and EOP. If you are able to do so, look through them and make a note of the information they contain.

Task 2

Select three different procedures used in the sports facility that you have investigated to promote and maintain a healthy and safe sporting environment. Write a report that describes, explains and analyses each procedure.

3.5 Planning a Safe Sporting Activity

 P5   M4   **D3**

When planning a sporting activity, you will need to determine the roles and responsibilities of each member of the group.

Roles and Responsibilities

The leader of the activity is responsible for the planning and preparation and the smooth running of the event. Prior to the activity, the leader should:

- Determine who will be taking part in the activity
- Undertake a risk assessment of the proposed activity
- Determine the staffing requirements of the activity – this should include an appropriate number of qualified first-aiders
- Ensure that you or your centre has adequate insurance to run the activity
- Plan transport arrangements, if required
- Visit the site or facility where you plan to hold the activity
- Plan contingency and emergency arrangements
- Inform parents of any children taking part in the activity and obtain parental and medical consent.

The Site, Equipment and First-aid Provision

The site chosen must be suitable for the activity. If it is an indoor event, you must ensure that the facility is an appropriate size, that it has suitable lighting, suitable changing facilities, first-aid provision, all the equipment you require, and so on. Basically, it has to suit the needs of the chosen activity and the needs of the participants, and still adhere to health and safety guidelines. If the activity is to be held outside, you should always take into account environmental factors that may adversely affect your activity. For example, a lot of rain could waterlog a sports field, which could then become dangerous to play on. Always have a contingency plan that allows you to run an activity but does not put the participants' health at risk. For example, a football game that was due to be played outside could be changed to a five-a-side match inside.

It is important that all equipment is checked prior to being used to ensure that it is complete, in working order and not faulty or damaged.

Adequate arrangements must be made for first aid, including responsible people, equipment and facilities.

You should always carry a basic first-aid kit with you, or ensure you have access to one when you are running a sports activity. A basic first-aid kit should contain:

- Ten plasters of various sizes

● Two large sterile dressings for the management of severe bleeding
● One medium sterile dressing for the care of larger wounds
● Four triangular bandages to support suspected broken bones, dislocations or sprains
● One eye pad in case of a cut to the eye
● Four safety pins to secure dressings
● Disposable gloves.

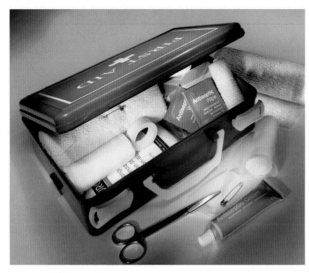

Fig 3.7 A first-aid kit

Suitability of Participants to the Activity

One of the main factors to help determine the suitability of a participant is to consider their age. If the participants are people of a different age to yourself, you should always speak to a person who has experience of dealing with this age group. You can then discuss your idea for your activity and determine whether it is suitable. From this you will be able to gauge what sort of equipment you should use, any adaptations required to make the activity more suitable and the staffing ratio required.

For example, if you wanted to run a cricket activity with (a) primary-school-aged children or (b) a group of 18-year-olds, you would have very different plans.

For the primary-school-aged children, you would use soft balls because hard balls would be more likely to cause injuries, as the children are less experienced in throwing and catching compared with most adults. You would probably adapt the game so that more people are active more of the time (e.g. you may have four teams of eight children playing quick cricket). You would need more staff to supervise the children to ensure their health and safety.

For a group of 18-year-olds you would use the usual cricket equipment, the game would be played to the usual cricket rules, and the only staffing required would be to umpire the event and ensure there is appropriate first-aid provision.

Health and Safety Review

After an event has taken place, you should always review your health and safety planning and procedures to see whether they were effective or if they could be improved. Examine if there were any injuries or near misses, how they occurred and if you could have done anything to reduce the likelihood of each incident happening. Determine if the participants were a suitable group for the activity: Were they the right age, of the right ability, and so on? Did the staff receive a suitable briefing so that they were able to carry out their roles and responsibilities effectively? Was the equipment suitable? Could you have used anything else to improve the health and safety of the participants during the activity?

This information will help you to improve your awareness of health and safety, and to ensure that you are doing everything possible to reduce risks and maintain the health and safety of yourself and others.

Key learning point 4

● In order to pay full attention to health and safety, a sporting activity should be planned effectively, with attention given to risk assessments, equipment, the site, the participants, first-aid provision, contingency plans, and the roles and responsibilities of each team member.

Student activity 3.5   60 minutes   P5   M4

Task 1

Select a sports activity of your choice. Produce and write a report to explain a plan for this sports activity that takes into account a range of different health and safety procedures.

Task 2

Write a report that reviews the plan you have produced, to determine how effective it is in managing the associated risks involved in the selected sports activity and the suitability of the participants, site and equipment used.

Useful websites

www.safesport.co.uk
Advice and safety tips on a wide range of sports & athletic abilities

http://www.uka.org.uk/governance/health-safety/
Advice on carrying out a risk assessment for sports; includes a sample template for an online incident report form

4: Fitness Training & Programming

4.1 Introduction

Developing the correct training programme is vital to the success of the individual athlete and the team. Top-class athletes build their life around the requirements of their fitness training and have a dedicated coach for this purpose. Fitness will be important to any individual who is involved in physical activity to give them the best chances to succeed.

By the end of this unit you should:

● know different methods of fitness training
● be able to plan a fitness training session
● be able to review a fitness training programme.

Assessment and grading criteria

To achieve a PASS grade the evidence must show that the learner is able to:	To achieve a MERIT grade the evidence must show that, in addition to the pass criteria, the learner is able to:	To achieve a DISTINCTION grade the evidence must show that, in addition to the pass and merit criteria, the learner is able to:
P1 describe one method of fitness training for six different components of physical fitness	**M1** explain one method of fitness training for six different components of physical fitness	
P2 produce training session plans covering cardiovascular training, resistance training, flexibility training and speed training	**M2** produce detailed session plans covering cardiovascular training, resistance training, flexibility training and speed training	**D1** justify the training session plans covering cardiovascular training, resistance training, flexibility training and speed training
P3 produce a six-week fitness training programme for a selected individual that incorporates the principles of training and periodisation		
P4 monitor performance against goals during the six-week training programme		
P5 give feedback to an individual following completion of a six-week fitness training programme, describing strengths and areas for improvement.	**M3** give feedback to an individual following completion of a six-week fitness training programme, explaining strengths and areas for improvement.	**D2** give feedback to an individual following completion of a six-week fitness training programme, evaluating progress and providing recommendations for future activities.

4.2 Different Methods of Fitness Training

Components of Fitness

Fitness can mean different things to different people and has been defined in different ways. When we examine fitness we need to ask 'What does this person have to be fit for?' or 'What functions does this person have to perform?' From this starting point we can build up a picture of their fitness requirements and then look at what can be done to develop their fitness.

Fitness is defined by the American College of Sports Medicine (ACSM) (1990) as:

> 'a set of attributes that people have or achieve that relate to their ability to perform physical activity.'

Fitness is clearly related to performance and developing the attributes to achieve this performance.

Physical Fitness

Physical fitness can be seen to be made up of the following factors.

Aerobic endurance is also called cardiovascular fitness or stamina. It is the individual's ability to take on, transport and utilise oxygen. It is a measure of how well the lungs can take in oxygen, how well the heart and blood can transport oxygen, and then how well the muscles can use oxygen. When working aerobically we tend to perform repetitive activities using large muscle groups in a rhythmical manner for long periods of time.

Muscular endurance is how well the muscles can produce repeated contractions at less than maximal (submaximal) intensities. When training for muscular endurance we usually do sets of 15 to 20 repetitions. Most movements we produce in sport and everyday activities will be at submaximal intensities and all people will benefit from muscular endurance training.

Flexibility is the range of motion that a joint or group of joints can move through. Flexibility is often not given the amount of attention it should have in a training programme because people do not always see its importance. However, improving flexibility

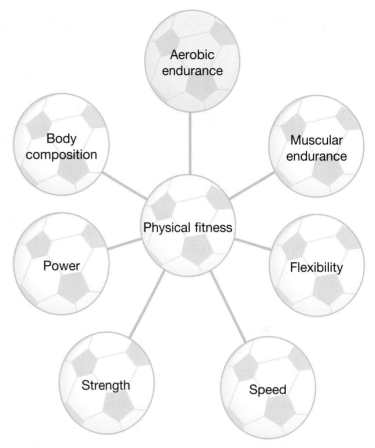

Fig 4.1 Physical fitness

can improve performance because a greater range of motion will result in greater power development and will help to prevent injury and pain caused through restrictions in movement.

Speed is the rate at which the body or individual limbs can move.

Strength is the maximum force a muscle or group of muscles can produce in a single contraction. Heavy weight lifting or moving a heavy object will require strength. For example, if you have to push-start a car the success or failure of this effort will be an expression of your muscular strength. To train for strength we usually do sets of 1 to 5 repetitions.

Power is the production of strength at speed and can be seen when we throw an object or perform a sprint start. To move a heavy load quickly we need to use our power. Activities such as jumping to head a ball or a long jump will require us to express our power.

4.3 Methods of Physical Fitness Training

P1 **M1**

Flexibility Training

Flexibility is the 'range of motion available at a joint' and is needed in sports to:

● enable the athlete to have the range of motion to perform the movements needed
● prevent the athlete from becoming injured
● maintain and improve posture
● develop maximum strength and power.

What Happens to Muscles When we Stretch?

The stretching of muscles is under the control of the sensory nerves. There are two types of sensory nerves which are involved in allowing muscles to stretch and relax. They are muscle spindles and Golgi tendon organs (GTOs). The sensory nerves work to protect the body from becoming injured and will contract if they think a muscle is at risk of becoming damaged. This is one of our basic survival instincts because when we were hunter-gatherers injury would render us incapable of finding food and our families would starve.

The muscle spindles are sensory receptors which become activated as the muscle lengthens (due to its potential danger). When the muscle has reached a certain length they tell the nervous system to contract the muscle and prevent it being stretched any further. This protects the muscle against damage. If you perform the patella knee tap test this activates the muscle spindles. When this test is conducted, the knee extends due to the contraction of the quadriceps muscle activated by the muscle spindle. This is also called 'the myotatic stretch reflex'.

When we stretch a muscle we try to avoid this by stretching in a slow and controlled manner. The muscle spindles contract the muscle, which makes it feel uncomfortable or slightly painful. This is called the 'point of bind' where the muscle has contracted to avoid any damage.

When the point of bind is reached the stretch should be held for around ten seconds. This is because after ten seconds the muscle will relax and the pain will disappear. This relaxation is brought on by the action of the GTOs. GTOs are found in tendons and they sense how much tension there is in the muscle. Once the GTOs sense that the muscle is not in danger of damage they will override the muscle spindles and cause the muscle to relax. This is the effect that you want a stretch to have; it is called 'the inverse stretch reflex'. Once the muscle has relaxed you can either stop the stretch there or stretch the muscle a bit more until the point of bind is reached again and the process starts again.

There are various methods of stretching muscles.

Static Stretching

This is when a muscle is stretched in a steady, controlled manner and then held in a static or still position. It is taken to the point where the muscle contracts and a slight pain is felt. This is called 'the point of bind'. At this point the stretch is held until the muscle relaxes and the discomfort disappears.

A static stretch can be a maintenance stretch or a developmental stretch. A maintenance stretch is held until the discomfort disappears and then the stretch is stopped. A developmental stretch is different because when the muscle relaxes and the discomfort disappears the stretch is applied further to a second point. It is taken to a point when the discomfort is felt again, it is held until the muscle relaxes and then applied again. It lasts for around 30 seconds while a maintenance stretch will last for around 10 seconds.

Proprioceptive Neuromuscular Facilitation

This type of stretching, known as PNF, is an advanced type of stretching in order to develop the length of the muscle. It needs two people to be involved: one person to do the stretching and one to be stretched.

It is carried out in the following way.

● The muscle is stretched to the point of bind by the trainer.
● At this point the trainer asks the athlete to contract the muscle and push against them at about 40 to 50 per cent effort.
● This contraction is held for 10 seconds.
● When the muscle is relaxed the trainer stretches the muscle further.
● Again a contraction is applied and then the muscle is re-stretched.
● This is done three times.

This is a more effective way of developing the length of the muscle as the contraction will actually cause the muscle to relax more quickly and more deeply.

Ballistic Stretching

This means a 'bouncing' stretch as the muscle is forced beyond its point of stretch by a bouncing movement. Ballistic stretches are performed in a rapid, repetitive bouncing movement. It is a high-risk method of stretching due to the risk of muscular damage but it may be used in specific sports such as gymnastics. It must never be used on people training for health and fitness reasons rather than sports.

Resistance Training

Resistance training means using any form of resistance to place an increased load on a muscle or muscle group. Resistance training can be done to develop muscular endurance, strength or power depending upon the number of repetitions chosen, resistance chosen and speed the movements are performed at. Muscular endurance training involves a high number of repetitions (12–20) performed with relatively low weights, while strength training involves low repetitions (1–5) with relatively heavy weights and power training is performed by moving weights at speed so involve low repetitions (1–5) with relatively heavy weights.

Resistance can be applied through any of the following methods:

- free weights
- resistance machines
- cable machines
- gravity
- medicine balls
- air
- water
- resistance bands
- manually.

The following are popular methods of resistance training:

- resistance machines
- free weights
- cables
- plyometrics
- circuit training.

A range of resistance machines have been developed to train muscle groups in isolation. They were

Fig 4.2 Resistance training with a machine

originally developed for body builders but their ease of use and safety factors make them a feature of every gym in the country. These machines target individual muscles and replicate the joint actions these muscles produce.

Free weights involve barbells and dumbbells and are seen to have advantages over resistance machines. Mainly, they allow a person to work in their own range of movement rather than the way a machine wants them to work. Also, when a person does free weights they have to use many more muscles to stabilise the body before the force is applied. This is particularly so if the person performs the exercise standing up. They also have more 'functional crossover' in that they can replicate movements that will be used in sports and daily life. This is seen as a huge advantage.

Cable machines are becoming increasingly popular because, again, they involve the use of many more muscles than resistance machines, and therefore burn up more calories. Once again, they can produce

Objective	Muscular strength	Muscle hypertrophy	Muscular endurance	Power
Repetitions or duration	1–5	6–12	12–20	1–2 for single-effort events 3–5 for multiple-effort events
Recovery period	3–5 mins	1–2 mins	30–60 secs	2–5 mins
Sets per exercise	2–6	3–6	2–3	3–5
Frequency per week	1–2 on each muscle group	1–2 on each muscle group	2–3 on each muscle group	1–2 sessions

Table 4.1 Shows the repetition ranges for targeting components of fitness.
(Adapted from Baechle and Earle, 2000)

Fig 4.3 Depth jumping is one example of plyometric activity

movements that are not possible on resistance machines. For example, a golfer will need to perform rotation-type movements and can do these on cable machines.

Plyometrics

Plyometric training develops power, which is producing strength at speed. It usually involves moving your body weight very quickly through jumping or bounding. Any sport that involves jumping in the air or moving the body forwards at pace will need power training.

Examples of plyometric training include:

- jumping on to boxes and over hurdles
- depth jumping
- vertical jumps and standing long jump
- medicine ball throws
- hopping
- bounding
- squat and jump
- press-up and clap.

It is a very strenuous type of training and an athlete must have well-developed strength before performing plyometrics. Before you take a plyometric session you must make sure the athlete is well warmed up and that you have checked the equipment and the surfaces thoroughly. Ideally, you should use a sprung floor or a soft surface.

Circuit Training

A circuit is a series of exercises arranged in a specific order and performed one after the other. There are normally eight to twelve stations set out and organised so that each muscle group is worked in rotation. Each exercise is performed for a certain number of repetitions or a set time period. Circuits are used predominantly to develop muscular endurance or aerobic fitness – this depends upon the resistances used, the speed of the movements and the length of time on each station. For muscular endurance the participant works flat out on each station for about 30 seconds, while to develop aerobic endurance the time period on each station is increased to 45 seconds with a slower speed of movement. They can be made specific to various sports by including exercises for the muscles used in that sport and some of the skills specific to that sport.

When planning a circuit you need to ask several questions:

- What is the objective of the session?
- How many participants will I have?
- What is their level of fitness?
- How much space have I got?
- What equipment is available?

A basic circuit session should contain exercise to improve aerobic fitness or raise the pulse rate, exercises to work the upper body, lower body and the core. When designing the circuit layout be careful not to place all the exercises for the same muscle group beside each other as this will cause undue fatigue. The circuit should follow the normal structure of a routine:

- warm-up
- main session
- cool-down
- flexibility.

The warm-up will include a pulse raiser, mobility and dynamic stretches. For example:

- walk
- walk with bicep curls and shoulder presses
- slow jog with shoulder circles
- jog
- dynamic stretches such as squat and press, step back and chest stretch
- jog with knee raises and heel flicks
- run
- jumps and hops
- sprint.

The main session should include eight to twelve exercises from Table 4.2.

Aerobic fitness or pulse raisers	Shuttle runs Skipping Box step-ups Box jumps Jumping jacks Star jumps Spotty dogs Grapevines
Upper body	Press-ups Bench press with dumbbells Cable seated rows Bent-over row Shoulder press Bicep curls Tricep curls Lateral raises Dumbbell pullovers Medicine ball chest passes Medicine ball chest pass & press-up Medicine ball overhead throws
Lower body	Squats Lunges Split squats Side lunges Squat thrusts Hurdle jumps Ladder work Step-ups with dumbbells
Core exercises	Swiss ball curls Swiss ball back extension Plank Bridge Superman Rotations with medicine ball Medicine ball rotate and throw

Table 4.2

The cool-down should progressively lower the pulse, but it can be combined with some stretching as well. It could follow this example:

- run (1 minute)
- jog (1 minute)
- brisk walk (1 minute)
- stretch trapezius, pectoralis major, latissimus dorsi, triceps, deltoids
- standing stretches of adductors, calves and quads
- kneeling stretches of hip flexors and lower back
- lying stretches of hamstrings and gluteus medius and minimus.

Aerobic Endurance Training

Continuous training is also called 'steady-state' training and involves an individual maintaining a steady pace for a long period of time. To be effective it needs to be done for a period of over 20 minutes. It is useful for developing a strong base of aerobic fitness, but it will not develop speed or strength.

While continuous training has a role to play it can be limited in its benefits, particularly if the athlete does the same session each time they train. While initially it will have given them fitness gains there will be limited benefits after about four weeks once the body has adapted to the work. It may also produce boredom and a loss of motivation to train.

Interval training is described as having the following features: 'a structured period of work followed by a structured period of rest'. In other words, an athlete runs quickly for a period of time and then rests at a much lower intensity before speeding up again. This type of training has the benefit of improving speed as well as aerobic fitness. Interval training also allows the athlete to train at higher intensities than they are used to, and thus steadily increase their fitness level and the intensity they can work at. The theory is that you will be able to run faster in competition only if you train faster – and interval training allows this to occur. Intervals can be used to improve performance for athletes and fitness levels for people involved in exercise.

Interval training can be stressful to the systems of the body and it is important to ensure that an individual has a good aerobic base before raising the intensity of the training.

Once an athlete has reached the limit of their aerobic system they will start to gain extra energy from their anaerobic system (lactic acid system); this is demonstrated by an increased accumulation of lactic acid in the blood. The point where blood lactic acid levels start to rise is called the lactate threshold. Interval training can be designed to push an athlete beyond their lactate threshold and then reduce the exercise intensity below the lactate threshold. This has the effect of enabling the athlete to become better at tolerating the effects of lactic acid and also increasing the intensity they work at before lactic acid is produced. Well-designed interval training sessions can produce this desirable effect.

The intensity of interval training is higher than continuous work and thus there will be more energy production to sustain this high-intensity work. More energy production equals more calories burnt during training, which could lead to a faster loss of body fat (if the nutritional strategy is appropriate). As the intensity is higher more waste products are built up, resulting in a greater oxygen debt and a longer period of recovery. This longer period of recovery results in more oxygen being used post-exercise and more energy used to recover. Therefore, more energy is used during exercise and also after exercise, multiplying the potential effects of fat loss.

The main benefits of interval training are:

- improved speed
- improved strength
- improved aerobic endurance
- improved ability to tolerate the effects of lactic acid
- increased fat burning potential
- increased calorie output
- improved performance.

Interval training can be used to develop aerobic fitness as well as anaerobic fitness. When designing interval training sessions you need to consider how long the periods of work are in relation to the periods of rest. The following are recommended guidelines for training with each of the three energy systems.

- Aerobic interval: 1 or half a unit of rest for every unit of work.
- Lactic acid intervals: 2 to 3 units of rest for 1 unit of work.
- ATP/CP intervals: 6 units of rest for 1 unit of work.

As the intensity increases, more rest is required to guarantee the quality of each interval. If you were training for aerobic fitness you may do four minutes' work then have two minutes' rest (1:1/2). If you were training for lactic acid intervals you would have one minute's work and two or three minutes' rest.

Sample Aerobic Interval Session

First estimate the maximum heart rate as 220 minus age and then you can work out the percentage of maximum heart rate.

For a 20 year old:
Maximum heart rate = 220 − 20 = 200 bpm
70% of max HR = 200 × 0.7 = 140 bpm
80% of max HR = 200 × 0.8 = 160 bpm
90% of max HR = 200 × 0.9 = 180 bpm

You will need to find out what workload (speed) produces each heart rate when you are running.

Basic interval
Work = 4 minutes   Rest = 2 minutes
4 sets of 4 minutes at 70% effort with 2 minutes' rest in between

Pyramid interval
Work = 3 minutes   Rest = 1.5 minutes

Warm-up
3 mins @ 80% of max HR

Rest
3 mins @ 85% of max HR

Rest
3 mins @ 90% of max HR

Rest
3 mins @ 85% of max HR

Rest
3 mins @ 80% of max HR

Cool-down

Treadmill hills pyramid
Find the speed that produces 70% of max HR and stay at this speed throughout the interval programme; then vary the gradient on the treadmill.

Work = 2 mins   Rest = 1 min

Warm-up
2 mins @ 2% gradient

Rest
2 mins @ 4% gradient

Rest
2 mins @ 6% gradient

Rest
2 mins @ 4% gradient

Rest
2 mins @ 2% gradient

Cool-down

Alternately the gradients could be set at 3%, 6%, 9%, 6% and 3%.

Sample Anaerobic Session

Lactic Acid System

6 sets of 45 seconds (or 300 m) at 90–95% effort with 90 seconds' rest
4 sets of 75 seconds (or 500 m) at 80–85% effort with 150 seconds' rest

ATP/PC System

10 sets of 50 metres at 100% effort with 1 minute rest

Fartlek is a Swedish term; it literally means 'speed play' and it involves an athlete going out and running at a range of different speeds for a period of 20 to 30 minutes. This type of training is excellent for replicating the demands of a sport such as football, rugby or hockey where different types of running are required at different times. It can be used to develop aerobic or anaerobic fitness depending on the intensity of the running. It can also be used in cycling or rowing training. Fartlek running involves finding a base speed at around 60 to 70 per cent of maximum intensity and then fast bursts of work at 75, 80, 85 and 90 per cent mixed up into longer or shorter time periods. It can be used to challenge the different energy systems and demands of sports as well as reducing the boredom of training for long periods of time.

Core Stability

If we were to take our arms and legs off our body we would be left with the body's core, which can be said to be the working foundation of the body and is responsible for providing the base to develop power. If we have a strong core we will be able to generate more force and power through the arms and legs; this is important when we kick a football or hit a tennis ball.

The body is made up of layers of muscles and the abdominal area is no different as it has deep, middle and outer layers which work together to provide stability.

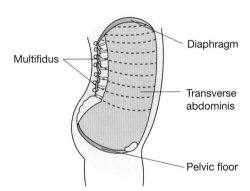

Fig 4.4 Outer layer of core muscles

The outer layer of muscles are the best known abdominal muscles with the rectus abdominis at the front, the erector spinae at the back and the internal and external obliques at the sides.

The middle layer is deeper muscle, which forms a cylinder or unit around the vertebrae. At the top we have the diaphragm and at the bottom the pelvic floor muscles, while across the back we have the multifidus, and around the front and sides we have the transverse abdominis (TVA). The TVA is the key muscle here and is described as being 'the natural weight belt' because a weight belt replicates its shape and function.

The role of the inner muscles is to stabilise the vertebrae, ribs and pelvis to provide the stable working base or foundation. These muscles contract a fraction of a second before the arms or legs are

moved when the body is functioning correctly. If this does not happen the chances of damaging the spine are increased.

The deep layer is tiny muscles which sense the position of the vertebrae and control their movement to keep them in the strongest position and prevent injury.

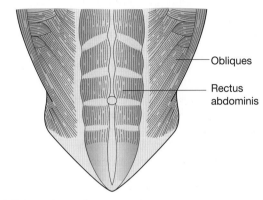

Fig 4.5 Inner layer of core muscles

Activating the core muscles can be done in two ways. First, by hollowing or pulling in the abdominals or by bracing, which means contracting the muscles without them moving out or in. Different trainers will recommend different techniques depending upon their own experiences and training.

Abdominal Training

The concepts of abdominal training are changing rapidly. The traditional method has been to do hundreds of sit-ups in pursuit of a perfect six-pack and then, in the late 1990s, abdominal cradles were introduced into gyms to aid people further. The 2000s have seen the introduction of Swiss balls and functional abdominal exercises into training programmes. There is still some confusion over what is the best way to train the abdominals. We need to look at a couple of misconceptions first before looking at what is the best way to train.

'Sit-ups will help me lose fat in the abdominal area'

No, you cannot spot-reduce fat because the muscle below the abdominal fat is separate from the fat itself and you can never be sure from where the losses in fat due to exercise will come. The way to lose abdominal fat is to increase activity level and have a correct nutritional strategy.

'Sit-ups will give me the six-pack I want'

Not necessarily, because overdoing abdominal work can cause a shortening of the abdominal muscles and pull your posture forwards, making the abdominal area shorter, squeezing the fat together and making you look fatter. In fact, if you perform back extensions it will make your posture more upright and help to keep the abdominals contracted and make them look more toned.

'Sit-ups are the best abdominal exercise'

This is debatable because sit-ups produce concentric and eccentric muscular contractions. The abdominals will contract isometrically when we train and move around in daily life. Therefore, surely we should replicate this isometric contraction when we train as it will have the best 'functional crossover' to daily life.

When we train the core muscles we need to target the deeper muscles; this is done by producing isometric or static contractions.

Any exercise where you are standing up or supporting your body weight will be a core exercise. For example, a press-up is an excellent core exercise because the core muscles work to keep the back straight and the back will start to sag when these muscles become fatigued. All standing free weight and cable exercises require the core to stabilise the vertebrae while they are being performed. However, there are some specific core exercises that can be performed (see Figure 4.6).

Fig 4.6b Side plank

Fig 4.6c Bridge

The use of a Swiss ball to perform exercises requires an extra load on the core muscles and works them harder, as will using cables to exercise.

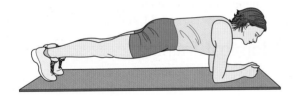

Fig 4.6a Plank

Fig 4.7 Swiss ball abdominal crunches

Q Quick quiz 1

Match the following: (a) the definition to the component of fitness and (b) the training method to the correct component of fitness that it works on.

Component of fitness	Definitions	Training methods
Aerobic endurance		
Muscular endurance		
Flexibility		
Speed		
Strength		
Power		

(a) Choices of definition

- The range of motion a joint or group of joints can move through
- The ability to take on, transport and utilise oxygen
- The rate that individual limbs can move
- The production of strength at speed
- The maximum force a muscle or group of muscles can produce in a single contraction
- The ability of muscles to produce repeated contractions

(b) Training methods

- plyometrics
- PNF stretching
- Resistance training (high weights, low repetitions)
- Resistance training (Low weights, high repetitions)
- Steady state running
- Interval training.

Student activity 4.1 40 minutes

Methods of fitness training

Complete the table below to describe and explain different methods of fitness training for six different components of fitness.

Component of fitness	Describe one method of fitness training for this component	Explain one method of fitness training for this component
Aerobic endurance		
Muscular endurance	E.g. Resistance training, which would be 8–10 exercises with a low weight but high repetitions.	E.g. Resistance training on free weights, resistance machines or cables using a low weight (about 60–70 of maximum) and high repetitions (12–20). Working all muscle groups and doing 2–3 sets per exercise.
Flexibility		
Speed		
Strength		
Power		

4.4 Planning a Fitness Training Session

Principles of Training

To develop a safe and effective training programme you will need to consider the principles of training. These principles are a set of guidelines to help you understand the requirements of programme design. The principles of training are:

- Frequency
- Intensity
- Time
- Type
- Overload
- Reversibility
- Specificity.

Frequency means how often the athlete will train per week, month or year. It is recommended that a beginner trains three times a week while a competitive athlete may train ten or twelve times a week.

Intensity is how hard the athlete works for each repetition. It is usually expressed as a percentage of maximum intensity. Intensity can be increased by adding more weight to be lifted, or increasing speed or gradient on the treadmill.

Time indicates how long they train for in each session. The recommended length of a training session is around 45 minutes before fatiguing waste products build up and affect training technique.

Type shows the type of training they will perform and needs to be individual to each person. A training effect can be achieved by varying the exercises an individual does – moving them from a treadmill to a rower, or a seated chest press to a free weight bench press.

Overload shows that to make an improvement a muscle or system must work slightly harder than it is used to. The weight that produces overload depends upon what the individual is currently used to at that moment. This may be as simple as getting a sedentary person walking for ten minutes or getting an athlete to squat more weight than they have previously. Overload can be achieved by changing the intensity, duration, time or type of an exercise. Reversibility says that if a fitness gain is not used regularly the body will reverse it and go back to its previous fitness level. Any adaptation which occurs is not permanent. The rule is commonly known as 'use it or lose it'.

Specificity states that any fitness gain will be specific to the muscles or system to which the overload is applied. Put simply, this says that different types of training will produce different results. To make a programme specific you need to look at the needs of the athletes in that sport and then train them accordingly. For example, a footballer would need to run at different speeds and have lots of changes of direction. A golfer would need to do rotational work but sprinting speed would not be so important. A runner would need to do running predominantly, and they may get some aerobic gain from swimming or cycling but it would not achieve the best result.

There are other principles too.

Progressive Overload

To ensure an athlete continues to gain fitness they need to keep overloading their muscles and systems. This continued increase in intensity (how hard they work) is called progressive overload. If you keep training at the same intensity and duration the body will reach a plateau where no further fitness gains are made. Therefore, it is important to keep manipulating all the training variables to keep gaining adaptations.

Who Will You Train?

You need to be prepared to train a range of individuals including elite performers, trained or well conditioned individuals and untrained or de-conditioned individuals. You may also train individuals who are training for a specific sport or have special requirements or medical conditions. You will have been able to identify the strengths and weaknesses of each individual by carrying out the health screening questionnaire, performing the static health tests and the dynamic fitness on the individual and then analysing their strengths and areas that need improvement.

Planning the Programme

Once you have identified the training needs of the individual through the screening process then you can design their training programme. Each programme will have a different content dependent upon the goals of the individual; however, the structure of the training programmes will be fairly similar. It should look like Table 4.3.

Type of training	Description of amount	Guidance
CV training – warm up	3–5 minutes	This involves a gradual increase of intensity to raise the heart rate steadily
Flexibility	2–3 dynamic stretches	These stretches involve moving the joints and muscles through the full range of movement in a controlled manner to replicate movements coming up in the main session
Resistance 1	4–5 exercises to cover the main muscle groups (pecs, lats, glutes, quads and hamstrings)	Sets and repetitions are dependent upon the training goals of the individual. Exercises could include free weights, resistance machines or cable exercises
CV training	Between 5 and 20 minutes, dependent upon the goals of the individual	Could involve steady state work or intervals. It may be done for speed or aerobic endurance and involve running, rowing or cycling
Resistance 2	4–5 exercises to cover a selection of the minor muscle groups (biceps, triceps, deltoids, claves)	Sets and repetitions are dependent upon the training goals of the individual. Exercises could include free weights, resistance machines or cable exercises
CV training	Between 5 and 20 minutes dependent upon the goals of the individual	Could involve steady state work or intervals. It may be done for speed or aerobic endurance and involve running, rowing or cycling
Core training	2–3 exercises to cover the abdominals, back muscles (erector spinae) and obliques	This could include dynamic exercises, such as sit ups, crunches or back extensions or static exercises, such as the plank or a bridge
CV training – cool down	3–5 minutes	This involves a gradual decrease of intensity to lower the heart rate steadily
Flexibility	8–10 stretches on all the muscles worked in the session	This would include developmental stretches on those muscles which are tight (e.g. pecs, hamstrings) and static stretches on all the other muscles worked

Table 4.3 The structure of a typical training programme

A typical training session for an untrained beginner may look like Table 4.4.

Type of training	Name of exercise	Amount
CV training – warm up	Treadmill	5 minutes
Flexibility	Dynamic stretches: chest, back, legs	×10 on each exercise
Resistance 1	Squats Bench press Seated row Leg extension Leg flexion	2 × 15 on each exercise with 20–30 seconds rest between sets and exercises
CV training	Rower	5–10 minutes
Resistance 2	Shoulder press Bicep curls Tricep press Calf raises	2 × 15 on each exercise with 20–30 seconds rest between sets and exercises
CV training	Static bike	3–5 minutes
Core training	Sit ups on stability ball Back extensions on stability ball	2 × 10 repetitions on each exercise
CV training – cool down	Treadmill	3–5 minutes
Flexibility	Quads Hamstrings (developmental) Pecs (developmental) Lats Glutes Biceps Triceps Deltoids Calves	All stretches to be held for 10 seconds, except the developmental stretches, which will be held for 30 seconds.

Table 4.4 A typical training session for an untrained beginner

Q Quick quiz 2

Match the components of fitness to their correct definition:

Component of fitness	Definition
Frequency	
Intensity	
Time	
Type	
Overload	
Reversibility	
Specificity	

Choice of definitions:

- if a fitness gain is not used it will be lost
- how often the athlete will train per week, month or year
- the individual's choice of training
- any training gain will only be of benefit to the muscles/energy system to which it is applied
- how hard the individual works
- working a muscle or system slightly harder than it is used to
- how long each session will last

4.5 Planning a Fitness Training Programme

Collecting Information

As an effective fitness coach it is important to be able to write an appropriate fitness training programme. There is a process that you need to go through to write an effective training session for a client.

Stage 1 – Gathering information: the first step is to gain relevant information about the person so that you can plan a personal training programme. The key is to build up a picture of the individual and what their life is like. Then you can look at what exercises you will plan for them. This is done through a questionnaire, which the client will fill out on your first meeting. (See Unit 8 Fitness Testing for Sport & Exercise, for a sample questionnaire.)

What a person does or does not do in their life will have an effect on their health and fitness levels as well as their chances of being able to keep the training programme going. The following factors need to be taken into consideration.

- Occupation – hours worked and whether work is manual or office-based.
- Activity levels – amount of movement they do on a daily basis.
- Leisure time activities – whether these are active or inactive.
- Diet – what, how much and when they eat.
- Stress levels – either through work or their home life and how they deal with it.
- Alcohol intake – how much they consume and how often.
- Smoking – whether they are a smoker or ex-smoker and the amount they smoke.
- Time available – the client needs to fit the training into their schedule and the fitness trainer needs to be realistic when planning the programme.
- Current and previous training history – this will give an idea of the current fitness level of the client and also their skill level.

Stage 2 – Establishing objectives: to ensure the success of the fitness programme it needs to be specific to the outcome a person wants. Once we have found this out we can establish goals. Their objective could be any of the following:

- cardiovascular fitness

75

- flexibility
- muscular strength
- muscular size
- muscle tone
- power.

Once the objectives have been established it is time to set goals to achieve these objectives.

Stage 3 – Goal setting: when setting goals it is important to ensure they follow the SMART principle – that they are specific, measurable, achievable, realistic and time-constrained. These goals should be set for the year or season, then for three months, one month and down to one week or one day. (For a full guide on how to set goals effectively see Unit 17: Psychology for Sports Performance, pp. 156–157.)

This goal-setting information should be kept in the training diary along with records of each training session.

Periodisation

Periodisation means a progressive change in the type of training that is being performed to gain maximum fitness benefits. It needs to be carefully planned and would show progression from one type of training to another. For example, a sprinter will focus on developing their strength base and muscular endurance in the autumn before working on improving power and speed as they get closer to the competitive season. All training for sports performance needs to be periodised. For people training in the gym, they can periodise their training by changing the volume and intensity of their training so that they train different energy systems and for different components of fitness.

For example, consider a competitive sports performer who has six weeks to prepare for the new season. They may realise that they need to train for aerobic endurance, anaerobic endurance and speed, as well as muscular endurance and power. They will periodise their cardiovascular training and their resistance training by manipulating the volume and intensity of their training. An example is provided in Table 4.5.

Macrocycle, mesocycle and microcycle are terminology specific to periodisation. The macrocycle is the largest unit of the training cycle and would cover the overall objective of the training. It will last for the length of a season or a training year. It is broken down into smaller units or mesocycles. A mesocycle is an individual phase of training and would cover a period of around a month depending upon the objective of the phase of training. A microcycle would represent each individual training session and its content. The plan would be periodised by looking at the big picture, or the macrocycle, then broken down into mesocycles, each contributing to the big picture and then the small detail of each session would be to consider how to achieve the aim of each mesocycle.

A Training Diary

A training diary is used to record all the training sessions completed, to enable the individual to monitor their progress. It should include the following details:

- date of each session
- detail of what was done in each session
- a record of the performances in training
- notes on how the athlete felt
- reasons as to why the athlete felt that way
- competition results
- fitness testing results
- performance reviews with their coach.

This can then be used to demonstrate progress, keep the athlete motivated and then to understand any improvements which have been made (or not).

Number of sets × number of repetitions	Week 1	Week 2	Week 3	Week 4	Week 5	Week 6
2 × 20	2 × 20					
2–3 × 15		2–3 × 15				
3 × 12			3 × 12			
3 × 10				3 × 10		
4 × 8					4 × 8	
5 × 5						5 × 5

Table 4.5 Example of a periodised six-week training plan for resistance training

Student activity 4.2   90 minutes   P2 P3 P4 M2 D1

Developing a six-week training programme

Read the following case study and then answer the questions that follow:

CASE STUDY

Harry is a 21-year-old who wants to start playing tennis again after having stopped playing when he left school 3 years ago. Since then he has been working in a sedentary job, which involves him sitting in front of a computer every day, and his favourite leisure activities are playing computer games and going to the cinema to watch horror films. He knows his diet is poor as he eats a lot of fried chicken and he is starting to put on a bit of weight around the middle. At his consultation he says he wants to get fit enough to start playing tennis again, and he is particularly worried that he gets breathless very easily.

At the consultation Harry and his trainer decide upon the following goals:

- Improve his aerobic fitness to help him keep going during his matches.
- Improve his speed so he can move around court quickly.
- Improve his muscular strength and endurance to his improve his hitting.
- Develop his flexibility so he can stretch for the ball.
- Develop his core strength so he can produce the strength and power he needs.

(a) Using the layout presented earlier in this unit, produce a training session for Harry covering cardiovascular training, resistance training, flexibility and speed training.

 P1

To gain a merit the programme needs to be produced with detail, and to gain a distinction you need to justify your training programme by explaining why you have chosen the exercises that you did for Harry.

M1 **D1**

(b) Harry has got 6 weeks until he has his first tennis match. Using the following template, show how his training will develop over this six-week period. You need to consider the principles of training and how frequency, intensity, time and type will change over the six weeks to ensure progressive overload on the muscles and energy systems.

(c) How will you monitor Harry's performance over the six weeks of the training programme?

 P4

This is an example for you to use as a practice before you prepare a six-week training programme for a selected individual, and then monitor their progress over the six weeks.

Component of fitness	Week 1	Week 2	Week 3	Week 4	Week 5	Week 6	Comments
Cardiovascular training							
Resistance training – Muscular endurance							
Resistance training – Strength							
Speed							
Flexibility							

77

Student activity 4.3 45 minutes | P5 | M3 | D2

Reviewing the training programme

Once the selected individual has completed the six-week training programme, you need to review their progress and then prepare to give them feedback. You can use the following information to base your review on:

- Information in the training diary on their progress over the six weeks.
- Progress towards their goal.
- Feedback from other people involved in the training.

To achieve a pass you need to give feedback and then describe their areas of strength and those that they need to improve on; to move to a merit you need to explain their areas of strength and those requiring improvement and to achieve a distinction you need to evaluate their progress by looking at the factors that have contributed to their progress or worked against it and then offer recommendations for future training activities.

4.6 Reviewing a Fitness Training Programme

The programme is planned out in detail and implemented with great energy and enthusiasm; likewise it must be evaluated in an organised manner. The athlete must keep a training diary for every session, whether it covered physical training, technical development or mental skills. Only then can it be accurately and systematically evaluated.

The athlete can evaluate the success and effectiveness of their training in the following ways:

- repeating their fitness tests
- evaluating performances
- reviewing their training diary
- measuring whether their goals have been achieved.

Based on all this information, the next stage of the training programme can be developed.

The diary can also be used to evaluate the reasons why the athlete did or did not achieve their goals, and any modifications or interventions can then be planned.

References

Baechle, T. and Earle, R. (2008) *Essentials of Strength Training and Conditioning*, Human Kinetics.

Elphinston, J. and Pook, P. (2009) *The Core Workout: a Definitive Guide to Swiss Ball Training for Athletes, Coaches and Fitness Professionals*, Core Workout.

Further reading

Ansell, M., (2008) *Personal Training*, Exeter: Learning Matters.

Baechle, T. and Earle, R., (2008) *Essentials of Strength Training and Conditioning*, Human Kinetics.

Coulson, M., (2007) *The Fitness Instructor's Handbook*, London: A&C Black.

Dalgleish, J. and Dollery, S. (2001) *The Health and Fitness Handbook*, Harlow: Longman.

Useful websites

www.topendsports.com/testing/tests.htm
Over 100 fitness tests to try, all divided into different fitness categories.

www.netfit.co.uk/previous.htm
Extensive range of exercise and training techniques, some sports specific, others more general

7: Fitness testing for sport & exercise

7.1 Introduction

The ability to conduct fitness testing is a vital skill for the sport scientist to possess. All athletes and people starting exercise need to know where they are at any point in time so they can work out how close they are to where they want to be.

This unit will start by looking at a battery of fitness tests that can be used with athletes and people taking exercise, and will consider any advantages or disadvantages with these methods. Then we will look at screening techniques and health-monitoring tests that are used to identify whether a person is healthy enough to perform these fitness tests, which can push an individual to the limits of their fitness. Once we have knowledge of the tests, we will look at how these tests can be administered safely and how the data you gain from the tests can be interpreted.

By the end of this unit you should:

● know a range of laboratory-based and field-based fitness tests
● be able to use health-screening techniques
● be able to administer appropriate fitness tests
● be able to interpret the results of fitness tests and provide feedback.

Assessment and grading criteria		
To achieve a PASS grade the evidence must show that the learner is able to:	To achieve a MERIT grade the evidence must show that, in addition to the pass criteria, the learner is able to:	To achieve a DISTINCTION grade the evidence must show that, in addition to the pass and merit criteria, the learner is able to:
P1 describe one test for each component of physical fitness, including advantages and disadvantages	**M1** explain the advantages and disadvantages of one fitness test for each component of physical fitness	
P2 prepare an appropriate health-screening questionnaire		
P3 devise and use appropriate health-screening procedures for two contrasting individuals		
P4 safely administer and interpret the results of four different health-monitoring tests for two contrasting individuals	**M2** describe the strengths and areas for improvement for two contrasting individuals using information from health-screening questionnaires and health-monitoring tests	**D1** evaluate the health screening-questionnaires and health-monitoring test results and provide recommendations for lifestyle improvement
P5 select and safely administer six different fitness tests for a selected individual, recording the findings	**M3** justify the selection of fitness tests, commenting on suitability, reliability, validity and practicality	
P6 give feedback to a selected individual, following fitness testing, describing the test results and interpreting their levels of fitness against normative data.	**M4** compare the fitness test results to normative data and identify strengths and areas for improvement.	**D2** analyse the fitness test results and provide recommendations for appropriate future activities or training.

7.2 Laboratory-based and field-based fitness tests

Tests are conducted to assess each different component of fitness. It is important to choose the components of fitness relative to the person you are working with. This will depend on their own goals and the activities they are involved in, be it sport or exercise.

Performance-related fitness

Performance in sport and exercise is dependent on a range of components of fitness. These are shown in Figure 7.1.

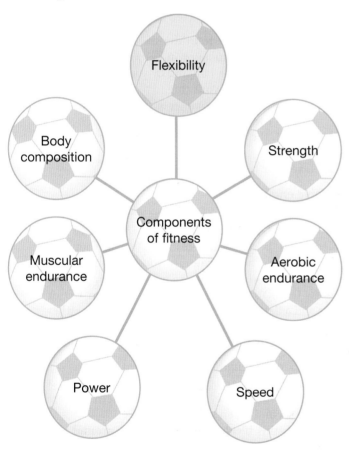

Fig 7.1 Components of fitness

Test protocols

The following is a list of test protocols:

- sit and reach
- one repetition maximum
- grip strength dynamometer
- multi-stage fitness test
- step test
- 40-metre sprint
- vertical jump
- wingate test
- one-minute press-up test
- one-minute sit-up test
- skinfold assessment
- bioelectrical impedance
- hydro-densitometry.

We will now look at each of these in turn.

Flexibility

The **sit and reach test** measures the flexibility of the muscles in the lower back and hamstrings. This test is safe to perform unless the athlete has a lower back injury, particularly a slipped disc. The test is performed in the following way:

1 Warm the athlete up with five minutes' jogging or cycling.
2 Ask the athlete to take off their shoes and any clothing that will limit movement.
3 The athlete sits with their legs straight and their feet against the board. Their legs and back should be straight.
4 The client reaches as far forward as they possibly can and pushes the marker forward.
5 Record the furthest point the marker reaches.

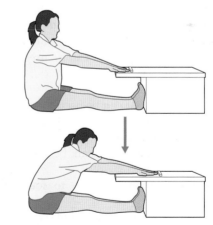

Fig 7.2 Sit and reach test

This test is quick and easy to administer and perform; however, it is a fairly non-specific test as it tells us something about the range of movement in the back, hamstrings and calves, but we may not be able to identify where there are restrictions or tight muscles. Also it tells us nothing about the range of movement in other important muscle groups, such as the chest, quadriceps or hip flexors.

81

Category	Males (cm)	Females (cm)
Elite	>27	>30
Excellent	17 to 27	21 to 30
Good	6 to 16	11 to 20
Average	0 to 5	1 to 10
Fair	−8 to −1	−7 to 0
Poor	−9 to −19	−8 to −14
Very poor	<−20	<−15

Table 7.1 Categories for sit and reach scores (adapted from Franklin, 2000)

Strength

The **one repetition maximum** (1 RM) is a measure of absolute strength and is the maximum weight that can be moved once with perfect technique.

This is clearly a dangerous test to perform unless the client is of an advanced skill level and is very well conditioned. The test will also require a thorough warm-up prior to its performance.

The test is performed in the following way:

1 Choose an exercise requiring the use of large muscle groups, such as a bench press or a leg press.
2 Warm up with a light weight for ten repetitions.
3 Give one minute rest.
4 Estimate a resistance that can be used for three to five repetitions.
5 Give two minutes' rest.
6 Estimate a load that can be used for two to three repetitions.
7 Give two to three minutes' rest.
8 Decide on a load that can be used for one repetition.
9 If successful, then give two to four minutes' rest.
10 Add a little more weight and complete one repetition.
11 Weight is gradually added until the client fails.
12 1 RM is the last weight that can be completed successfully.

There are no normative tables for 1 RM tests as they are used to monitor progress and strength gains. They can also be used to decide on training loads for the individual.

The **grip strength dynamometer** is a static test to assess muscular strength in the arm muscles. Unfortunately, it will give no indication as to the strength of other muscle groups. The test involves squeezing a hand-grip dynamometer as hard as possible. The test is conducted in the following way:

1 Adjust the handle to fit the size of your hand.
2 Hold the dynamometer in your strongest hand and keep the arm hanging by your side with the dynamometer by your thigh.
3 Squeeze the dynamometer as hard as you can for around five seconds.
4 Record the results and repeat after about a minute.
5 Take your best recording.

Aerobic endurance

The **multi-stage fitness test** was developed at the University of Loughborough and is known as the 'bleep' test because athletes have to run between timed bleeps. The test will give you an estimation of your VO_2max, which is the measure of your aerobic fitness level. You will need the pre-recorded CD or tape and a flat area of 20 metres, with a cone at either end. This test can be used with large groups, as all the athletes will run together. The procedure is as follows:

1 Mark out a length of 20 metres with cones.
2 Start the tape and the athletes run when the first bleep sounds. They will run the 20 metres before the second bleep sounds.
3 When this bleep sounds, they turn around and run back.
4 They continue to do this and the time between the bleeps gets shorter and shorter, so they have to run faster and faster.
5 If an athlete fails to get to the other end before the bleep on three consecutive occasions, they are out.
6 Record at what point the athlete dropped out.
7 Using Table 7.2, you can find out the athlete's predicted VO_2max.

This is an excellent field-based test which can be used to assess and monitor the fitness levels of individuals and groups of people. The results are dependent on the motivation level of the participants and how willing they are to drive themselves to their limits.

The **Canadian step test** is a simple and straightforward test to perform, and measures how heart rate increases with steady-state exercise.

You need a step 30 cm high, a heart-rate monitor and a stopwatch. This test is carried out in the following way:

1 The client steps up and down for three minutes while you monitor their heart rate.
2 You keep the client at a steady state by saying 'up, up, down, down' at a normal speech rate. The client should complete 24 steps per minute.
3 At the end of the third minute, record their heart rate.
4 Compare the result to the normative data for males and females shown in Tables 7.3 and 7.4.

This is a safe test to use with clients and provides a

Category	Males (mm/O2/kg/min′′′1)	Females (mm/O2/kg/min′′′1)
Extremely high	>70	>60
Very high	63–69	54–59
High	57–62	49–53
Above average	52–56	44–48
Average	44–51	35–43

Table 7.2 Categories for predicted VO$_2$max scores (adapted from Baechle and Earle, 2008)

Age	Excellent	Good	Above average	Average	Below average	Poor	Very poor
18–25	<79	79–89	90–99	100–105	106–116	117–128	>128
26–35	<81	81–89	90–99	100–107	108–117	118–128	>128
36–45	<83	83–96	97–103	104–112	113–119	120–130	>130
46–55	<87	87–97	97–105	106–116	117–122	123–132	>132
56–65	<86	86–97	98–103	104–112	113–120	121–129	>129
65+	<88	88–96	97–103	104–113	114–120	121–130	>130

Table 7.3 The classification for males measured in b.p.m. (adapted from Franklin, 2000)

Age	Excellent	Good	Above average	Average	Below average	Poor	Very poor
18–25	<85	85–98	99–108	109–117	118–126	127–140	>140
26–35	<88	88–99	100–111	112–119	120–126	127–138	>138
36–45	<90	90–102	103–110	111–118	119–128	129–140	>140
46–55	<94	94–104	105–115	116–120	121–129	130–135	>135
56–65	<95	95–104	105–112	113–118	119–128	129–139	>139
65+	<90	90–102	103–115	116–122	123–128	129–134	>134

Table 7.4 The classification for females measured in b.p.m. (adapted from Franklin, 2000)

Fig 7.3 Canadian step test

useful means to monitor progress. It will not provide any information regarding their maximal aerobic capacity.

Speed

The **40-metre sprint** is a test for pure speed. You will need a flat running surface and a tape measure to ensure the distance is correct. You also require a stopwatch and a person who can time the run. The test is conducted in the following way:

1 The athlete warms up for several minutes.
2 They then do the 40-metre run at a speed less than their maximum.
3 The athlete starts the test behind the line, with one or two hands on the ground.
4 The starter will shout 'go' and the athlete sprints the 40 metres as quickly as possible.

5 This run should be repeated after two or three minutes and the average of the two runs taken.

This test is a good, accurate test of pure speed; it is dependent on the competence of the testers to accurately record the times of the performers.

Power

The **vertical jump** is a test of power, with the aim being to see how high the athlete can jump. It is important that you find a smooth wall, with a ceiling higher than the athlete can jump. A sports hall or squash court is ideal. The test is conducted in the following way:

1 The athlete rubs chalk on their fingers.
2 They stand about 15 cm away from the wall.
3 With their feet flat on the floor, they reach as high as they can and make a mark on the wall.
4 The athlete then rubs more chalk on their fingers.
5 They then bend their knees to 90 degrees and jump as high as they can up into the air.
6 At the top of their jump they make a second chalk mark with their fingertips.
7 The trainer measures the difference between their two marks – this is their standing jump score.
8 This test is best done three times, so the athlete can take the best of their three jumps.

Category	Males (seconds)	Females (seconds)
Elite	<4.6	<7.5
Excellent	4.6–4.7	7.5–7.7
Good	4.8–7.0	7.8–6.3
Average	7.1–7.5	6.4–6.7
Below average	>7.6	>6.7

Table 7.5 Categories for the 40-metre sprint test (adapted from Franklin, 2000)

Rating	Males (cm)	Females (cm)
Excellent	>70	>60
Very good	61–70	51–60
Above average	51–60	41–50
Average	41–50	31–40
Below average	31–40	21–30
Poor	21–30	11–20
Very poor	<21	<10

Table 7.6 Ratings for males and females in the vertical jump test (adapted from Franklin, 2000)

Fig 7.4 Vertical jump test

Fig 7.5 Wingate test

Anaerobic Capacity

The **Wingate test** is a maximal test of anaerobic capacity and is thus suitable only for highly conditioned clients. It is used to measure peak anaerobic power and anaerobic capacity. It is carried out in the following way:

1 The client warms up for around two to three minutes at increasing intensities until their heart rate is 180 b.p.m.
2 Once they are ready, the client cycles as fast as they can for 30 seconds at a calculated load. The load is calculated for use on the Monark cycle ergometer. For a person aged under 15 years, the load is their body weight in kilograms × 0.35 g. For an adult, it is their body weight in kilograms × 0.75 g. A 70 kg adult's workload would be worked out in the following way: 70 × 0.75 = 52.5 kg.
3 The client is instructed to start and then given two seconds to achieve their maximum speed, at which point the workload is added.

4 The client pedals for 30 seconds as fast as they can, and the tester needs to count the number of revolutions of the flywheel every five seconds.
5 There needs to be a second tester who records the scores as they are called out for each five seconds.
6 At the end of the 30 seconds, the client cools down at a light workload.

To work out the power for each five-second interval, you need to use the following equation:

Power = load (kg) × revolutions of flywheel in five seconds × radius of flywheel × 12.33

This score is then divided by their body weight in kilograms to calculate the power per kilogram of body mass.

To analyse the results you need to do the following:

● Plot a graph with power in watts (y-axis) against time in seconds (x-axis).
● The peak anaerobic power is the highest power score in a five-second period.

85

- The minimum anaerobic power is the lowest score in a five-second period.
- The power decline can be calculated in the following way:

$$\text{Power decline} = \frac{\text{Peak power} - \text{Minimum power}}{\text{Peak power} \times 100}$$

You will need to use Table 7.7 to record the results and then work out the power achieved.

This is a test of maximal aerobic capacity and should be used only with advanced, well-conditioned performers. Again, its accuracy is dependent on the motivation of the individual to push themselves to their maximum capacity.

Muscular endurance

The **one-minute press-up test** is a test of muscular endurance in the chest and arms. You will need a mat and a stopwatch.

It is carried out in the following way:

1 This test involves the male starting in the press-up position, with their hands facing forwards and below the shoulders, back straight and pivoting on their toes. Females will perform the test from their knees, with their knees, hips and shoulders all in line and their lower legs resting on the ground.

2 The subject will go down until their chest is 2 cm off the floor and push up to a straight elbow. They must maintain a straight back.

3 The number of press-ups performed in one minute without rest is recorded.

4 If a client is unable to maintain good technique or shows undue fatigue, the test must be stopped.

Time (s)	Number of revolutions of flywheel	Power (watts)	Power per kg of body mass
0–2			
2–7			
7–12			
12–17			
17–22			
22–27			
27–32			

Table 7.7 Recording the information from the Wingate test

Age	Excellent	Very good	Good	Fair	Needs improvement
20–29	36	29–35	22–28	17–21	<17
30–39	30	22–29	17–21	15–20	<15
40–49	25	17–24	13–16	8–12	<8
50–59	21	13–20	10–12	7–9	<7
60–69	18	11–17	8–10	5–7	<5

Table 7.8 Categories for males measured in the number of completed press-ups (adapted from Franklin, 2000)

Age	Excellent	Very good	Good	Fair	Needs improvement
20–29	30	21–29	15–20	10–14	<10
30–39	27	20–26	13–19	8–12	<8
40–49	24	15–23	11–14	5–10	<4
50–59	21	11–20	7–10	2–6	1
60–69	17	12–16	5–11	2–4	1

Table 7.9 Categories for females measured in the number of completed press-ups (adapted from Franklin, 2000)

Age	High	Above average	Average	Below average	Low
17–19	>49	44–48	37–43	24–36	<24
20–29	>44	39–43	32–38	20–31	<20
30–39	>39	34–38	27–33	16–26	<16

Table 7.10 The classification for males measured in the number of completed sit-ups (adapted from Franklin, 2000)

Age	High	Above average	Average	Below average	Low
17–19	>42	32–41	25–31	19–24	<19
20–29	>36	27–35	21–26	15–20	<15
30–39	>30	22–29	17–21	11–16	<11

Table 7.11 The classification for females measured in the number of completed sit-ups (adapted from Franklin, 2000)

The **one-minute sit-up test** is a test of muscular endurance in the abdominals. You will need a mat and a stopwatch.

The test procedure is as follows:

1 The athlete lies on the floor with their fingers on their temples and their knees bent.
2 On the command of 'go', the athlete sits up until their elbows touch their knees.
3 They then return to the start position, with the back of their head touching the floor. That will be one repetition.
4 The athlete does as many repetitions as they can in one minute.

Body composition

In very simple terms, a person's body weight or mass can be split into two categories: fat mass and lean body weight (all that is not fat).

- Fat mass is made up of fat (adipose tissue).
- Lean body weight consists of:
  - muscle
  - water
  - bone
  - organs
  - connective tissue.

This shows that you can lose weight by reducing any of the components of the body. However, lean body weight could be seen as healthy weight, as it contributes to the performance of the body. Fat weight in excess would be unhealthy weight, as it would cause a loss in performance as it requires oxygen without giving anything back to the body.

It is necessary to take a body fat measurement to show that the weight loss is fat and not muscle.

It is impossible to turn muscle into fat or fat into muscle. This is because they are completely different types of tissue in the body. A good training programme will produce a loss of fat or excess fat and a gain in muscle tissue. So while it may look like one is turning into the other, this is not the case. This happens particularly when an athlete does weight training.

87

1. **Triceps brachii**
With the client's arm hanging loosely, a vertical fold is raised at the back of the arm, midway along a line connecting the acromion (shoulder) and olecranon (elbow) processes.

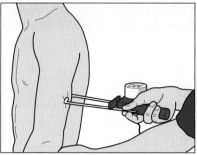

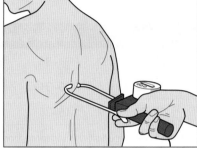

2. **Biceps brachii**
A vertical fold is raised at the front of the arm, opposite the triceps site. This should be directly above the centre of the cubital fossa (fold of the elbow).

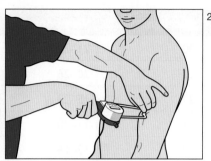

3. **Subscapular**
A fold is raised just beneath the inferior angle of the scapula (bottom of the shoulder blade). This fold should be at an angle of 45 degrees downwards and outwards.

4. **Anterior suprailiac**
A fold is raised 5–7 cm above the spinale (pelvis), at a point in line with the anterior axillary border (armpit). The fold should be in line with the natural folds downward and inwards at up to 45 degrees.

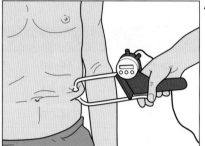

Fig 7.6 Body fat measurement

Area	Description of site
Triceps	This is taken halfway between the shoulder and elbow on the back of the arm. It is a vertical pinch.
Biceps	This is taken 1 cm above the site for the triceps on the front of the arm. It is a vertical pinch.
Subscapular	This is taken 2 cm below the lowest point of the shoulder blade. It is taken at a 45-degree angle.
Suprailiac	This is taken just above the iliac crest (hip bone), directly below the front of the shoulder.

Table 7.12 Description of four sites for measuring body composition

The **skinfold assessment** test is carried out using skinfold calipers. It is conducted using the Durnin and Wormsley sites, and is carried out as follows:

1 Take the measurements on the left-hand side of the body.
2 Mark up the client accurately.
3 Pinch the skin 1 cm above the marked site.
4 Pull the fat away from the muscle.
5 Place the calipers halfway between the top and bottom of the skinfold.
6 Allow the calipers to settle for one or two seconds.
7 Take the reading and wait 15 seconds before repeating for accuracy.
8 Add up the total of the four measurements.
9 Calculate body fat percentage using Table 7.13.

This test has proved to be an accurate method of assessing and monitoring body composition; however, it is very dependent on the tester's competence to correctly identify the skinfold sites and then to take the measurement accurately. This does involve a fair amount of skill and practice.

The **bioelectrical impedance** technique involves placing electrodes on one hand and one foot and then passing a very small electrical current through the body. The theory is that muscle will conduct the electricity, while fat will resist the path of the electricity. Therefore, the more electricity that comes out of the body, the more muscle a person has, and the less electricity that comes out, the more fat a person has.

This technique has benefits over skinfold measurement because it is easier to do and does not mean that the client has to remove or adjust any clothing. However, it has been shown to be not such an accurate measure of body fat percentage, as it is dependent on how well hydrated the individual is at any point.

Hydro-densitometry, or underwater weighing, is a technique based on the Archimedes principle.

Males		Females	
Sum of skinfolds	Body fat %	Sum of skinfolds	Body fat %
		14	9.4
		16	11.2
		18	12.7
20	7.1	20	14.1
22	9.2	22	17.4
24	10.2	24	16.5
26	11.2	26	17.6
28	12.1	28	17.6
30	12.9	30	19.5
35	14.7	35	21.6
40	16.3	40	23.4
45	17.7	45	27.0
50	19.0	50	26.5
55	20.2	55	27.8
60	21.2	60	29.1
65	22.2	65	30.2
70	23.2	70	31.2
75	24.0	75	32.2
80	24.8	80	33.1
85	27.6	85	34.0
90	26.3	90	34.8
95	27.0	95	37.6
100	27.6	100	36.3
110	27.8	110	37.7
120	29.9	120	39.0
130	31.0	130	40.2
140	31.9	140	41.3
150	32.8	150	42.3
160	33.6	160	43.2
170	34.4	170	44.6
180	37.2	180	47.0

Table 7.13 Body fat measurements for males and females (adapted from Franklin, 2000)

It involves a person being weighed on land and then when fully submerged in water. Muscle and bone are denser than water, while fat is less dense. A person with more bone and muscle will weigh more in water, have a higher body density and therefore less fat. Once the weight on land and weight in water are taken, a formula is used to work out percentage body fat.

This technique involves the use of a large pool of water and significant amounts of equipment. It is impractical for use outside a sport science laboratory.

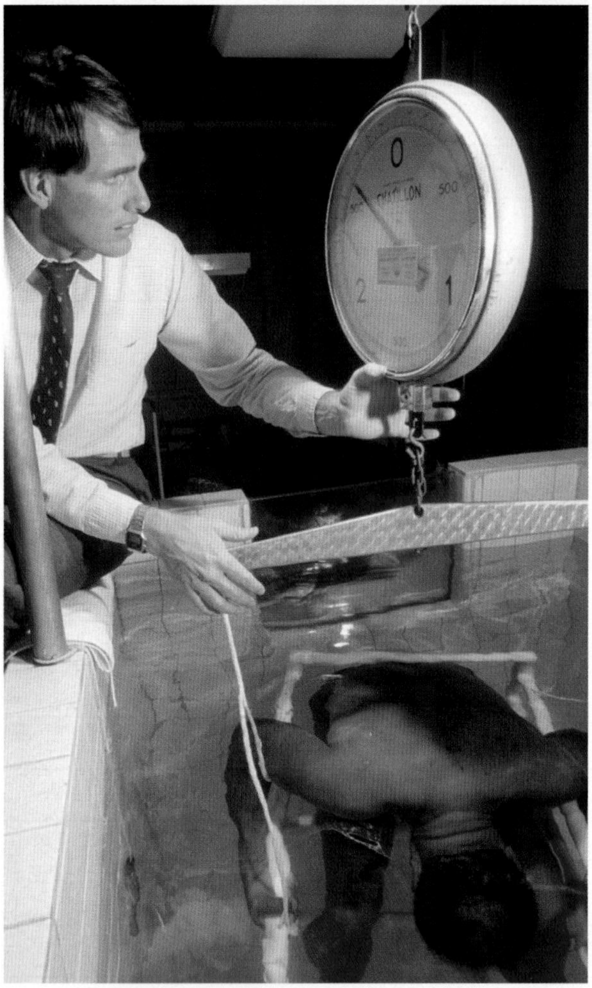

Fig 7.7 Underwater weighing

Key learning points 1

- Blood pressure, resting heart rate, lung function, body mass index and hip-to-waist ratio are all static tests which are performed to see if the client is healthy enough to perform the dynamic fitness tests.
- Performance-related fitness is made up of the following components: flexibility, strength, aerobic endurance, speed, power, muscular endurance and body composition.
- Flexibility is measured by a sit and reach test.
- Strength is measured by one repetition maximum and grip strength dynamometer.
- Aerobic endurance is measured by the multi-stage fitness test and the step test.
- Anaerobic capacity is measured by the Wingate test.
- Speed is measured by the 40-metre sprint test.
- Power is measured by the vertical jump test.
- Muscular endurance is measured by the one-minute press-up test and the one-minute sit-up test.
- Body composition is measured by skinfold assessment, bioelectrical impedance and hydro-densitometry tests.

Classification	Males (% body fat)	Females (% body fat)
Under-fat	<6	<14
Athletes	6–13	14–20
Fitness	14–17	21–24
Acceptable	18–25	25–30
Overweight	26–30	31–40
Obese	>30	>40

Table 7.14 Calculating your body fat percentage (adapted from Franklin, 2000)

Student activity 7.1   ⏱ **45 minutes**   P1   M1

Fill in the following table to demonstrate your knowledge of the tests for the different components of fitness and their advantages and disadvantages.

Component of fitness	Description of a test for component of fitness	Description of test's strengths and weaknesses	Explanation of test's strengths and weaknesses
Flexibility	Sit and reach test – where the person sits with their feet against a board and slowly bends forwards to see how far they can reach.	It is an easy-to-use test for flexibility, but it does not give us very specific scores.	The test is easy to explain and easy for the participant to perform. It is safe and we can get the results quickly. However, it gives us a score that measures flexibility in the back, hamstrings and calves, but cannot be used to identify range of movement specifically in one of the areas or any other joint/muscle in the body. It gives us a general measure of flexibility but lacks specificity.
Strength			
Aerobic endurance			
Speed			
Anaerobic endurance			
Muscular endurance			
Body composition			

Ⓠ Quick quiz 1

Match each fitness test in the table below to the component of fitness that it tests, choosing from the following:
- flexibility
- strength
- aerobic endurance
- speed
- anaerobic capacity
- muscular endurance
- body composition.

Name of test	Component of fitness tested
Wingate test	
Bioelectrical impedance	
I RM	
One-minute press-up test	
40-metre sprint	
Sit and reach test	
Multi-stage fitness test	

7.3 Using health-screening techniques

Before you start to conduct fitness tests with an athlete or a person who wants to start exercising, you will need to conduct a detailed fitness consultation. This will consist of the following:

- health-screening questionnaire
- informed consent form
- identification of coronary heart disease risk factors
- identification of any causes for medical referral.

Health-screening questionnaire

You will need to have prepared a detailed questionnaire to cover areas such as medical conditions, illnesses and injuries, as well as history of exercise and lifestyle factors. A sample questionnaire is shown here.

Section 1: Personal Details

Name_____

Address _____

_____

_____

_____

Home telephone _____

Mobile telephone _____

Email _____

Occupation _____

Date of birth _____

Section 2: Sporting Goals

1 What are your long-term sporting goals over the next year or season?

_____

_____

2 What are your medium-term goals over the next three months?

_____

_____

_____

3 What are your short-term goals over the next four weeks?

_____

_____

_____

_____

Section 3: Current Training Status

1 What are your main training requirements?

(a) Muscular strength.

(b) Muscular endurance.

(c) Speed.

(d) Flexibility.

(e) Aerobic fitness.

(f) Power.

(g) Weight loss or gain.

(h) Skill-related fitness.

(i) Other (please state).

_____

2 How would you describe your current fitness status?

_____

_____

3 How many times a week will you train?

_____

4 How much time do you have available for each training session?

_____

Section 4: Your Nutritional Status

1 On a scale of 1 to 10 (1 being very low quality and 10 being very high quality), how would you rate the quality of your diet?

_____

2 Do you follow any particular diet?

(a) Vegetarian.

(b) Vegan.

(c) Vegetarian and fish.

(d) Gluten-free.

(e) Dairy-free.

_____

3 How often do you eat? Note down a typical day's intake.

_____

_____

_____

_____

4 Do you take any supplements? If so, which ones?

_____

_____

Section 5: Your Lifestyle

1 How many units of alcohol do you drink in a typical week? _____

2 Do you smoke? _____ If yes, how many a day? _____

3 Do you experience stress on a daily basis? _____

4 If yes, what causes you stress (if you know)?

_____

_____

_____

5 What techniques do you use to deal with your stress?

_____

Section 6: Your Physical Health

1 Do you experience any of the following?

   (a) Back pain or injury.

   (b) Knee pain or injury.

   (c) Ankle pain or injury.

   (d) Swollen joints.

   (e) Shoulder pain or injury.

   (f) Hip or pelvic pain or injury.

   (g) Nerve damage.

   (h) Head injuries.

2 If yes, please give details.

_____

_____

_____

3 Are any of these injuries made worse by exercise?

_____

4 If yes, what movements in particular cause pain?

_____

_____

5 Are you currently receiving any treatment for any injuries? If so, what?

_____

Section 7: Medical History

1 Do you have or have you had any of the following medical conditions?

   (a) Asthma.

   (b) Bronchitis.

   (c) Heart problems.

   (d) Chest pains.

   (e) Diabetes.

   (f) High blood pressure.

   (g) Epilepsy.

   (h) Other.

2 Are you taking any medication? If yes, state what, how much and why.

_____

_____

Section 8: Informed Consent

Name   Signature

Trainer's name   Trainer's signature

Date

Notes

1 Explanation of the tests.
You will perform a series of tests which will vary in their demands on your body. Your progress will be observed during the tests and stopped if you show signs of undue fatigue. You may stop the tests at any time if you feel unduly uncomfortable.

2 **Risks of exercise testing.**
During exercise certain changes can occur, such as raised blood pressure, fainting, raised heart rate and, in a very small number of cases, heart attacks or even death. Every effort is made through screening to minimise the risk of these occurring during testing. Emergency equipment and relevantly trained personnel are available to deal with any extreme situation that occurs.

3 **Responsibility of the participant.**
You must disclose all information in your possession regarding the state of your health or previous experiences of exercise, as this will affect the safety of the tests. If you experience any discomfort or unusual sensations, it is your responsibility to inform your trainer.

4 **Benefits to expect.**
The results gained during testing will be used to identify any illnesses and the types of activities that are relevant for you.

5 **Freedom of consent.**
Your participation in these tests is voluntary and you are free to deny consent or stop a test at any point.
I have read this form and understand what is expected of me and the tests I will perform. I give my consent to participate.

Client's signature   Trainer's signature

Print name   Print name

Date   Date

Informed consent

An informed consent form lets a client know what to expect during the exercise test, and the associated risks involved in exercise or training. It also stresses that any participation in the tests is voluntary and that they have the choice to stop at any point.

An example of an informed consent form is shown at the end of the health-screening questionnaire above.

Risk of coronary heart disease

Coronary heart disease (CHD) is a leading cause of death in all industrialised countries. It is caused by a narrowing of the coronary arteries, which limits the amount of blood flowing through the arteries.

> ### Key term
>
> **Coronary arteries:** blood vessels that bring oxygenated blood to nourish the muscle cells of the heart muscle.

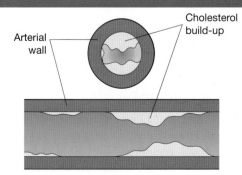

Fig 7.8 Build-up of cholesterol in an artery

95

Arteries losing their elasticity is part of the ageing process. However, there are many lifestyle factors that cause damage or narrowing of the arteries. Obstructions are created as cholesterol and fatty plaques are laid down in the artery, causing a narrowing of the artery space.

The coronary arteries are found only in the heart and they supply the heart with oxygen to enable it to pump. When these arteries narrow or become blocked, the blood supply to the heart is reduced. As a result, carbon dioxide builds up in the heart muscle and this causes pain, which is called angina. Angina feels like a crushing pain on the chest. If this pain becomes a shooting pain into the left arm and the neck, the person is having a heart attack.

The following lifestyle factors will increase an individual's chance of having CHD:

- diet high in fat (particularly deep-fat fried foods)
- diet high in table salt (sodium chloride)
- obesity (particularly abdominal fat)
- smoking
- excess alcohol consumption
- older age
- male gender
- high blood pressure
- type 2 diabetes.

Fig 7.9 Smoking will increase an individual's chance of having CHD

If you consider that a person has a high risk of CHD, it is best to refer them for GP clearance before you start to train them.

Medical referral

To ensure that you offer a proper 'duty of care' to your client, you will need to refer them to a GP if you have any doubt regarding how safe it is for them to exercise. If your client has any of the following, they must be referred to their GP:

- high blood pressure (over 160/100)
- poor lung function
- excess body fat (40 per cent or more for a female, 30 per cent or more for a male)
- high resting heart rate (100+ b.p.m.)
- medication for a heart condition (e.g. beta blockers).

Likewise, if they experience any of the following, they must also be referred to their GP:

- Muscle injuries
- Chest pain or tightness
- Light-headedness or dizziness
- Irregular or rapid pulse
- Joint pain
- Headaches
- Shortness of breath.

Health-monitoring tests

Tests can be split into two clear categories: those that measure health and those that measure fitness. Health tests are carried out to see if the individual is healthy enough to do the fitness tests or whether they need to receive GP clearance. Health tests will be static in nature while fitness tests will be dynamic and involve bodily movement and exertion.

The health tests conducted are:

- heart rate
- blood pressure
- lung function
- waist-to-hip ratio
- body mass index (BMI).

Resting heart rate

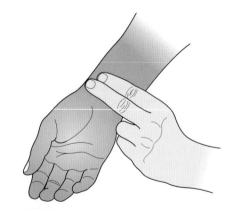

Fig 7.10 Taking a pulse rate

To measure the resting heart rate, you can use a heart rate monitor or do it manually. The best time to take a person's resting heart rate is before the person gets out of bed and experiences the stresses of the day. To perform it manually, complete the following steps:

1 Let your client sit down and rest for about five minutes.
2 Find their radial pulse (wrist) or brachial pulse (front of elbow).
3 Place your middle and index fingers over the pulse. The thumb has a pulse of its own and will produce an inaccurate reading.
4 Count the pulse for 60 seconds and record the result before repeating for another 60 seconds.
5 If there is a large variation in readings you should take a third reading.

Here is a reference for resting heart rates for men and women:

Category	Males (b.p.m.)	Females (b.p.m.)
Normal	60–80	60–80
Average	70	76
Proceed with caution	90–99	90–99
GP referral	100+	100+

Table 7.15 Heart rate reference tables for males and females (adapted from Franklin, 2000)

Blood Pressure

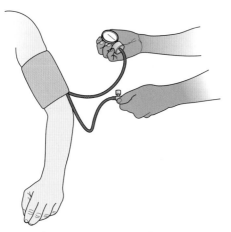

Fig 7.11 Taking a blood pressure reading

Blood pressure is the pressure blood exerts on the artery walls and is a clear indication of general health. It is vital to measure blood pressure before a client exercises, because it will tell you whether they are at risk of having a heart attack.

We need to split this up into the short-term and long-term. Short-term means the blood pressure rises for a period and then falls again, while long-term means that the blood pressure remains high all the time.

Blood pressure is taken by a blood pressure meter and stethoscope, or it can be done using an electronic blood pressure meter.

1 Allow the client to be relaxed for about five minutes.
2 Ask the client to sit down, with their left arm resting on a chair arm. Their elbow should be at 45 degrees, with the palm of the hand facing up.
3 Find the brachial pulse – it should be on the inner side of the arm, just under the biceps muscle.
4 Place the cuff just clear of the elbow (about 2–3 cm above the elbow). The bladder of the cuff (the part which inflates) should be directly over the pulse.
5 Place the earpieces of the stethoscope in your ears and place the microphone over the brachial pulse.
6 Inflate the cuff up to 200 mmHg.
7 Slowly open the valve by turning it anticlockwise and release the pressure.
8 Listen out for the first time you hear the thud of the heart beat and make a mental note of it. This is the systolic blood pressure reading.
9 Keep deflating the cuff, and when the heart beat becomes muffled or disappears, this is your diastolic reading.
10 Keep deflating the cuff and, if necessary, repeat after around 30 seconds.

Lung function

We need to assess lung function to see whether the airways between the mouth and the alveoli are clear and conducive to good air flow. Poor lung function will limit the amount of oxygen that can be delivered to the bloodstream and the tissues.

Lung function can be measured using a micro-spirometer or a hand-held peak flow meter.

To use a peak flow meter, work through the following steps:

1 Ask the client to hold the peak flow meter directly in front of their mouth.
2 Ask them to turn their head to the side and take three deep breaths.
3 On the third breath, ask them to put their mouth around the end of the tube and, ensuring a good lip seal, blow as hard as they can into the tube.
4 Say that it should be a short, sharp blow, as if they were using a pea shooter.
5 Repeat twice more and take the highest reading. This is called their peak expiratory flow rate (PEFR).

97

Age	1.55 m	1.60 m	1.65 m	1.70 m	1.75 m	1.80 m	1.85 m	1.90m
25	515	534	552	570	589	607	625	644
30	502	520	539	557	576	594	612	632
35	489	508	526	544	563	582	600	619
40	476	495	513	531	550	568	586	606
45	463	482	501	519	537	556	574	593
50	450	469	487	505	524	543	561	580
55	438	456	475	493	511	530	548	567
60	424	443	462	480	498	517	535	545
65	412	430	449	460	486	504	522	541
70	399	417	436	454	472	491	509	528

Table 7.16 PEFR for males (adapted from Franklin, 2000)

Age	1.45 m	1.50 m	1.55 m	1.60 m	1.65 m	1.70 m	1.75 m	1.80m
25	365	383	400	416	433	449	466	482
30	357	374	390	407	423	440	456	473
35	348	365	381	398	414	431	447	464
40	339	356	372	389	405	422	438	455
45	330	347	363	380	397	413	429	446
50	321	338	354	371	388	404	420	437
55	312	329	345	362	379	395	411	428
60	303	320	336	353	370	386	402	419
65	294	311	327	344	361	377	393	410
70	285	302	318	335	352	368	384	401

Table 7.17 PEFR for females (adapted from Franklin, 2000)

The PEFR is a measurement of the power of the lungs. It is a hypothetical figure which tells us how much air would pass through our lungs if we breathed in and out at our maximum power for one minute. It is hypothetical because it cannot really be measured, as we would faint after about 15 seconds of breathing at maximum power.

You will need to know the gender, age and height of the client to work out their acceptable score.

The PEFR for males and for females are shown in Tables 7.16 and 7.17.

If your client's score is 100 below the acceptable figure, this is classified as poor lung function and they should be referred to their GP before they exercise.

Body mass index

Body mass index is used to give us an idea of whether a client is obese. It then gives the extent of their obesity.

This is worked out by using the following formula:

Body mass index (BMI) = weight in kilograms divided by height in metres squared.

For a male who weighs 75 kg and is 1.80 m tall: $75 \div 1.80^2 = 23.1$. Thus his body mass index will be 23.1 kg/m^2.

What does this mean? Table 7.18 shows the classification for overweight and obesity.

The body mass index has serious limitations because it does not actually measure body composition. It can be used as a quick measure to see if a person is over-fat, but it is inaccurate because it does not make a distinction between muscle and fat. Thus, someone with a lot of muscle may come out as fat!

Hip-to-waist ratio

Hip-to-waist ratio is taken as an indicator of the health risks associated with obesity, and in particular the risk of coronary heart disease. Fat stored in the abdominal area is a greater risk factor for CHD because it is closer to the heart and can more easily be mobilised and taken to the heart.

Hip-to-waist ratio is calculated in the following way, using a tape measure.

● Waist measurement is taken at the level of the navel, with the stomach muscles relaxed and after a normal expiration. The tape measure is put around the waist and a horizontal reading is taken.
● Hip measurement is taken with the client standing up and is the widest measurement around the hips. It is usually taken at the level of the greater trochanter, which is at the top of the femur.

The ratio is worked out by dividing the waist measurement by the hip measurement. For a male with a 26" waist and 30" hips, this would be: $26 \div 30 = 0.87$.

What do these scores mean? Table 7.19 shows the classification for hip-to-waist ratio.

A male with a score above 0.90 and a female with a score above 0.80 will have an increased risk of developing CHD.

	Obesity class	BMI (kg/m2)
Underweight		< 17.5
Normal		17.5–24.9
Overweight		25–29.9
Obesity	I	30–34.9
Obesity	II	35–39.9
Extreme obesity	III	>40

Table 7.18 BMI classification of overweight and obesity

	Hip-to-waist ratio	Classification
Males	> 1.0	High risk
	0.90–0.99	Moderate risk
	< 0.90	Low risk
Females	> 0.85	High risk
	0.80–0.85	Moderate risk
	< 0.80	Low risk

Table 7.19 CHD risk classification from hip-to-waist ratio scores

Key learning points 2

● Before a fitness test is conducted, a health-screening form and an informed consent form must be completed.
● A client must be screened for risk of CHD. Risk factors include poor diet, obesity, smoking, excess alcohol intake, male gender and type 2 diabetes.

Student activity 7.2   **90 minutes**   P2 P3 P4 M2 D1

- Using the health-screening questionnaire provided as a template, design your own questionnaire that covers personal details, goals, current activity levels, lifestyle factors and medical history.

- Use the health-screening questionnaire for two individuals who have different goals and a different health status (e.g. conditioned and unconditioned).

- Use the following table to record and analyse the results of four health-related tests for the two individuals:

Name of test	Result of test	Interpretation of test: fit and healthy/proceed with caution/ GP referral
Resting heart rate		
Blood pressure		
Lung function		
Body mass index		
Strengths:		
Areas for improvement:		

Evaluate the information gained from the health-screening questionnaire and the fitness tests and make recommendations on how each individual could improve their lifestyle.

Q Quick quiz 2

1 Describe why coronary heart disease develops.
2 State three occasions when you would refer someone to the GP before letting them start exercising.
3 What is the difference between a static test and a dynamic test?
4 A high hip-to-waist ratio may indicate a raised risk of which medical condition?

7.4. Administering appropriate fitness tests

In order to administer fitness tests safely and effectively, you need to follow certain procedures. The test protocols have been described in Section 7.2, but you also need to ensure that the tests are valid and reliable, and that the individual being tested is appropriately prepared. You also need to be aware of any signs that would suggest that you ought to terminate the test.

Validity and reliability

These two terms must be considered before a test is conducted. The two questions you must ask yourself are:

1 Does this test actually test what I say it tests?
2 If this test were to be repeated, would I get the same results?

The first question tests validity. For example, a speed test using a shuttle run may actually test a person's ability to turn, which is more about agility than speed.

The second question tests its reliability. The conditions of the test must always be identical, making it most likely that the same results will be produced. However, there are many factors that may change, such as the temperature of the environment, the physical state of the athlete and the technique of the tester. All these may alter the results produced.

The purposes of fitness testing

The purposes of fitness testing are to:

- ensure that the person is safe to exercise
- find out their current position in terms of the components of fitness
- identify the strengths and weaknesses of each of their components of fitness
- gain information to allow a specific training programme to be written
- be able to monitor any changes in fitness
- provide an opportunity to educate individuals about health and fitness.

Pre-test procedures

When testing people, it is important that the tests are safe for the client, and also that the conditions the tests are performed in are consistent and stable.

The following should be taken into consideration in relation to the client:

- They should have medical clearance for any health conditions.
- They should be free of injuries.
- They should be wearing appropriate clothing.
- They should not have had a heavy meal within three hours of the test.
- They should have had a good night's sleep.
- They should not have trained on the day and should be fully recovered from previous training.
- They should have avoided stimulants such as tea, coffee or nicotine for two hours before the test.

The following should be taken into consideration regarding the environment:

- Heating in the area should be at room temperature (around 18 °C).
- The room should be well ventilated.
- The room should be clean and dust-free.

Test sequence

The order in which tests are conducted must be considered because it may change the accuracy of the results you produce. You may even have to do different tests on different days to produce the best results.

Your knowledge of sport science can help you to decide which tests should be done first and for how long the athlete will have to rest between tests. For example, a test that requires effort over a long period of time or works to failure will require one to two hours of recovery. A test requiring a high level of skill or coordination needs to be done first because skill level decreases when a person is tired. The correct order to follow would be:

- sedentary tests – height, weight, body composition, flexibility
- agility tests
- maximum power and strength tests
- sprint tests
- muscular endurance tests
- aerobic endurance tests.

Reasons to terminate a fitness test

There will be occasions when it becomes unsafe to continue with a test due to physiological changes within the client. The following is a list of specific situations when a test should be stopped:

- chest pains or angina-like symptoms
- excessive increase in blood pressure (250/115)
- shortness of breath and wheezing
- leg cramps or pain
- light-headedness, nausea or pale, clammy skin

- heart rate does not rise with exercise intensity
- irregular heart beat
- client requests to stop
- signs and symptoms of severe exhaustion
- equipment fails.

Key learning points 3

- Tests can be split into two types: those which test health and are static in nature and those which test fitness and are dynamic in nature.
- Before conducting a test, you must consider whether both the client and the environment are in an appropriate state for the test to take place.
- A valid test is one that tests what it says it will test.
- A reliable test is one that would yield the same results if it were to be repeated.

Q Quick quiz 3

Fill in the blank spaces to complete the following sentences, choosing from the list of words below.

- Safe
- Reliable
- Sedentary
- Strengths
- Valid
- Coordination
- Maximal
- Weaknesses.

When administering a fitness test, you must make sure it is _____ by considering whether it tests what it says it is testing, and also how to make it _____, which means that if you did the test again you would get the same results. Fitness testing is done to make sure the person is _____ to exercise and to identify their _____ and _____. It is important to do the _____ tests first and then tests requiring _____, and finally tests requiring _____ effort.

7.7. Interpreting the results of fitness tests and providing feedback

Once you have completed a fitness test, it is important to give detailed feedback to the individual. Before you conduct a test, you need to say what you are testing and explain how the test will be conducted. Feedback is given once you have conducted the test, written down the result and then worked out how the result compares with the normative tables.

Feedback should be given in the following format:

- Repeat the component of fitness that has been tested.
- Tell the individual what the result of the test was.
- Explain what you have tested and what the score represents.
- Tell the individual where they fit within the population norms.
- Tell the individual what the implications of the result are in terms of their health and fitness.
- Discuss what recommendations you would make for the future.

If you have carried out a blood pressure test, for example, you would give feedback in this specific way:

- 'I have just taken your blood pressure.'
- 'Your blood pressure was 120/80 mmHg.'
- 'Blood pressure is the pressure of blood in the arterial system. 120 mmHg is the pressure during the contraction phase of the heart beat, and 80 mmHg is the pressure during the relaxation phase of the heart beat.'
- 'This score is within the normal healthy range.'
- 'It means you are healthy enough to take part in sport and exercise.'

The scores of all fitness tests must be recorded in writing to ensure you have the information available in the future when you come to retest.

Recommendations

Once you have completed all the tests, you will be able to write an action plan or a report on the individual. This should cover the following information:

- current situation, highlighting strengths and weaknesses
- client's aims and objectives
- changes to be made, with options
- actions – a step-by-step guide to achieving aims.

Key learning points 4

● When giving feedback, you must let the individual know what you were testing, what score they achieved, what their score means and any implications this score may have.

● Once fitness tests have been completed, you can write an action plan for the individual, with recommendations for them to improve their health and fitness.

Student activity 7.3   ⏱ **3 hours**   P5 P6 M3 M4 D2

Task 1

• Choose six fitness tests specifically identified for the individual that you have selected to test.

• Justify why you chose these six tests for this individual (think about choosing tests specific to the goals and fitness needs of that individual).

• Develop a table and record the scores for each of the six tests.

Task 2

• Once your selected individual has done the fitness tests and you have recorded their results, you should prepare and then present feedback to the individual in the form of a consultation. You should have worked out how their score fits into the normative data for each test, and what the implications of the results are.

• As part of the consultation, summarise by identifying the individual's strengths and weaknesses and then provide recommendations for their future training activities.

References

Baechle, T. and Earle, R. (2008) *Essentials of Strength Training and Conditioning*, Human Kinetics.

Davis, R., Bull, C., Roscoe, J. and Roscoe, D. (2005) *Physical Education and the Study of Sport*, Elsevier Mosby.

Franklin, B. (2005) *American College of Sports Medicine's (ACSM) Guidelines for Exercise Testing and Prescription*, 6th edn, Lippincott, Williams and Wilkins.

Wesson, K., Wiggins-James, N., Thompson, G. and Hartigan, S. (2005) *Sport and PE: A Complete Guide to Advanced Level Study*, Hodder Arnold.

Further reading

Baechle, T. and Earle, R. (2008) *Essentials of Strength Training and Conditioning*, Human Kinetics.

Coulson, M. (2007) *The Fitness Instructor's Handbook*. A & C Black.

Sharkey, B.J. and Gaskill, S.E. (2006) *Fitness and Health*, Human Kinetics.

Useful websites

www.topendsports.com/testing/tests.htm
Over 100 fitness tests to try, all divided into different fitness categories

www.teachpe.com
Extensive range of online resources that cover the major sports, their skills and techniques, coaching tips, and physiology and anatomy

www.bases.org.uk
Membership website for sports professionals, providing details of job vacancies, careers advice, forums for coaching and sports science-related topics; limited access to non-members

www.1st4sport.com
Provides qualifications for sports professionals covering a wide range of sports-related activities

11: Sports nutrition

11.1 Introduction

As we seek to gain an extra edge in our sporting performances and to maximise the effects of our training, so the spotlight has fallen on areas other than training. Nutrition has been shown to be an area of increasing interest. We know that training brings benefits and we know that eating properly brings benefits. So if we combine the correct training with the correct nutritional strategy, the gains are multiplied. Nutrition is as important for people who are seeking to improve their sporting performance as it is for those seeking fitness gains or weight-management objectives.

By the end of this unit you should:

- know the concepts of nutrition and digestion
- know energy intake and expenditure in sports performance
- know the relationship between hydration and sports performance
- be able to plan a diet appropriate for a selected sports activity.

Assessment and grading criteria

To achieve a PASS grade the evidence must show that the learner is able to:	To achieve a MERIT grade the evidence must show that, in addition to the pass criteria, the learner is able to:	To achieve a DISTINCTION grade the evidence must show that, in addition to the pass and merit criteria, the learner is able to:
P1 describe nutrition, including nutritional requirements, using recommended guidelines from public health sources associated with nutrition		
P2 describe the structure and function of the digestive system		
P3 describe energy intake and expenditure in sports performance	**M1** explain energy intake and expenditure in sports performance	
P4 describe energy balance and its importance in relation to sports performance	**M2** explain the importance of energy balance in relation to sports performance	**D1** analyse the effects of energy balance on sports performance
P5 describe hydration and its effects on sports performance		
P6 describe the components of a balanced diet	**M3** explain the components of a balanced diet	
P7 plan an appropriate two-week diet plan for a selected sports performer for a selected sports activity.	**M4** explain the two-week diet plan for a selected sports performer for a selected sports activity.	**D2** justify the two-week diet plan for a selected sports performer for a selected sports activity.

11.2 Nutrients

P1

> ### Key term
>
> **Nutrients:** chemical substances obtained from food and used in the body to provide energy, as well as structural materials and regulating agents to support growth, maintenance and repair of the body's tissues.

Nutrients can be divided into two main groups: macronutrients and micronutrients. The three macronutrients are:

- carbohydrate
- protein
- fat.

Macronutrients are needed in large amounts in the diet and all provide energy for the body. They are also used to build the structures of the body and produce functions needed to sustain life.

The two micronutrients are:

- vitamins
- minerals.

They are needed in smaller amounts in the diet and contain no energy themselves. They work in conjunction with the macronutrients to produce life-sustaining functions and are needed to unlock the energy present in the macronutrients.

There are other food groups such as water and fibre. Water is not usually regarded as a nutrient because it has no nutrient value despite being highly important in sustaining life. Fibre is a type of carbohydrate so it would be part of that food group.

Carbohydrate

Almost every culture relies on carbohydrate as the major source of nutrients and calories – rice in Asia, wheat in Europe, the Middle East and North Africa, corn and potato in the Americas.

Carbohydrate should provide between 50 and 60 per cent of calorie intake and its main role is to supply energy to allow the body to function. The energy content of carbohydrate is that 1 g provides 4 kcals.

There are many sources of carbohydrate, such as bread, rice, pasta, potatoes, fruit, vegetables, sweets and biscuits. They all differ in form slightly but are all broken down into glucose because that is the only way the body can use carbohydrate.

The functions of carbohydrate are to provide energy for:

- the brain to function
- the liver to perform its functions
- muscular contractions at moderate to high intensities.

When carbohydrate foods are digested they are all broken down into glucose which is then absorbed in the small intestine and enters the bloodstream. From the bloodstream it can either be used immediately as energy or stored in the liver and muscles. Glucose is stored in the form of glycogen, which is bound to water (1 g of glucose needs 2.7 g of water) for storage. However, the glycogen molecule is bulky and difficult to store in large amounts. The body can store around 1600 kcals of glycogen, which would enable us to run for around two hours.

> ### Key terms
>
> **Glucose:** the smallest unit of a carbohydrate.
> **Glycogen:** stored glucose in the muscles and liver attached to water molecules.

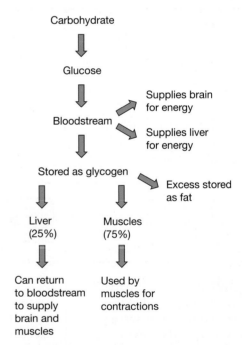

Fig 11.1 What happens to carbohydrate when it is digested

Forms of carbohydrate

Carbohydrates come in a variety of forms, but they are all made up of molecules of sugar. These molecules of sugar are called saccharides; they come in different forms depending upon the foods in which they are found. Eventually through the process of digestion they all become glucose. These saccharides are found as one of the following:

● monosaccharides
● disaccharides
● polysaccharides.

Monosaccharides are one saccharide molecule on its own. There are three types of monosaccharide:

● glucose – occurs naturally in most carbohydrate foods
● fructose – occurs in fruit and honey
● galactose – does not occur freely but is a component of the sugars found in milk products.

Disaccharides are two saccharide molecules joined together by a bond:

● sucrose = glucose + fructose – most commonly found as table sugar
● lactose = glucose + galactose – found in milk and milk products
● maltose = glucose + glucose – found in malt products, beers and cereals.

Mono- and disaccharides are commonly known as simple carbohydrates because they are in short simple chains – existing as individual molecules.

Polysaccharides are long, complex chains of glucose molecules containing ten or more molecules. Due to their complicated structures they are called 'complex carbohydrates'.

To digest polysaccharides, the bonds need to be broken down through the process of digestion so that they can become individual glucose molecules and be absorbed into the bloodstream. If a complex carbohydrate is processed or cooked in any way these bonds will start to be broken down before they enter the digestive system.

Polysaccharides or complex carbohydrates can come in either their natural or refined forms. Wheat and rice are naturally brown in colour due to their high levels of fibre, vitamins and minerals. Therefore, the brown varieties of bread, rice and pasta are of greater nutrient value than the white, refined varieties.

Good sources of polysaccharides:

● wholemeal, wholegrain or granary breads
● wholemeal pasta
● wholegrain rice
● potatoes
● sweet potatoes
● vegetables
● pulses.

Poorer choices of polysaccharides:

● white bread
● white pasta
● white rice
● rice cakes.

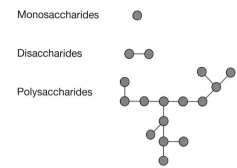

Fig 11.2 Structure of saccharides

Glycaemic index

The rate at which carbohydrate foods are broken down and how quickly they raise blood glucose levels is measured via the glycaemic index (GI). It is a ranking system that shows how quickly the carbohydrate is broken down and enters the blood as glucose in comparison with the speed at which glucose would enter the blood if consumed. Foods with a high glycaemic index break down quickly and rapidly increase blood glucose levels. Table sugar is a good example. Pasta would have a lower glycaemic index, breaking down into glucose more slowly. It would also have less of an immediate effect on blood glucose levels, causing a slower increase over a longer period.

The glycaemic index is one of the most important principles in nutrition currently. We deal best with foods of a low glycaemic index that release their energy slowly and over time. Foods of a high glycaemic index cause a rapid release of glucose into the bloodstream, followed by a rapid drop in blood glucose, causing hunger and fatigue. The person who eats high glycaemic index foods will experience fluctuating blood glucose levels and be tempted to overeat the wrong type of food. High glycaemic index foods, such as sweets, cakes, biscuits, fizzy drinks, white breads and sugary cereals, are linked to obesity and the development of type 2 diabetes. If a person eats low glycaemic index foods they will find that their stable blood glucose levels give them energy and enable them to concentrate throughout the day.

In the glycaemic index foods are either high, moderate or low.

High	Moderate	Low
Above 85	60–84	Below 60

Table 11.1 Glycaemic index for foods

The speed at which a food is broken down and enters the bloodstream is dependent on a range of factors. The following will lower the speed at which glucose enters the bloodstream:

● the presence of fibre in the food
● the presence of fat in the food
● the presence of protein in the food
● the type of saccharides present in the food
● the amount of carbohydrate eaten.

The following will increase the speed at which glucose enters the bloodstream:

● the length of the cooking process
● the amount the food has been refined or processed
● the riper the fruit has become.

Fig 11.4 Refined white foods

Soluble fibre dissolves into a gel in water and is found in the fleshy part of fruit and vegetables, oats, barley and rice. For example, when you make porridge the oats partly dissolve into a sticky gel and this is the soluble fibre.

Soluble fibre has two main roles to play:

● it slows down how quickly the stomach empties and how quickly glucose enters the bloodstream
● it binds to fat and blood cholesterol, thus decreasing the risk of heart disease.

Insoluble fibre will not dissolve in water and is found in the skin of fruit and vegetables, wheat, rye, seeds and pips of fruit. Insoluble fibre passes through the digestive system without being altered in any way. Its main roles are as follows:

● It adds bulk to faeces and speeds its passage through the large intestine.
● It helps to keep the large intestine clean and prevent bowel disease.
● It stretches the stomach and makes you feel full for longer.

Fig 11.3 Unrefined brown foods

Fibre

Dietary fibre is the part of a plant that is resistant to the body's digestive enzymes. It is defined as 'indigestible plant material', and although it is a carbohydrate and contains calories, the digestive system cannot unlock them from the plant. As a result, fibre moves through the gastrointestinal tract and ends up in the stool. The main benefit in eating fibre is that it retains water, resulting in softer and bulkier stools that prevent constipation and haemorrhoids. Research suggests that a high-fibre diet also reduces the risk of colon cancer. All fruits, vegetables and grains provide some fibre.

There are two types of fibre – soluble and insoluble – that perform slightly different functions.

● It slows down the release of glucose into the bloodstream.

It is recommended that we eat around 18 g of fibre a day. This can be done by eating foods in their natural form rather than in their processed or refined states.

Recommended daily intake of carbohydrate

A minimum recommended daily intake of at least 50 per cent of total kilocalories consumed should come from complex carbohydrate sources. The British Nutrition Foundation found that in Britain the average intake of carbohydrate is 272 g for men and 193 g for women, providing just over 43 per cent of the energy in the diet.

As with most nutrients, eating excess amounts can lead to problems. Excessive consumption of sugar (for example sucrose) can lead to tooth decay and is linked to a number of major diseases, such as diabetes, obesity and coronary heart disease. Excess carbohydrate in the diet will be converted to and stored as fat. Thus it is possible to gain body fat even on a low-fat diet.

Key learning points I

● Carbohydrate provides energy for:
 – brain function
 – liver function and digestion
 – muscular contractions.
● Carbohydrates are made up of saccharides, of which there are three types:
 – monosaccharides – single units of saccharides known as 'simple sugars'
 – disaccharides – two units of saccharides joined by a bond called 'simple sugars'
 – polysaccharides – long chains of saccharides called 'complex carbohydrates'.
● Glycaemic index (GI) is the rate at which a carbohydrate food enters the bloodstream as glucose:
 – high GI = above 85
 – moderate GI = 60–85
 – low GI = less than 60.
● Fibre is 'indigestible plant material' which cannot be digested. It protects against heart disease and diseases of the colon by keeping the colon clean and the waste moving through quickly.

Q Quick quiz I

Look at the list of carbohydrate-rich foods and put them into the appropriate column (some of them can go into more than one column).

Monosaccharide	Disaccharide	Polysaccharide	Fibre

Apple	Milk	Pasta
Cereal	Rice	All Bran
Bread	Cabbage	Banana
Honey	Potatoes	Cream
Sweetcorn	Beer	

Protein

The word 'protein' is derived from Greek and means 'prime importance'. Proteins are of prime importance because they are the building blocks that make up the structures of the body. Muscle, skin, bones, internal organs, cartilage and ligament all have a protein component. We gain our protein by eating protein-rich foods such as red meat, fish, chicken, eggs and dairy products.

The diet should consist of between 10 and 20 per cent protein depending upon the specific needs of the individual. Protein also provides a source of energy: 1 g of protein provides 4 kcals.

Amino acids

The smallest unit of a protein is an amino acid. Proteins are made up of long chains of amino acids which are formed into structures. Amino acids are the smallest unit of a protein and there are 20 amino acids in total. Amino acids can be seen to be like the alphabet. In the English language we have 26 letters from which we can make up millions of words. The protein alphabet has 20 amino acids from which can be produced approximately 50,000 different proteins present in the body. Just as different words are made up of different orders of letters, so different structures are made up of different orders of amino acids.

They can be split into essential and non-essential amino acids. An essential amino acid is one that must be gained through eating it in the diet, while a non-essential amino acid can be made in the liver if all essential amino acids are present. This means to produce all the structures of the body we must gain all the essential amino acids on a daily basis.

There are eight essential amino acids to be gained from the diet:

- isoleucine
- leucine
- lysine
- methionine
- phenylalanine
- threonine
- tryptophan
- valine.

There are 12 non-essential amino acids which are synthesised in the liver if all eight essential amino acids are gained from the diet:

- cystein
- yrosine
- histidine
- glutamine
- glutamic acid
- glycine
- alanine
- serine
- proline
- aspartic acid
- asparagine
- arginine.

Foods that contain all eight essential amino acids are described as being complete, while a food that is missing one or more essential amino acid is described as being incomplete. Table 11.2 shows sources of complete and incomplete proteins.

With the exception of the soya bean, the sources of complete protein are from animals, while incomplete proteins come from plant sources. To gain all eight essential amino acids from incomplete protein sources you need to eat a range of sources or combine protein sources. This is called 'complementary protein' and examples are:

- wheat and pulses (beans on toast)
- nuts and vegetables (nut roast)
- rice and lentils (vegetarian chilli).

All protein sources contain different amounts of amino acids. The greater the quantity of the essential amino acids in the food, the higher the biological value. Eggs have the highest quality or biological

Complete protein	Incomplete protein
Chicken	Wheat
Eggs	Oats
Fish	Rice
Red meat	Pulses
Dairy products	Nuts
Soya beans	Vegetables

Table 11.2 Complete and incomplete proteins

Fig 11.5 Complete protein

Fig 11.6 Incomplete protein

value of all foods and are given a protein rating of 100. All other proteins are compared with eggs in terms of their quality and quantity of amino acids. This is shown in Table 11.3.

Functions of protein

When we eat protein it is digested in the digestive system and then delivered to the liver as individual amino acids. The liver then rebuilds the amino acids into long chains to make up proteins. The proteins that the liver produces depend upon the needs of the body at that time. If we need to replace muscle the liver will produce the relevant proteins to replace muscle tissue.

Proteins have three specific roles in the body:

● to build structures (structural)
● to perform functions (functional)
● to provide fuel.

Protein forms a part of the following structures:

● muscle (skeletal, smooth and cardiac)
● bone
● internal organs (heart, kidneys, liver)
● connective tissue (tendons and ligaments)
● hair
● nails.

Protein forms part of the following structures which perform specific functions in the body:

● hormones (which send messages to cells – insulin and adrenaline)
● enzymes (biological catalysts which speed up reactions in cells)
● part of the immune system (white blood cells are made partly of protein)
● formation of lipoproteins (these help to transport fats around the body).

Protein is not the body's first choice of fuel but it can be used as energy. It is heavily used during endurance training and events, or at times of starvation.

Food	Protein rating
Eggs	100
Fish	70
Beef	69
Cow's milk	60
Brown rice	57
White rice	56
Soya beans	47
Wheat	44
Peanuts	43
Beans	34

Table 11.3 Protein ratings of different foods
Source: Adapted from McArdle *et al.* (2009)

Recommended intakes of protein

The average daily intake of protein in the UK is 85 g for men and 62 g for women. The recommended daily amount of protein for healthy adults is 0.8 g per kilogram of body weight, or about 15 per cent of total kilocalories. Protein needs are higher for children, infants and many athletes.

Key learning points 2

- Proteins are long chains of amino acids. There are 20 amino acids in total: eight are essential amino acids which need to be eaten in the diet, and 12 are non-essential amino acids which can be synthesised by the liver if all eight essential amino acids are present.
- Foods containing all eight essential amino acids are described as being complete protein. Foods missing one or more essential amino acid are described as being incomplete.
- Protein has the following main functions:
  - to build structures of the body
  - to perform specific functions
  - to provide fuel.

Q Quick quiz 2

Liver	Isoleucine	20	Nuts	8
Muscle	Aspartic acid	Soya bean	Eggs	Hormone

Choose the correct word or words to match the following descriptions.

1 This is an essential amino acid.

2 This is a complete protein.

3 This is an incomplete protein.

4 This body structure contains protein.

5 There are this number of amino acids in total.

6 There are this number of essential amino acids.

7 This is a non-essential amino acid.

8 This organ rebuilds amino acids into long chains.

9 This food has a very high protein rating.

10 Protein forms part of this structure.

Fats

Fats are often perceived as being bad or a part of the diet to be avoided. In fact, fats are vital to health and perform many important functions in the body. The intake of certain fats does need to be minimised and excess consumption of fats will lead to health problems.

The functions of fat are as follows:

- formation of the cell membrane
- formation of the myelin sheath which coats the nerves
- a component of the brain and nervous system
- protection of internal organs (brain, kidneys, liver)
- production of hormones (oestrogen and testosterone)
- transportation and storage of vitamins A, D, E and K
- constant source of energy
- store of energy
- heat production.

Fats and oils belong to a family called 'lipids' and they perform a variety of important roles in the body. Predominantly fats supply energy for everyday activities and movement. They are described as being 'energy-dense' because they contain a lot of energy per gram: 1 g of fat provides 9 kcals.

If we compare this figure to the 4 kcals which carbohydrates and protein provide (see Table 11.4) then we can see that it is significantly higher.

The difference between a fat and an oil is that a fat is solid at room temperature while an oil is liquid at room temperature.

The smallest unit of a fat is called a 'fatty acid'. There are different types of fatty acid present in the foods we ingest. In particular, a fatty acid can be

Macronutrient	Kcals per gram
Carbohydrate	4
Protein	4
Fat	9

Table 11.4 Kcalories per gram of macronutrients

saturated or unsaturated; this is important because they will be shaped differently. In chemistry shape matters because it influences the function performed. Therefore, different fatty acids perform different functions in the body.

Triglycerides

Triglycerides are dietary fats in that they are how the fats we ingest are packaged. A triglyceride is defined as 'three fatty acids attached to a glycerol backbone'. Glycerol is actually a carbohydrate which the fatty acids attach to. During digestion the fatty acids are broken off from the glycerol backbone to be used by the body as required. The glycerol is used as all carbohydrates are used, to produce energy.

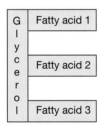

Fig 11.7 Structure of a triglyceride

Types of fatty acid

Fatty acids can be divided into:

● saturated fatty acids
● monounsaturated fatty acids
● polyunsaturated fatty acids.

A fatty acid consists of long chains of carbon atoms with an acid group (COOH) at one end and a methyl group (CH_3) at the other. The structure of the chains of fatty acids attached to the glycerol molecule determines whether the fat is classed as saturated, monounsaturated or polyunsaturated. If you think of different types of fats, such as butter, lard, sunflower oil and olive oil, you will notice that they differ in terms of their colour, texture and taste. This is because of the different types of fatty acids attached to the glycerol backbone.

A saturated fat is one where all the carbon atoms are attached to hydrogen molecules. The chain is said to be saturated with hydrogen.

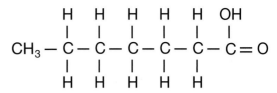

Fig 11.8 Saturated fatty acid

We can see that the carbon atoms each have single bonds between them and each carbon atom has four bonds. The hydrogen atoms possess a very slight charge and gently push away from each other. This has the effect of making the chain straight in shape. In chemistry shape matters as it affects function and it also makes the saturated fat solid at room temperature. This is because the fatty acids can pack tightly together with little space between each one. Saturated fats are also described as being stable or inert. This means that their structure will not change when they are heated. They will melt but the structure of the fatty acid chain stays the same.

The majority of saturated fats come from animal sources (see Table 11.5).

Source	
Animal	**Plant**
Red meat	Coconut oil
Poultry	Palm oil
Eggs	
Dairy products	

Table 11.5 Sources of saturated fats

The Department of Health recommends a person should have a maximum of 10 per cent of daily kilocalories from saturated fat.

An unsaturated fat is one where there are hydrogen atoms missing from the carbon chain, causing the carbon atoms to attach to each other with double bonds. This is because carbon has to have four bonds and if there is no hydrogen present they will bond to each other. In this case the carbon chain is not saturated with hydrogen atoms and is therefore 'unsaturated'.

A monounsaturated fat is one where there is just one double bond in the carbon chain (see Figure 11.9).

Due to the slight charge the hydrogen atoms contain, they push each other away. Now that there are hydrogen atoms missing, it causes the chain to bend and become curved. The curved fatty acids cannot pack so tightly together, so their appearance

113

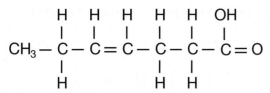

Fig 11.9 Monounsaturated fatty acid

changes and they will be in liquid or oil form. They will also be less stable or more reactive. This is because of the double bonds between the carbon atoms. Carbon attaches to itself only if there is nothing else to be attached to and it will take the opportunity to break off and attach to something else if it can. If monounsaturated fats are heated they change their structure.

Examples of monounsaturated fats are:

● olive oil
● peanut oil
● avocados
● rapeseed oil (canola oil)
● almond oil.

The Department of Health recommends a person should have a maximum of 12 per cent of daily kilocalories from monounsaturated fat.

A polyunsaturated fat is one where there are many double bonds in the carbon chain due to a shortage of hydrogen ions in the chain.

This has the effect of making the fatty acid even more curved and highly reactive in nature. They are also in oil or liquid form. Polyunsaturated fats are highly unstable when heated to high temperatures and will change their structure.

Examples of polyunsaturated fats are:

● sunflower oil
● safflower oil
● corn oil
● fish oils
● nuts
● seeds.

The Department of Health recommends a person should have a maximum of 10 per cent of daily kilocalories from these polyunsaturated fats.

$$CH_3 - \overset{\overset{\displaystyle H}{|}}{C} - \overset{\overset{\displaystyle H}{|}}{\underset{\underset{\displaystyle H}{|}}{C}} = \overset{\overset{\displaystyle H}{|}}{C} - \overset{\overset{\displaystyle H}{|}}{C} = \overset{\overset{\displaystyle H}{|}}{C} - \overset{\overset{\displaystyle OH}{|}}{C} = O$$

Fig 11.10 Polyunsaturated fatty acid

Saturated versus unsaturated fats

Saturated fats have always received bad press until recently when people realised that they have an important role in the diet. Due to their stable nature they always retain their structure. This is important because when they enter the fat cells, the cells will recognise them and know what to do with them. Saturated fats are always stored as fat in the fat cells.

Naturally occurring unsaturated fats, such as olive oil, have very beneficial effects when they are stored in fat cells – they improve circulation, lower cholesterol levels and improve the health of hair, skin and nails. The problem comes when unsaturated fats are heated or processed in any way because they then change their structure and start to look like saturated fats. They become 'hydrogenated' or altered structurally and when they enter the body they are accepted into the fat cells because they look like saturated fats. Once inside the fat cells, they start to cause damage to the cell and stop positive reactions occurring. The two most dangerous types of fats are:

● hydrogenated vegetable oil
● trans fats.

These have been linked to heart disease and cancer and are present in processed foods and deep-fat-fried foods.

Butter versus margarine?

In terms of fat content these two products are pretty similar. However, due to the margarine being an unsaturated fat (sunflower oil), it would appear to be beneficial to health. Sunflower oil is naturally a liquid and margarine is a solid product, which means it has been processed in some way and thus changed structurally.

The butter will not be changed structurally because it is predominantly saturated fat. For these reasons the butter is a better health choice because it is a more naturally occurring product. In particular, it is the cheap margarines that need to be avoided. If choosing a margarine, check the contents for hydrogenated vegetable oil and trans fats.

Essential fatty acids

The body can make all the fatty acids it needs except for two, the essential fatty acids (EFAs), which must be supplied in the diet. These fatty acids are omega 3 and omega 11.

Sources of omega 3 and 6 are as follows.

Omega 3 fatty acids:

● oily fish (e.g. salmon, mackerel, herring)
● flax oil

- walnuts
- soya beans.

Omega 6 fatty acids:

- sunflower oil
- pumkin seeds
- sesame seeds
- safflower oil.

Research into omega 3, and in particular fish oils, has shown that eating oily fish protects against heart disease. This is because the omega 3s may prevent the formation of blood clots on the artery walls and lower the levels of triglycerides circulating in the bloodstream.

The essential fatty acids are also thought to improve the function of the brain and promote learning as well as being beneficial for arthritics because they reduce swelling in the joints.

Cholesterol

Cholesterol can either be ingested or made in the body. It is found only in animal products and never in plants. It has some useful functions including building cell membranes and helping the function of various hormones.

There are two types of cholesterol: low-density lipoproteins (LDLs) and high-density lipoproteins (HDLs). LDLs are responsible for the deposits lining the walls of arteries and lead to an increased risk of coronary heart disease. HDLs actually reduce this risk by transporting cholesterol away to the liver and so are beneficial to health.

Recommended daily intake of fat

Fat intake should make up no more than 30 per cent of total kilocalories. Only 10 per cent of kilocalories should come from saturated fat. Dietary cholesterol should be limited to 300 mg or less per day.

There are many health problems related to eating an excess of fat, especially saturated fats. These include obesity, high blood pressure and coronary heart disease, although it is important to distinguish between the different types of fat eaten in a person's diet. Consumption of certain fatty acids (omega 3 fish oils found in tuna) is linked to a decreased risk of coronary heart disease.

As fat provides just over twice as much energy per gram as carbohydrate, a diet high in fat can make over-consumption more likely. It is thought that excess dietary fat may be more easily converted to body fat than excess carbohydrate or protein. Research suggests that more people are obese today than ever before. Obese people are more likely to suffer from a range of illnesses including coronary heart disease, adult-onset diabetes, gallstones, arthritis, high blood pressure and some types of cancer. However, most of the health problems associated with obesity are removed once the extra weight is lost.

Key learning points 3

- Fat performs some vital functions in the body:
  - formation of the cell membrane
  - formation of the myelin sheath which coats the nerves
  - a component of the brain and nervous system
  - protection of internal organs (brain, kidneys, liver)
  - production of hormones (oestrogen and testosterone)
  - transportation and storage of vitamins A, D, E and K
  - constant source of energy
  - store of energy
  - heat production.
- Saturated fats occur when all the carbon atoms are saturated with hydrogen. They are solid at room temperature, stable and unreactive. Examples of saturated fats include:
  - animal fats
  - fat of red meat and poultry
  - dairy products
  - eggs
  - coconut oil
  - palm oil.
- Unsaturated fats occur when there is a double bond in the carbon chain due to a shortage of hydrogen. They are liquid at room temperature, unstable and reactive. There are two types of unsaturated fats:
  - monounsaturated fats, which have one double bond in the chain and include olive oil and peanut oil
  - polyunsaturated fats, which have more than one double bond and include sunflower oil and fish oils.

Quick quiz 3

1 Name three functions of fat.

2 What is the name of the family that fats and oils are in?

3 How many kcalories are there in 1g of fat?

4 What is the difference between fats and oils?

5 What is the smallest unit of a fat called?

6 What is a triglyceride?

7 Name the three categories that fatty acids can be placed in.

8 Describe the structure of an unsaturated fat.

9 What are the problems associated with saturated fats?

10 What is an essential fatty acid? Give three examples of one.

Vitamins

Vitamins are organic substances that the body requires in small amounts. The body is incapable of making vitamins for its overall needs, so they must be supplied regularly by the diet.

Vitamins are not related chemically and differ in their physiological actions. As vitamins were discovered, each was identified by a letter. Many of the vitamins consist of several closely related compounds of similar physiological properties.

Vitamins may be subdivided into:

● water soluble – C and B (complex)
● fat soluble – A, D, E and K.

The water-soluble vitamins cannot be stored in the body so they must be consumed on a regular basis. If excess quantities of these vitamins are consumed, the body will excrete them in the urine. Fat-soluble vitamins are stored in the body's fat so it is not necessary to consume these on such a regular basis. It is also possible to overdose on fat-soluble vitamins, which can be detrimental to health.

Varying amounts of each vitamin are required. The amount needed is referred to as the recommended daily allowance (RDA).

Fat-soluble vitamins

Vitamin A

● **Function:** to help maintain good vision, healthy skin, hair and mucous membranes, and to serve as an antioxidant; also needed for proper bone and tooth development

● **Source:** liver, mackerel and milk products
● **RDA:** 1.5 mg

Vitamin D (calciferol)

● **Function:** essential for calcium and phosphorus utilisation; promotes strong bones and teeth
● **Source:** sunlight, egg yolk, fish, fish oils and fortified cereals
● **RDA:** 0.01 mg

Vitamin E

● **Function:** antioxidant, helps prevent damage to cell membranes
● **Source:** wheat germ, nuts, whole grains and dark green leaf vegetables
● **RDA:** 15 mg

Vitamin K

● **Function:** used in the formation of blood clots
● **Source:** leafy green vegetables
● **RDA:** 70 mg

Water-soluble vitamins

B vitamins are not chemically related, but often occur in the same foodstuff. Their main function is to aid in the metabolism of food.

Vitamin B1 (thiamine)

● **Function:** helps convert food to energy and aids the nervous and cardiovascular systems
● **Source:** rice, bran, pork, beef, peas, beans, wheat germ, oatmeal and soya beans
● **RDA:** 1.5 mg

Vitamin B2 (riboflavin)

● **Function:** aids growth and reproduction, and helps to metabolise fats, carbohydrates and proteins; promotes healthy skin and nails
● **Source:** milk, liver, kidneys, yeast, cheese, leafy green vegetables, fish and eggs
● **RDA:** 1.7 mg

Vitamin B3 (niacin)

● **Function:** helps to keep the nervous system balanced and is also important for the synthesis of sex hormones, thyroxine, cortisone and insulin
● **Source:** poultry, fish, peanuts, yeast extract (for example Marmite), rice bran and wheat germ
● **RDA:** 20 mg

Vitamin B5 (pantothenic acid)

● **Function:** helps in cell building and maintaining normal growth and development of the central nervous system; helps form hormones and antibodies; also necessary for the conversion of fat and sugar to energy

● **Source:** wheatgerm, green vegetables, whole grains, mushrooms, fish, peanuts and yeast extract (for example, Marmite)
● **RDA:** 10 mg

Vitamin B6 (pyridoxine)

● **Function:** helps in the utilisation of proteins and the metabolism of fats; also needed for production of red blood cells and antibodies
● **Source:** chicken, beef, bananas, yeast extract (for example Marmite), eggs, brown rice, soya beans, oats, whole wheat, peanuts and walnuts
● **RDA:** 2 mg

Vitamin C (ascorbic acid)

● **Function:** essential for the formation of collagen; helps to strengthen tissues, acts as an antioxidant, helps in healing, production of red blood cells, fighting bacterial infections and regulating cholesterol; also helps the body to absorb iron
● **Source:** most fresh fruits and vegetables
● **RDA:** 60 mg

Folic acid (folacin)

● **Function:** helps the body form genetic material and red blood cells, and aids in protein metabolism; also acts as an antioxidant; research has shown that if folic acid is taken on a daily basis 30 days before conception, the fetus is less likely to suffer from birth defects such as spina bifida
● **Source:** green vegetables, kidney beans and orange juice
● **RDA:** 400 mg

Minerals

There are several minerals required to maintain a healthy body. Some are needed in moderate amounts, others in only very small amounts; the latter are referred to as trace minerals.

Calcium

● **Function:** needed to build strong bones and teeth, helps to calm nerves and plays a role in muscle contraction, blood clotting and cell membrane upkeep; correct quantities of calcium consumption have been shown to significantly lower the risk of osteoporosis
● **Source:** milk and milk products, whole grains and unrefined cereals, green vegetables and fish bones
● **RDA:** adults 1200 mg
● **Deficiency:** fragile bones, osteoporosis, rickets, tooth decay, irregular heartbeat and slowed nerve impulse response; vitamin D is essential for proper calcium absorption and utilisation

Magnesium

● **Function:** aids the production of proteins and helps regulate body temperature; helps lower blood pressure and assists with the proper functioning of nerves and muscles
● **Source:** whole grain foods, wheat bran, dark green leafy vegetables, soya beans, fish, oysters, shrimp, almonds and peanuts
● **RDA:** 350 mg
● **Deficiency:** decreased blood pressure and body temperature, nervousness, interference with the transmission of nerve and muscle impulses

Phosphorus

● **Function:** essential for metabolism of carbohydrates, fats and proteins; aids growth and cell repair, and is necessary for proper skeletal growth, tooth development, proper kidney function and the nervous system
● **Source:** meat, fish, poultry, milk, yoghurt, eggs, seeds, broccoli and nuts
● **RDA:** 800 mg
● **Deficiency:** bone pain, fatigue, irregular breathing and nervous disorders

Potassium

● **Function:** in conjunction with sodium helps to maintain fluid and electrolyte balance within cells; important for normal nerve and muscle function and aids proper maintenance of the blood's mineral balance; also helps to lower blood pressure
● **Source:** bananas, dried apricots, yoghurt, whole grains, sunflower seeds, potatoes, sweet potatoes and kidney beans
● **RDA:** 2500 mg
● **Deficiency:** decreased blood pressure, dry skin, salt retention and irregular heart beat

Sodium

● **Function:** works in conjunction with potassium to maintain fluid and electrolyte balance within cells
● **Source:** virtually all foods contain sodium, for example celery, cheese, eggs, meat, milk and milk products, processed foods, salt and seafood
● **RDA:** 2500 mg
● **Deficiency:** confusion, low blood sugar, dehydration, lethargy, heart palpitations and heart attack

Trace minerals

Copper

- **Function**: assists in the formation of haemoglobin and helps to maintain healthy bones, blood vessels and nerves
- **Source**: barley, potatoes, whole grains, mushrooms, cocoa, beans, almonds and most seafoods
- **RDA**: 2 mg
- **Deficiency**: fractures and bone deformities, anaemia, general weakness, impaired respiration and skin sores

Iron

- **Function**: required for the production of haemoglobin
- **Source**: liver, lean meats, eggs, baked potatoes, soya beans, kidney beans, whole grains and cereals, and dried fruits
- **RDA**: males 10 mg, females 18 mg
- **Deficiency**: dizziness, iron deficiency anaemia, constipation, sore or inflamed tongue

Selenium

- **Function**: a powerful antioxidant, aids normal body growth and fertility
- **Source**: seafood, offal, bran and wheat germ, broccoli, celery, cucumbers and mushrooms
- **RDA**: 1 mg
- **Deficiency**: heart disease, muscular pain and weakness

Zinc

- **Function**: necessary for healing and development of new cells; an antioxidant, plays an important part in helping to build a strong immune system
- **Source**: beef, lamb, seafood, eggs, yoghurt, yeast extract (for example Marmite), beans, nuts and seeds
- **RDA**: 15 mg
- **Deficiency**: decreased learning ability, delayed sexual maturity, eczema, fatigue, prolonged wound healing, retarded growth and white spots on nails

Water

One of the major chemicals essential to life is water, although it has no nutritional value in terms of energy. Water is used by the body to transport other chemicals. It also plays a major role in maintaining the body at a constant temperature. About 2.5 litres a day are needed to maintain normal functions in adults. This amount depends heavily on environmental conditions and on the amount of energy expenditure. In the heat a greater amount of water is needed, and exercise requires an increased intake of water due to the loss of fluid via sweating.

Only half of the body's water requirement comes in the form of liquid. The other half is supplied from food (especially fruit and vegetables) and metabolic reactions (the breakdown of food results in the formation of carbon dioxide and water).

Fig 11.11 Taking in water during a match

Key learning points 4

- Vitamins and minerals play key roles in sustaining life and the health of the body.
- Vitamins B and C are water soluble.
- Vitamins A, D, E and K are fat soluble.

Student activity 11.1 60 minutes P1

Nutrition and nutritional requirements

Good nutrition is important for every person and is even more important for athletes if they want to be able to perform at their optimal level.

Task 1

Design a poster that illustrates a person's normal nutritional requirements. These include:

- carbohydrates
- proteins – including essential and non-essential
- fats – including essential fatty acids

- vitamins
- minerals.

Task 2

Write a leaflet to go with your poster that describes nutrition and the nutritional requirements of people. Include in your leaflet the common terminology used to express how much of each type of macro- and micronutrient we should be consuming, for example RDA, and describe the meaning of each.

11.3 Digestion

The digestive system is where foods are broken down into their individual nutrients, absorbed into the bloodstream and the waste excreted. It works through processes of mechanical and chemical digestion. Mechanical digestion starts before the food enters the mouth as we cook the food and then cut it up or mash it to make it more palatable. In the mouth we chew the food to tear it apart further, then digestive juices continue this process. The chemical digestion of foods occurs through the digestive enzymes which are present in the mouth and the organs the food passes through. Enzymes are defined as biological catalysts that break down the large molecules of the nutrients into smaller molecules which can be absorbed.

The aim of the digestive system is to break down the nutrients into their smallest units (see Table 11.6).

Nutrient	Smallest unit
Carbohydrate	Glucose
Protein	Amino acid
Fats	Fatty acid

Table 11.6 Nutrients and their smallest units

The digestion, absorption and elimination of nutrients take place in the gastrointestinal tract, which is a long tube running from the mouth to the anus. It includes the mouth, oesophagus, stomach, small intestine and large intestine.

Mouth

The technical term for the mouth is the buccal cavity and this is where the food's journey begins. The teeth and jaw produce mechanical digestion through a process of grinding and mashing up the food. The jaw can produce forces of up to 90 kg on the food. Saliva acts to soften and moisten the food, making it easier to swallow and more like the internal environment. Saliva contains the digestive enzyme amylase, which starts the breakdown of carbohydrates. The tongue is also involved in helping to mix the food and then produce the swallowing action.

Oesophagus

When the food has been swallowed it enters the oesophagus, which delivers the food to the stomach through a process of gravity and peristalsis. Amylase continues to break down the carbohydrates.

Stomach

The stomach is situated in the upper left of the abdominal cavity and is behind the lower ribs. The stomach continues the process of chemical digestion, but no absorption of nutrients occurs in the stomach because the pieces are still too large. The only substance absorbed in the stomach is alcohol, which can enter the bloodstream here. The stomach is made up of three layers of smooth muscle which help to mix up the food. The parietal cells that line the inside of the stomach release hydrochloric acid which helps to dissolve the food and kill off the bacteria present. These cells also release another digestive enzyme, pepsinogen, which produces protein breakdown. The stomach takes around one to four hours to empty completely, depending upon the size of the

119

meal. Carbohydrates leave the stomach most quickly, followed by proteins and then fats.

Small intestine

Around 90 per cent of digestion occurs in the upper two-thirds of the small intestine with help from the pancreas, liver and gall bladder. The small intestine is between five and six metres long and consists of three areas:

● the duodenum, the first 25 cm
● the jejunum, the next 2 m
● the ileum, around 3 to 4 m long.

The partly digested foods (called chime) move through the small intestine partly by gravity and mainly through the peristaltic action of the smooth muscle present in the intestine walls. The peristaltic action is also aided by the action of the villi and microvilli, which pushes the food along. These structures line the walls of the intestine and absorption of nutrients occurs between the villi. Any waste is passed into the large intestine.

Pancreas

The pancreas is an important organ in digestion because it secretes around 1.5 litres of a juice that contains three digestive enzymes. These are amylase to digest carbohydrates, lipase to digest fats and trypsin to digest protein.

Liver

The liver is bypassed by the food but it does secrete bile, which helps to emulsify and digest fats. Bile is synthesised in the liver and is stored in the gall bladder, which sits just below the liver.

Large intestine

The large intestine, or colon, performs the following functions:

● storage of waste before elimination
● absorption of any remaining water
● production of vitamins B and K
● breakdown of any toxins that might damage the colon.

The colon contains many millions of bacteria that work to keep the colon healthy through detoxifying the waste and producing vitamins. They are intestinal micro-flora and there are as many of these present in the colon as there are cells in the body. These can be supplemented by yoghurt drinks that promote and increase the number of friendly bacteria.

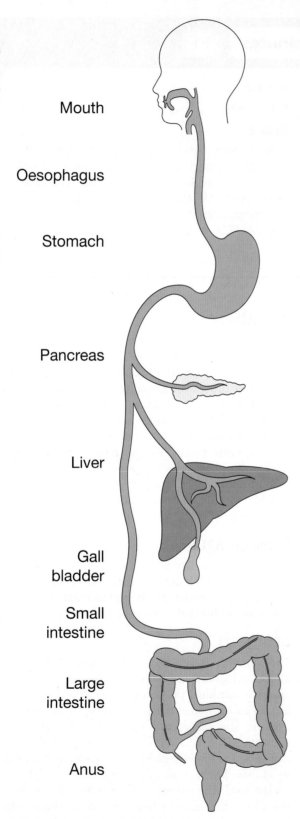

Mouth

Oesophagus

Stomach

Pancreas

Liver

Gall bladder

Small intestine

Large intestine

Anus

Fig 11.12 Structure of the digestive system

Anus

The anus is the end of the gastrointestinal tract and is the opening to allow the elimination of waste products of digestion.

Key learning points 5

- The aim of the digestive system is to produce the mechanical and chemical breakdown of the nutrients into their smallest units.
  - Carbohydrates are broken down into glucose.
  - Proteins are broken down into amino acids.
  - Fats are broken down into fatty acids.
- The main structures of the digestive tract are:
  - mouth
  - oesophagus
  - stomach
  - small intestine (duodenum, jejunum, ileum)
  - large intestine
  - anus.
- Other organs are vital in releasing digestive juices to aid in the chemical breakdown of foods.
  - The pancreas releases amylase to digest carbohydrates, lipase to digest fats and trypsin to digest proteins.
  - The liver produces bile to digest fats.

Student activity 11.2 30 minutes P2

Digestion

In order for our body to use the foods that we have eaten, they need to be digested. The digestive system consists of many different parts.

Task 1

By hand, draw a diagram of the digestive system and include in your drawing:

- mouth
- oesophagus
- stomach
- small intestine
- pancreas
- liver
- large intestine
- anus.

Task 2

Write a paragraph that describes the structure and function for each part of the digestive system.

11.4 Energy intake and expenditure in sports performance

P3 M1

Energy intake and expenditure can be measured in either calories or joules. One calorie is defined as the amount of energy, or heat, needed to raise the temperature of one litre of water by 1°C.

A calorie should be referred to as a kilocalorie (kcal). Whereas in Britain we use calories, the international unit for energy is a joule or, more specifically, a kilojoule. To convert a kcalorie into a kjoule you need to use the following calculation: 1 kcal = 4.2 kjoules.

Energy value of food

To discover how much energy foods contain, a scientist in a laboratory would use a bomb calorimeter which is used to burn foods completely and see how much energy is liberated. We know that different nutrients provide different amounts of energy:

1 g of carbohydrate = 4 kcals
1 g of protein = 4 kcals
1 g of fat = 9 kcals

Energy produced by the body

The amount of energy produced by the body can be measured through direct and indirect calorimetry. Direct calorimetry involves having an athlete working in an airtight chamber or human calorimeter. There are coils in the ceiling that contain water circulating at a specific temperature. The athlete has a mouthpiece leading outside the chamber to enable them to breathe. As they work, the circulating water heats up, dependent on the amount of heat and energy the athlete gives off during their activity.

Indirect calorimetry is done by working out how much oxygen an athlete consumes. This works because all reactions in the body that produce energy need oxygen to be present.

Measuring body stores of energy

Our body stores any excess food that we consume as fat. This fat can be stored in and around our body organs and also just underneath the skin (subcutaneous fat). A store of too much body fat is not good for us and can lead to a variety of other health problems, including CHD, diabetes and cancer. In order to help determine whether a person has too much body fat there are different measuring techniques that can be used.

Skinfold analyses

The skinfold assessment test is done using skinfold callipers. It is done using the Durnin and Wormsley sites, as described below. It is carried out as follows:

1 Take the measurements on the left-hand side of the body.
2 Mark up the client accurately.
3 Pinch the skin 1 cm above the marked site.
4 Pull the fat away from the muscle.
5 Place the callipers halfway between the top and bottom of the skinfold.
6 Allow the callipers to settle for one or two seconds.
7 Take the reading and wait 15 seconds before repeating for accuracy.
8 Add up the total of the four measurements.
9 Calculate body fat percentage using the table on the opposite page.

Bioelectrical impedance

The bioelectrical impedance technique involves placing electrodes on one hand and one foot and then passing a very small electrical current through the body. The theory is that muscle will conduct the electricity while fat will resist the path of the electricity. Therefore, the more electricity that comes out of the body, the more muscle a person has; the less electricity that comes out, the more fat a person has.

This technique has benefits over skinfold measurement because it is easier to do and does not mean that the client has to remove or adjust any clothing. However, it has been shown to be not such an accurate measure of body fat percentage.

Hydro densitometry

Hydro densitometry or underwater weighing is a technique that is based on the Archimedes principle. It involves a person being weighed on land and then when fully submerged in water. Muscle and bone are denser than water while fat is less dense. A person with more bone and muscle will weigh more in water, have a higher body density and therefore less fat. Once the weight on land and weight in water are taken, a formula is used to work out percentage body fat.

This technique involves the use of a large pool of water and significant amounts of equipment. It is impractical for use outside a sport science laboratory.

Energy balance

Basal metabolic rate

Basal metabolic rate (BMR) is the minimal caloric requirement needed to sustain life in a resting individual. This is the amount of energy your body would burn if you slept all day or rested in bed for 24 hours. A variety of factors affects your basal metabolic rate. Some speed it up so you burn more kilocalories per day just to stay alive, whereas other factors slow down your metabolic rate so that you need to eat fewer kilocalories just to stay alive.

● Age: as you get older you start to lose more muscle tissue and replace it with fat tissue. The more muscle tissue a person has, the greater their BMR, and vice versa. Hence, as you get older this increased fat mass will have the effect of slowing down your BMR.
● Body size: taller, heavier people have higher BMRs. There is more of them so they require more energy.
● Growth: children and pregnant women have higher BMRs. In both cases the body is growing and needs more energy.

- Body composition: the more muscle tissue, the higher the BMR, and the more fat tissue, the lower the BMR.
- Fever: fevers can raise the BMR. This is because when a person has a fever, their body temperature is increased, which speeds up the rate of metabolic reactions (to help fight off an infection) and results in an increased BMR.
- Stress: stress hormones can raise the BMR.
- Environmental temperature: both heat and cold raise the BMR. When a person is too hot, their body tries to cool down, which requires energy. When a person is too cold they shiver, which again is a process that requires energy.
- Fasting: when a person is fasting, as in dieting, hormones are released which act to lower the BMR.
- Thyroxin: the thyroid hormone thyroxin is a key BMR regulator – the more thyroxin produced, the higher the BMR.

Student activity 11.3 30 minutes

Working out your BMR

Task 1

Use the BMR calculations in the box below to estimate your BMR.

BMR Method 1

There is a very basic calculation that takes into account your body weight and gender. This calculation does not take physical activity or age into consideration.

Males: BMR = kg (body weight) × 24 = kcal/day

Females: BMR = kg (body weight) × 23 = kcal/day

BMR Method 2

This method is called the Harris–Benedict equation. It is a more accurate method of assessing a person's BMR because body size (weight and height) and age both affect your BMR.

Males: BMR = 66 + (13.7 × wt in kg) + (5 × ht in cm) − (11.8 × age in yrs)

Females: BMR = 655 + (9.6 × wt in kg) + (1.8 × ht in cm) − (4.7 × age in yrs)

BMR Method 3

This calculation takes into account a person's activity levels. The more active they are, the more calories they will burn on a daily basis.

Males

0–3 yrs (60.9 × wt) − 54

3–10 yrs (22.7 × wt) + 495

10–18 yrs (17.5 × wt) + 651

18–30 yrs (15.3 × wt) + 679

30–50 yrs (11.6 × wt) + 879

over 60 yrs (13.5 × wt) + 487

Females

0–3 yrs (61.0 × wt) − 51

3–10 yrs (22.5 × wt) + 499

10–18 yrs (10.2 × wt) + 746

18–30 yrs (14.7 × wt) + 496

30–60 yrs (8.7 × wt) + 829

over 60 yrs (10.5 × wt) + 596

To include exercise – multiply BMR by the appropriate activity factor:

Level type of activity factor

A Very light cooking, driving, ironing, painting, sewing, standing		1.3 men, 1.3 women
B Light walking at 3 mph, electrical trades, sailing, golf, childcare, house-cleaning		1.6 men, 1.3 women
C Moderate walking 3.5–4.0 mph, weeding, cycling, skiing, tennis, dance		1.7 men, 1.6 women
D Heavy manual digging, basketball, climbing, football, soccer		2.1 men, 1.9 women
E Exceptional training for professional athletic competition		2.4 men, 2.2 women

Task 2

Which method do you think gives the most accurate estimate of your BMR and why?

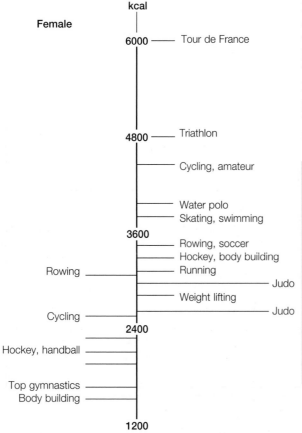

Figure 11.13 shows how differing athletes expend different amounts of energy. Here you can clearly see that a male cyclist on the Tour de France is expending by far and away more kcals than many other athletes. The reason behind this is that athletes on the Tour de France are exercising at high intensities for prolonged periods of time. Athletes who are body-building are at the bottom of this list as they exercise at very high intensity but for relatively short periods of time.

Key learning points 6

- Fat contains the most amount of energy per g compared with protein and carbohydrate.
- Direct calorimetry involves measuring the heat production of an athlete directly; indirect calorimetry involves working out how much oxygen a person consumes.
- Body fat stores can be measured by skin folds, bioelectric impedance and hydro densitometry.
- Basal metabolic rate can be affected by age, body size, body composition, fever, stress, environment, fasting and thyroxine.

Fig 11.13 Daily energy expenditure
(Source: van Erp-Baart *et al.*, 1989)

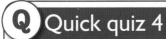

Quick quiz 4

Answer the following questions:

1 What is the definition of a calorie?
2 What is the international unit for energy?
3 Which macronutrient contains the most kcalories per gram?
4 Describe the process of direct calorimetry.
5 Name and describe factors that can affect a person's BMR.
6 Name three different methods of measuring a person's body fat.
7 Where is body fat stored?
8 What are the problems associated with having too much body fat?
9 Name five different types of sports where excess body fat does not affect performance.

Student activity 11.4   ⏱ 60–90 mins   P3   P4   M1   M2   D1

Energy intake and expenditure

In order to train and compete, most athletes need to make sure they are taking in sufficient amounts of energy, but not too much energy that they store excess as body fat.

Task 1

Prepare a written report that:

- describes and explains energy intake
- describes and explains energy expenditure.

Task 2

Describe and explain the importance of energy balance in relation to an athlete's sporting performance.

Task 3

Analyse the effects of energy balance on an athlete's sporting performance – for this task you may like to consider three different athletes who take part in different sports and how energy balance affects each of their sporting performances.

For example:

- Usain Bolt – 100 m sprinter
- Steve Backley – javelin thrower
- Stefka Kostadinova – female high jump world record holder.

11.5 Hydration and its effect on sports performance

It is possible to survive for six or seven weeks without food because the body stores energy in the form of fat, protein and a small amount of carbohydrate. However, you could survive for only two or three days without drinking water. Every day we lose roughly two litres of water through breathing, sweating and urine production. This is increased if we train or compete as water is sweated out to control the heat produced as a waste product of energy production. Therefore, we need to drink at least two litres of water

a day – and more if we train or drink caffeinated or alcoholic drinks. The advice is that we should continually sip water throughout the day or take two or three mouthfuls of water every 15 minutes.

Dehydration

Dehydration is a condition that occurs when fluid loss exceeds fluid intake. The signs and symptoms of dehydration are:

- thirst
- dizziness
- headaches
- dry mouth
- poor concentration
- sticky oral mucus

125

- flushed red skin
- rapid heart rate.

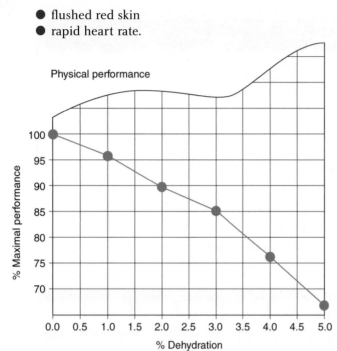

Fig 11.14 Dehydration index

Dehydration causes a significant loss of performance. This is because dehydration, also called hypo hydration, causes a loss of blood plasma affecting blood flow and the ability to sweat. Thus temperature starts to increase steadily. When we sweat it is predominantly blood plasma that is lost and thus cardiac output (the amount of the blood leaving the heart per minute) is reduced. Therefore, dehydration affects the circulation of the blood and the body's ability to control temperature.

Hyper hydration

Hyper hydration is when an athlete drinks extra water before exercising. This is done when they are exercising in a hot environment to prevent the negative effects of dehydration and to minimise the rise in body temperature. The advice is to increase fluid intake over the preceding 24 hours and then drink around 500 ml of water 20 minutes before the event starts. This does not replace the need to continually top up water levels during the competition.

Fluid intake

It is advised that an athlete continually takes on enough fluid to cover the 'cost' of their training or competition. This may involve them consuming around 2.5 to 3 litres of water a day. It should be taken on continually and then some extra taken on 20 minutes before the event. During the event they should top up their water levels when they have a chance. Finally, they should drink water steadily for around one to two hours after their performance, depending upon the demands of the event.

Choices of fluid intake

Water is a good choice, particularly bottled water served at room temperature. Chilled drinks, although refreshing, need to be warmed up in the stomach before they can leave the stomach to be absorbed in the small intestine. This slows down the speed of their absorption.

Sports drinks have a benefit over water in that they provide energy as well as fluid replacement.

Sports drinks are now a common sight at all sports grounds and there are three types of sport drink.

- Isotonic: these drinks have a similar concentration of dissolved solids as blood and as a result are absorbed very quickly. They contain 6 mg of carbohydrate per 100 ml of water and thus provide a good source of fuel as well as being good for hydration. These drinks are useful before, during and after performance, and are the most commonly used.
- Hypotonic: these drinks have a lower concentration of dissolved solids than blood and are absorbed even more quickly than isotonic drinks. With only 2 g of carbohydrate per 100 ml of water they are a relatively poor source of energy. They are used to hydrate after performance.
- Hypertonic: these drinks have a higher concentration of dissolved solids than blood and are absorbed relatively slowly. They contain 10 g of carbohydrate per 100 ml of water and are a very good source of energy but relatively poor for

Student activity 11.5   15 minutes   P5

Sports drinks

Task

Name as many different sports drinks as you can. Look through magazines, on the internet or in

sports shops to help you. Note down the prices of these drinks and any claimed benefits of consuming them.

hydration. They are mostly used in endurance events of over an hour and a half.

These drinks also contain the correct amounts of the electrolytes, which ensure optimum speed of absorption. On the negative side, they often contain additives such as sweeteners and colourings which have a negative effect on health. They are also relatively expensive when compared with water.

An easy and cheaper alternative is to make your own sports drinks by taking 500 ml of unsweetened fruit juice, 500 ml of water and a pinch of salt to aid absorption. You will have made yourself an isotonic sports drink which is cheaper and without the additives.

Student activity 11.6   60 minutes   P5

Designing a sports drink

The aim of this practical is to make a sports drink. You need to decide which athletes you are making the drink for, and when it should be consumed (i.e. if you want to make an isotonic, hypertonic or hypotonic drink).

For this experiment, if you are using equipment taken from the science lab, it must have been thoroughly sterilised. You will need:

- measuring cylinders
- beakers
- weighing scales
- glucose
- sweeteners
- flavourings – your choice
- colourings – your choice
- tasting cups
- drinking water
- salt.

Method

Isotonic drink

- If you are designing an isotonic drink, you need to ensure that the carbohydrate content of your drink is between 6 and 8 per cent. To do this, for every 100 ml of water, you need to add between 6 and 8 g of glucose.

- You can then add other flavourings to your drink to make it taste better. These flavourings should not contain any carbohydrates, so use things that contain sweeteners, such as reduced-sugar squash.

Hypertonic drink

- If you are designing a hypertonic drink, it should contain at least 9 per cent carbohydrates. This means for every 100 ml of water, you need to add at least 9 g of glucose.

- You can then add other flavourings which can contain carbohydrates.

Hypotonic drink

- If you are designing a hypotonic drink, it should contain 5 per cent or fewer carbohydrates. To do this, to every 100 ml of water add 5 g of glucose or less.

- You can then add other flavourings, but these should not contain any carbohydrates, so you could use things that contain sweeteners.

Experiment with different flavours and quantities of flavour. Ensure that, each time, you write out exactly how much of each ingredient you use. When you have made a drink that you think tastes acceptable, place it in a beaker.

Results

Go around the class and sample other people's sports drinks. Do this by pouring their drink from the beaker into your own tasting cup. Ensure that you rinse out your cup after each tasting. Draw up a table for your findings.

Conclusion

In your conclusion answer the following questions:

1 Who was your drink designed for?

2 Did your drink taste acceptable?

3 Would people buy your drink?

4 What could you have done to improve the taste of your drink?

5 Out of the class tasting session, which drinks tasted the best and why?

Key learning points 7

- We need to drink at least 2 litres of water a day to keep hydrated, and 2.5 to 3 litres if we are active. It is best to regularly sip water, taking two or three mouthfuls every 15 minutes.
- There is a range of sports drinks available to provide fuel and rehydration:
  - Isotonic drinks are of the same concentration as blood and provide good fuel and good hydration.
  - Hypotonic drinks are less concentrated than blood and provide good hydration but will be a poor source of fuel.
  - Hypertonic drinks are more concentrated than blood and provide a good source of fuel but will be poor for hydration.

Q Quick quiz 5

Hypo hydration	2 litres	Dizziness
Hyper hydration	Hypotonic	Isotonic
Hypertonic	2.5–3 litres	Blood plasma

Select a word or words from the table to match the correct statement below:

1 This is how much water we lose per day through breathing, sweating and urine production.
2 This is a symptom of dehydration.
3 This is another name for dehydration.
4 This occurs when a person drinks excessive water.
5 An athlete should aim to drink this quantity of water per day.
6 This type of sports drink has similar concentration of dissolved solids as blood.
7 This type of sports drink has lower levels of dissolved solids than blood.
8 This type of sports drink has higher levels of dissolved solids than blood.
9 Sweat is produced from this.

Student activity 11.7 30 minutes P5

Hydration and its effects on sports performance

As you now know, hydration levels are very important as dehydration can have a significant impact upon an athlete's performance.

Task 1

Design a leaflet that could be given to athletes that describes hydration and its importance in relation to sports performance.

11.6 Planning a diet for a selected sports activity

A balanced diet consists of the following quantities:

- 50–60 per cent of kcals from carbohydrates
- 10–20 per cent of kcals from proteins
- 30 per cent of kcals from fats
- a plentiful supply of vitamins and minerals from fruit and vegetables
- 2 litres of water.

For an athlete these percentages are slightly different:

- 65–70 per cent of kcals from carbohydrates
- 10–20 per cent of kcals from proteins
- 30 per cent of kcals from fats.

Fig 11.15 A body builder

When choosing foods there are some guidelines that will help you make a good choice:

- eat foods which are naturally occurring rather than processed
- eat foods that look as they occur in nature
- limit processed or take-away foods
- the best foods will not have a label containing ingredients
- avoid additives or E numbers
- eat organic foods where possible as they will contain more vitamins and minerals.

Basically what you eat will become a part of your body or affect the way your body functions, so be very particular about what you choose to eat.

When deciding upon a nutritional strategy for any person, you need to look at the physiological demands placed upon them and the effect these have on their body structures and fuel consumption. You may also have to make a decision about whether to use food alone or to combine food with supplements, protein shakes or multi-vitamins.

Student activity 11.8   ⏱ **60 minutes**   P6   M3

Components of a balanced diet

A balanced diet that includes carbohydrates, fats, proteins, water, fibre, vitamins and minerals is important for all people, athletes and non-athletes.

Task

Write a report that describes and explains the components of a balanced diet – you will need to include details on:

- carbohydrates
- fats
- proteins
- water
- fibre
- vitamins
- minerals.

Aerobic athletes

The physiological demands on the aerobic athlete are considerable and you will have to consider the following:

● replacing the energy lost during training
● maintaining high energy levels
● repairing any damage done to the body's structures during training
● the need for vitamins and minerals to ensure correct functioning of all the body's systems
● replacement and maintenance of fluid levels.

Anaerobic or power athletes

The physiological demands on the anaerobic athlete differ from the aerobic athlete and they will be:

● repairing the considerable damage occurring to the muscles and other structures of the body during training
● replacing the energy lost during training
● the need for vitamins and minerals to ensure correct functioning of all the body's systems
● replacement and maintenance of fluid levels.

Catabolism and anabolism

Catabolism refers to the breaking down of the structures of the body. Training, especially weight training, is catabolic in nature because it causes damage to the muscles being trained. We know this has occurred because we tend to feel sore and stiff the next day until the body has repaired itself. The process of catabolism releases energy.

Anabolism refers to the building up of the structures of the body. When the body is resting and recovering it will be in an anabolic state. Eating also promotes anabolism. While training is the stimulus to improving our fitness and strength of the body's structures, it is actually when we rest that the body builds up and becomes stronger. The process of anabolism requires energy.

When looking at different athletes' diets we need to give advice on two of the nutrients specifically. They are carbohydrate to replace the energy used and protein to repair the damage that has occurred to the structures. Each performer will still require around 30 per cent of kcals to come from fats, with 10 per cent from saturated fats, 10 per cent from monounsaturated and 10 per cent from polyunsaturated. They will each require at least five to nine portions of fruit and vegetables a day and enough water to replace their fluid loss.

Recommended protein intake

The amount of protein recommended is dependent upon the activity in which the individual is involved. Table 11.7 gives estimated recommended amounts.

Therefore, if you have a sedentary person of 70 kg you would work out their requirements in the following way:

$$70 \times 0.8 = 56 \text{ g of protein}$$

Or a body builder at 90 kg:

$$90 \times 2.0 = 180 \text{ g of protein}$$

Protein is best utilised if it is taken on in amounts of 30 to 35 g at a time. If any more is taken on it is

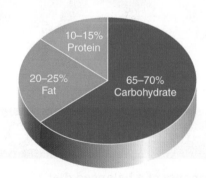

Fig 11.16 Pie chart showing how an athlete's calorie intake should be balanced

Activity	Grams of protein per kg of body weight
Sedentary adult	0.8 g
Recreational exerciser	0.8–1.5 g
Endurance athlete	1.2–1.6 g
Speed/power athlete	1.7–1.8 g
Adult building muscle (hypertrophy)	2 g

Table 11.07 Estimated recommended amounts of protein intake based on activity (Source: Adapted from Franklin, 2000)

either excreted in the urine or stored as body fat. A chicken breast, tin of tuna or a small steak gives 30 g of protein. The best advice for the body builder would be to consume six portions of 30 g of protein rather than three large protein meals.

Recommended carbohydrate intake

The amount of carbohydrate recommended is based on the activity level of the individual in terms of its length and intensity.

An endurance athlete would need 10 g a day, mainly from complex carbohydrate sources.

The continuum in Figure 11.14 shows an estimated calorie intake and clearly depends upon the size and weight of the individual.

Athlete group	Carbohydrate %	Protein %	Fat %	Kcals per kg of body weight
Triathlete:				
Male	611.2	11.6	21.2	62.0
Female	59.2	11.8	29	57.4
Cyclist:				
Male	54.3	13.5	31.7	411.2
Female	511.5	14.0	29.5	59.1
Swimmer:				
Male	50.3	15.0	34.7	45.5
Female	49.3	14.2	311.5	55.6
Runner:				
Male	48.0	14.0	38.0	42.2
Female	49.0	14.0	311.0	42.9
Basketball:				
Male	49.0	15.0	311.0	32.0
Female	45.3	160	34.7	45.6
Gymnast:				
Male	49.8	15.3	34.9	37.8
Female:	44.0	15.0	39.0	53.3
Dancer:				
Male	50.2	15.4	34.4	34.0
Female	38.4	111.5	45.1	51.7
Rower:				
Male	54.2	13.4	23.7	
Female	55.8	15.3	30.3	
Footballer:				
Male	47	14	39	
Weight lifter:				
Male	40.3	20.0	39.7	411.5
Marathon runner:				
Male	52	15	32	51

Table 11.8 Percentage of macronutrients needed by different types of athletes

Daily intake of carbohydrate, protein and fat

Table 11.8 shows a summary of the studies done into male and female athletes to show the percentage of macronutrients different types of athletes should be consuming in order to maximise their sporting performance.

Protein shakes

Recently there has been a boom in the use of protein shakes as a supplement to training. They are employed by athletes who want to lay down more muscle and need to gain more protein on a daily basis. Protein shakes are usually high in whey protein because it contains high levels of three essential amino acids: leucine, isoleucine and valine. These are important because they are the amino acids that are broken down most during training.

Protein shakes contain plentiful supplies of amino acids and are quick and convenient to use. However, there are several issues to consider:

● The human body has evolved to gain its protein from natural rather than processed sources (meats rather than powders).
● They often contain additives such as sweeteners, sugars and colourings.
● The process of drying the proteins into powder form damages the structure of the amino acids, making them unusable by the body.
● They are often very expensive.

Diet plans

If the amount of energy taken in (via food) equals the amount expended (physical activity and BMR) then a person will remain at the same weight. To lose weight, energy intake must be less than energy expenditure and to gain weight energy intake must exceed expenditure. Therefore, in order to lose weight a person needs to reduce intake (eat less) and increase expenditure (do more physical activity).

To lose one pound in body weight (approximately 0.45 kg) the energy deficit needs to be around 3500 kcals per week. If you expended 250 kcals per day and consumed 250 kcals less you would have a daily deficit of 500 kcal. In seven days you would have a deficit of 3500 kcals and hence you would have lost eleven pounds in body weight.

Weight loss

We have established that in order to lose weight it is necessary to consume fewer calories than your body needs. Athletes may not be overweight, but may need to lose excess weight to compete in a lower weight category. Excess weight in the form of fat usually acts to hinder a person's performance because a heavier body requires more energy for transport. Therefore, athletes may diet to get rid of any unessential fat. The best type of diet to help the person lose weight but still have enough energy to train seems to be a low-fat diet.

Low-fat diets

A low-fat diet recommends low-fat options whenever possible, plus regular consumption of complex carbohydrates like potatoes and brown bread. Low-fat diets are usually quite filling because they involve eating large amounts of complex carbohydrates, which include fibre. Weight loss is steady at about 1.5–2 pounds (0.5–1 kg) per week. Most experts agree that faster weight loss is not sustainable as the weight lost is from the glycogen stores and not from the fat stores of the body.

Here is an example of what you might eat on a low-fat diet.

A typical breakfast:

● glass of freshly squeezed orange
● large bowl of cereal with fat-free milk
● toast with no margarine, and yeast extract (for example Marmite) or jam
● tea/coffee.

A typical lunch:

● large brown bread sandwich with lean meat, and large salad with low-fat dressing
● low-fat yoghurt.

A typical dinner:

● 4 oz lean chicken with potatoes (no butter) and two helpings of vegetables
● chopped fruit topped with low-fat ice cream or low-fat fromage frais.

Typical snacks:

● fruit
● whole-wheat sandwiches
● low-fat yoghurts
● cereal.

Key learning points 8

- A typical athlete's diet should consist of:
  - 65–70 per cent of kcals from carbohydrates
  - 10–20 per cent of kcals from proteins
  - 30 per cent of kcals from fats.
- An aerobic athlete's diet should be designed to provide sufficient energy, repair damage and maintain fluid levels – these are usually high carbohydrate diets.
- An anaerobic athlete's diet should repair muscle damage, replace energy and maintain fluid levels – these are usually high protein diets.
- In order to lose weight a person needs to consume fewer calories than their body needs – this can be achieved through a low-fat diet.

Q Quick quiz 6

Answer the following questions.

1 What percentage of macronutrients should a typical athlete consume?
2 Describe catabolism and how it affects athletes.
3 Describe what anabolism is and how it affects athletes.
4 What is the main function of carbohydrates for athletes?
5 What is the main function of proteins for athletes?
6 Work out your recommended amount of protein per day.
7 Work out your recommended amount of carbohydrates per day.
8 What are the benefits of taking a protein shake?
9 Which athletes may benefit from protein shakes and why?
10 How many kcals are there in a pound of body fat?

Student activity 11.9 60–90 mins P7 M4 D2

Planning a two-week diet plan for a sports performer

Select a sports person of your choice – they could be an aerobic or an anaerobic athlete.

Task 1

(a) Think about what sort of foods your athlete should consume and the percentages of each.

(b) Draw a spider diagram to show the different types of foods your athlete could consume, for example carbohydrates – rice, pasta, baked potato.

Task 2

Produce a two-week plan for your selected athlete of all the meals, snacks and drinks they should eat that meets with their dietary requirements.

Task 3

Write a report that explains and justifies your choice of foods and drinks in your two-week diet plan for your selected sports person.

References

Burke, L. and Deakin, V. (1994) *Clinical Sports Nutrition*, McGraw-Hill.

Clark, N. (2003) *Sports Nutrition Guidebook*, Human Kinetics.

Eisenman, P., Johnson, S. and Benson, J. (1990) *Coaches' Guide to Nutrition and Weight Control*, Leisure Press.

Franklin, B. (2000) American *College of Sport Medicine's (ACSM) Guidelines for Exercise Testing and Prescription*, 6th edn, Lippincott, Williams and Wilkins.

McArdle, W.D., Katch, F.I. and Katch, V.L. (1999) *Sports and Exercise Nutrition*, Williams & Wilkins.

McArdle, W.D., Katch, F.I. and Katch, V.L. (2001) *Exercise Physiology: Energy, Nutrition and Human Performance*, Williams & Wilkins.

van Erp-Baart, A., Saris, W., Binkhorst, R., Vos, J. and Elvers, J. (1989) nationwide survey on nutritional habits in elite athletes, *International Journal of Sports Medicine*, 10, 53.

Useful websites

www.ausport.gov.au/ais
Provides invaluable tips on nutrition for sports participants, including suitable recipes that can be downloaded easily

www.netfit.co.uk/nutrition/nutrition/index.htm
Free useful food facts with the focus on health and fitness.

www.nutrition.org.uk/healthyliving/lifestyle/how-much-physical-activity-do-i-need
Nutrition tips relating to physical activity from the British Nutrition Foundation

17: Psychology for sports performance

17.1 Introduction

Success in sport is derived from a series of variable factors. The athlete must be prepared physically, have the correct nutritional strategy, and ensure that they are appropriately recovered and in a positive mental state. Sport psychology deals with ensuring that the performer has this correct mental state and is able to control this state during training and training periods.

By the end of this unit you should:

- know the effect of personality and motivation on sports performance
- know the relationship between stress, anxiety, arousal and sports performance
- know the role of group dynamics in team sports
- be able to plan a psychological skills training programme to enhance sports performance.

Assessment and grading criteria

To achieve a PASS grade the evidence must show that the learner is able to:	To achieve a MERIT grade the evidence must show that, in addition to the pass criteria, the learner is able to:	To achieve a DISTINCTION grade the evidence must show that, in addition to the pass and merit criteria, the learner is able to:
P1 define personality and how it affects sports performance	**M1** explain the effects of personality and motivation on sports performance	**D1** evaluate the effects of personality and motivation on sports performance
P2 describe motivation and how it affects sports performance		
P3 describe stress and anxiety, their causes, symptoms and effect on sports performance		
P4 describe three theories of arousal and the effect on sports performance	**M2** explain three theories of arousal and the effect on sports performance	
P5 identify four factors which influence group dynamics and performance in team sports	**M3** explain four factors which influence group dynamics and performance in team sports	**D2** analyse four factors which influence group dynamics and performance in team sports
P6 assess the current psychological skills of a selected sports performer, identifying strengths and areas for improvement (IE2)		
P7 plan a six-week psychological skills training programme to enhance performance for a selected sports performer.	**M4** explain the design of the six-week psychological skills training programme for a selected sports performer.	**D3** justify the design of the six-week psychological skills training programme for a selected sports performer, making suggestions for improvement.

17.2 The Effects of Personality and Motivation on Sports Performance

P1 **P2** **M1** **D1**

The key concept that underpins all studies in sport psychology is personality. It is clear that each person has the same brain structure and that their senses will all work in the same way to provide the brain with information. However, each person appears to be different in the decisions they make and how they behave in specific situations. Personality looks at these individual differences and how they affect performance.

There is a range of definitions of personality, each with its merits and drawbacks. It has been suggested that we all have traits and behaviour that we share with other people, but we also have some particular to ourselves. However, this idea does lack depth of information, as does Cattell's (1965) attempt to define personality: 'that which tells what a man will do when placed in a given situation.'

This suggests that if we know an individual's personality, we can predict their behaviour. However, human beings tend to be less than predictable and can act out of character, depending on the situation. Their behaviour may also be affected by their mood, fatigue or emotions.

Eysenck (1964) sought to address the limitations of previous definitions: 'The more or less stable and enduring organisation of an individual's character, temperament, intellect and physique which determines their unique adjustment to the environment.' Eysenck's statement that personality is more or less stable allows the human element to enter the equation and explain the unpredictable. He also makes the important point that personality is 'unique'. We may have behaviour in common with other people, but, ultimately, every person has a set of characteristics unique to themselves.

In summary, most personality theories state the following: personality is the set of individual characteristics that make a person unique and will determine their relatively consistent patterns of behaviour.

By giving labels to a person's character and behaviour, you have started to assess personality. By observing sportspeople, we are using a behavioural approach – assessing what they are like by assessing their responses to various situations. In reality, our observations may be unreliable because we see sportspeople in only one environment, and although we see them interviewed as well, we do not know what they are truly like. A cognitive psychologist believes we need to understand an individual's thoughts and emotions, as well as watching their behaviour. This we cannot do without the use of a questionnaire or an interview.

Personality Theories

Jarvis (2006) identifies four factors that will determine how an individual responds in a specific situation:

1   Our genetic make-up – the innate aspect of our personality that we inherit from our parents.
2   Our past experiences – these are important because if we have acted in a certain way in the past and it had a successful outcome, it is likely that we will act in the same way in the future; or if we have had a negative experience in the past, the same experience in the future will be seen as being threatening or stressful.
3   The nature of the situation in which we find ourselves – this will cause us to adapt our behaviour in a way that suits the situation.
4   Free will – a difficult concept in psychology, which suggests we have control over our thinking and thus our behaviour; it can be difficult to separate whether a person has chosen to behave in that way or is programmed by their genetics or past experiences.

Martens' Schematic View of Personality

Martens views personality as having three different depths or layers:

● Level 1 – the psychological core is the deepest component of personality and is at its centre. It includes an individual's beliefs, attitudes, values and feelings of self-worth. It is 'the real you' and, as a result, it is relatively permanent and seen by few people.
● Level 2 – typical responses are how we usually respond to situations and adapt to our environment. It is seen as the relatively consistent way we behave. Our typical responses are good indicators of our psychological core, but they can be affected by the social environment. A person who is very outgoing and sociable with his rugby-playing friends may become more reserved at a party with people he does not know.
● Level 3 – role-related behaviour is the shallowest level of our personality, and this level shows how we change our behaviour to adapt to the situation we are in. For example, throughout the day, we may play the roles of sportsperson, student, employee, friend, son/daughter, coach, and so on. In order to survive, we need to adapt our personalities, as it

137

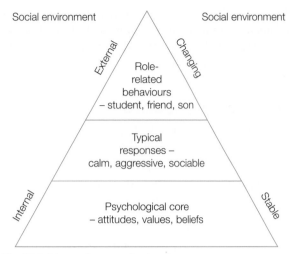

Social environment   Social environment

External   Changing

Role-related behaviours – student, friend, son

Typical responses – calm, aggressive, sociable

Psychological core – attitudes, values, beliefs

Internal   Stable

Fig 17.1 Martens' personality levels

would not be appropriate to behave on the sports field in the same manner as when studying in class. We need to modify our personalities to suit the situation.

Trait Theory

The trait approach to personality relates to the first factor of personality. Jarvis (2006) identifies that personality is based in genetics. This is called the nature approach and says that we inherit personality at birth. This has some validity. For example, we can observe how different babies have different personalities from a young age. A trait is defined as 'a relatively stable way of behaving', suggesting that if a person shows a trait of shyness in one situation, they will be shy across a range of situations. Across a population, the traits people have are the same, but they show them to a greater or lesser extent, and this dictates their personality. This theory was very popular in the 1960s, but it is continually criticised for not considering that the situation may influence an individual's behaviour.

Situational Approach

The situational approach, or social learning theory, takes the view that personality is determined by the environment and the experiences a person has as they grow up. Other theories (e.g. trait theory) take the nature or biological approach to personality in that they see it as being largely genetic or inherited. The social learning theory sees personality as the result of nurture or past experiences.

Cox (2007) outlines the two mechanisms of learning: modelling and social reinforcement:

● Modelling: as we grow up, we observe and imitate the behaviour of significant others in our lives. At first, this is our parents and siblings, then our friends, teachers, sports stars and anyone we regard as a role model.

● Social reinforcement: this means that when behaviour is rewarded positively, it is more likely that it will be repeated. Conversely, behaviour negatively rewarded is less likely to be repeated. At an early age, our parents teach us right and wrong by positively or negatively rewarding behaviour.

In sport, there is a system of negative reinforcement to discourage negative behaviour on the sports field. Thus, rugby players are sent to the sin bin, cricketers are fined part of their match fee, and footballers are shown yellow and red cards. In particular, this theory shows why people behave differently in different situations. For example, an athlete may be confident and outgoing in a sporting setting, but shy and quiet in an educational setting. The athlete may have chosen positive role models in the sporting environment and had their successful performances rewarded. In the educational setting, they may have modelled less appropriate behaviour and had their behaviour rewarded negatively.

Interactional Approach

The trait theory of personality is criticised for not taking into account the situation that determines behaviour. The situational approach is criticised because research shows that while situation influences some people's behaviour, other people will not be influenced in the same way. The interactional approach considers the person's psychological traits and the situation they are in as equal predictors of behaviour.

$$behaviour = f\ (personality,\ environment)$$

Thus, we can understand an individual's behaviour by assessing their personality traits and the specific situation they find themselves in. Bowers (1973) says the interaction between a person and their situation could give twice as much information as traits or the situational approach alone.

An interactional psychologist would use a trait–state approach to assess an individual's personality traits and then assess how these traits affect their behaviour in a situation (state). For example, an athlete who exhibits high anxiety levels as a personality trait would have an exaggerated response to a specific situation.

Neither personality traits nor situations alone are enough to predict an individual's behaviour. We must consider both to get a real picture.

Type A and Type B Personalities

Friedman (1996) developed a questionnaire to diagnose people who were prone to stress and

Type A behaviour:

- Highly competitive and strong desire to succeed
- Achievement orientated
- Eat fast, walk fast, talk fast and have a strong sense of urgency
- Aggressive, restless and impatient
- Find it difficult to delegate and need to be in control
- Experience high levels of stress.

Type B behaviour:

- Less competitive
- More relaxed
- Delegate work easily
- Take time to complete their tasks
- Calm, laid-back and patient
- Experience low levels of stress.

Name of researcher/s	Questionnaire used and groups studied	Research findings
Schurr, Ashley and Joy (1977)	16PF: 1500 American students – athletes versus non-athletes	Athletes were more: • Independent • Objective • Relaxed. Athletes who played team sports were: • More outgoing and warm-hearted (A) • Less intelligent (B) • More group-dependent (Q2) • Less emotionally stable (C). Athletes who played individual sports were: More group-dependent (Q2) Less anxious (Q4) Less intelligent (B).
Francis *et al.* (1998)	EPQ: 133 female hockey players versus non-athlete students	Hockey players were: • More extroverted • Higher in psychoticism.
Ogilvie (1968)	16PF: athletes versus non-athletes	Athletic performance is related to: • Emotional stability • Tough-mindedness • Conscientiousness • Self-discipline • Self-assurance • Trust • Extroversion • Low tension.
Breivik (1996)	16PF: 38 elite Norwegian climbers	Research showed: • High levels of stability • Extroversion • Adventure seeking.
Williams (1980)	Female athletes versus female non-athletes	Athletes were: • More independent • More aggressive and dominant • More emotionally stable.

Table 17.1 **Trait theory research (from Weinberg and Gould, 2007)**

stress-related illnesses. However, it has some application to sport and exercise.

Type Bs will exhibit the opposite types of behaviour to type As. In sport, we see both personality types being equally successful. However, with people exercising recreationally, we see higher levels of retention on their exercise programmes. Type As would benefit from exercise, as it promotes type B-related behaviour. Type A behaviour is seen as causing a rise in a person's blood pressure and increasing the risk of coronary heart disease (CHD).

Personality and Sports Performance

The majority of research using trait theory was carried out in the 1970s and 1980s. Table 17.1 summarises this research.

Motivation

If a sports psychologist were asked why athletes of similar talents achieve different levels of performance, they would consider several factors, such as personality and ability to cope with stress. However, if one subject could be said to influence everything in sports psychology, it would be motivation – the reasons why we do what we do and behave and respond in the manner particular to us.

Psychologists would say that there is a reason for everything we do in life, and that some of these motives are conscious and some are unconscious. As a result, it can be difficult to assess our own motivating factors, let alone anyone else's.

Motivation is important to coaches and managers as they seek to get the best performances out of their athletes. Arsene Wenger and Alex Ferguson are two football managers who are seen as being great motivators of people.

Motivation can be a difficult subject to pin down and deal with because it is not steady and constant and depends on many factors. Most people will experience fluctuations in motivation. Some days they are fully prepared for the competition mentally, and on other days they just cannot seem to get themselves in the right frame of mind. This applies to everything we may do in a day, as sometimes it takes all our powers of motivation just to get out of bed!

When examining motivation, five terms come up again and again:

- Fulfilling a need – all motivation arises as we seek to fulfil our needs. These may be basic biological needs, such as finding food and shelter, or more sophisticated needs, such as self-esteem or the need to belong and be loved.
- Internal state – a state is 'how we feel at any point in time', and this will be subject to change. As we see and feel things, they will trigger an internal state that will need actions to fulfil any needs.
- Direction – the direction of effort refers to the actions we take to move towards what we feel motivated by and feel we need.
- Intensity – the intensity of effort refers to how much effort the person puts into achieving their goal or into a certain situation.
- Energise behaviour – this shows how the power of the brain and the thoughts we have can give us the energy we need to produce the behaviour that is required to be successful in a certain situation.

Intrinsic and Extrinsic Motivation

To expand on Sage's definition, we can see motivation as coming from internal mechanisms or sources inside the body. We can call these intrinsic factors, or rewards coming from the activity itself. These include motives such as fun, pleasure, enjoyment, feelings of self-worth, excitement and self-mastery. They are the reasons why we do a sport and keep doing it.

> Those who are intrinsically motivated engage in an activity for the pleasure and satisfaction they experience while learning, exploring or trying to understand something new.
> (Weinberg and Gould, 2007)

The external stimuli, also called extrinsic rewards, come from sources outside the activity. This would include the recognition and praise we get from other people, such as our coach, friends and family. It could also be the approval we get from the crowd who support us. Extrinsic motivating factors would also include trophies, medals, prizes, records and any money derived from success.

> Those who are extrinsically motivated engage in the activity because of the valued outcome rather than the interest in the activity solely for itself.
> (Weinberg and Gould, 2007)

Theories of Motivation

Achievement motivation

> I do not play to win; I play to fight against the idea of losing. (Eric Cantona, Manchester United, 1997)

Key terms

Motivation:
- 'Motive – a desire to fulfil a need' (Cox, 2007)
- 'The internal mechanisms which arouse and direct behaviour' (Sage, 1974)
- 'The direction and intensity of one's effort' (Sage, 1977).

Achievement motivation is seen as a personality factor and describes our persistence in striving for success, irrespective of the bad experiences and obstacles that are put in our way. It can be seen as our level of 'competitiveness' or desire for success. Achievement motivation is not that simple, however, as the quote from Eric Cantona shows. Some people are driven to success and have no fear of failure, while others are driven to succeed because they have a deep-rooted fear of failure. This paradox was addressed by McClelland *et al.* (1953) in their theory of the need for achievement.

In certain sporting situations, we may have conflicting feelings: on the one hand, we want to take part and achieve success; on the other hand, we are motivated to avoid the situation by our need to avoid failure. The relative strength of these emotions influences our achievement motivation:

Achievement motivation = need to achieve (nACH) − need to avoid failure (naF)

If our nACH outweighs our naF, we are said to be high in achievement motivation; if our naF outweighs our nACH, we are said to be low in achievement motivation. This will influence our behaviour in sport and the types of challenges we seek.

A sportsperson with a high need to achieve will choose competitive situations and opponents close to their skill level who will challenge them. A person with a high fear of failure will choose opponents of much higher skill or much lower skill because these people are less threatening to them; they will also tend to avoid situations involving personal challenges.

The situation will also affect achievement motivation. If the probability of success is high, it tends to weaken the need to achieve because the reward for success is low; if the probability of success is low and failure is likely, it tends to weaken the need to avoid failure.

Weiner's attribution theory

The reasons we give for an outcome are called attributions. We are attributing that outcome to a certain factor. We all make attributions about our own performances, as well as those of other people. It is important for us to make attributions because:

● they affect our motivation levels
● we need to understand the outcome so that we can learn from our experiences
● they will affect our future expectations of success and failure.

Attributions fall into four categories:

1 **Ability or skill** – a performer's capability in performing skills.
2 **Effort** – the amount of physical or mental effort put into a task.
3 **Task difficulty** – the problems posed by the task, such as the strength of the opposition or the difficulty of a move.
4 **Luck** – factors attributed to chance, such as the effect of the weather, the referee or the run of the ball.

As shown in Table 17.2, these four categories can be classified as internal (inside an individual), external (outside the individual), stable (not subject to change) or unstable (continually changing).

	Internal	External
Stable	Ability	Task difficulty
Unstable	Effort	Luck

Table 17.2 Categories of attributions

Research findings

Research shows that winners tend to give internal attributions and take responsibility for their successes. They will usually say, 'I won because I tried hard', or 'I am more talented'. Losers, meanwhile, tend to give external attributions and distance themselves from their failures. For example, they will say, 'The task was too difficult', or 'The referee was against me'. These attributions can be seen as ego-enhancing and ego-protective, respectively. Winners give internal attributions to make themselves feel even better; losers give external attributions so they do not feel so bad.

Attributions and self-confidence

If we make a more stable attribution – that is, to ability or task difficulty – it is more realistic and gives a clearer indication of future expectations and confidence. However, attribution to unstable factors can act to protect the ego and reduce loss of self-confidence.

This is important because confidence levels will influence motivation – the more confidence we have, the more motivation we will have for a task.

The Motivational Climate

Creating a motivational climate means influencing the factors that affect motivation in a positive way, to help increase the motivation levels of the participants in that environment. Three of the most influential factors are:

1 The behaviour of the leader.

2 The environment itself.

3 The influence of other people in the environment.

Behaviour of the leader

The leader's behaviour can seriously affect the behaviour of other people because the leader will set an example. If the people who are being led think that the leader does not care, then they may not care either; however, if the leader behaves in an upbeat and energetic way, this behaviour may be modelled.

The environment

Think about going to a gym that has grey walls and no decoration; it is cold and there are no staff. Compare this to walking into a gym that is painted brightly and has pictures of athletes achieving great feats, the staff are welcoming and there is upbeat music playing. The second environment is much more appealing to us, and we will be motivated to train there and also to return regularly.

The influence of other people

The motivation of an individual can be affected by social influences, in that other people will offer either approval or disapproval of their behaviour. The support and encouragement an individual receives from their family, friends, teachers and coaches can be vital in maintaining their motivation.

Key learning points I

- Personality theories focus on whether personality is based in genetics (trait theory) or is learned from our environment (social learning theory).
- Motivation is defined as the direction and intensity of one's effort (Sage, 1974).
- Motivation can be intrinsic (coming from sources within the individual) or extrinsic (coming from sources outside the individual).

Student activity 17.1   ⏱   I hour   P1   P2   M1   D1

Choose three performers in three different sports, then fill in the following table to show how their personality affects performance.

Sports performers	Define personality and describe motivation and how they affect sports performance (P1, P2)	Explain the effects of personality and motivation on sports performance (M1)	Evaluate the effects of personality and motivation on sports performance (D1)
I			
2			
3			

Q Quick quiz 1

Decide whether each of the following statements is an example of intrinsic or extrinsic motivation:

- I want to win medals.
- I want to earn an England cap.
- I want to reach my full potential.
- I want to make money.
- I want to play in a good team.
- I want to play in front of large crowds.
- I want to give the public enjoyment.
- I want to feel good about my performance.
- I want to be recognised by the public for my ability.
- I want to feel mastery in my own ability.
- I want to feel the joy of winning.

17.3 The Relationship Between Anxiety, Arousal, Stress and Sports Performance

Stress

Stress is usually talked about in negative terms. People complain that they have too much stress or are stressed out. Sportspeople claim that the stress of competition is too much for them. However, we should not see stress as an entirely negative thing, because it provides us with the mental and physical energy to motivate us into doing things and doing them well.

Stressors are anything that causes us to have a stress response, and these are invariably different for different people. If we did not have any stress in our lives, we might not bother to do anything all day. We need stressors to give us the energy and direction to get things done. This type of positive stress is called eustress (good stress). If we have too much stress it can become damaging, and we call this distress (bad stress).

- **Eustress** (good stress):
  - gives us energy and direction
  - helps us to be fulfilled and happy.
- **Distress** (bad stress):
  - causes discomfort
  - can lead to illness
  - can cause depression.

Too much stress in our lives over a long period of time can seriously damage our health, causing coronary heart disease, high blood pressure, ulcers, impotence, substance addiction, mental health problems and suicidal tendencies.

Sport is a source of stress for some sportspeople. This is related to the experience of the performer, the importance of the competition, the quality of the opposition, the size of the crowd or previous events. The stress response will be specific to the individual.

The feelings you have are the symptoms of stress, and they can be separated into physical (the effects on your body), mental (the effect on your brain) and behavioural (how your behaviour changed).

Key terms

Stress: any factor that changes the natural state of the body.

The classic definition of stress sees the body as having a natural equilibrium or balance, when the heart rate and breathing rate are at resting levels and blood pressure is at normal level. Anything that changes these natural levels is a stressor. Theoretically, we could say we become stressed as soon as we get out of bed, as our heart rate, breathing rate and blood pressure all rise. Indeed, to some people, the alarm going off is a real source of stress!

The Stress Process

McGrath (1970) sees the stress response as a process and defines stress as 'a substantial imbalance between

143

demand (physical and psychological) and response capability, under conditions where failure to meet the demand has important consequences'.

Stress will occur when the person does not feel they have the resources to deal with the situation and that this will have bad consequences.

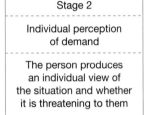

Stage 1
Cause of stress
An emotional demand places physical or psychological pressure

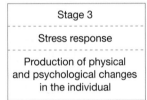

Stage 2
Individual perception of demand
The person produces an individual view of the situation and whether it is threatening to them

Stage 3
Stress response
Production of physical and psychological changes in the individual

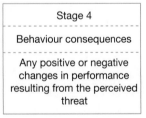

Stage 4
Behaviour consequences
Any positive or negative changes in performance resulting from the perceived threat

Fig 17.2 The four stages of the stress process

Causes of Stress

The causes of stress are many and varied, but, crucially, they are specific to an individual. For example, you can have two people in the same event, each with a different stress response.

The sources of stress can generally be divided into four categories:

- internal: things we think about, such as past memories and experiences, current injuries, past injuries, our feelings of self-worth, and so on
- external: things in our surroundings and our environment, such as competition, our opponents, the crowd, the weather, spiders and snakes, transport problems
- personal factors: people we share our lives with, such as friends, family, partners; and life factors such as money and health
- occupational factors: the job we do, the people we work with and our working conditions; in sport, this could include our relationships with teammates and coaches/managers.

Stress levels also depend on personality. Those people who have a predominantly type A personality will find more situations stressful, as will people who have a high N score using Eysenck's personality inventory.

The Physiology of Stress

When we perceive ourselves to be in a situation that is dangerous, our stress response is activated. This has been developed as a means of ensuring our survival, by making us respond to danger. For example, if we are walking home at night through dark woods and we hear noises behind us, the body will instigate physiological changes, called the fight-or-flight response, as the body is preparing to turn and fight the danger or run away as fast as it can.

The response varies depending on how serious we perceive the threat to be. The changes take place in our involuntary nervous system, which consists of two major branches:

- sympathetic nervous system
- parasympathetic nervous system.

The sympathetic nervous system produces the stress response, and its aim is to provide the body with as much energy as it can to confront the threat or run away from it. The sympathetic nervous system works by releasing stress hormones, adrenaline and cortisol, into the bloodstream. The sympathetic nervous system produces the effects listed in Figure 17.3.

The parasympathetic nervous system produces the relaxation response, its aim being to conserve energy. It is activated once the stressor has passed.

It is not healthy for the body to be in a constant state of stress because of the activation of the sympathetic nervous system. The excess production of adrenaline is dangerous because the body requires more cholesterol to synthesise adrenaline. This excess cholesterol production raises blood cholesterol levels and is a risk factor for coronary heart disease.

Sympathetic nervous system	Parasympathetic nervous system
Increased adrenaline production	Decreased adrenaline production
Increase in heart rate	Slowed heart rate
Increase in breathing rate	Slower breathing rate
Increased metabolism	Slower metabolism
Increased heat production	Lower body temperature
Muscle tension	Muscle relaxation
Dry mouth	Dry skin
Dilated pupils	Smaller pupils
Hairs on the skin stand on end (to make us look bigger)	
Digestive system slows down	Digestion speeds up
Diversion of blood away from internal organs to the working muscles	

Table 17.3 Nervous systems

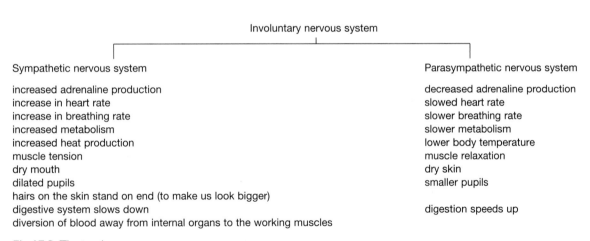

Fig 17.3 The involuntary nervous system

Symptoms of Stress

Stress has a threefold effect on the body, causing cognitive (mental), somatic (physical) and behavioural responses, as outlined in Table 17.4.

Arousal and Anxiety

Arousal and anxiety are terms related to stress. Arousal is a response to stress and shows how motivated we are by a situation. The more aroused we become, the more interested and excited we are by a situation. We can see this when we watch a football match involving a team we support. We are so aroused that we are engrossed in the action to the point that we don't hear noises around us and time seems to go by very quickly. During a match that does not arouse us to the same extent, we find that our attention drifts in and out as we are distracted by things happening around us.

We can look at levels of arousal on a continuum that highlights the varying degrees of arousal:

Deep sleep → Mild interest → Attentive → Absorbed → Engrossed → Frenzied

Cognitive response	Somatic response	Behavioural response
Reduced concentration	Racing heart rates	Talking, eating and walking quickly
Less interested	Faster breathing	Interrupting conversations
Unable to make decisions	Headaches	Increased smoking, drinking and eating
Sleep disturbances	Butterflies in the stomach	Fidgeting
Making mistakes	Chest tightness and pains	Lethargy
Unable to relax	Dry cotton mouth	Moodiness and grudge bearing
Quick losses of temper	Constant colds and illness	Accidents and clumsiness
Loss of sense of humour	Muscular aches and pains	Poor personal presentation
Loss of self-esteem	Increased sweating	Nervous habits
Loss of enthusiasm	Skin irritations	

Table 17.4 Symptoms of stress

Arousal and Attention Span

As arousal levels increase, they can affect a performer's attention span. If a performer has a broad attention span, they are able to pick up information from a wide field of vision. The narrower the attention span becomes, the less information the performer will pick up and the more they will miss. The attention span can be too broad, as the performer may try to pick up too much information.

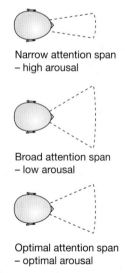

Narrow attention span
– high arousal

Broad attention span
– low arousal

Optimal attention span
– optimal arousal

Fig 17.4 Three attention spans

Anxiety

Anxiety can be seen as a negative aspect of stress, and it may accompany high levels of arousal. It is not pleasant to be anxious. It is characterised by feelings of nervousness and worry. Again, the stress and anxiety responses are unique to each individual.

Trait and State Anxiety

Trait anxiety means that a person generally experiences high levels of anxiety as part of their personality. They tend to worry and feel nervous in a range of situations and find them threatening. State anxiety is anxiety felt in response to a specific situation. It is anxiety related to a specific mood state. Usually, a person who has high trait anxiety will also experience higher levels of state anxiety. This is important for athletes because their levels of trait anxiety will determine their state anxiety in competition and, as a result, their performance.

Arousal and Performance

Arousal levels will have an influence on performance, but it is not always clear-cut what this relationship is. The following theories help to explain the relationship.

Drive Theory

Drive theory, initially the work of Hull (1943), states that as arousal levels rise, so do performance levels. This happens in linear fashion and can be described as a straight line.

The actual performance also depends on the arousal level and the skill level of the performer. Arousal will exaggerate the individual's dominant response, meaning that if they have learned the skill well, their dominant response will be exaggerated positively. However, if they are a novice performer, their skill level will drop to produce a worse performance.

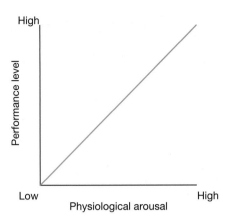

Fig 17.5 Drive theory

The Inverted U Hypothesis

This theory is based on the Yerkes and Dodson law (1908) and seeks to address some of the criticisms of the drive theory. This theory agrees that arousal does improve performance, but only up to a point, and once arousal goes beyond this point, performance starts to decline. Figure 17.6 shows the curve looking like an upside-down U.

This theory's main point is that there is an optimum level of arousal before performance starts to diminish. This is also called the ideal performing state (IPS) and is often referred to as the zone. At this point, the arousal level meets the demands of the task, and everything feels good and is going well.

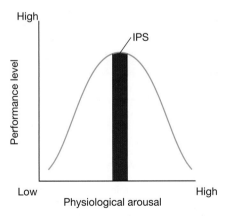

Fig 17.6 The inverted U hypothesis

Catastrophe theory

This theory has been taken a step further by Fazey and Hardy (1988), who agree with the inverted U hypothesis, but say that once arousal level has passed, the IPS will drop off drastically rather than steadily. The point where performance drops is called the point of catastrophe. The Americans refer to this phenomenon, when performance drops, as choking. The history of sport is littered with examples of people or teams throwing away seemingly unassailable positions.

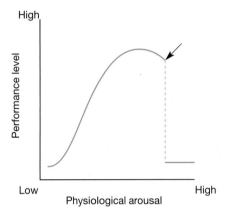

Fig 17.7 Catastrophe theory

Key learning points 2

- Stress is any factor that changes the natural balance of the body.
- Symptoms of stress can be cognitive, somatic or behavioural.
- Arousal is a response to stress that describes how interested and motivated an individual becomes in a situation.
- Anxiety is a negative response to a stressful situation, characterised by nervousness and apprehension.
- The theories of arousal show that changing levels of arousal will influence performance.
- The drive theory of arousal says that increases in arousal level will cause an increase in performance level, while the inverted U hypothesis suggests that increases in arousal level will cause an improvement in performance, but only up to a certain point; after this point, increases in arousal level will cause decrements in performance level.

Student activity 17.2 90 minutes | P3 | P4 | M2

Read the case study and answer the questions below.

1 Using Oliver as an example, describe how stress and anxiety affect him and what their causes are.

2 Describe how Oliver experiences arousal and, using the theories of arousal, what effect changes in arousal have on his performance.

3 Explain how Oliver experiences arousal and, using the theories of arousal, what effect changes in arousal have on his performance.

Oliver is a 16-year-old tennis player whose play is characterised by moments of brilliance mixed with temper tantrums. When Oliver trains in the gym, he loves to lift weights to increase his strength, and he finds that the more up for it he is, the heavier weights he can lift, so he spends time psyching himself up before lifting weights. Oliver loves the excitement of playing a match and feels that it gives him energy and helps to focus his attention. When Oliver plays tennis, he always starts off quite relaxed, but sometimes he is too relaxed to play well and will start to lose points. However, when he is in a losing situation, he starts to become worried and gets butterflies in his stomach, and this spurs him on to play better and get back into the match. Sometimes he wants to win so much that he starts to miss the service box or the base line, often by quite large margins. This can make him really angry, and when he loses his temper he quickly loses the match.

Q Quick quiz 2

1 Match each of the terms in the table below to the appropriate description.

Term	Description
Stress	An individual tends to get worried in most situations
Arousal	Feelings of worry associated with uncomfortable thoughts
Trait anxiety	Any force that changes the natural balance of the body
State anxiety	Racing heart rate and butterflies accompany feelings of worry
Cognitive anxiety	An individual experiences feelings of apprehension in certain situations
Somatic anxiety	Feelings of motivation and excitement produced in a situation

2 Fill in the blanks in the following paragraph.

According to drive theory, increased _____ levels will result in an increase in _____ levels; however, this works best for _____ performers, as arousal will exaggerate the dominant response, while for a novice it can produce a _____ in performance level. The inverted U hypothesis disagrees with drive theory, as it says that increased arousal levels will improve performance, but once arousal gets to a certain point, _____ will start to decline. The point at the top of the curve is called the _____ _____ _____.

17.4 The Role of Group Dynamics in Team Sports

  P5 **M3** **D2**

Throughout our sporting and social lives, we are involved in working in groups, such as our families, school groups, friendship groups and the sports teams in which we play. Sports teams have different characteristics – an athletics team will have different teamwork demands to a rugby or cricket team. However, all groups rely on the fundamental characteristic of teamwork.

Defining a group is not easy, but the minimum number of people required is two. A group can be seen as two or more like-minded people interacting to produce an outcome they could not achieve on their own. Groups involve interaction or working with other people in order to influence the behaviour of other people and, in turn, be influenced by them.

Key term

Group: a group should have:

- a collective identity
- a sense of shared purpose or objectives
- structured modes of communication
- personal and/or task interdependence
- interpersonal attraction.

(Weinberg and Gould, 2007)

A Group or a Team?

Generally speaking, an instructor will call people who are involved in an exercise class or dance class a group, and people playing cricket or rugby a team. People involved in the group have a similar sense of purpose and may share common objectives. However, a team's members will actually be dependent on one another to achieve their shared goals and will need to support each other.

So why is the outcome of the group not always equal to the sum of its parts? For example, we can see in football that the teams with the best players do not always get the results they should. In 2006, the very talented Brazil and Argentina teams were knocked out at the quarter-final stage of the World Cup, and in 2004 the European Championships were won by Greece rather than the individually talented Portugal team. In cricket, the England one-day side is continually changing its players, as it seeks to find a

team rather than a group of individuals. We can even see the importance of a team when individual players come together in an event such as the Ryder Cup in golf. In 2004 and 2006, the British and European team beat the Americans emphatically, due to the team feeling that had developed.

Stages of Group Development

A group of people coming together does not form a team. Becoming a team demands a process of development. Tuckman and Jensen (1977) proposed a five-stage model of group development:

1. Forming.
2. Storming.
3. Norming.
4. Performing.
5. Adjourning.

Each group will go through the five stages. The length of time they spend in each stage is variable.

Forming

The group comes together, with individuals meeting and familiarising themselves with the other members of the group. The structure and relationships within the group are formed and tested. If it is a team, the coach may develop strategies or games to break the ice between the group members. At this point, the individuals are seeing whether they fit in with this group.

Storming

A period of conflict will follow the forming stage, as individuals seek their roles and status within the group. This may involve conflict between individual members, rebellion against the leader or resistance to the way the team is being developed or managed, or the tactics it is adopting. This is also a period of intense inter-group competition, as group members compete for their positions within the team.

Norming

Once the hostility and fighting have been overcome, by athletes either leaving the group or accepting the common goals and values of the group, a period of norming occurs. Here, the group starts to cooperate and work together to reach common goals. The group pulls together and the roles are established and become stable.

Performing

In the final stage, the group members work together to achieve their mutual goals. The relationships within the group have become well established, as have issues of leadership and strategies for play.

It is unrealistic to see the group as being stable and performing in a steady way. The relationships within the group will change and develop with time, sometimes for the good of the group and sometimes to its detriment. As new members join the group, there will be a new period of storming and norming, as each person is either accepted or rejected. This re-evaluation of the group is often beneficial and stops the group becoming stale. Successful teams seem to be settled and assimilate two or three new players a year to keep them fresh. Bringing in too many new players can disrupt the group and change the nature of the group completely.

Adjourning

Once the group has achieved its goals or come to the end of its useful purpose, the team may break up. This may also be caused by a considerable change in the personnel involved or the management and leadership of the group.

Group Effectiveness

The aim of a group is to be effective by using the strengths of each person to better the effectiveness of the group. However, the outcome is often not equal to the sum of its parts. Steiner (1972) proposed the following model of group effectiveness:

Actual productivity = Potential productivity − Process losses

- Actual productivity = the actual performance achieved.
- Potential productivity = the best possible performance achievable by that group, based on its resources (ability, knowledge, skills).
- Process losses = losses due to working as part of a group (coordination losses, communication problems, losses in motivation).

For example, in a tug-of-war team, each member can pull 100 kg individually, and as a team of four they pull 360 kg in total. Why do you think this would happen?

Social Loafing

One of the problems of working in groups is that it tends to affect motivation. People do not seem to work as hard in groups compared with working on their own. Research shows that rowers in larger teams put in less effort than those in smaller teams:

1 person = 100 per cent effort
2 people = 90 per cent effort
4 people = 80 per cent effort
8 people = 65 per cent effort.

This phenomenon is called the Ringelman effect, or social loafing, and is defined as the tendency of individuals to lessen their effort when part of a group.

Cohesion

Cohesion is concerned with the extent to which a team is willing to stick together and work together. The forces tend to cover two areas:

- the attractiveness of the group to individual members
- the extent to which members are willing to work together to achieve group goals.

To be successful in its goals, a group has to be cohesive. The extent to which cohesion is important depends on the sport and the level of interaction needed.

Key term

Cohesion: 'The total field of forces which act on members to remain in the group' (Festinger *et al.*, 1950).

Types of Cohesion

There seem to be two definite types of cohesion within a group:

- task cohesion – the willingness of a team to work together to achieve its goals
- social cohesion – the willingness of the team to socialise together.

It would appear that task cohesion comes first, as this is why the team has formed in the first place. If the group is lucky, they will find that they develop social cohesion as well, and this usually has a beneficial effect on performance. This is because if you feel good about your teammates, you are more likely to want success for each other as well as yourself.

Research says that cohesion is important in successful teams, but that task cohesion is more important than social cohesion. It does depend on the sport being played, as groups that need high levels of interaction need higher levels of cohesion. Research also suggests that success will produce increased cohesion, rather than cohesion coming before performance. Being successful helps to develop feelings of group attraction, and this will help to develop more success, and so on. This can be seen with the cycle of success, in that once a team has been successful it tends to continue being successful – success breeds success.

Leadership in Sport

The choice of a manager, coach or captain is often the most important decision a club's members have to make. They see it as crucial in influencing the club's chances of success. Great leaders in sport are held in the highest regard, irrespective of their talent on the pitch.

> ## Key term
>
> **Leadership:** 'The behavioural process of influencing individuals and groups towards goals' (Barrow, 1977).

Leadership behaviour covers a variety of activities, which is why it is described as multi-dimensional. It includes:

- decision-making processes
- motivational techniques
- giving feedback
- establishing interpersonal relationships
- confidently directing the group.

Leaders are different from managers. Managers plan, organise, budget, schedule and recruit, while leaders determine how a task is completed.

People become leaders in different ways; not all are appointed. Prescribed leaders are appointed by a person in authority – a chairman appoints a manager, a manager appoints a coach, a principal appoints a teacher. Emergent leaders emerge from a group and take over responsibility. For example, John Terry emerged to become the leader of the England football team, just as Andrew Strauss emerged to become the new England cricket captain. Emergent leaders can be more effective, as they have the respect of their group members.

Theories of Leadership

Sport psychologists have sought to explain leadership effectiveness for many years, and they have used the following theories to help understand effective leadership behaviour.

Trait Approach

In the 1920s, researchers tried to show that characteristics or personality traits were stable and common to all leaders. Thus, to be a good leader, you needed to have intelligence, assertiveness, independence and self-confidence. Therefore, a person who is a good leader in one situation will be a good leader in all situations.

Behavioural Approach

The trait approach says that leaders are 'born', but the behavioural approach says that anyone can become a good leader by learning the behaviour of effective leaders. Thus, the behavioural approach supports the view that leadership skills can be developed through experience and training.

Interactional Approach

Trait and personal approaches look at personality traits. The interactional approach looks at the interaction between the person and the situation. It stresses the following points:

- Effective leaders cannot be predicted solely on personality.
- Effective leadership fits specific situations, as some leaders function better in certain circumstances than others.
- Leadership style needs to change to match the demands of the situation. For example, relationship-orientated leaders develop interpersonal relationships, provide good communication and ensure everyone is feeling good within the group. However, task-orientated leaders are concerned with getting the work done and meeting objectives.

Social Facilitation

Social facilitation is the change in performance that occurs due to the presence of others – whether the presence is an audience or fellow competitors. There is no doubt that our performances change as the result of the presence of other people. Think about how you feel when your parents or friends come to watch you, or when you start to perform in front of an audience.

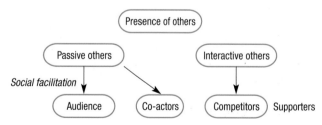

Fig 17.8 Social facilitation model

Zajonc (1965) defined the different types of people present, separating them into those people who are competing against you and those people who are merely present and not competing.

> ## Key term
>
> **Social facilitation:** 'The consequences upon behaviour which derive from the sheer presence of other individuals' (Zajonc, 1965).

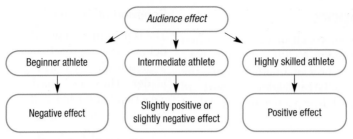

Fig 17.10 Audience effect and the standard of performer

Co-actors are people involved in the same activity, but not competing directly. Triplett (1898) did some of the earliest experiments in sport psychology. He examined co-action in the following three conditions, using cyclists:

1 Unpaced.
2 Paced (co-actor on another bike).
3 Paced competitive (co-actors pacing and competing).

Triplett's findings were that cyclists in condition 2 were 34 seconds per mile faster than cyclists in condition 1, while cyclists in condition 3 were 39 seconds per mile faster than cyclists in condition 1.

The reasons for social facilitation are not always clear. Triplett concluded that in his experiment it was due to the physical effects, such as suctioning and sheltering resulting from travelling behind another rider; and psychological effects, such as encouragement, anxiety, pressure and competitiveness, which are felt as the result of cycling with someone else. Triplett concluded that it did not matter if the cyclists were competing. What was important was that 'the bodily presence of another rider is stimulus to a rider in arousing the competitive instinct'.

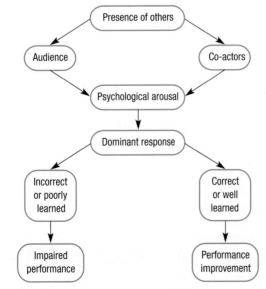

Fig 17.9 Zajonc's expanded model (1965)

Zajonc's expanded model (Figure 17.9) showed that whether the audience or co-actors have a positive or negative effect on performance depends on how well the skill has been learnt. A poorly learnt skill will become worse, while a well-learnt skill will be improved. This links in well with the effect of stress on performance, and it can be seen that the presence of others would cause more stress.

Zajonc also looked at the relationship between the audience effect and the standard of the performer. His results are shown in Figure 17.10.

The effect also depends on the nature of the task – whether it is strength- or skill-related. Strength tasks will usually be enhanced by the presence of others. However, skilled tasks (especially poorly learnt skills) may suffer. Social facilitation effects tend to disappear as the individual gets used to them.

Cottrell (1968) said that it is not the mere presence of an audience that creates arousal, but that the type of audience is also very important. For example, a blindfolded audience had no facilitation effect. The following factors will affect social facilitation:

● audience expertise: an expert audience will increase arousal level
● type of audience: a pro-winning audience will have more of a facilitation effect than a pro-enjoyment audience
● performer's evaluation of the audience: the performer decides what they think the audience wants and is aroused accordingly
● size: a larger audience will have more of a facilitation effect.

Home advantage

Home advantage is the view that the team playing at home has a disproportionately higher chance of winning in relation to the team playing away from home. This phenomenon was apparent in cricket, as home teams are more often successful in test matches. For example, England beat Australia to win the Ashes in 2005 and 2009, yet they were beaten 5–0 in Australia in 2006 when they tried to retain the Ashes. In the football World Cup of 2006, which was held in Germany, all four semi-finalists were European countries.

There are many reasons why home teams are more successful. Some of these are physical and some are psychological:

- familiarity with the surroundings and the surfaces
- a supportive home crowd who give positive approval
- less intimidation from opposing supporters
- the territory is theirs and claimed by display of their playing colours
- there is less travel involved in getting to the match
- travel can cause boredom and staleness
- players do not have to stay in unfamiliar surroundings and eat unfamiliar food
- home teams are more likely to play offensively
- away teams may not be treated well by their opponents
- referees and officials may unconsciously favour the home team to seek the crowd's approval.

Home advantage may be seen as being a disadvantage to the away team rather than an advantage to the home team. It is the job of the coach and psychologist to find ways of minimising this away disadvantage.

Key learning points 3

- A group is defined as two people who have to work together to achieve an outcome they could not achieve individually.
- Members of a team will have greater dependence on each other to achieve their outcome than members of a group.
- The model of group effectiveness states that the actual productivity of a group will equal the potential productivity (best possible outcome of the group) minus process losses (losses due to the problems of working as a group).
- Process losses include problems with coordination, communication and motivation of individuals in the group.
- Social loafing describes the tendency of individuals to exert less effort when working as a part of a group than they would individually.
- Cohesion is described as the total sum of forces that cause individuals to remain in a group.
- The leader in the group can influence its effectiveness, especially if they are able to adapt their personality to the demands of the situation they find themselves in.

Q Quick quiz 3

Match each of the terms in the table below to the appropriate description.

Term	Description
Social loafing	The degree of attraction an individual feels towards a group
Task cohesion	Loss of performance caused by working as part of a group
Leadership	The presence of other people can have a beneficial effect on performance
Social cohesion	The tendency for an individual to give less effort when part of a group
Process losses	The process of influencing individuals or groups towards achieving their goals
Social facilitation	The extent to which team members want to work together

Student activity 17.3 | 1 hour | P5 M3 D2

Read the case study, in which Patrick, a former professional player, talks about two teams he played for in his career, then answer the questions below.

1 From Patrick's explanation, identify four factors that influence group dynamics and performance in team sports.

2 Using Patrick's explanation, explain four factors that influence group dynamics and performance in team sports.

3 Using Patrick's explanation, analyse four factors that influence group dynamics and performance in team sports.

I played for several teams in my career, but when I was a young player I was lucky to have a brilliant manager. At the beginning of the season, he would tell each player what their role was in the team, and then he would bring the team together and tell us how he wanted us to play together. We each knew our individual role, and as long as we performed it we were kept in the team. I remember the manager taking players off early in matches because they were not doing their job. He was a hard manager to please, but his methods worked well and we were very successful. My second team was managed by an ex-player who I knew from the first club, and he put together a team of players that he had played with and trusted. We were never the most talented group of individuals, but once we were on the pitch, we all worked for each other and achieved more than the individual sum of our talents should have achieved. The manager always took us out on Monday nights, when we would go for a meal, go bowling or play darts, which helped to build a solid bond between us, and we cared for each other on and off the pitch. This manager was so successful that he moved to a bigger club; he was replaced by a new manager who was not successful because he didn't understand how the club worked and he could never explain how he wanted us to play.

17.5 Planning a Psychological Skills Training Programme to Enhance Sporting Performance

Assessing Psychological Strengths and Weaknesses

An assessment of an individual's mental strengths and weaknesses can be made in different ways. We will look first at the use of a questionnaire, but it could also be done through performance profiling.

Example Questionnaire

Name:

Sport played:

● Explain any past experience you have of psychological skills training.

● Explain your involvement in sport and any important competitions or events coming up.

● What do you consider to be your psychological strengths and weaknesses?

Below is a list of statements. Circle the answer appropriate to your experience.

1 **I always feel motivated to succeed, whatever activity I am doing.**
Don't know Never Sometimes Usually Always

2 **I always work towards clear goals.**
Don't know Never Sometimes Usually Always

3 **I set myself goals on a weekly basis.**
Don't know Never Sometimes Usually Always

4 **I always make full use of my skills and abilities.**
Don't know Never Sometimes Usually Always

5 **When I am involved in my physical activity, I often find my attention wavering.**
Don't know Never Sometimes Usually Always

6 **I am easily distracted during whatever activity I am involved in.**
Don't know Never Sometimes Usually Always

7 **I perform much better when I am under a lot of pressure.**
Don't know Never Sometimes Usually Always

8 **I become very anxious when I am under pressure.**
Don't know Never Sometimes Usually Always

9 **If I start to become tense, I can quickly relax myself and calm down.**
Don't know Never Sometimes Usually Always

10 **I find it easy to control my emotions, whatever the situation.**
Don't know Never Sometimes Usually Always

11 **I am always able to remain upbeat and positive, whatever the situation.**
Don't know Never Sometimes Usually Always

12 **If I am criticised by a coach or trainer I tend to take it very badly.**
Don't know Never Sometimes Usually Always

13 **I am easily able to deal with unforeseen situations.**
Don't know Never Sometimes Usually Always

14 **I have my own set of strategies for dealing with difficult situations.**
Don't know Never Sometimes Usually Always

Analysing the results:

- Questions 1–4 relate to motivation
- Questions 5–6 relate to concentration
- Questions 7–10 relate to arousal and anxiety
- Questions 11–14 relate to self-confidence.

There is no scoring system as such, but the questions are designed for you to establish areas of strength and areas of weakness.

Identifying the Psychological Demands of a Sport

Each sport will have an individual psychological demand on it which is also constantly open to change. The main categories of psychological demands are:

- Motivation
- Arousal control
- Confidence
- Concentration
- Emotional control

By using techniques such as performance profiling, we can assess why each one of these is important in our sport, how important it is and our current level of competence at the skill. Once our current competence level and the importance of the skill to the sport have been identified, you can lay down the aims of the training programme and begin to identify the content and the techniques needed to address these skills.

Techniques to Influence Motivation: Goal Setting

The main way that sports psychologists develop motivation is through the use of goal setting. In reality, goals are the dreams we have for ourselves, but goal setting gives these dreams legs and starts moving us towards them. A goal usually represents a situation we want to be in, which involves us moving away from the situation we are currently in.

Key term

Goal: what an individual is aiming to achieve. It is the outcome they desire from their actions.

Why Does Goal Setting Work?

Goal setting works because it gives our wants and desires a specific outcome and provides us with the steps we need to move towards this outcome. It gives our daily actions a meaning or framework to work within and gives us direction in life. Goals will work to direct our energy and efforts.

What you focus on you will move towards.

155

Short-term, Medium-term and Long-term Goals

Short-term goals are set over a brief period of time, usually from one day to one month. A short-term goal may relate to what you want to achieve in one training session or where you want to be by the end of the month.

Short-term goals may be:

- one session
- one day
- one week
- one month.

Medium-term goals will bridge the gap between short- and long-term goals and are set from one to three months.

Long-term goals will run from three months to several years. You may even set some lifetime goals, which run until you retire from your sport. In sport, we set long-term goals to cover a season or a sporting year.

Long-term goals may be:

- four months
- six months
- nine months
- one year
- one season
- three years
- lifetime.

Usually, short-term goals are set to help achieve the long-term goals. It is important to set both short-term and long-term goals, particularly short-term goals, because they will give a person more motivation to act now. If you have to give in a piece of coursework tomorrow, it will make you work hard tonight, but if you have to submit it in one month, you are unlikely to stay in tonight and complete the work!

Outcome and process goals

An outcome goal focuses on the outcome of an event or performance, such as winning a race or beating an opponent.

A process goal focuses on the process or actions that an individual must produce to perform well – for example, train three times a week or get eight hours' sleep a night.

Both types of goal are important, and we find that short-term goals are normally process goals, while long-term goals are outcome goals.

The process goals will be the small steps we take towards the big outcome or goal. A marathon race is the result of millions of small steps, and it is each individual step that is most important at that time.

SMART Goals

When goals are set you need to use the SMART principle to make them workable. SMART stands for:

- Specific
- Measurable
- Achievable
- Realistic
- Time-constrained.

Specific

The goal must be specific to what you want to achieve. This may be an aspect of performance or fitness. It is not enough to say, 'I want to get fitter'; you need to say, 'I want to improve strength, speed or stamina, etc.'

Measurable

Goals must be stated in a way that is measurable, so they need to state figures. For example, 'I want to improve my first serve percentage' is not measurable. However, if you say, 'I want to improve my first serve success by 20 per cent', it is measurable.

Achievable

It must be possible to actually achieve the goal.

Realistic

We need to be realistic in our goal setting and look at what factors may stop us achieving our goals.

Time-constrained

There must be a time-scale or deadline on the goal. This means you can review your success. It is best to state a date by which you wish to achieve the goal.

How to set goals

The best way to do this is to answer three questions:

1 What do I want to achieve? (Desired state)
2 Where am I now? (Present state)
3 What do I need to do to move from my present state to my desired state?

Then present this on a scale:

Present state				Desired state
1	2	3	4	5

1 Write in your goal at point 5 and your present position at point 1.
2 Decide what would be halfway between points 1 and 5; this is your goal for point 3.
3 Then decide what would be halfway between your present state and point 3; this is your short-term goal for point 2.
4 Then decide what would be halfway between point 3 and the desired state; this is your goal for point 4.

5 All these goals are outcome goals and must be set using the SMART principle.

6 Work out what needs to be done to move from point 1 to point 2. These are your process goals and, again, must use the SMART principle.

It is best to use a goal-setting diary to keep all goal-setting information in the same place, and to review the goals on a weekly basis.

Techniques to Influence Motivation: Performance Profiling

Performance profiling is a way of getting the athlete to analyse their strengths and weaknesses. It can be a way of monitoring improvements in psychological skills as well as being used to motivate and energise athletes.

The benefits of performance profiling are as follows:

- it considers what the individual feels is important
- the individual is actively involved and will feel some sense of possession of their performances
- it is used to motivate and monitor improvements
- it is specific for each athlete
- the visual display helps to give it more power
- it enables the athlete and coach to identify areas of weakness.

Process of Performance Profiling

Introduce the idea of performance profiling

This may be a new concept for the athlete and a period of explaining the process will be valuable. You will need to cover the following information:

- explain performance profiling
- explain the benefits and how the results can be applied
- emphasise that there are no wrong or right answers and that what is important is the individual's view
- show them examples of completed performance profiles (these should be anonymous).

Elicit the constructs

The sports psychologist will need to ask the athlete to come up with ten psychological factors that are vital to their performance. You may ask a question such as: What psychological factors do you consider to be most important in helping you to achieve your best performance?

The sports psychologist may assist the process by making relevant suggestions if the athlete is struggling to come up with good responses.

The ten factors they come up with are called 'constructs'.

Assess the constructs

The athlete is asked to complete the following tasks:

- Rate themselves on a scale of 1–10 to show their current level of competence at each construct. A rating of 10 would represent their idea of perfection.
- Rate how far they would like to progress towards their idea of perfection; they may feel that a score of 10 is not necessary and they would be happy to get to 17.

Plot the performance profile

Once the above tasks have been completed, you can present the information on a grid, with dark bars showing current levels of competence and lighter bars showing desired levels.

You can then use this information in different ways:

- assess their strengths and weaknesses
- see what they feel is important in their sport
- as their coach, you may have different ideas about what is important and their level of skill. This exercise will highlight any differences in your points of view.

You can identify the following information from the profile:

- areas of perceived strength – where they score 5 or more (e.g. Aggression control)
- areas of perceived weakness – where they score less than 5 (e.g. Arousal control)
- areas resistant to change – where there is little difference between their current rating and the rating they would like to achieve (e.g. Attitude).

Imagery

Imagery is one of the most important techniques in sports psychology because the pictures and thoughts that we have in our head will influence how we feel and how we behave. If we can have positive thoughts and images, they are going to be beneficial to our performance.

What Is Imagery?

Imagery is the creation or re-creation of an image or experience in your mind rather than physically practising the skill. It will involve the employment of all the senses in actually re-creating the experience. Imagery is used extensively by many athletes, particularly golfers and track and field athletes. Jack Nicklaus, one of the most successful golfers of all time, explains how he uses visualisation:

Before every shot I go to the movies in my head. Here is what I see. First I see the ball where I want it to finish, nice and white, sitting up high on the bright green grass. Then I see the ball going there – its path and trajectory and even its behaviour on landing. The next scene shows me making the kind of swing that will turn the previous image into reality. These home images are the key to my concentration and to my positive approach to every shot. (Nicklaus, 1976)

Imagery is a skill and some people will be better at it than others. If you find developing images difficult, you will need to use the practices later to help you with this skill.

Why does imagery work?

Imagery works because when you imagine yourself performing a skill, the brain is unable to differentiate between a real experience and an imagined experience. As a result, the brain sends impulses to the muscles via the nervous system; these impulses are not strong enough to produce a muscular contraction, although you may see twitches. As the impulses are passed down the nervous system, so the pattern becomes imprinted on the nervous system and is there for whenever you physically perform the skill. It is as if you have been there without actually going there.

Imagery can be used for the following skills:

● management of mental state
● mental rehearsal
● relaxation techniques
● developing confidence
● concentration skills.

Mental Rehearsal

Mental rehearsal is taking time to sit down and think about your sport. It is seeing, feeling and hearing yourself playing your sport. It can be utilised in different ways:

● developing and practising skills
● reducing anxiety about an event.
● practising 'what if…' scenarios
● developing confidence before an event
● replaying and reviewing performance.

Rather than just physical practice, mental rehearsal can complement your skill development. However, you need to have well-developed imagery skills to be able to perform mental rehearsal effectively.

Developing and Practising Skills

Mental rehearsal can be used before, during and after competitions to ensure the best performance. Roger Black, who won the 400 m silver medal in the 1996 Olympics, talks about the power of mental rehearsal:

For the Olympic Games I walked around the stadium four months prior and I kept that picture in my mind every day. I ran it from every lane. I could close my eyes now and run the 400 m race and I would feel how I would feel. (Black, in Grout and Perrin, 2004)

Here are some guidelines for mental rehearsal:

● Precede the session with a short relaxation session.
● Bring up the picture and make sure it is big, colourful, sharply focused and as bright as a film.
● Employ all your senses, by hearing the sounds and experiencing the feelings associated with performing.
● Visualise at the correct speed (same speed as the action).
● Always visualise yourself successfully executing the skills.
● Visualise from inside your head looking out.
● Practise in intervals of five to ten minutes a day.

Developing Confidence Before an Event

Self-confidence is the extent to which you expect to be successful. If you can, use imagery to recall times when you were sure about being successful, or you can use the following techniques to help you experience what it would be like to be completely self-confident.

Techniques to Control Arousal Levels

According to the inverted U hypothesis, our performance is related to our arousal level. If we are over-aroused, we need to reduce arousal by using relaxation techniques; conversely, if we find ourselves under-aroused, we need to use energising techniques to raise our arousal level.

Relaxation Techniques

There is a range of relaxation techniques which addresses different aspects of the effects of stress and anxiety. These techniques are:

● progressive muscular relaxation (PMR)
● mind-to-muscle techniques (imagery)
● breathing control.

Certainly, relaxation techniques will control arousal before and during performance, and they can also be used for other purposes:

● to lower levels of trait and state anxiety
● to help the athlete fall into a deep sleep before or after a competition
● to keep the athlete calm and reduce energy lost through nervous worry before a competition

- to relax and recover during breaks in play or between races or matches
- to help recovery from illness and injury
- to help them enjoy their life in general.

When performing relaxation techniques, it is important to follow these instructions:

1 Find a place where you will not be disturbed.
2 Sit or lie down in a comfortable place.
3 Close your eyes and turn down the lighting.
4 Put on some relaxing music.
5 Enjoy the experience.

Progressive muscular relaxation (PMR)

This technique is excellent for people who are experiencing the symptoms of somatic anxiety, such as tension in the muscles and butterflies in the stomach. PMR involves listening to a recording of a script, or a psychologist reading out a script where muscle groups are sequentially contracted and then relaxed. This starts from the hands and arms, up to the face, upper body and then the lower body.

Mind-to-muscle techniques (imagery)

These techniques will work with a person who is experiencing cognitive anxiety. It works best with people who have well-developed imagery skills. This technique involves listening to a recording of a script or a psychologist reading out a script where you develop pictures in your head. These pictures will be of a relaxing place or room where you can go to rest and relax when you need to.

Breathing control

Breathing control is a method often used by athletes to reduce muscle tension and lower anxiety levels. When we become stressed and anxious, we experience short and shallow breathing; when we are relaxed, our breathing deepens.

To aid relaxation, we can teach the athlete to breathe deeply and slowly from the diaphragm to produce mental and physical relaxation. If they are focusing on their breathing, it will shift their attention from whatever is causing them stress. It can be done in a standing or sitting position. Get the individual to place their hands on their stomach and see how the hands move out and fall back as they breathe in and out.

Once they have learnt how to breathe properly, they can use it at the appropriate time during a competition.

Energising techniques

If the athlete is feeling under-aroused, there are ways of raising the arousal level. For example, many coaches will use music to psych up their athletes and raise their energy levels. This can be a personal choice or a team may develop a theme tune that they play before performing in order to lift them. Also, scripts, similar in style to relaxation scripts, can be employed to raise arousal and energy levels.

Self-talk to develop confidence

Self-talk is what we say to ourselves when we have internal conversations, and this affects our mental state at any time. If we have positive thoughts and say positive things to ourselves, we will maintain high levels of confidence. However, if we say to ourselves that we are useless and no good, that is how we will act and we will get poor outcomes as a result. We need to keep building our confidence by reframing any negative thoughts we have in a positive way. For example, rather than saying, 'I always perform poorly against Sheena', you might say, 'Playing Sheena is a good challenge for me'.

Key learning points 4

- Before looking at techniques to improve performance in sport, you need to identify the psychological demands of the sport.
- Goal setting and performance profiling can be used to influence motivation.
- Imagery can be used for mental rehearsal, developing confidence and to promote relaxation.
- Relaxation techniques can be used to lower arousal levels, while energising techniques can increase them.

Student activity 17.4 2 hours   P6 P7 M4 D3

Choose a sports performer from your fellow students and then plan and carry out a consultation with this performer. You could use the sample questionnaire provided and any other methods you feel are important. You might watch them perform to see how they behave during competition or plan an interview with them.

Once you have found out as much information as you can, use the following template to plan a six-week psychological skills training programme.

Current situation:
[Write a description of the athlete and what sport they play, and summarise their main issues/problems, as in the case study of Sarah]
Aims of the psychological skills training:
[What areas are you going to address/improve?]
1
2
3

Action plan:
[The steps you will take to achieve the aims (e.g. set goals or teach relaxation skills)]
1
2
3
4

Training plan:
[What you will do week by week]
Week 1:
Week 2:
Week 3:
Week 4:
Week 5:
Week 6:

Comments on progress:

(To achieve M4, explain why you have planned the training programme for your selected performer. To achieve the first part of D3, you need to justify your training programme. You can do this by showing why you have chosen each technique you recommended. To achieve the second part of D3, you need to review your training programme and make suggestions for its improvement.)

References

Barrow, J. (1977) The variables of leadership: a review and conceptual framework. *Academy of Management Review*, 2, 231–51.

Bowers, K.S. (1973) Situationism in psychology: an analysis and a critique. *Psychological Review*, 80, 307–36.

Cattell, R.B. (1965) *The Scientific Analysis of Personality*, Penguin.

Cottrell, N.B. (1968) Performance in the presence of other human beings: mere presence, audience and affiliation effects, in E. Simmell, R. Hoppe and G. Milton (eds), *Social Facilitation and Imitative Behaviour*, Allyn & Bacon.

Cox, R. (2007) *Sports Psychology: Concepts and Applications*, Wm C. Brown Communications.

Eysenck, H. (1964) *Manual of Eysenck Personality Inventory*, University of London Press.

Fazey, J. and Hardy, L. (1988) *The Inverted U Hypothesis: A Catastrophe for Sport Psychology?* British Association of Sports Sciences Monograph, no. 1, NCF.

Festinger, L.A., Schachter, S. and Back, K. (1950) *Social Pressures in Informal Groups: A Study of Human Factors in Housing*, Harper.

Friedman, M. (1996) *Type A Behaviour: Its Diagnosis and Treatment*, Plenum Press.

Gill, D. (2000) *Psychological Dynamics of Sport and Exercise*, Human Kinetics.

Grout, J. and Perrin, S. (2004) *Mind Games*, Capstone.

Hull, C.L. (1943) *Principles of Behaviour*, Appleton-Century-Crofts.

Jarvis, M. (2006) *A Student's Handbook*, Routledge.

McClelland, D.C., Atkinson, J.W., Clark, R.W. and Lowell, E.J. (1953) *The Achievement Motive*, Appleton-Century-Crofts.

McGrath, J.E. (1970) Major methodological issues, in J.E. McGrath (ed.), *Social and Psychological Factors in Stress*, Holt, Rinehart & Winston.

Nicklaus, J. (1976) *Play Better Golf*, King Features.

Sage, G. (1974) *Sport and American Society*, Addison-Wesley.

Sage, G. (1977) *Introduction to Motor Behaviour: A Neuropsychological Approach*, Addison-Wesley.

Schurr, K., Ashley, M. and Joy, K. (1977) A multivariate analysis of male athlete characteristics: sport type and success. *Multivariate Experimental Clinical Research*, 3, 53–68.

Steiner, I.D. (1972) *Group Processes and Productivity*, Academic Press.

Triplett, N. (1898) The dynamogenic factors in pacemaking and competition. *American Journal of Psychology*, 9, 507–33.

Tuckman, L. and Jensen, M. (1977) *Stages of Small Group Development Revisited*, Group and Organisational Studies.

Weinberg, R.S. and Gould, D. (2007) *Foundations of Sport and Exercise Psychology*, Human Kinetics.

Williams, J.M. (1980) Personality characteristics of the successful female athlete, in W.M. Straub, *Sport Psychology: An Analysis of Athlete Behavior*, Movement.

Yerkes, R.M. and Dodson, J.D. (1908) The relationship of strength and stimulus to rapid habit formation. *Journal of Comparative Neurology and Psychology*, 18, 459–82.

Further reading

Cox, R. (2007) *Sports Psychology: Concepts and Applications*, Wm C. Brown Communications.

Thatcher, J., Thatcher, R., Day, M., Portas, M. and Hood, S. (2009) *Sport and Exercise Science*, Learning Matters.

Weinberg, R.S. and Gould, D. (2007) *Foundations of Sport and Exercise Psychology*, Human Kinetics.

Useful websites

www.bbc.co.uk/wales/raiseyourgame

A wealth of advice and tips on improving focus, motivation and performance

www.5min.com/Video/How-to-Develop-Motivation-for-Sport-34094922

A short video explaining how to develop motivation

www.5min.com/Video/How-to-Change-Negative-Thoughts-to-Positive-Thoughts-in-Sport-Part-2-34095006

A short video explaining how you can improve performance by changing negative thoughts into positive thoughts

27: Technical & Tactical Skills in Sport

27.1 Introduction

This unit will demonstrate the range and types of skills and tactics in sports.

Having established the key techniques and tactics in sports, the unit will describe the ways in which techniques and tactics may be analysed, with a view to performance enhancement of elite athletes and your own performance. Finally, this unit looks at designing a development plan or action plan for the improvement of performance.

By the end of this unit you should:

● understand the technical skills and tactics demanded by selected sports
● be able to assess the technical and tactical ability of an elite sports performer
● be able to assess your own technical and tactical ability.

Assessment and grading criteria

To achieve a PASS grade the evidence must show that the learner is able to:	To achieve a MERIT grade the evidence must show that, in addition to the pass criteria, the learner is able to:	To achieve a DISTINCTION grade the evidence must show that, in addition to the pass and merit criteria, the learner is able to:
P1 explain the technical and tactical demands of three contrasting sports	**M1** compare and contrast the technical and tactical demands of three contrasting sports	
P2 produce an observation checklist that can be used to assess the technical and tactical ability of a performer in a selected sport		
P3 use an observation checklist to assess the technical and tactical ability of an elite performer, in a selected sport, identifying strengths and areas for improvement	**M2** explain strengths and areas for improvement, in technical and tactical ability, of the selected elite sports performer, and make suggestions relating to development	**D1** justify development suggestions made for the selected elite sports performer regarding areas for improvement
P4 use an observation checklist to assess own technical and tactical ability, in a competitive situation for a selected sport, identifying strengths and areas for improvement	**M3** explain strengths and areas for improvement, in own technical and tactical ability in a competitive situation	
P5 complete a four-week log of own technical and tactical ability in a selected sport, identifying strengths and areas for improvement	**M4** explain identified strengths and areas for improvement of own technical and tactical ability in a selected sport	
P6 produce a development plan of own technical and tactical ability, based on identified strengths and areas for improvement.	**M5** relate development plan to identified strengths and areas for improvement in own technical and tactical ability.	**D2** justify suggestions made in personal development plan.

27.2 Understanding the Technical Skills and Tactics Demanded by Selected Sports

Improvement in sport is at the core of this unit. All performers and in particular elite performers strive to improve their performance in a variety of ways.

Attention to technical ability and tactical awareness are the keys to performance improvement, along with specific training, nutrition, fitness, psychology and the use of technology.

All sports require some form of technical ability and, in order to use these technical abilities and to be able to perform, tactics are required. The performer of a sport should be aware of both the technical and tactical requirements.

Some skills can be general and can be used across all sports; these include running, jumping, throwing and catching. Other skills are specific to only a few sports, or even just one sport; these include the volleyball serve, the golf swing and the sprint start used in athletics.

Tactics are actions and strategies planned to achieve an overall objective – in sport, that objective is predominantly to win. Tactics can depend on a number of factors, such as opposition, players available for selection, the importance of the game/ match and possibly even weather. Even the greatest players in the world must have tactical awareness and consider such factors.

Technical Skills

All sports have a demand in terms of the level of performance. Consider the performance of a beginner in any sport and compare that performer with an elite performer from the same sport. There will be many differences in the quality of their performance.

The skills of sports are of course very different, but sports can be categorised into groups that largely contain the same range of skills, with notable exceptions, e.g. the basic techniques of badminton and tennis are similar, such as body positioning, the importance of grip and overhead smash shots, but some techniques are distinctly different, such as the service.

- **Racket sports** – tennis, badminton, table tennis, squash, etc.
- **Team sports** – football, basketball, rugby, volleyball, handball, etc.
- **Individual sports** – trampolining, trekking, climbing, swimming, skiing, etc.

Each of the sports has its own set of techniques and skills, which can be learnt and assessed.

Continuous/Discrete/Serial Technical Skills

Continuous Technical Skills

Continuous technical skills do not have clear beginnings and endings, e.g. cycling, walking, running, canoeing, race walking or cross-country skiing. They cannot be split up into sub-routines or easily distinguishable parts but last a relatively long time.

Batting	Bowling
Straight drive	Line
Pull shot	Length
Front foot defensive	Movement
Square or late cut	Flight/pace
Drive to mid-wicket or covers	Googly
Hook shot	Swing
Running between wickets	Top spin/flipper
Leg glance	Off or leg spin
Back foot drive	Off or leg cutter
Sweep	

Table 27.1 Techniques required for a team sport such as cricket

Fig 27.1 A skill continuum

Discrete Technical Skills

Discrete technical skills have clear beginnings and endings, e.g. a free throw in basketball, a golf swing, board diving or a throw-in in football. They can be performed by themselves without being linked to other skills. The skill can be repeated but the performer starts again.

Serial Technical Skills

Serial technical skills are made up of a number of discrete skills put together. They often make up a routine or sequence, e.g. the triple jump, or a gymnastics or trampolining routine. Serial skills have a number of discrete skills which are linked together into a performance consisting of several phases.

Discrete, serial and continuous skills are often shown on a continuous diagram known as a continuum like the one shown in Figure 27.1.

Tactics

Tactics are plans and actions to achieve a goal. Tactics in sport are usually focused directly or indirectly on winning. Tactics can depend upon the opposition, players of the other team or opponents, the importance of the competition and maybe the weather.

Strategy and tactics are key features in all sports. There are many examples of different kinds of tactics and how and when they might be employed. It is important to remember that tactics are only effective if the performer(s) are able to execute them.

Tactics can be:

● **Pre-event tactics** – a particular plan before the event, e.g. target specific players or aspects of a team that are seen as a weakness, or
● **In-event tactics** – a plan implemented during the game, such as switching from man-to-man to zone defence in basketball, or changing bowlers in cricket due to the weather or playing surface changes.

Tactics can be successful and unsuccessful. It is important to understand what determines the success of a tactic or tactics.

Tactics can fail if the opposition work them out too easily, if they are employed too late or if the player or players are simply not able to understand or execute the necessary tactic(s).

Consider the range of options that a tennis player has at their disposal. First, where should they stand while waiting for their opponent's return? If the ball is likely to come over the net in the middle and low, then the player might consider standing close to the net to make a volley. In this way the player has selected a tactical position and shot selection. The same player might also consider serving the ball to the forehand and backhand of their opponent, some serves with spin, some without and some faster than others. This is known as variation.

If the conditions of the match are such that the player is losing then that player might start to play defensive 'percentage' (fewer risk-taking) shots in an attempt to encourage the opponent to be more forceful, possibly taking more risks, and potentially making more errors, allowing you 'back into the match'.

It is easy to think of tactics and strategies used in team games, e.g. full court pressure defence in basketball, chip and charge in tennis, kick and chase in rugby or playing the offside trap in football. In racket sports such as badminton an example of a tactic to use against a taller, less mobile player could be to make a lot of drop shots and push the shuttle to all corners of the court.

Key learning points I

● Continuous technical skills do not have clear beginnings and endings.
● Discrete technical skills have clear beginnings and endings.
● Serial technical skills are made up of a number of discrete skills put together; they often make up a routine or sequence.
● Techniques can be unique to a sport or transferable, such as in the case of several techniques common to racket sports.
● A strategy is a plan designed to meet a specific objective, either during a performance or as a part of a longer-term plan.
● A tactic can be defined as the actions that you need to make the strategy work.

Quick quiz 1

Give five examples of each of the following:

- A continuous skill
- A serial skill
- A discrete skill.

Select two sports of your choice, then describe the tactics required for each.

Student activity 27.1   🕐 **1–2 hours**   P1   M1

For this activity, you need to select three different sports.

Task 1

Draw a spider diagram for each of your selected sports which illustrates the tehcnical and tactical demands of each.

Task 2

Prepare a written report that explains, compares and contrasts the technical and tactical demands of each of your three selected sports.

27.3 Assessing the Technical and Tactical Ability of an Elite Sports Performer

P2   P3   M2   D1

Elite Performers

Sporting performance at its very best is often described as elite performance. Because of the range of sports and the way that they have developed and have been funded there is a range of descriptions that outline elite provision for different sports.

1 Professional athletes are those who are technically employed by the sport, and as such are paid to participate in their sport. Examples include basketball players, footballers, tennis players, golfers and motor racing drivers. This kind of performer has the most available time and resources at their disposal.

2 National representatives can also be professional, but are often amateur, in the sense that while they may receive some funding to cover costs, they are employed in other professions. Recent political changes in sport in the UK have meant that national stars in rugby union and athletics are now professional, while a few

remain amateur, as in the case of sports that have a limited following such as water polo, canoeing or volleyball. Since national athletes of this type have less time available to train and compete, because they must balance careers and the demands of their sport, analysis and future planning should consider these challenges.

Analysis of Performance

Analysis forms an important part of the performance; it reflects on the previous performances and helps shape future practices. For example, a basketball team does not take many defensive rebounds in a game; the observer takes note of this and builds some drills into the next practice in order to improve that performance. It is important to note that this process can be applied to opponents and that knowledge of the opponent's strengths and weaknesses can be as useful in planning practices and preparation.

Observation

Observation involves the gathering of data – this could be the number of blocked shots in basketball, successful overhead smashes in badminton or the distance travelled from the cross in a trampoline routine. There are a number of ways of observing and recording this data, which will be discussed later in this unit.

Fig 27.2 A basketball coach

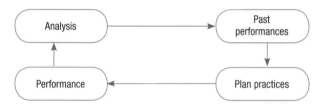

Fig 27.3 Simple model of the coaching process

Analysis

Analysis is about deciding what has happened and is a complete skill in itself. A trampoline coach can see that a front somersault has over-rotated, but the real skill is in determining why this has happened. An analyst will understand the techniques and tactics of their sport and also what the causes are of good and poor performance.

Fig 27.4 A performance analysis model

Evaluation

Evaluation is the end product of observation and analysis. It is the final process where decisions are made and feedback is given to the performer. For this there must be effective communication between the coach and the performer, and an understanding of the methods and effect of feedback on the performer. Some performers will enjoy lots of descriptive feedback about their performance, while others will respond better to simple vocal feedback. This kind of information can then be used to help in the planning of subsequent training sessions (see Table 27.2).

Observation Checklists

Checklists can be used to assess a range of parameters, e.g. technical skills, skill selection, the application (tactics) of skill and shot selection.

Checklists are often best used accompanying a video recording of the leadership experience.

Tables 27.3 and 27.4 show two examples of observation checklists – one for technique analysis and the other for performance analysis.

Technique	Problem	Observation	Correction
Basketball – 3-point shot	Ball drops short on shot	Shooter using only upper body to shoot	Use legs and lower body to generate more efficient use of ground reaction force
Trampolining – swivel hips	Poor shape in flight	Body not straightened before twisting	Straighten body by pushing hips forward and lifting arms and upper body

Table 27.2 Evaluation

	Strengths	Developmental aspects
Student:		**Shot:**
Aim of shot:		
Grip		
Stance		
Footwork		
Stroke action		
Impact point		
Weight transfer		
Follow through		
Accuracy/success		
Effectiveness		

Table 27.3 Racket sports shot analysis – technique analysis

Qualitative Analysis

Qualitative analysis is the most common simple observation and is usually performed by a coach, but also by spectators and performers. This method is largely subjective, meaning that it is open to personal interpretation and is therefore subject to bias or error. The more knowledgeable the observer, the more valid the observations are likely to be.

Think of a sports pundit such as Alan Hansen (football) or Jonathan Davies, who, with the benefit of experience as a player and recording/replay technology at his disposal, can make a detailed analysis of performance based on the observation of the key parts of a match.

Quantitative Analysis

Quantitative analysis is more involved and scientific, and involves the direct measurement of a performance or technique. These methods are more time-consuming but generally produce more reliable results. In basketball matches it is possible to record a number of match statistics, both while the game is in progress, called real-time, and after the game using a camera, for example. This is called lapsed-time analysis.

Student:		Sport:	Date:
Skill (basic description):			

Preparation	Strengths	Developmental aspects
Footwork		
Arm action		
Body position		
Balance		
Execution		
Contact/strike		
Follow through		
Accuracy		
Effectiveness		
Recovery		
Footwork		
Arm action		
Body position		
Balance		

Table 27.4 Performance analysis

It is very difficult when observing a game in real-time not to make a few errors. For instance, while recording a loss of possession in football there could be a successful completed pass immediately afterwards, followed by a piece of link-up play. All this can happen in the blink of an eye and can be very difficult to record all at once. One of the many advantages of recording performances is that it can be played back after the event to ensure greater accuracy.

As technology advances and equipment becomes more affordable, so coaches and observers have access to computers, image capture software and digital cameras. This equipment, with the right kind of training, can help to produce valuable information for the coach and performer.

This technology can be used to measure the following:

● Patterns of movement or tactics
● Efficiency of skills or techniques
● How hard a performer is working
● The psychological state of the performer, e.g. anxious, concentrating.

Examples of the kinds of factors measured could be as follows:

● How close to the centre the trampolinist is while completing a ten-bounce routine
● How many steals or turnovers there are in a basketball game.

In individual sports such as singles tennis it can be useful to compare one player's profile with another's, so measuring first-serve percentage and forehand winners and comparing results could show trends and patterns in the match.

Individual data can be presented in three ways in a performance evaluation:

1 In comparison with their opponent.
2 In comparison with someone of the same level of performance.
3 In comparison with their own previous experiences.

Notation

Notation is a way of collecting data and can be done by hand or with a computer.

Hand notation is a system of recording detailed analysis of a sport and literally noting the data on a paper sheet using a pre-defined set of symbols. Systems like this exist for many sports, such as tennis, archery and football.

The advantage of these systems is that they are inexpensive and, if completed by a skilful recorder, will produce information quickly in real-time, so that the coach or performer can have instant access to detailed information. The main disadvantages of this system are that it is open to human error, can be difficult to interpret and can be hard to use in certain conditions, e.g. bad weather.

Team sport match analysis			
Date	**Opponent**	**Result**	
Analysis area		**Mark**	**Target**
Positional play			
Tactical awareness/ decision making			
Fitness levels			
Skills/techniques			
Cooperation/teamwork			
Concentration/ psychological factors			
Diet/nutrition			
This could be administered by the performer, a peer or a neutral observer, scoring 1–10 for both achieved and target scores.			

Table 27.5 Example of a match analysis sheet for a team sport

Technology in Performance Analysis (including Computerised Notation)

As digital recording technology improves, new software packages are developed that can analyse all physical activities. Packages such as Kandle and Dartfish are capable of producing a range of exciting analysis tools, including:

● Delayed replay systems
● Distance and angle measurement
● Overlays and comparators that compare other performances, e.g. Jonny Wilkinson's kicking pattern and success
● Multi-frame sequencing that breaks down complex skills
● Drawing and annotation tools.

Due to their decreasing cost, these packages are becoming available in schools and colleges as well as professional sports clubs.

Critical Analysis and Self-Reflection

Self-reflection allows you to explore your perceptions, decisions and subsequent actions to work out ways in which performers can improve technical, tactical or physical ability.

Diaries

Diaries can act as a permanent source of information to record your own thoughts and feelings, and serve as a true account of what happened and when. Diaries or logs can certainly help with self-reflection and form the basis of action plans for improvement.

Performance Profiling

Performance profiling is a method that can be self-employed or, more typically, applied by a leader or observer. Put simply, it is an inventory of attributes/ skills/techniques that form the basis of an assessment grading model.

Performance profiling can be used to analyse and record technical or tactical factors as well as, for example, psychological attributes.

Performance Profile and Technique

Example – hockey skills/techniques. Figure 8.5 (on page 220) shows a sample profile of a hockey player. The darker column is the assessment of the level of performance by the performer and the lighter column is the assessment of the level of performance as identified by the coach.

If you look at the results, it is clear that there are differences in opinion as to level of performance. It is important, if there is a difference in opinion, that coach and performer discuss the issues and decide on what needs development in practice and game situations and how this can be achieved.

Performance Profile of Tactical Awareness

Example – basketball tactical awareness. Figure 8.6 (on page 220) shows a sample profile of a basketball player. Again, the darker column is the assessment of the level of tactical awareness identified by the performer and the lighter column is the assessment by the coach.

Looking at the profile produced, it would seem that there is a difference in how the coach perceives the player's ability to recognise opponents' tactics. A discussion could follow where the coach and performer discuss their differences of opinion openly, providing examples that will help improve the understanding between coach and performer.

Scouting

This is a process where an expert observer can either identify a talented individual or produce a report about an opponent.

In the first case it could be bringing a new player to a team to strengthen the existing squad.

Knowledge of how your opponent performs is an underused system in this country. A simple observation and a few notes can be very useful in deciding how to prepare for the next match. For example, if a tennis player knows that their opponent has a fast, hard service but is poor on their backhand, then their preparation should have a greater emphasis on service returns under pressure and returning the ball to their opponent's weaker side.

Sports Performance Analysts – Computerised Notational Analysis

Examples of this type of system and its uses can be seen particularly at the Wimbledon Tennis Championships and during cricket Test matches.

Tennis analysis can visually display the ball placement and speed (m.p.h. or k.p.h.) of the first and second services, as well as the percentage success/effectiveness of the serves. Similarly, service returns can also be reviewed regarding the placement and percentage success.

Cricket coaches, players and analysts also use the technology. For example, a bowler can have their delivery patterns reviewed for line and length (accuracy) and the subsequent success in taking wickets. For a batsman, the systems can display the shots selected and where the player has scored his runs.

Key learning points 2

- Observation involves the gathering of data. Analysis is about deciding what has happened and is a complete skill in itself. Evaluation is the end product of observation and analysis.
- Checklists can be used to assess a range of parameters, e.g. technical skills, skill selection, the application (tactics) of skill, shot selection, etc.
- Qualitative analysis is the most commonly used simple observation, usually by a coach but also by spectators and performers.
- Quantitative analysis is more involved and scientific and involves the direct measurement of a performance or technique.
- Notation is a way of collecting data and can be done by hand or with a computer.
- Performance profiling is an inventory of attributes/skills/techniques that form the basis of an assessment grading model.
- Assessment of elite athletes should be focused on the following: strengths, areas for improvement and development plans.

Q Quick quiz 2

1 What are the main differences between a professional sports person and an amateur?

2 Draw a model to show the processes for the analysis of performance.

3 Describe qualitative analysis.

4 Describe quantitative analysis.

5 Explain what self-reflection is and how it can be carried out.

6 Describe what 'scouting' means.

7 Describe ways in which computerised notational analysis can be used to monitor performance.

Student activity 27.2 — 2–3 hours

For this activity, you will need to select a sport that you are familiar with in relation to the technical and tactical skills required.

technical and tactical ability of an elite performer in your selected sport. You can observe your performer either live or through film, TV or video footage.

Task 1

Prepare an observation checklist that you could use to assess the technical and tactical ability of a performer in the sport that you have selected.

Task 2

Use your observation checklist to assess the

Task 3

Write a report that identifies and explains your performer's strengths and areas for improvement. Produce and justify appropriate development suggestions for your performer based on your report.

27.4 Assessing your own Technical and Tactical Ability

Before undertaking any assessment, it is important to consider the assessment environment. In most cases, it would be best to assess your own performance in a competitive environment, where all the elements of pressure and stress are in place, to create a more realistic and valid set of measurements or observations.

Assessment should be focused on the following aspects.

1 **Strengths** – this is usually a list of the best performed skills, or the correct application of them, and could include tactical awareness, such as shot selection, spacing or the ability to read the game. Fitness and diet and nutrition assessment may form the basis of a scientific analysis.

2 **Areas for improvement** – could also be termed

'action points', indicating that these elements should form the focus for any improvement following an analysis. These could include the following:

(a) Attacking skills.

(b) Defending skills.

(c) Specific techniques, e.g. overhead shots in tennis.

(d) An aspect of fitness such as flexibility or power.

3 **Development** – this is the actual changes made or a plan that lays out what should be done, and could include the following:

(a) A modification to training or equipment.

(b) Coaching on key technical or tactical points, possibly one to one.

(c) Further and more detailed observational analysis that could be concentrated into key areas, such as in the case of a video analysis that could be focused on, for example, a cricket bowler's arm action, split into three phases.

(d) Nutritional guidance, advice on what and when to eat, how to refuel or rehydrate, etc.

(e) Psychological guidance that may concentrate on relaxation, stress reduction, mental toughness or team cohesion.

(f) Fitness guidance, typically an adaptation to current training that demonstrates the component that needs to be developed, e.g. anaerobic endurance.

27.5 Devising a Development Plan

In addition to the methods described for the assessment of elite performers, there are other means of assessment that may be used by the performers themselves.

● **Recording performances** – this is an excellent way of improving your own effectiveness. Recordings can be used to produce an objective review of a performance.

● **Critical analysis and self-reflection** – self-reflection allows you to explore your perceptions, decisions and subsequent actions to work out ways in which performance can improve technically or tactically.

● **Logbooks** – these can act as a permanent source of information to record your own thoughts and feelings, and serve as a true account of what happened and when. Diaries or logs can certainly help with self-reflection and form the basis of action plans for improvement.

Development Plans

Once analysis is completed, the next stage should be to design a plan that should improve one or more aspects of performance.

Setting SMART Goals

It is a good idea to use the SMART principle when planning your sessions/season.

● **Specific** – this means that the session meets the objectives that you want it to meet, and is specific to that sport. For example, you could focus a cricket batting session on dealing with short-pitched, fast deliveries, thus being explicit and specific.

● **Measurable** – this is the way in which you measure your results. If you have identified that you want to improve your jump shooting as a basketball player, then you might measure this by counting how many shots are successful in a training or game situation and then measure again after the training programme.

● **Achievable** – what you set out to improve must be possible. It would not be fair to ask a beginner in trampolining to complete a complicated routine with multiple somersaults.

● **Realistic** – it must be possible and realistic to achieve what you intend to achieve.

● **Time-constrained** – there should be a reasonable amount of time to achieve the learning goal. Some goals will be short term in nature and established to be achieved in the next session; others will be longer term and established for the entire season.

Types of Goals

Goal setting can be used for motivating ourselves in life as well as for sport. The main categories of goals are as follows.

1 **Personal goals** – these relate to our personal life, such as family life, social life, sporting aims, health and fitness and things that give us pleasure.

2 **Business/career/economic goals** – these relate to the development of our careers and financial rewards.

3 **Self-improvement goals** – these relate to personal growth and development.

Goals can also be split into short-term, medium-term and long-term goals.

● **Short-term goals** – these are goals that are set over a period of time that might be between one day and one month. A short-term goal might relate to what you aim to achieve in one session, but will usually relate to a period of around one month.

● **Medium-term goals** – these fill the gap between short-term and long-term goals and would cover a period of between one and six months.

● **Long-term goals** – these goals relate to periods that might run from six months to several years. Some people set 'lifetime goals', which cannot be assessed until retirement. Most long-term goals are set for achievement over the course of either a year or a competitive season.

It is important to set long-term, medium-term and short-term goals. The fulfilment of short-term goals will contribute to the achievement of long-term goals.

Key learning points 3

- When analysing your own performance, you should examine your strengths and your areas for improvement.
- Goal setting should be SMART: specific, measurable, achievable, realistic, time-constrained.
- Goals can be personal, business, career, economic or self-improvement in nature.
- Logbooks can be used to keep a record of assessments and performances, and show improvement over time.

Student activity 27.3   ⏱ **4–5 hours**   P4 P5 P6 M3 M4

In order to help you to assess your own technical and tactical ability, it is a good idea to track your progress over a period of time and explore areas for development.  M4 **D2**

Task 1

Complete a logbook which contains information on your technical and tactical ability in both training and competition over a four-week period. Make entries into your logbook after any type of training or competition related to your selected sport. At the end of each entry, try to make a note of areas that you thought you did well in and areas for improvement.

Task 2

After your four-week period, write a report that identifies and explains your strengths in your selected sport and areas for improvement.

Task 3

Based on the information in your report from Task 2, produce a development plan to help you to improve your own technical and tactical ability and, where possible, justify your suggestions in this plan.

References

Franks, I. M. and Millar, G. (1991) 'Training coaches to observe and remember', *Journal of Sport Sciences*, 9, 3, 285–97.

Further reading

Badminton England (2008) *Badminton – Know the Game*, 4th edn, London: A & C Black.

British Canoe Union (2008) *Canoe and Kayak Handbook*, 3rd edn, Polskabook.

Crisfield, P. (2001) *Analysing your Coaching*, Coachwise.

England Basketball (2006) *Basketball – Know the Game*, 3rd edn, London: A & C Black.

England Netball (2009) *Netball – Know the Game*, 5th edn, London: A & C Black.

English Table Tennis Association (2006) *Table Tennis – Know the Game*, 4th edn, London: A & C Black.

England and Wales Cricket Board (2009) *Cricket – Know the Game*, 5th edn, London: A & C Black.

The Football Association (2006) *Soccer – Know the Game*, 5th edn, London: A & C Black.

The Lawn Tennis Association (2008) *Tennis – Know the Game*, 5th edn, London: A & C Black.

Mattos, B. (2007) *Kayaking and Canoeing for Beginners (A practical guide to paddling for novices and intermediates)*, Anness Publishing Ltd.

Miles, A. (2004) *Coaching Practice*, Coachwise.

Stafford-Brown, J., Rea, S., Janaway, L. and Manley, C. (2006) *BTEC First Sport*, Hodder Arnold.

Useful websites

www.elitesoccerconditioning.com/FitnessTraining/FitnessTraining.htm

Drills, tips and ideas to help you maximise your footballing fitness and techniques.

www.coachesinfo.com/index.php

Free access to a number of regularly updated articles on a wide range of sports, describing methodology of research; registration necessary for full access.

28: The Athlete's Lifestyle

28.1 Introduction

To be successful at sport, clearly an athlete must get the right training, the most appropriate nutritional advice, psychological support, technical and skills training and, ultimately, the correct competition. However, how they spend their time away from the sporting environment is also crucial to their success or failure. How they live their life and the choices they make or what lifestyle they have will have a bearing on the outcomes they achieve.

Every choice an athlete makes will have one of two outcomes:

1   It will contribute in a *positive* way to improving their chances of success
2   It will contribute in a *negative* way to their chances of success or will increase their chances of failure.

While it is important that the athlete is able to lead a full and rounded life, it is also important that they take responsibility for the outcomes of their own actions.

By the end of this unit you should:

● Know how lifestyle can affect athletes
● Know the importance of appropriate behaviour for athletes
● Know how to communicate effectively with the media and significant others
● Be able to produce a career plan.

Assessment and grading criteria		
To achieve a PASS grade the evidence must show that the learner is able to:	**To achieve a MERIT grade the evidence must show that, in addition to the pass criteria, the learner is able to:**	**To achieve a DISTINCTION grade the evidence must show that, in addition to the pass and merit criteria, the learner is able to:**
P1 describe five different lifestyle factors that can affect athletes	**M1** explain five different lifestyle factors that can affect athletes	**D1** analyse five different lifestyle factors that can affect athletes
P2 describe the importance of appropriate behaviour for athletes	**M2** explain the importance of appropriate behaviour for athletes	**D2** justify the importance of appropriate behaviour for athletes.
P3 describe strategies that can be used by athletes to help deal with three different situations that could influence their behaviour		
P4 describe the factors to be considered when giving two different types of media interview		
P5 describe the factors to be considered when communicating with significant others		
P6 produce a career plan covering an individual's career as an athlete and their career outside competitive sport.	**M3** explain factors involved in career planning for an athlete.	

28.2 How lifestyle factors can affect athletes

Athletes will increasingly find that they have many demands on their time. Their success is dependent upon their managing this time appropriately so that they allocate the right amount of time for training, eating, rest and recovery as well as activities that form their leisure time.

Any person's life could be divided into three areas:

1 Work
2 Survival
3 Leisure

Leisure time activities

Leisure time is the time which is left after all work and survival activities have been performed. For a busy athlete this may be as little as one hour a day; or it may be much longer if they are only required to train in the morning and then have the rest of the day to themselves. How athletes choose to spend their time can have a dramatic bearing on their performances.

Appropriate leisure activities

While athletes train they will impart physical stress in the form exercise by loading muscles and joints to result in positive adaptations and mental stress in terms of the pressure they put on themselves every day to get the best from their training and during competition. This has an effect on the body of breaking down structures and placing demands on the organs in the body such as the glands which produce hormones such as adrenaline and cortisol. The athletes training scheduled will be periodised and tapered to ensure that they are well rested before competition and at their optimum performance level. However, rest and recovery will occur during their leisure time and what they do during their leisure will affect the quality of the rest and recovery they receive. A useful creed to remember is:

An athlete does not get fit by training, but by resting

While training is the stimulus for adaptation, training will actually *lower* an athlete's fitness level. When we leave the gym we are less fit than when we went in because we have broken down muscle and bone and have lowered our stores of energy. However, over the next two to three days the body will recover by laying down more protein in the muscles and replacing bone and other damaged tissue as well as replacing energy stores in the form of glycogen. The athlete has to ensure that they provide the best conditions for these adaptations to occur. During their leisure time they will need to perform all three of the following activities:

- rest
- relaxation
- eating

Activity	Definition	Examples
Work	Activities done as employment to make money or to provide the basic needs for living	Training Competition Education Study Paid employment Voluntary employment
Survival	Activities performed to maintain health and life	Eating Drinking Sleeping Washing Cleaning Personal hygiene
Leisure	Activities which are freely chosen and done for pleasure, rest and relaxation	Relaxing Socialising Watching television Going to the cinema Going to the pub Hobbies

Table 28.1 The three areas of an athlete's lifestyle

Rest

While training breaks down the structures of the body (catabolism) so resting will build up the structures of the body (anabolism). This includes gaining 7-8 hours sleep and rest periods during the day.

Relaxing

When we relax we produce an internal environment that is conducive to building up the structures of the body. When we are stressed we produce hormones that are catabolic, such as adrenaline and cortisol, and these will break down the structures of the body.

Eating

To rebuild the body we need to provide the cells with top quality nutrients or building blocks. If we have good health at the cellular level, this will contribute to good health for the overall body. Consuming high levels of foods containing toxins such as preservatives, colourings, thickeners, emulsifiers and pesticides can cause stress to the digestive system and body overall.

Inappropriate leisure activities

Leisure activities can also be very damaging to the athlete in terms of their health and ultimately their performance. These would include:

- alcohol
- smoking
- drugs
- gambling
- unruly behaviour.

Alcohol

Alcohol in small quantities may have benefits in terms of promoting relaxation and reducing the risk of heart disease. However, due to its toxicity and addictiveness, in larger quantities alcohol can actually damage the health of the individual. The toxicity will damage all the structures it passes through such as the throat, stomach, intestines, blood and liver. It will also place stress on other organs such as the heart, brain, liver and pancreas. The problem for athletes is more short term in that it will produce the effects of a hangover, which is caused by dehydration, presence of toxins in the bloodstream and the loss of vitamins and minerals. The athlete will feel tired and nauseous, which will seriously affect performance.

It is recommended that a male drinks no more than 21 units of alcohol a week and a female drinks no more than 14 units a week. A unit is half a pint of beer, lager or cider or a pub measure of sprits such as gin, vodka or whiskey.

Acceptable levels of alcohol for males and females to consume can be found in Table 28.2.

Smoking

Cigarette smoke contains more than 4000 different chemicals of which around 400 are toxic and 60 are cancer-forming. Nicotine, the drug in tobacco is highly addictive and it is this that causes the dependency. A cigarette will reduce the craving for nicotine for 20-30 minutes after which point the smoker will want another cigarette to make them feel normal again. The major problem for athletes is the tar that cigarette smoke contains, as this will accumulate in the airways (bronchioles) and restrict the flow of air to the alveoli, thus reducing available oxygen. Also, due to the presence of carbon monoxide in the smoke, smoking will be attracted to the haemoglobin in the red blood cells taking the place of the oxygen. Hence, smoking will affect the fitness level of an athlete in the short term and in the long term cause life-threatening diseases.

Drugs

Each governing body of sport provides a list of drugs to show which drugs can or cannot be taken by an athlete or the limit to which a drug may be present. Legal drugs may be taken by an athlete for a positive outcome. This may be for health reasons or to address a medical condition. On the list of banned substance are illegal drugs, which may be used by the athlete for social reasons. All of these illegal drugs have side effects that will seriously impair the

Male	Category	Female
1–2 units a day	Beneficial	1–2 units a day
3–4 units a day (21/week)	Acceptable	2–3 units a day (14/week)
>21 units a week	Unhealthy	>14 units a week
>35 units a week	Harmful	>21 units a week

Table 28.2 Acceptable levels of alchol for male & females
(Source: NHS, 2002)

Drug	What are the effects?	What are the risks?	What is the legal position?
Amphetamines	Cause an adrenaline rush creating energy and increased confidence.	Can lead to addiction, paranoia, delusions and hallucinations. Can lead to mental illness.	*Class B drug:* possession without prescription and supply is an offence.
Cannabis	Creates a feeling of relaxation increasing sociability and heightens senses.	Causes cancers, affects short-term memory, ability to concentrate and may cause anxiety and paranoia or nausea.	*Class C drug:* illegal to grow, possess or supply.
Cocaine	Has a stimulant effect and gives users a sense of well-being, confidence and alertness.	Dependence, depression and fatigue. Habit can cost thousands of pounds a year and drug causes panic attacks and paranoia.	*Class A drug:* possession can lead to seven years in prison and supplying means a prison sentence of life.
Heroin	Causes a feeling of well being and pain release leading to relaxation and drowsiness	A highly addictive drug that leads users to take larger doses to feel normal again. High risk of infection through needles and damage to veins.	*Class A drug:* possession can lead to seven years in prison and supplying means a prison sentence of life.
Ketamine	Alters perception creating hallucinations.	Users can suffer heart failure and due to its pain killing qualities the user can suffer injury without knowing it.	*Class C drug:* illegal to possess and supply it.

Table 28.3 Summary of the effects of illegal drugs

athlete's performance. If an athlete is found guilty of having consumed these substances, they can expect a long ban, financial penalties and even the cancellation of their contract.

Gambling

As athletes are now being paid more, so they have started to find new ways of spending their money. Gambling is an activity that offers similar qualities as sport in that it provides a sense of excitement and feelings of success and failure. The media is quick to report the amount of money that footballers spend on card-schools and horse racing. Gambling can lead to addictive behaviour that can result in severe financial problems and a loss of focus from their sport.

Unruly behaviour

There is a certain level of conduct that is expected from athletes and which is demanded by their clubs or governing bodies. In the UK we have a media that is quick to report on any misdemeanours of well-paid athletes. Poor behaviour is again acted upon by imposing fines and bans.

Pressures on athletes

Athletes do not live their life on paper nor is the world organised around them. They have to live in an unpredictable world full of people who try to pull them one way or another. Pressures can be split up into the following categories:

- pressure from other people
- social pressures
- sport pressures
- financial pressures.

People

Everyone has a network of people they deal with on a weekly basis. Such a network may include the following:

- peers
- friends
- training partners
- family
- coaches
- advisors
- selectors

181

- teachers
- lecturers.

While most of these people will act to support the efforts of an athlete, nevertheless, the athlete may feel that these people are pulling them in different directions. For example, a friend may have the best intentions when they invite you out for a drink because they want to spend some time with you. However, once you are out they could persuade you to have a couple of drinks and stay out later than you intended. The result of this is that you get less sleep and do not feel so energised in the morning for training.

The people in your network will fall into one of two categories:

1 **Supporter:** whose actions will support your intended behaviour and positive lifestyle
2 **Saboteur:** whose actions will sabotage your attempts to behave in a set way

As an athlete, you need to choose to spend time with supporters and limit the damage caused by saboteurs.

Social pressures

Social pressures can be caused by the conflict in interests of the athlete's friends and social group and their own interests. You will want your friends to behave like yourself and do what you enjoy doing, and you will persuade them consciously and unconsciously in this way. The athlete is acting in a way that improves their chances of success as an athlete, but you may want them to behave in different ways and this could cause a clash or a conflict of interests. Consider a time when you knew that you had to study to get a piece of work in by a particular deadline and you had a friend who was persuading you to go out and spend the time in another way. This conflict is one of roles between being a student and being a friend, and can create pressure on you.

Training and competition

The demands of training and competition will have a physiological, psychological and social pressure. These demands should be foremost in the athlete's mind and be the central issue when they make decisions about how to spend their time and, in particular, their leisure time.

Financial

At some point in our lives everyone will feel financial pressure as it is fundamental to our survival as human beings and being able to pay for food, drink, shelter and clothing (the most basic human needs). Spending money for leisure will be what is left over after all the essentials have been paid for and money has been put aside for savings, paying taxes and investments.

Key learning points 1

An athlete's life can be split up into:

- **Work:** activities done as employment to make money
- **Survival activities:** activities performed to maintain life and health
- **Leisure:** activities freely chosen for pleasure, rest and relaxation

An athlete does not get fit by training, but by resting

During leisure time an athlete will need to perform three activities:

- rest
- relaxation
- eating

Leisure activities can be very damaging to the athlete in terms of their health and their performance. These would include:

- alcohol
- smoking
- drugs
- gambling
- unruly behaviour

Pressures on athletes can be split up into four categories:
- pressure from other people
- social pressures
- sport pressures
- financial pressures

Q Quick quiz 1   ⏱ 10 minutes

1 Fill in the blank spaces by choosing from the words that follow this paragraph.

It is important for an athlete to _____, _____ and _____ during their leisure time and avoid inappropriate activities such as _____, drinking _____ and taking _____. It is acceptable for a male to consume _____ of alcohol and a female to consume _____ spread over one _____. Most banned drugs should be avoided because they are _____ and have harmful _____ on your performance.

- drugs
- rest
- effects
- 21 units
- 14 units
- week
- smoking
- eat
- Alcohol
- illegal
- relax

Student activity 28.1   ⏱ 60 minutes   P1   M1   D1

Use the following table to show your knowledge of how lifestyle factors can affect an athlete:

Lifestyle factor	Describe how these factors can affect an athlete	Explain how these factors can affect an athlete	Analyse how these factors can affect an athlete
Rest/relaxation			
Drinking alcohol			
Smoking			
Taking drugs			
Gambling			

183

28.3 Appropriate behaviour for an athlete

Behaviour by athletes is an area of constant coverage by the media. Most of the time the bad behaviour of athletes is focused on rather than the positive aspects.

Behaviour is analysed in a range of situations:

- During competition and performances
- During the training periods
- In social situations away from the sporting environment

What is acceptable behaviour?

All athletes and other professions will have a code of conduct which they are expected to abide by and will include at least the following:

- Adherence to the rules of the sport
- Respecting peers and other athletes
- Wearing clothing appropriate to the situation
- Abiding by the code of ethical practice
- Accepting personal responsibility for one's actions.

Why is the behaviour of athletes so important?

There are many reasons why athletes' behaviour is important.

- **They are role models for future generations:** whether athletes like it or not they are role models who are copied by millions of young people. We can clearly see that people learn by copying the behaviour of people they respect whether this behaviour is seen as being positive or negative.
- **They are ambassadors for their sport:** this means that the way that athletes behave will influence the public's perception of the sport and how they feel about it. An ambassador is someone who will present a positive image of what they represent.
- **Their behaviour can enhance the status of their sport:** again, how athletes within a certain sport behave will colour the perception people have of that sport. For example, during the 1990s the poor behaviour of certain footballers off the field gave the sport a bad name. More recently the sports of cycling and athletics have become damaged due to revelations of widespread use of performance enhancing drugs.
- **They can stimulate interest in the sport:** and, as a result, increase participation rates among the general public.

Coping and management strategies

How can an athlete deal with these pressures? The athlete must make sure that they have resources which will help them to deal with the pressures they face.

Fig 28.1 Coping & management stategies

Resources can come in many forms. They may be any of the following:

- Support network of supporters, e.g. coach or advisor
- Clear goals and strategy of how to achieve their goals
- Use of role models, e.g. people who have achieved their goal and the means by which they achieved that goal
- Use of diaries or training logs to accurately track progress
- Development of psychological skills to influence their own behaviour
- Development of your own personal qualities

Mentoring and coaching

A mentor is a person that you trust who has experience of what you are currently experiencing and is able to offer you guidance and advice. The term 'coach' initially occurred in sport and is now applied to a range of situations such as business coaching or career coaching. A coach makes you conscious of where you are currently, where you want to go and how to get there. The athlete will need a mentor or coach to help them work towards their goals and decide upon the best path to take. Coaching is a fast growing profession and the athlete and coach can work together to support any changes that need to be made in the athlete's lifestyle. A coach can help an athlete get an understanding their life and their behaviour and the outcomes they achieve. If they are happy with their outcomes they can continue these, and if they are not happy they can change them. If you wanted to examine a house you would need to stand well back from it to get a good view of the overall picture, rather than stand with your nose pressed up against the front door. Often an individual can be too close to his or her own life and, as a result, be unable to see the overall picture. A coach can help that person to stand back from their life and get a better view of the bigger picture, so that they can see for themselves what needs to be changed and what should be left alone. This is the role of coaching and it usually occurs in a one-to-one situation or it may occur as group activity if the group as a whole needs direction.

Routines and lifestyle

Human beings perform the daily activities in their lives in the form of routines or unconscious strategies. The way that we get up in the morning, get washed, prepare our breakfast and then get to work or college is done in much the same manner every day. Have you noticed that it usually the same people who are on time for college and the same ones who are late? This is because they are each using their own routine in the morning, one of which is successful and one of which is unsuccessful. If they had a different routine then they would get a different result. For example, taking an earlier bus would increase their chances of getting to college on time. Managing our lives effectively means developing effective routines that produce a positive outcome. Coaching can help athletes to change their routines and, as a result, their lifestyle for the good.

Behaviour in certain situations

Athletes may find themselves in some of the following situations:

- on the sports field
- off the sports field
- dealing with the media
- dealing with the general public
- dealing with sport-related people.

The media would include people such as journalists, interviewers, reporters and commentators. The general public would include fans and supporters (both supportive and hostile). Sport-related people would include agents, sponsors, colleagues, managers and coaches.

Key learning points 2

Pressures can be split up into four categories:
- pressure from other people
- social pressures
- sport pressures
- financial pressures.

Reasons why athletes' behaviour is important include:
- They are role models for future generations
- The are ambassadors for their sport
- Their behaviour can enhance the status of their sport
- They can stimulate interest in the sport and increase participation rates

Acceptable behaviour for an athlete includes:
- Adherence to the rules of the sport
- Respecting peers and other athletes
- Wearing clothing appropriate to the situation
- Abiding by the code of ethical practice
- Accepting personal responsibility for one's actions.

Q Quick quiz 2

1 List four reasons why athletes' behaviour is important.
2 Describe four resources an athlete may have to support them.

Student activity 28.3   45 minutes   P2   P3   M2   D2

Prepare a poster presentation that illustrates the importance of appropriate behaviour for the athlete. To achieve P2 you need to *describe*, for M2 *explain* and for D2 you need to *justify*, the importance of appropriate behaviour.

Add to the poster a description of strategies that can be used by athletes to deal with three different situations that could influence their behaviour.

28.4 Communicating effectively with the media and significant others

To develop a relationship with anyone we must be able to communicate accurately and clearly. This seems fairly obvious until we understand that the process of communication is different for each individual. For example, the words we use may have different meanings for each person, as do the gestures we use and the body language we employ.

Communication is important for the following reasons:

- It is essential to the development of any relationship
- It is needed to convey our thoughts and knowledge to other people
- It is the basis of developing understanding and rapport.

Communication is done in two ways:

- verbally
- non-verbally

See Table 28.4 for examples of verbal and non-verbal communication.

Table 28.3 Examples of verbal & non-verbal forms of communication

Verbal	Non-verbal
talking	body language
giving commands	gestures
asking questions	listening.
explaining.	

Verbal communication

Communication is a two-way process and in any situation we will have three components: a sender, a receiver and a message. The sender puts their thoughts and feelings into words and the receiver will interpret these words to find the meaning of the message. Communication is difficult because everyone gives different meaning to words and interprets messages in different ways.

Active listening skills

It is easy to pretend that you are listening, but much more difficult to *really* listen. To show that you are listening you can use the following skills:

- Show you are giving undivided attention by maintaining eye contact. Look away occasionally and do not stare.
- If you lean forward slightly it will encourage the other person to talk, as will smiling occasionally and nodding your head.
- Ask open-ended questions to help them to talk.
- If you are unclear about what is being said, then check your understanding by asking the speaker 'Can I check that I understand you? I think that you mean…'
- Summarise occasionally to show you understand as this will help you to keep listening.

How not to listen.

All of the following will show you are not listening and do not care:

- Show boredom or impatience.
- Being condescending or patronising.
- Passing judgement or laughing inappropriately.
- Talking too much.
- Using distracting body gestures or fiddling with paper or pens.
- Interrupting.
- Not giving a person time to answer a question.

Asking questions

Questions broadly come in two types: **open** and **closed.**

An **open** question is used to find out more information and will begin with words such as:

- Why…?
- How…?
- Where.?
- What…?
- When.?

Closed questions are used to make a situation clear and can be answered with s simple 'yes' or 'no'.

Non-verbal communication

Body language is an important component of communication and helps to develop a relationship. People tend to like people who are like them and you will notice that people who get on will copy each other's body position. This is a good rule to follow. If you copy a person's body position in terms of whether they are sitting forward, back or to the side, also, give them as much eye contact as they give you and if they smile a lot, then you should smile a lot too. Gestures are important to people as well. If they use gestures then use the same gestures back to them. They will not notice you are doing this and it will help to build rapport.

Writing clearly and effectively

Reading efficiently is a great skill to have as it will save us a great deal of time. We read for different purposes, for example, we may read a novel from cover to cover and let the story take us where it is going. Or we read to pick out relevant detail and information.

There are different reading styles:

Skimming involves going through a text at two or three times normal reading speed and focusing on the introduction, conclusion, first line and first paragraph. This type of reading gives us a flavour of the text to see if we want to buy it or read it in full.

Scanning is done when you are looking for information such as an address or a topic from a glossary or index.

Searching is done when you know what you are looking for. It involves you picking out key words or phrases to find the relevant information.

A guide to reading

1   Ask yourself what is the aim of your reading.
2   Ask what exactly you are finding out.
3   Using skimming, scanning or searching.
4   Be methodical and stop reading a text once you have found what you need.
5   Prioritise information and decide what is relevant and what is irrelevant.
6   Be flexible and put a text down as soon as you know it is not relevant.
7   Do not get side tracked by other interesting information.
8   Make sure your environment is set up comfortably and with good lighting.

A guide to writing clearly and effectively

- Know who your target group are and use the appropriate language.
- Check spelling and punctuation as mistakes are embarrassing and damage your image.
- Keep paragraphs and sentences short as long blocks of words are hard to follow.
- Start with the main points and then break down into the smaller detail. Imagine a pyramid and start at the top not the bottom.
- Make sure you have an introduction, main body and conclusion. This means you will tell your reader what you are going to say; then you will say and finally you will tell them what you have told them!

Preparation for communication

Before you address a group of people or are put in a situation where you will be asked questions, it is necessary to make preparations. This can be done by asking the following questions:

- What is the purpose of this situation?
- What content will be covered?
- What is the level of the audience in terms of age, experience and knowledge?
- What are their expectations?
- What information do I need over and above what I already have?
- What research do I need to conduct?

Once all these questions have been answered you can prepare your material and develop a script or prompt sheet (whichever is most appropriate). Once the communication has been prepared, you may want to rehearse the material in full or have a peer ask you the questions so you can practise responding to these.

Personal delivery

When communicating with another person or group of people you will need to adapt your communication to the other person. Communication is your responsibility and the response you receive will depend upon the quality of your communication.

Body language

Although we present most of our body language without consciously thinking about this, we can be aware of what how we look says about us. To present a confident image when seated, you should sit in an upright posture with your shoulders pulled back in a relaxed way. Your facial expressions should be relaxed and your hands should be held in front of you. Crossing your arms or legs suggests that you feel insecure or uncomfortable; as does fidgeting and moving around. When standing up, you should hold an upright and relaxed posture with your shoulders pulled back.

Language and speech

While most of our body is presented without our conscious knowledge, the words we choose represent the thoughts and feelings we are experiencing. We choose them to describe the pictures in our heads. As a result they form our representation of reality and this will be individual to each person. When choosing words with which to communicate we need to consider how the other person communicates. As a person speaks they will employ differences in the following methods of delivery:

- technicality or simplicity of vocabulary
- pace or speed
- tonality (high, medium or deep)
- loudness.

When communicating with one person you can match the above criteria and attempt to use similar words to the ones they use. You will also need to be clear in your explanations and give people time to assimilate and understand the words and information you are communicating.

Appearance:

Attention to appearance is never wasted and it will say something about what type of person you are or conveying that you are. You will always need to portray an image of excellence in everything that you do. It is not by chance that the teams who play in the FA Cup Final each year take time to choose their suits and have them specially made. They understand that if they look the part they will feel the part as well and this puts them in a positive frame of mind. We need to consider this too, that if we take time over our appearance we will feel better about ourselves and this will be conveyed in our body language and facial expressions. Also, consider that our appearance must be adapted to the situation in which we find ourselves.

Communicating effectively with significant others

An athlete does not operate alone and must be prepared to communicate with a network of people. These will include their coaching staff, employers, agent, manager, sponsors, fellow athletes and media professionals.

These different groups of people will require different things from the athlete and communication must be done in different ways.

Media

The term 'media' relates to all groups of people responsible for reporting action and events to the general public. Now, all events can be distorted to meet the ends of any group of people as all events can be looked at more than one way. Likewise, the words an individual uses can be interpreted in many different ways.

Look at two or three reports of an event in a newspaper and see if you can show how different journalists have changed the events. Ask yourself why has this been done and in whose interests. It may be best to compare a tabloid newspaper to a broadsheet; for example, *The Sun* against *The Daily Telegraph*.

The media comes in many different forms. Currently sporting events are reported through these different media:

- Newspapers
- Television
- Radio
- Internet
- Magazines
- Teletext services

Newspapers can be seen to fall into two categories:

1 Tabloids
2 Broadsheets

Tabloids are the 'small' papers which have the highest sales figures. Tabloids would include *The Sun*, *The Mirror*, *The Daily Mail* and *The Daily Express*. These newspapers are clearly aimed at certain groups; for example, *The Sun* aims at men who like football, while *The Daily Mail* aims at women. You can see this by looking at the content of each newspaper and guessing which person each article is aimed at.

Broadsheets are newspapers that tend to be printed on broad sheets of newspaper, which are larger than the pages of a tabloid. However, recently both *The Times* and *The Independent* can be found in a smaller tabloid form. These newspapers are aimed at people who want to know more than just the facts of a story or a sports event. They will include analysis of events. The main difference in the way they report sports is that they will focus on a large range of sports rather than the most popular three or four sports on which the tabloids focus.

Evaluation of communication

'The meaning of communication is the response you receive'

When you evaluate communication you need to ask the simple question: 'Did I get the response I wanted?' If you are able to answer 'yes', then the feedback you give yourself is to carry on in that way; if the answer is 'no', then the feedback you give yourself is to change the way you communicate.

Gathering feedback

You can only improve if you gather feedback and then modify your behaviour based on the feedback you receive. You are looking to find out your strengths and weaknesses and then address these weaknesses (your strengths will always remain your strengths). You can gather feedback in the following ways:

Developing sensory acuity: this simply means using the senses of vision and hearing to see the response you receive in terms of the body language and facial expressions of the people with whom you communicate. Listen to what they have to say and process this information. Most people are able to sense an atmosphere when boredom, tension or satisfaction develops; if a negative atmosphere develops, make it your responsibility to change the mood.

Questioning peers and tutors: using open questions can elicit some excellent information from supportive others who have observed the communication.

Video analysis: by producing a video of yourself you can uncover information which you were not consciously aware of previously. Our body language is presented in unedited form and signs of tension or nervousness may be observed which you were unaware of at the time. Also, through video analysis you can observe facial expressions and gestures you were unaware of and decide whether they are beneficial to the image you are portraying.

Once you have evaluated the effectiveness of your communication you can prepare an action plan which will identify the following:

- Areas of strengths and weakness
- Appropriate modifications to be made if necessary

Key learning points 3

Communication is important for the following reasons:
- It is essential to the development of any relationship
- It is needed to convey our thoughts and knowledge to other people
- It is the basis of developing understanding and rapport

Communication is done in two ways:
- Verbally
- Non verbally

Verbal communication includes:
- talking
- giving commands
- asking questions
- explaining.

Non-verbal communication includes:
- body language
- gestures
- listening

Different forms of the media:
- newspapers
- television
- radio
- internet
- magazines
- teletext services

28.5 Career plan

Goal setting

Clearly, for success as an athlete you must have a clear plan of where you are going and how you are going to get there. There is a detailed discussion of how to set goals in **Unit 17:** *Psychology for Sports Performance* (see pages 155–157) and the principles that can be applied to any aspect of life.

Key term

Goal: what an individual is trying to achieve; an objective or aim of an action.

Why is it important to set goals?

- **Persistence:** goals can help us as individuals to persist at a task over time and keep sight of what we are trying to achieve.
- **Attention:** goals can help us to keep our attention directed to the important aspects of what we are trying to achieve.
- **Effort:** goals can help us to mobilise and direct the intensity of our effort towards a certain task or outcome.
- **Strategies:** goals may help us to develop new strategies to help us achieve our desired outcomes.

Student activity 28.5   ⏱ 30 minutes   P4   P5

Imagine that you are advising a top level performer in a sport of your choice. Prepare a briefing document that covers the following points:

- Describe the factors to be considered when giving two types of media interview

- Describe the factors to be considered when communicating with significant others

Types of goals

Goal-setting can be used for motivating ourselves in life as well as for sport. The main categories of goals are:

- **Personal:** which relate to our personal life, such as family life, social life, sporting aims, health and fitness and things that give us pleasure.
- **Business/Career/Economic:** which relate to the development of our careers and financial rewards.
- **Self-improvement:** relate to personal growth and development.

Goals can also be split into **short-term** and **long-term** goals:

- **Short-term:** set over a period of time that might be between one day and one month. These might relate to what you aim to achieve in one session, but will usually relate to a period of around one month.
- **Medium-term:** fill the gap between short term and long term goals and would cover a period of between one to six months.

- **Long-term:** goals that relate to periods that might run from six months to several years. Some people set 'lifetime goals', which cannot be assessed until retirement. Most long-term goals are set for achievement over the course of either a year or a competitive season.

It is important to set both long-term, medium-term and short-term goals. The fulfilment of short-term goals will contribute to the achievement of long-term goals.

For a full examination of how to set goals look at **Unit 17:** *Psychology for Sports Performance.*

Planning an athletic career

Once you as an athlete have set your goals, you have taken steps to plan your career. Within goal-setting you have placed your key dates for the reviews at least four times in the year; you will also have looked at your current expectations of success and where you expect to be at certain points of the season.

Due to the uncertain nature of an athlete's life you need to be aware that you may need to adapt or

191

alter the goal-setting. Goals are often achieved before their time once we have set our course on something. Transitions will also have to be considered, such as:

- change of coach
- change of club
- attaining national or international standard.

Once these changes happen it is matter of re-aligning goals to fit in with your new current position.

It is of key importance that you will have put in place measures to ensure that, should you become ill or injured, you have professionals by whom you can be treated immediately. As an athlete you should also make contingency plans in case of an injury or accident that threatens your career. This is why it is important to have plans for a second career.

Planning a second career

As an athlete you are in a special situation because you have to focus on your primary career as an athlete, but also keep an eye on the future. The life of an athlete is unpredictable as it may flourish or end at any time so you have to be prepared for the future.

While as an athlete you will have a network of people to ensure your success and your goals so you know where you are headed, you must also make plans for things that may go wrong. These are called *contingency plans* and the following situations need to be considered:

- illness
- injury
- accidents
- falling out with your coach
- falling out with your club.

Whether you like it or not you need to prepare for a second career of your choice. This can be seen in many colleges where provision is made for various football schemes from professional and semi-professional clubs. Professional clubs who achieve academy status are contracted to provide twelve hours education a week to their scholars; the PACE scheme is run for non-league football clubs to combine their training with their education. All full-time athletes are encouraged to study for degrees and diplomas, and special arrangements are made for this provision.

There is a full range of careers available to athletes and with the introduction of internet-based courses a wide range of courses is available. However, most people choose to study sport-related courses due to their interests and the easy availability of information for research and case studies.

What careers may you as an athlete choose?

Sports Coach

As a practitioner of a sport at a high level it is a natural progression to want to share this knowledge. There are opportunities to coach at all levels of the sport and to all age groups. Each governing body will have a scheme to enable you to become qualified to coach at different levels.

Sports Teacher

Teaching or lecturing can be done at schools, colleges or universities and you will notice that all sports teachers have a keen practical interest in their subject. Teaching may be in Physical Education (PE) or diplomas and degrees in Sport or Sport Science. As a teacher you will need to develop your academic knowledge as well and should hold a degree in Sport or Teaching, as well as a Certificate in Education. Full-time study will take four years, at least.

Journalist

Many former sportspeople work in broadcasting as sports journalists or write for newspapers and magazines. With the growth of online publications and specialist websites there are new areas where writing can be published. A journalist usually has a degree and belongs to professional body such as the NUJ.

Sports Development Officer

Local authorities employ sports development officers to increase participation in their local area. They usually target certain groups of people for specific reasons. There is often a large choice of schemes for children in particular to help them become interested in sport. A local authority will be looking for people with sports qualifications and, in particular, with a range of coaching awards.

Physiotherapist

General and sports physiotherapy is a popular choice for athletes to consider due to its practical nature. Physiotherapists need a degree and, while there are many universities offering degrees, competition for places is fierce. Because of this, you should work towards the highest grades to gain a place. The work itself is interesting and varied and often takes place in hospitals or at sports venues.

Sports Scientist

A sports scientist works to improve the performance of any athlete and this may include physiology, biomechanics, nutrition and psychology. Fitness testing and evaluation is a key part of this work to highlight areas of weakness. Sports scientists will need a degree in their subject and are often researching towards a higher degree.

Strengths	Weaknesses
A good relaxed swing	Not accurate with driving clubs
Excellent body positioning in relation to the ball	Putting is inconsistent
A low-risk safety-first approach	Poor technique in short iron game (head up too early)
Opportunities	**Threats**
Short game practice has been improved recently	Can be prone to getting annoyed easily and letting it
Has learnt how to mentally rehearse	spoil their game
Opponent has no knowledge of the course	Environment – windy day
	Opponent is a better player

Fig 28.1 Swot analysis grid

Self- and Needs analysis through SWOT

Once you have identified what your goals as an athlete are and the second career path you may wish to take, then you can start to look at what you need to do to succeed in that direction. This can be done by using a SWOT analysis. SWOT stands for:

Strengths
Weaknesses
Opportunities
Threats

You should look at the skills you currently possess and those that you may need. Skills can broadly fall into three categories:

● Technical skills (what techniques that can be performed)
● Practical skills (coaching, teaching and instructing)
● Key skills (IT, working in teams and communication)
● Basic skills (literacy and numeracy)

You may come up with the following audit of your skills:

Strengths
● Knowledge of techniques within the sport
● Experience of coaching children
● High level of literacy achieved

Weaknesses
● Teaching in a formal situation to a large group
● Presenting information to a group of people
● Poor IT skills
● Poor financial management

Opportunities
● Access to large groups of young athletes who need teaching and coaching
● Access to education as part of their training scheme

● Time available for learning and gaining experience

Threats
● Competition from other people
● Maintaining their health and fitness

Key learning points 4

A goal is what an individual is trying to achieve; an object or aim of an action.

Goals are set for the following reasons:
● Persistence
● Attention
● Effort
● Strategies

Types of goals include:
● Personal goals
● Business/career/economic goals
● Self-improvement goals

Goals can be split into **short-term** and **long-term** goals:
● Short-term goals: 1 day to 1 month
● Medium-term goals: 1 month to 6 months
● Long-term goals: 6 months to lifetime goals

An athlete needs to plan a second career in case of the following:
● Illness
● Injury
● Accidents

Possible careers could include:
● coaching
● teaching
● journalism
● sports development
● physiotherapy
● sport scientist

193

Q Quick quiz 3

1 Match the following careers to their appropriate descriptions

Careers	Description
Sports coach	Employed by a local authority to increase sports participation
Sports teacher	Due to their performances in sport at high levels they are well equipped to pass their knowledge on to other performers
Sports development officer	They work to improve the performance of athletes in all sports
Sport scientist	Because they have a keen interest in sport they work at schools or colleges to pass this information on

Student activity 28.6 60 minutes P6 M3

Using the following template complete a career plan for yourself or an athlete of your choice

Name: Chosen sport:
Athletic career goals Short term: Long term:
Needs analysis Technical skills Practical skills
Second career goals Short term: Long term: Qualifications needed Experience needed

References

(2001). *Sports*. London: (2000). Harlow: Barbara Woods (1998). *ort*. London:

Further reading

Bell, B. (2009). *Sport Studies*. London: Learning Matters.

Dixon, B. (2007). *Careers uncovered: Sport, Exercise and Fitness*. Trotman.

Mottram, D.R. (2005). Drugs in Sport. London: Routledge.

Useful websites

http://www.bbc.co.uk/ethics/sport/debate/types_1.shtml

General information on performance-enhancing drugs in sport

http://www.uksport.gov.uk/pages/living-as-an-athlete/

Extensive range of articles to help athletes make the most of their lifestyle; topics range from financial advice to time management

5: Sports coaching

5.1 Introduction

Sports coaches are vital to the success of a number of programmes across a range of sports. They are at the heart of participation and performer development. Whether the coach of an after-school club or a top international coach with support staff, coaches are at the very centre of the development of sport.

This unit will assist those starting on the coaching ladder to learn the rules and responsibilities, the qualities and characteristics of sports coaches. It will provide an understanding of the role of the coach in promoting a positive coaching experience.

By the end of this unit you should:

- know the roles, responsibilities and skills of sports coaches
- know the techniques used by coaches to improve the performance of athletes
- be able to plan a sports coaching session
- be able to deliver and review a sports coaching session.

Assessment and grading criteria

To achieve a PASS grade the evidence must show that the learner is able to:	To achieve a MERIT grade the evidence must show that, in addition to the pass criteria, the learner is able to:	To achieve a DISTINCTION grade the evidence must show that, in addition to the pass and merit criteria, the learner is able to:
P1 describe four roles and four responsibilities of sports coaches, using examples of coaches from different sports	**M1** explain four roles and four responsibilities of sports coaches, using examples of coaches from different sports	**D1** compare and contrast the roles, responsibilities and skills of successful coaches from different sports
P2 describe three skills common to successful sports coaches, using examples of coaches from different sports	**M2** explain three skills common to successful sports coaches, using examples of coaches from different sports	
P3 describe three different techniques that are used by coaches to improve the performance of athletes	**M3** explain three different techniques that are used by coaches to improve the performance of athletes	**D2** evaluate three different techniques that are used by coaches to improve the performance of athletes
P4 plan a sports coaching session		
P5 deliver a sports coaching session, with tutor support	**M4** independently deliver a sports coaching session	
P6 carry out a review of the planning and delivery of a sports coaching session, identifying strengths and areas for improvement.	**M5** evaluate the planning and delivery of a sports coaching session, suggesting how improvements could be reached in the identified areas.	**D3** justify suggestions made in relation to the development plan.

5.2 The roles, responsibilities and skills of sports coaches

P1 **P2** **M1** **M2** **D1**

Effective coaches tend to find new ways of improving existing practices or theories. Some adapt the way in which they practise, others deal with how to play specific strategies in differing situations. Other coaches integrate new developments or technologies to improve performance. Consider the trampoline coach who adapts a harness that supports a performer for use while learning somersaults, allowing them the freedom to twist at the same time and add to the range of skills and techniques achievable. Performers who work with innovative coaches speak about how they are never bored and always trying something new.

Trainer, educator and instructor

The difference between a teacher, educator and instructor is hard to discern. Teaching implies a

Fig 5.1 A tennis coach and player

transfer of learning through demonstration, modelling or instruction. Coaches can also teach emotional and social skills. Young performers in particular can be encouraged to increase their social awareness, learn to cope with losing and winning, and develop self-confidence. Good coaches will be aware that people learn in different ways. They then adapt and use a range of techniques to ensure that learning takes place.

In some cultures trainers and coaches are taken to mean the same thing. Since all sport requires some kind of physical exertion, it is important that these physical demands are recognised and that allowance for these demands is incorporated into coaching programmes.

A sound knowledge of anatomy, physiology and fitness theory is essential for coaches. In the role of trainer, you might expect to design and implement training programmes for your performers.

Motivator

Motivation can come merely by providing a stable environment in which to learn, in a positive and safe atmosphere. Performers who constantly find negativity are certain at some point to become despondent and suffer a reduction in self-confidence and improvement.

Evidence suggests that performers who receive praise and positive feedback are likely to get more from their performances. When providing feedback to performers you would employ the following technique: KISS, KICK, KISS.

This technique would be applied in providing feedback such as in skill learning. When communicating with performers, the emphasis with this technique would be to start your feedback with a positive comment. There is nearly always something that is positive in any performance. Second, a corrective comment can be presented in as positive a manner as possible. Finally, leave the interaction with a positive comment and possibly an action plan. Consider a tennis player struggling to make a particular shot:

KISS – 'Good positioning prior to the shot and you watched the ball well.'
KICK – 'You should consider how you back-lift the racket; you could prepare your grip earlier.'
KISS – 'If you practise these changes you will almost certainly improve.'

Role model

In almost every coaching situation players will look mostly, if not entirely, to the coach as their source of inspiration and knowledge, never more so than when working with children. Children often imitate the behaviour and manner of their coach. For this reason it is vital that coaching is safe and responsible, and that behaviour is considered good practice.

The coach can influence player development in a number of ways.

- Social – sport offers a code of acceptable social behaviour, teamwork, citizenship, cooperation and fair play.
- Personal – players can be encouraged to learn life skills, promote their self-esteem, manage personal matters like careers or socialising, and develop a value system including good manners, politeness and self-discipline.
- Psychological – coaches can create environments that help performers control emotions and develop their own identities. Confidence, mental toughness, visualisation and a positive outlook on life can be developed or improved.
- Health – in taking care to design coaching or training sessions to include sufficient physical exercise, good health and healthy habits can be established and maintained.

The responsibilities of a coach

Many expectations are put upon a coach. Some of these responsibilities are clear-cut, others less so. Coaching and playing sport should always be enjoyable, and to that end coaches should not be overburdened by expectation. Common sense and a good knowledge of safety and ethics will provide the basis of a responsible coach.

As coaching is now considered a profession, so coaches will increasingly be measured and assessed, whether paid or voluntary, and increasingly expected to work to a code of practice.

A coaching code of practice

So that performers achieve their potential, coaches should:

- remain within the bounds of adopted codes of practice
- maintain safe and secure coaching environments
- make best use of all facilities and resources
- establish good working relationships with all involved
- control the behaviour of participants where possible.

Many sports governing bodies and sports coach UK have established a code of conduct for sports coaches, which includes the following sections.

- Rights – coaches must respect and champion the right of every individual to participate in sport. Coaches should ensure that everyone has an equal opportunity to participate, regardless of age, gender, race, ability, faith or sexual orientation.
  For example, you would organise sessions in a place that has childcare arrangements, and you would be sensitive to religious festivals of all denominations and make allowances for the absences of performers on notable religious dates.
  Coaches also have a responsibility to ensure that no discriminating behaviour occurs during their working sessions. Every member of the coaching group should have the right to feel part of the group, free from prejudice.
- Relationships – coaches need to establish relationships with performers that are based on openness, trust and mutual respect. This is not just about effective communication. Good coaches understand how their performers think and what is best for them. Performers will also learn better in an atmosphere of trust and respect for their coach. Involving performers in the decision-making process is an excellent way of establishing an effective relationship with a performer. When deciding what is best for a performer or group of performers, an example could be a situation where the coach presents the performers with information about their performance, such as a particular phase of play in a tennis competition. Having supplied that information and perhaps offering their opinion, the coach could present the performer with a range of options that relates to the best course of action – how to improve on the last period of play. The performer who has an input into the decision in this process will come to appreciate the knowledge and analytical skills of the coach and over time their relationship will develop based on trust and respect.

Coaches should also anticipate and deal with potential relationship problems such as:

- dealing with parents
- dropping players from squads
- assuming control as a carer.

Personal standards

Coaches should demonstrate model behaviour at all times. Their influence should always be positive and would usually mean working to a code.

Professional conduct

It is not enough to achieve a coaching qualification. Coaches should have a commitment to continual and ongoing learning or professional development. This could include:

- attaining higher-grade qualifications
- attending workshops and seminars
- being aware of changes to their sport.

Skills of sports coaches

The essential skills required of a sports coach are illustrated in Figure 5.2.

Fig 5.2 Skills of sports coaches

Management

The key ways to demonstrate good leadership in coaching are:

- checking that participants are well prepared and organised
- checking that participants and appropriate others are well deployed
- safe management and coordination of equipment and facilities
- safe and well-delivered sessions
- maintaining support and guidance to participants
- establishing and maintaining effective communication with appropriate others within the coaching environment.

It is important that coaches motivate participants by ensuring that they remain interested and challenged. Coaches will get the best from their sport if they are self-motivated and working in an atmosphere that allows them to:

- enjoy their coaching sessions

- share their experiences with others and socialise with peers and friends
- compete in a safe and non-threatening environment
- achieve negotiated goals
- remain fit and healthy
- achieve success or reward
- please others and receive praise
- create a positive self-image.

Organisation

Planning and organisation are critical to the success of coaching. When planning a session there is much to consider, but the main points are to:

- have identified a set of goals for the session
- have an awareness of the resources available
- have enough information about the participants
- have developed a plan that allows participants to achieve.

During a session coaches need to be constantly making judgements about the following:

- Is the practice working?
- What could be adapted and how?
- Are the facilities being used to full advantage?

Many coaches now keep records, usually in the form of logbooks. Many coaching qualifications require candidates to complete logbooks as part of the formal assessment process. Few coaches have the privilege of just turning up, coaching and going home. Often coaches are also involved in booking facilities, arranging equipment or contacting participants,

Role	Responsibilities
Coach	Team selection
Assistant coach	Warm-up, cool-down & general preparation
Player 1	Calling players to arrange meeting place for away fixtures
Player 2	Washing & looking after kit
Player 3	Contacting officials prior to games
Player 4	Maintaining website & making travel arrangements
Player 5	All communication with league
Player 6	Introducing new players & schools liaison
Player 7	Seeking sponsorship

Table 5.1 Responsibilities and roles within a senior women's volleyball team

which involves a great deal of organisation. Some coaches delegate these responsibilities as in the example for a senior women's volleyball team shown in Table 5.1.

In some clubs such as this, some or all of these responsibilities and others are undertaken by appropriate others, usually with the coach in control of exactly who is capable and most responsible for the task.

Communication

Perhaps the single most valuable skill is the ability to convey your thoughts and ideas in such a way as to be easily understood. It is not enough to just present your opinions: you must be able to send effective messages – these are mostly non-verbal signals. Consider the body language of a coach in a variety of scenarios. The main feedback a performer receives in almost every sport is non-verbal body language from their coaches.

Talking too much can lead to confusion. The pace, tone and volume of the spoken word will all have a marked effect on participants. The coach who spends most of their time shouting abuse will quickly lose the respect of their participants and will be less likely to be successful.

You must also be able to receive incoming messages. This particular skill is concerned with understanding and interpreting the signs and signals of other players, officials, etc. You must also listen to opinions from players regarding tactical decisions, drills in practice or perhaps even concerning opponents.

You must also be able to check message reception. Good coaches will question their players and check their understanding. If an instruction is not understood, this is the fault of either the performer lacking concentration or the coach in the quality of the message. One way of ensuring understanding is to ask players to explain a concept in their own words.

Teaching

One of the key processes of teaching is an understanding of how people learn. Drills and practices need to be designed in a way that allows participants to progress at an appropriate pace. As a rule of good practice, the following model is useful when teaching skills:

- introduce and explain the technique
- demonstrate the technique
- practise (allow performers to experience the technique)
- observe and analyse the participants
- identify and correct errors.

It is vital that learning is achieved in simple, short and logical steps. The most valuable knowledge that a coach can gain is through learned experience, judging for themselves and from their performers what is effective and what is not.

Coaching is a continuous process which lends itself to self-reflection and evaluation. Since the knowledge and skills required to be a successful coach are constantly changing and developing with the sport, it is unlikely that coaches will ever reach the point where they will know all that there is to know!

Key learning points 1

- The roles of a sports coach are many and varied, and include teacher, trainer, motivator and instructor.
- Coaches can have a direct influence on the lives of their performers in terms of their social, psychological, personal and health development.
- Most coaches in the UK work to a code of conduct or practice that is established to set the parameters of acceptable behaviour and effective coaching.
- The essential skills toolkit of a successful sports coach includes:
  - management
  - communication
  - teaching
  - organisation.

Quick quiz 1

Fill in the blanks in the following paragraph.

Coaches will perform many different roles as they work with their performers. They will act as a _____ as they demonstrate and model skills. They will need to have a good knowledge base, including _____ and _____ . Coaches will need to pick out the good points so that performers remain motivated and also act as a _____ _____ so they influence performers in a positive way.

Student activity 5.1   ⏱ 60 minutes   P1   P2   M1   M2   D1

Roles and responsibilities of a sports coach

Part 1

Investigate the roles, responsibilities and skills of the sports coach by filling in the following table.

Role/Responsibility	Describe each of the roles/responsibilities, using examples of coaches from different sports	Describe each of the roles/responsibilities, using examples of coaches from different sports	Compare and contrast the roles, responsibilities and skills of successful coaches from different sports
Role 1: Trainer			
Role 2: Educator			
Role 3: Role model			
Role 4: Motivator			
Responsibility 1: Working within a code of practice			
Responsibility 2: Maintain a safe and secure environment			
Responsibility 3: Equal opportunities			
Responsibility 4: Professional conduct			

Part 2

Take three coaches of your choice:

(a) Describe how they use the skills of communication, organisation and analysis to improve the performance of athletes:

Coach	Communication	Organisation	Analysis
Coach 1:			
Coach 2:			
Coach 3:			

(b) To achieve a merit you need to explain these three techniques.

(c) To achieve a distinction you need to evaluate the effectiveness of each of the three techniques.

5.3 Techniques used by coaches to improve performance

Coaches in all sports have a number of techniques at their disposal that they can use to improve the performance of their athletes.

Coaching diaries/logbooks

Diaries come in different sizes, paper or electronic. They can be used to record personal thoughts, make appointments or log training sessions. Diaries can be useful in aiding self-reflection, planning and evaluation of coaching sessions.

Guidelines for getting the most from your diary are as follows:

- Complete the diary soon after the coaching session.
- Write down what happened in order.
- Focus on what went well first.
- Describe what needs improvement.
- Action plan to develop what needs to be improved.

The benefits of diaries are that they can show progress over a period of time and are usually honest and describe how you felt about a situation at that time.

Performance profiles

If a trampolinist is not performing a somersault correctly or is not coping with the physical demands of the sport, the coach or trainer can design a suitable exercise or coaching programme. But what if the trampolinist has trouble with their nerves before the start of the competition, or they have some kind of mental block that stops them from executing a skill?

Although not always obvious, the following psychological factors can affect sporting performance:

- confidence: belief in yourself and your abilities

- concentration: the ability to attend to relevant cues, not being distracted
- control: the extent to which you feel able to influence events
- commitment: the level to which you apply yourself
- re-focusing after errors: the ability to adjust to negative outcomes in a positive way
- enjoyment: the amount of fun that you can have.

To use a performance profile you would talk with the performer and ask them to tell you how they feel about their sport. Do they ever feel anxious, and if so, when? Do they understand the terms above and if so, how do they rate them?

In Table 5.2, a performer has been asked to rate out of ten the importance of each of the factors and then rate their own proficiency in that factor.

It seems that the performer's main emphasis for any intervention should be focused on the areas that they identify as a weakness, in this case re-focusing after errors and concentration.

> ### Key term
>
> **Intervention:** an interruption that brings about change (in sporting performance).

In the same way, coaches can adapt this approach and apply it to their own coaching (as in the example below).

Observation and analysis

It is possible to be observed and analysed by your team or club mates, your coach and yourself, particularly if you have access to a video of your performance.

Interviews

It is possible to get a great deal of information from an interview. You could ask a performer about what

Performance factors	Importance to performer	Self-assessment
Confidence	9	9
Commitment	10	10
Concentration	9	6
Control	9	8
Re-focusing after error	10	6
Enjoyment	7	9

Table 5.2 Factors and proficiency

Strengths	Weaknesses
A good relaxed swing	Not accurate with driving clubs
Excellent body positioning in relation to the ball	Putting is inconsistent
A low-risk safety-first approach	Poor technique in short iron game (head up too early)
Opportunities	**Threats**
Short game practice has improved in recent weeks	Can be prone to getting annoyed easily and letting it spoil their game
Has learned how to mentally rehearse	Environment – windy day
Opponent has no knowledge of the course	Opponent is a better player

Table 5.3 SWOT analysis of a golfer

they consider to be their strengths and weaknesses, or you could ask them about what tactics they might use against a particular opponent.

SWOT analysis

This is a subjective analysis of a performance or a performer's ability. Table 5.3 shows an example of a SWOT analysis carried out on a golfer.

Simulation or conditioned practice

This is about artificially creating a competition-like situation in a practice session, or a particular condition that may be likely to happen in a competitive situation. A basketball coach might consider the merits of initially removing defenders, or outnumbering them in a practice situation that is aimed at improving a particular attacking focus. Defenders

Coaching factors	Importance to coach	Self-assessment
Planning & preparation	9	9
Needs of participants considered	10	10
Technical progression & sequencing	9	6
Health & safety observed	9	8
Goals defined at start of session	10	6
Technically accurate instructions/demonstrations	7	9
Appropriate content & structure		
Variety of drills		
Monitored progress		
Skills related to game situation		
Errors identified & corrected		
Control & behaviour of group		
Time management		
De-brief & feedback to participants		
Checked player understanding		
Stopped & brought group together		
Evaluated against objectives set		
Made provisions for future planning		

Table 5.4 Assessment of factors for coaching

can be added when the techniques are well practised. Or, conversely, extra defenders could be added so that the attacking technique could be practised under greater pressure. Similarly, defenders in these practices could be asked to take one of three roles according to the conditions required by the coach:

- passive, offering little resistance other than presence
- active, playing under normal conditions, tempo, intensity
- pressure, playing with extra intensity.

Conditioned games are used when a coach wants to create a situation that is likely to happen in a game, such as practising defending free kicks in football. Or simply adding a condition that emphasises a teaching point, such as choosing a target area on a tennis court with a chalk circle or hoop where the player is expected to return the balls in a practice drill.

Video analysis

Video gives the person who watches it an objective record of a performance. The greatest benefit of video is the playback feature, including slow motion, which can be used to demonstrate skill execution, tactical efficiency or a more general generic performance evaluation.

Here are some guidelines on the use of video analysis in sport:

- Do not try to film your performers and coach them at the same time. Ask someone reliable to do the filming and brief them on what you want – follow the player or the ball, try to capture tactics or specific techniques, etc.
- Try to pick up all of the sound as it can provide useful feedback.
- Start the recording before the action and end it well after, judging players' body language before and after performance.
- Label and date the film immediately, to keep a record.

Notation

Notation is a way of collecting data and can be done by hand or with a computer. Hand notation is a system of recording detailed analysis of a sport and literally noting the data on a sheet of paper using a predefined set of symbols. Systems like this exist for many sports, such as tennis, archery and football.

The advantage of these systems is that they are inexpensive and, if completed by a skilful recorder, will produce quick information in real time, so that the coach or performer can have instant access to detailed information. The main disadvantages of this system are that it is open to human error, can be difficult to interpret and can be difficult in certain conditions such as bad weather.

On the next page there is an example of a match analysis sheet for a team sport. This could be filled in by the performer, a peer or a neutral observer, scoring 1 to 10 for both achieved and target scores.

Key learning points 2

- Coaches can make good use of reflective diaries in order to improve their coaching performance.
- Performance profiles can be used for performers and coaches alike.
- Coaches are expected to make interventions to improve performance, having identified areas for development.
- Coaches can condition games to facilitate the teaching of a specific skill or tactic.

Q Quick quiz 2

Which coaching techniques are the following sentences a description of?

(a) Watching the individual performing skills.

(b) Identifying strengths and weaknesses.

(c) Recording data about performance by hand or using a computer package.

(d) Getting a performer to rate different aspects of their performance out of 5.

(e) Creating similar conditions to those of competition.

Possible answers:

SWOT analysis, performance profiling, observation, simulation, notational analysis.

Student activity 5.2   ⏱ 45 minutes   P3   M3   D2

Techniques used by a sports coach

Fill out the following table to show your understanding of different techniques used by coaches.

Coaching technique	Describe the techniques used by coaches to improve the performance of athletes	Explain the techniques used by coaches to improve the performance of athletes	Evaluate the techniques used by coaches to improve the performance of athletes
Observation analysis			
Performance profiling			
Coaching diaries			

5.4 Plan a coaching session

Planning can be separated into the following stages:

- collecting and reviewing relevant information
- identifying participant needs
- goal setting
- identifying appropriate resources
- identifying appropriate activities to enable goals to be achieved
- planning coaching sessions and/or programmes.

Before you coach any session you need to answer the following questions:

- What is the starting point, what are their skill levels, who are they?
- Where do they want to be and what do they want from you?
- How will you achieve this?
- What will you need to do this – facilities, equipment, etc.?
- How will you/they know if they have improved?

To plan an effective coaching session or programme of sessions, the coach needs to establish:

- the number of participants, as this will affect the kinds of practices that the coach can employ
- the age of participants, as this will affect the kinds of practices that the coach can use, and even how they might approach coaching that group
- the level of experience and ability of the participants
- whether the participants have any special requirements relating to diet, health, culture or language.

An example of a session planner is reproduced in Table 5.5.

Setting SMART goals

It is a good idea to use the SMART principle when planning your sessions or season.

Key terms

Specific: this means that the session meets what you want it to meet, and is specific to the sport. For example, you could focus a cricket batting session on dealing with short-pitched, fast deliveries, thus being explicit and specific.

Measurable: this is the way in which you measure your results. If you have identified that you want to improve a basketball player's jump shooting, then you might measure this by counting how many shots are successful in a training or game situation and then measure again after the training programme.

Achievable: what you set out to improve must be possible. It would not be fair to ask a beginner in trampolining to complete a complicated routine with multiple somersaults.

Realistic: it must be possible and realistic to achieve what you intend to achieve.

Time-constrained: there should be a reasonable amount of time to achieve the learning goal. Some goals will be short term in nature and established to be achieved in the next session, others more long term and established for the entire season.

Session planner	
Date	Venue
Time	Duration
Group	No. of participants
Equipment required	Aims of session
Safety checks required	
TIME	CONTENT
	Warm-up
	Fitness work
	Main technical skills work
	Game play/tactical work
	Cool-down
Injuries/issues arising	
Evaluation of session	

Table 5.5 Example of a session planner

Health and safety

The health and safety of all involved in sport should be the most important of the coach's considerations. In most cases it is necessary to ensure that facilities and equipment are safe and well maintained, and that performers are adequately aware of key health and safety issues, particularly relating to their own safety and the safety of others.

Coaches should consider the following as a checklist, though it is by no means exhaustive.

- The context in which the sport will take place – the facilities and equipment. Does the provider have a normal operating procedure and emergency action plan? This should cover number of players allowed, coach:learner ratio, conduct and supervision, hazardous behaviours, fire and evacuation procedures.
- The nature of the sport, for playing and training:
  - what to do when rules are not observed
  - what to do with injured players
  - not teaching activities beyond the capabilities of the performers
  - in competitive situations, matching performers where appropriate by size, maturity or age.
- The players:
  - are you aware of any special individual medical needs, and the types of injuries common to the sport?
  - safety education – informing players of inherent risks and establishing a code of behaviour
  - teammates and opponents to be aware of their responsibilities to each other
  - players should be discouraged from participating with an existing injury.
- The coach:
  - safe practices
  - safe numbers for the area
  - arranging appropriate insurance
  - dealing with and reporting accidents
  - being aware of emergency actions.

Risk assessments

Risk assessments are not just forms to fill out. A risk assessment is a skill that helps prevent accidents or serious events. You need to consider what could go wrong and how likely it is.

Risk assessments should be kept and logged, and stored in a safe place. Examples of risk assessments for sporting activities are wide ranging and will depend upon who they are prepared for, the nature of the sport and the competence of the person making the assessment.

Contingency planning

Nothing ever goes completely to plan and for that reason it is good practice to plan for the unexpected so that everyone remains safe and continues to learn. Consider the following as examples of what can happen and what you could plan for.

- Weather threatens your outside session.
- You fall ill and are no longer able to continue as coach.
- There are not enough participants for the session.
- The facility is double-booked when you arrive for the session.
- The group is not responding to your style of coaching or the practices that you have chosen.

The components of a session

While the demands of the structure of sessions for different sports are quite different, the general rules for the layout of sessions are common to all sports.

Key terms

Warm up: to physically and mentally prepare and focus the performers.

Skill learning phase: the objectives of the session are established and employed through a series of drills or practices, perhaps with a competition, followed by an evaluation.

Cool-down: the final and often ignored phase that is concerned with restoring normality to body functions and that has a role to play in injury prevention and emotional control.

Key learning points 3

- Planning is the first stage of coaching and requires the gathering of information relating to performers, facilities and resources.
- Effective coaches use session planners to show what they have planned for a session and to maintain a record.
- Health and safety is the most important consideration in the planning and delivery of coaching sessions.
- Contingency plans are back-up plans that can be used in the event of an unforeseen circumstance that threatens the safety or quality of the coaching session.

Student activity 5.3 45 minutes P4

Planning a coaching session

Using the session planner provided, plan a sports coaching session for a group or individual of your choice.

5.5 Deliver a coaching session

This is concerned with the actual 'doing' part of coaching, and will help with the principles of coaching sessions.

Like the planning of a session, delivering a session follows a logical path.

- Ensure the session plan fits all.
- Identify any risks to the delivery of the session.
- Introduce and start planned activities.
- Manage the behaviour of all involved.
- Monitor and adapt the session as it progresses.
- Summarise and conclude the coaching session.

Once the session is under way, the coach should work to maintain what is going well, and the role of the coach changes to become more of a manager/supervisor.

Skills should be introduced, followed by an explanation which could help performers understand their relevance and when they could be used in a competitive situation.

A competent demonstration should follow, which could be from the coach or with the aid of a video model. This must be a technically correct example and should be thorough, without too much explanation. There should be a balance between verbal instruction and visual demonstration. There will also need to be a balance between activity, instruction and discussion depending on the age, experience and maturity of performers. It is essential for the coach to note the differing rates of learning of individuals.

Performers will then need time to practise the skill or technique. Coaches can use questions to check understanding. The role of the coach changes again to become one of observer/analyst, and it is here that the coach will be looking to assist learners and correct any faults.

To improve performance the coach must have highly developed awareness relating to how to identify errors, compare to a perfect model example and, most importantly, knowledge of how to bridge the gap using feedback, observation and application of a range of suitable techniques.

There is no substitute for practice at this stage. A session that is continually interrupted by a coach for whatever reason is less likely to be successful. It is also important that a coach does not attempt too much in one session.

Most coaches enjoy this part of the coaching process the most, but it is too easy to forget what the aims of the session are and how to keep track of achievement.

Reviewing a session

It is important to consider that coaching does not finish at the end of a session when everyone has cooled down or even gone home. Coaching is a continuous process, and the best coaches reflect on what happened and, more importantly, how to improve. A well-considered evaluation should aid the improvement of subsequent sessions.

The process is as follows:

- Collect, analyse and review – information about the session from feedback, self-reflection and from others.
- Session effectiveness – identify the effectiveness of the session in achieving objectives.
- Review key aspects – drills or practices.
- Identify development needs and take steps to action them.

When evaluating a session a coach should consider the following:

- Performance against pre-set goals: effective coaches will be familiar with the goals for the season, both long and short term. There should be an opportunity to decide to what extent, if at all, the session objectives were met and to what extent this matched the other goals.
- Participants' progress: the review will enable coaches to monitor the performer's progress over a period of time, and help plan for future sessions. Typical review questions could be:
  - How well did the performers learn the skills or techniques introduced to them?
  - What performance developments were evident for each participant?
  - Are the performers ready to progress to the next session?
- Coaching ability: this is the part where the coach can review their own performance:
  - What went well?
  - What went less well?
  - How did the performers respond?
  - Were the performers bored or restless?
  - Did the coach behave acceptably?
- Future targets: this is all about planning for future goals and objectives based on achievements and progress made by participants.

Tools for the review process

There are a number of tools that coaches can use.

- Videos – an excellent way of improving your coaching effectiveness. Videos can be used to judge coaching actions, interaction with your performers, facial expressions and gestures, as well as what you say.
- Critical analysis and self-reflection – self-reflection allows you to explore your perceptions, decisions and subsequent actions to work out ways in which performers can improve technical, tactical or physical ability.
- A mentor – a mentor coach can help provide you with a role-model figure who can offer you practical solutions, work as a sounding board and generally provide you with a range of support.
- Coaching diaries – these can act as a permanent source of information to record your thoughts and feelings, and serve as a true account of what happened and when. Diaries or logs can certainly help with self-reflection and form the basis of action plans for improvement.

Formative and summative reviews

A formative review occurs during the process of coaching and changes can be made immediately. A summative review is done at the end of the coaching session as you reflect on the process overall.

Student activity 5.4 45 minutes | P5 | P6 | M4 | M5 | D3

Delivering a sports session

Part 1

Once you have planned your session, arrange with your tutor when you are going to deliver your session.

Part 2

When you have delivered your coaching, you need to carry out a review of the planning and delivery of the session in the following manner:

1 Gain as much feedback/information as you can about the planning and delivery of your session by asking open questions to:

- the participants in your session
- your tutor
- other people who were observing your session.

You want to find out what was good and what was not so good about your session.

Then think deeply about your session and the parts that you thought were good and not so good.

2 What will you ask them about? The more specific you can be in your questioning, the better information you will receive and the more you will learn.

First, ask them:

- whether the aims and objectives of the session were met

- what parts went particularly well
- what parts went particularly badly.

Then, ask them about the skills you used to coach during the session:

- communication
- organisation
- observation
- decision-making
- time management.

3 Once you have gained the information to achieve a pass you need to identify the strengths and weaknesses of your session.

To achieve a merit you need to dig a bit deeper and think about what it was about each of these factors that made it a strength or a weakness. For example, if you felt your communication was good, what was it about your communication that was good? Did you use the right tone of voice, did you explain things well, did you use language that was appropriate? When you have evaluated all your strengths and weaknesses, you can then make suggestions about how you could improve your performance for the next session.

To achieve a distinction you need to justify the improvements you have suggested and say how they will improve the skills that you felt needed improving.

Further reading

Crisfield, P. (2001) *Analysing Your Coaching*, Coachwise.

Gordon, D.A. (2009) *Coaching Science*, Learning Matters.

Martens, R. (2004) *Successful Coaching*, Human Kinetics.

Miles, A. (2004) *Coaching Practice*, Coachwise.

Useful websites

www.coachesinfo.com/index.php

Free access to a number of regularly updated articles on a wide range of sports, describing methodology of research; registration necessary for full access.

http://www.brianmac.co.uk/coaching.htm

Offers an introduction to coaching and its process, with links to related topics

8: Practical Team Sports

8.1 Introduction

Sport and sports participation are on the increase in the UK. Sport has many purposes: to improve health, for enjoyment and the natural human urge to compete among others. There are many different types of sports, and this unit includes details of how to improve your performance in sport and your knowledge of the rules and regulations, as well as the ways in which you can measure and assess performance.

By the end of this unit you should:

- be able to use a range of skills, techniques and tactics in selected team and/or individual sports
- understand the rules and regulations of selected team and/or individual sports
- be able to assess your own performance in selected team and/or individual sports
- be able to assess the performance of a team in two selected team sports or other individuals in selected individual sports
- be able to use a range of skills, techniques and tactics in selected team and individual sports.

Assessment and grading criteria		
To achieve a PASS grade the evidence must show that the learner is able to:	**To achieve a MERIT grade the evidence must show that, in addition to the pass criteria, the learner is able to:**	**To achieve a DISTINCTION grade the evidence must show that, in addition to the pass and merit criteria, the learner is able to:**
P1 describe skills, techniques and tactics required in two different team/individual sports	**M1** explain skills, techniques and tactics required in two different team/individual sports	
P2 describe the rules and regulations of two different team/individual sports, and apply them to three different situations for each sport	**M2** explain the application of the rules and regulations, of two different team/individual sports, in three different situations for each sport	
P3 demonstrate appropriate skills, techniques and tactics in two different team/individual sports		
P4 carry out a self-analysis using two different methods of assessment, identifying strengths and areas for improvement in two different team/individual sports	**M3** explain identified strengths and areas for improvement in two different team/individual sports, and make suggestions relating to personal development	**D1** analyse identified strengths and areas for improvement in two different team/individual sports, and justify suggestions made
P5 carry out a performance analysis using two different methods of assessment, identifying strengths and areas for improvement in the development of a team/an individual in a team/individual sport.	**M4** explain identified strengths and areas for improvement in the development of a team/an individual in a team/individual sport, and make suggestions relating to development of a team.	**D2** analyse identified strengths and areas for improvement in the development of a team/an individual in a team/individual sport, and justify suggestions made.

8.2 Team and Individual Sports

P1 **P3** **M1**

Team sports are those in which two or more players compete together with a single aim. They include sports such as football, rugby, netball and lacrosse.

Individual sports are those in which the competitor usually competes on their own and is solely responsible for their own actions. These include sports such as gymnastics, judo, trampolining and golf.

Sports can be further classified as follows:

● **Invasion sports**: games such as football, netball, basketball and rugby, where the object of the sport is to invade the opponent's territory

Fig 8.2 Taekwon do – an example of a martial art

Fig 8.1 Netball is an example of an invasion sport

● **Court sports**: non-contact sports because opponents are normally on opposite sides of a net, such as badminton, volleyball and tennis
● **Target sports**: involve the use of marksmanship and include golf and archery
● **Striking/fielding**: games with a batting and a fielding team, e.g. cricket, baseball and rounders
● **Martial arts**: these come from different ancient fighting methods, many of which originated in the Far East, such as judo, taekwon do and karate
● **Water sports**: activities undertaken on or in water, including swimming, sailing and water polo
● **Athletic sports**: take place on the field or track
● **Field sports**: hunting sports associated with the outdoors, such as shooting and fishing.

Skills and Techniques in Team and Individual Sports

A skill is the ability to do something well and requires lots of practice. Technique is a way of undertaking a particular skill. If a basketball player is able to perform a jump-shot well, it is said that they have a good technique in playing the shot.

There are many shared skills in different team sports, and having the awareness and ability to undertake them will be an advantage to your team. They include:

● Passing – moving the ball around your teammates
● Receiving – being able to receive a pass from a teammate
● Shooting – aiming at a specific target, such as a goal or a basket
● Dribbling – moving around with the ball
● Throwing – there are many ways of throwing an object, normally specific to the sport being played
● Intercepting – this is where a player stops the ball from reaching its intended place; this could be through a block or a tackle
● Creating space – this means moving away from opponents so that you are in a position in which you can receive a pass or create a shooting opportunity.

In addition to the skills and techniques required of a sport, players may also be judged on other criteria, such as their performance over the duration of a game.

All sports are made up of a range of specific skills. In tennis there are a number of different shots that you can play at different times during a game. Playing these effectively will allow you to win points. They include:

- Forehand drive with spin variation
- Forehand volley
- Service
- Lob
- Smash
- Return of service.

Tactics

Key term

Tactic: a plan of action to achieve a goal.

Tactics in sport are usually focused directly or indirectly on winning. Tactics can depend on the opposition, players of the other team or opponents, the importance of the competition and maybe the weather.

Tactics can be:

- Pre-event tactics – a particular plan before the event
- In-event tactics – a plan implemented during the game, such as switching from man-to-man to zone defence in basketball.

Tactics can fail if the opposition work them out too easily, if the tactic is employed too late or if the player or players are simply not able to understand or execute the necessary tactic(s).

Consider the range of options that a tennis player has at their disposal. First, where should they stand while waiting for their opponent's return? If the ball is likely to come over the net in the middle and low, then the player might consider standing close to the net to make a volley. In this way, the player has selected a tactical position and shot selection. The same player might also consider serving the ball to the forehand or backhand of their opponent, some with spin, some without and some faster than others. This is known as variation.

If the conditions of the match are that the player is losing, that player might start to play defensive shots in an attempt to prevent them from falling further behind.

Tactics can include playing precise formations against specific opponents. Football teams may play more defensively away from home and opt to play with more defending players rather than strikers. In certain sports, opposing players may be marked to stop them having a positive effect for their team.

Other tactics may include working on specific set plays, such as line-outs in rugby, and corners and free kicks in football.

In order to improve your performance, it is a good idea to actually watch yourself perform the skill. Ask a friend or coach to video you while you perform a set skill. You can then analyse your performance and see what you are doing. You may be surprised and realise your body is not doing what you thought it was! You will then need to amend the skill, practise it and video yourself again, to check that you are now performing the skill properly.

Key learning points

- Sports can be classified as:
  - Invasion games
  - Court sports
  - Target sports
  - Striking/fielding
  - Martial arts
  - Water sports
  - Field sports.
- A skill is the ability to perform something well.
- Techniques are a way of undertaking a particular skill.
- A tactic is a plan of action to achieve a goal.
- Team and individual sports are different, not just in terms of numbers, but also in terms of the skills and techniques to be developed and assessed.

Quick quiz 1

1 Place the following sports into their correct classification:
   (a) Tennis.
   (b) Judo.
   (c) Clay-pigeon shooting.
   (d) Windsurfing.
   (e) 400 m running.
   (f) Shot put.
   (g) Squash.
   (h) Lacrosse.
   (i) Curling.
   (j) Mountain biking.
2 What skills do you need to perform well for your favourite sport?
3 Name three different tactics used in your favourite sport.

Student activity 8.1      **60 minutes**   **P1**   **M1**

Select two individual or two team sports for the following tasks.

Task 1

Draw a spidergram for two sports which illustrates the skills, techniques and tactics required for each.

Task 2

Write a report that describes and explains the skills, techniques and tactics for each of your two selected sports.

Task 3

Take part in your two selected sports and demonstrate appropriate skills, techniques and tactics in each sport.

8.3. Rules and Regulations

The rules and regulations of any sport are normally set and amended by its national governing body (NGB) and international sports federations (ISFs). These are set to ensure that the sport is played fairly and that the opponents are aware of how to win.

International sports federations and national governing bodies may change the rules and regulations periodically, as they look to improve the sport. For example, FIBA, the international governing body for basketball, meets every four years at a world congress, with a view to changing or clarifying rules to the benefit of the sport.

Time

Many team sports have time constraints and are split into periods of play:

● Ice hockey has three periods of 20 minutes.
● Basketball has four periods of 10 minutes.
● Rugby union has two halves of 40 minutes.

Usually the team with the most points or goals is declared the winner, and if the scores are tied, the game is normally declared a draw. For sports like rugby and football, the timing is described as real time, since the start and finish times are exact (except for added time), whereas basketball and ice hockey are played in artificial time, because the game clock is stopped on a regular basis for a variety of reasons, meaning that the whole of the running game time is spent on the court/field of play.

In some sports, a winner can be declared before the allocated time has elapsed. Often in test match cricket, a team will have bowled out a team twice and scored the required number of runs before the five days are completed.

Few individual sports are constrained by time, the outcome of the event usually being determined by the success of the competition, and usually by accruing points to a critical point.

Scoring

Each sport has a different scoring system, with the team or individual with the most points usually being declared the winner. An exception to this is golf, where the player who has taken the fewest strokes is the winner. Scoring may include putting the ball into a goal in football and handball.

Facilities and Equipment

Specific sports require certain facilities to enable play to take place. Different surfaces can be used for different sports, and often sports are played on a range of surfaces. Tennis is a good example, as it can be played on grass, clay and hard surfaces, and can be played inside or outdoors. Occasionally, rules may be adapted for sports played on different surfaces.

Many sports require the participants to wear or use specialist equipment. In football, the laws of the game insist that all players must wear shin guards to protect their lower legs. In sports such as hockey, rugby and cricket, players may wear specific equipment to reduce the risk of injury. This could include arm guards, helmets and padding.

You can find the rules and regulations of each sport via its national governing body. The NGB looks after many aspects of a sport, including organising major competitions, running coaching schemes and dealing with the development of the sport at all levels.

Unwritten Rules and Etiquette

Unwritten rules cover those situations in sports where the normal rules of the sport are unclear or require the discretion or cooperation of the competitors. Examples include the following:

- **Football**: when a player appears to be injured, the opposition often put the ball out of play, and in an act of fair play the other team returns the ball to its generous opponents.
- **Fencing**: points in fencing are scored when an opponent strikes another. In a fast-moving sport, the electronic scoring apparatus can misinterpret an inaccurate contact, such as the blade contacting the floor. Sporting opponents often either concede the point or suggest that the contact was not eligible for scoring.
- **Cricket**: a batsman can choose to 'walk' on appeal. In other words, if a fielder appeals for a dismissal decision, the batsman can choose to walk from the field of play, effectively admitting that they were out.
- **Golf**: players can 'give' competitors shots, usually when their opponent's ball is very close to the

hole. In doing so, they allow them to score that shot without actually playing it.

Officials

Officials in sport have wide-ranging roles and duties, including football fourth officials, trampoline judges, athletics markers, cycle marshals, netball umpires and cricket third umpires. The role of these officials varies in terms of their physical nature, their proximity to the event and the support that they receive from their co-officials.

Playing Surfaces

The amount and type of surfaces played on in sports are many and varied. While some surfaces can be used for a variety of sports, others are more specialised. The level of competition can also have a bearing. Artificial surfaces come in many varieties – with rubber crumbs or sand drainage.

Fig 8.4 Playing tennis on clay

Situations

Rules and regulations are often used to describe what should be done in certain situations, such as what to do if a player handles the ball in football, or when a ball is out of bounds in golf. Where rules are broken, officials have a predetermined course of action and a penalty may follow.

Football Rules

Football rules are known as the 'laws of the game'. There are 17 laws, which have changed marginally over the years. The international sports federation, FIFA, adapts them as it considers necessary. Recent examples of this include changing the offside law to encourage more attacking football.

The following is a summary of the 17 laws:

- **Field of play**: this law looks at the surface, dimensions, layout and markings of the football pitch.
- **Ball**: the shape and dimensions of the football are covered, as well as replacing the ball should it burst during a match.

Fig 8.3 A cricket umpire indicating a leg bye during a match

- **Number of players**: there should be 11 players at the start of a match, including a designated goalkeeper; the use of substitutions is also looked at.
- **Players' equipment**: the health and safety considerations of what players wear is mentioned. No jewellery should be worn and all players must wear shin guards. The goalkeeper must also wear a top that distinguishes him from the other players.
- **Referee**: this law looks at the responsibilities of the referee, which include enforcing the laws, taking responsibility for the safety of the players, acting as a timekeeper, punishing serious offences and providing a match report to the relevant authority.
- **Assistant referees**: assistant referees assist the referee to control the game, signalling when the ball goes out of play and any offences that the referee may miss.
- **Duration of the match**: a football match is played over two equal periods of 45 minutes. This time may be reduced for youth football. Time can be added for substitutions, injuries and time wasting, at the referee's discretion.
- **Start & restart of play**: the team that wins the toss of a coin can choose which goal they want to attack. The game starts with a kick-off, where all players must be in their own half of the pitch; this method is also used after a goal has been scored.
- **Ball in & out of play**: the ball is out of play when the whole ball crosses one of the perimeter lines or when the referee blows his whistle to stop play.
- **Method of scoring**: the rule states that a goal is scored when the ball crosses the line between the posts and under the crossbar. The team with the most goals wins.
- **Offside**: a player is offside if 'he is nearer to his opponent's goal line than both the ball and the second last opponent' and receives a pass from one of his teammates. The player also needs to be in his opponent's half and interfering with the game. However, you cannot be offside if you receive the pass from a goal kick or throw-in.
- **Fouls & misconduct**: fouls and misconduct are penalised by either a direct or indirect free kick. There are ten offences that result in a direct free kick, including kicking, tripping or pushing an opponent. Indirect free kicks are given for infringements such as a goalkeeper picking up a back pass or throw-in, or for impeding an opponent. Direct free kicks are given for offences that are committed by a player in their own penalty box and are awarded as a penalty kick.
- **Free kicks**: following a foul, a free kick is awarded, which will be either direct or indirect. Opponents must be a minimum of ten yards away from the ball. A direct free kick shot directly into the opponent's goal will be awarded a goal, while a goal can be scored from an indirect free kick only if it has touched another player before going into the goal. A referee will signal an indirect free kick by raising one arm into the air above their head.
- **Penalty kick**: awarded when an offence is committed by a player in their own penalty area. The goalkeeper must remain on their line until the ball has been kicked. A penalty taker cannot touch the ball until it has touched another player if they miss.
- **Throw-in**: the ball is thrown back on to the pitch when the ball goes out of play on either side of the pitch. A throw-in is taken with two hands on the ball and the ball must be released from behind the player's head.
- **Goal kick**: the ball is kicked back into play from within the goal area when the ball crosses the goal line and was last touched by an attacking player. The ball must leave the penalty area before it can be played again.
- **Corner kick**: a corner is awarded when the ball crosses the goal line and was last touched by a defending player. The kick is taken from within the corner arc. A goal can be scored direct from a corner kick.

The FA has set a number of regulations to help the running of football in England. Regulations are rules controlled by the organising bodies. The FA has included regulations on:

- The control of youth football
- The doping control programme
- Disciplinary procedures.

Key learning points 2

- Rules are established and controlled by national governing bodies (NGBs), such as the Rugby Football Union (RFU).
- Sports can be played in real time, like one-day cricket, or in artificial time, like basketball.
- Unwritten rules are situations that can occur when players and officials can choose to demonstrate fair play.
- Governing bodies are responsible for any necessary changes to rules or changes to interpretations of rules.

Student activity 8.2   ⏱ 60–90 mins   P2   M2

Select two team or two individual sports of your choice to carry out the following:

- List the rules and regulations of each of your selected sports.
- Describe and explain the rules and their application for each of your two selected sports.

- Demonstrate your ability to apply these rules in three different situations for each of your selected sports.

Q Quick quiz 2

1 Name three sports that take more than one day to complete.

2 Name three sports that can be completed in two hours.

3 Describe why sports need rules.

4 Give four examples of where you have witnessed fair play.

5 Name six different types of playing surfaces.

6 Give the name for the leading official(s) in the following sports (e.g. for football, it is referee).

   (a) Tennis.

   (b) Netball.

   (c) Athletics.

   (d) Gymnastics.

8.4 Assessing Own and Other People's Performance in a Team or Individual Sport

P4   P5   M3   M4   D1

D2

Performance Assessment

Performances can all be assessed. Assessment should always be conducted with a view to improve future performances.

   Some assessors try to correct errors in performance by simply shouting instructions, like 'You are not trying hard enough' or 'Get more aim on your shot' in basketball. These instructions give the sportsperson an idea of what they should be doing, but not how to achieve this. To analyse techniques from a coach's viewpoint, it is important to:

- Sort the effective techniques from the less effective
- Break down complete movements into simple parts
- Concentrate on the techniques that need the most improvement, in the right order.

There are many different factors to consider when evaluating a team's or individual's performance:

- How well do they perform specific skills?
- Are they using the correct techniques?
- Are they using appropriate tactics?
- Are they successful at employing these tactics?

There are several ways in which to assess performance:

- Assessment can be completed by the individual, known as self-assessment.
- Peer assessment is the assessment of an individual or a group of individuals on performance.
- Other observers could be teachers, coaches or judges.

Here are some key terms in assessing performance:

- **Observation** – watching sporting performances
- **Analysis** – deciding what has happened
- **Evaluation** – the end-product of observation and analysis, where decisions are made and feedback is given to the performer
- **Qualitative analysis** – largely subjective, meaning that it is open to personal interpretation and is therefore subject to bias or error; the more knowledge the observer has, the more valid the observations
- **Quantitative analysis** – more involved and scientific, and involves the direct measurement of a performance or technique; match statistics recorded while the game is in progress are called 'real-time', while match statistics recorded after the events are called 'lapsed-time' analysis.

There are a number of methods of assessment that can be used to assess performance.

Video Analysis

Video gives the person who watches it an objective record of a performance. The greatest benefit of video is the playback feature, including slow motion, which can be used to demonstrate skill execution, tactical efficiency or a more general generic performance evaluation.

Here are some guidelines on the use of video analysis:

- Do not try to film your performers and coach them at the same time. Ask someone reliable to do the filming, and brief them on what you want – follow the player or the ball, try to capture tactics or specific techniques, and so on.
- Try to pick up all the sound, as it can provide useful feedback.
- Start the recording before the action and end it well after, judging players' body language before and after performance.
- Label and date the film immediately to keep a record.

Table 8.1 is an example of a match analysis sheet for a team sport. This could be filled in by the performer, a peer or a neutral observer, scoring 1 to 10 for both achieved and target scores.

Notation

Notation is a way of collecting data and can be done by hand or with a computer.

Hand notation is a system of recording detailed analysis of a sport and literally noting the data on a sheet of paper using a predefined set of symbols.

Systems like this exist for many sports, such as tennis, archery and football.

The advantage of these systems is that they are inexpensive and, if completed by a skilful recorder, produce quick information in real time, so that the coach or performer can have instant access to detailed information. The main disadvantages of this system are that it is open to human error, can be difficult to interpret and can be difficult in certain conditions, such as bad weather.

Figure 8.5 gives an example of a profile of a hockey player's skills and techniques. The darker column is the assessment of the level of performance by the performer, and the lighter column is the assessment of the level of performance as identified by the coach.

If you look at the results, it is clear that there are differences in opinion as to level of performance. It is important that, if there are such differences, the coach and performer discuss the issues and decide on what needs development in practice and game situations and how that can be achieved.

Technology in Performance Analysis

As video and sound technology improve, new software packages have been developed that can analyse all physical activities. Packages such as Kandle and Dartfish are capable of producing a range of exciting analysis tools, including:

- Video delay systems
- Distance and angle measurement
- Overlays and comparators that compare other performances
- Multi-frame sequencing that breaks down complex skills
- Drawing and annotation tools.

Date	Opponent	Result	
		Mark	Target
Analysis area			
Positional play			
Tactical awareness/decision-making			
Fitness levels			
Skills/techniques			
Cooperation/teamwork			
Concentration/psychological factors			
Diet/nutrition			

Table 8.1 Match analysis of an individual sport

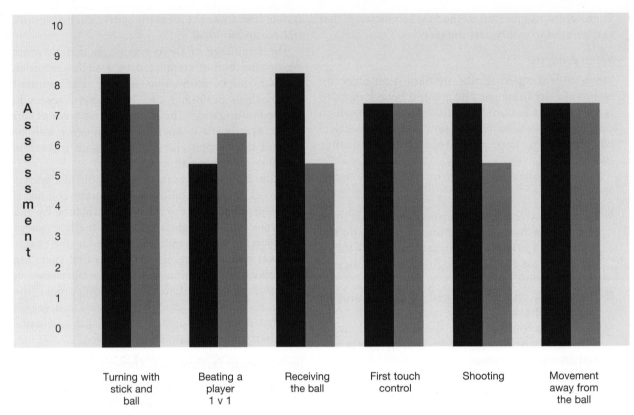

Fig 8.5 Profile of hockey player's skills & techniques

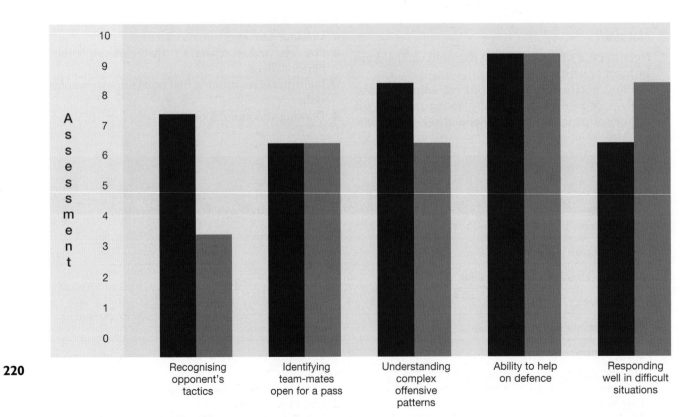

Fig 8.6 Profile of basketball player's skills & techniques

Thanks to ever decreasing costs, these packages have become available in schools and colleges, as well as at professional sports clubs.

Critical Analysis and Self-reflection

Self-reflection allows a performer to explore their perceptions, decisions and subsequent actions, to work out ways in which they can improve technical, tactical or physical ability.

A Mentor

A mentor should be someone who is a role-model figure, who can help provide practical solutions, work as a sounding board and generally provide a range of support.

Coaching Diaries

Coaching diaries can act as a permanent source of information to record thoughts and feelings, and serve as a true account of what happened and when. Diaries or logs can certainly help with self-reflection and form the basis of action plans for improvement.

SWOT Analysis

An example of a SWOT analysis carried out on a golfer is shown in Table 8.2.

Performance Profiling

Performance profiling is a method that can be used by a performer or, more typically, applied by a coach or observer. Put simply, it is an inventory of attributes, skills and techniques that form the basis of an assessment grading model.

Performance profiling can be used to analyse and record technical or tactical factors as well as psychological attributes.

Scouting

This is a process where an expert observer can identify either a talented individual or produce a report about an opponent. In the first case it could result in bringing a new player to a team to strengthen the existing squad. The second aspect – gaining knowledge of how your opponent performs – is an underused approach in the UK. A simple observation and a few notes can be very useful in deciding how to prepare for the next match. If a tennis player knows that their opponent has a fast, hard service, but is poor on their backhand, their preparation should have a greater emphasis on service returns under pressure and returning the ball to their opponent's weaker side.

Development

The last stage is what to do once performance has been assessed. In other words, what you should do about what you have discovered, be it strengths or points for improvement.

Aims and Objectives

Following analysis, it is important to collate the information relating to the performance improvement. Having done this, there needs to be an established set of priorities that will form the basis of the plan of action. These aims or objectives need to be the foundation of the targets to be set.

It is a good idea to use the SMART principle in designing an action plan. SMART stands for:

- **S**pecific
- **M**easurable
- **A**chievable
- **R**ealistic
- **T**ime-constrained.

Specific

This means that the action plan meets what you want it to meet. For example, instead of saying that attacking play is a technical weakness in football, you could say that running off the ball, pass completion and beating a defender are weaknesses.

Measurable

This is the way in which you measure your results. If you have identified that you want to improve a basketball player's jump-shooting, you might measure this by counting how many shots are successful in a

Strengths	Weaknesses
A good relaxed swing	Not accurate with driving clubs
Excellent body positioning in relation to the ball	Putting is inconsistent
A low-risk safety-first approach	Poor technique in short iron game (head up too early)
Opportunities	**Threats**
Short game practice has been improved recently	Can be prone to getting annoyed easily and letting it
Has learnt how to mentally rehearse	spoil their game
Opponent has no knowledge of the course	Environment – windy day
	Opponent is a better player

Table 8.2 An example of a SWOT analysis

training or game situation, and then measure again after additional training sessions.

Achievable

What you set out to improve must be possible. It would not be fair to ask a beginner in trampolining to complete a complicated routine with multiple somersaults.

Realistic

It must be possible and realistic to achieve what we intend to achieve.

Time-constrained

There should be a reasonable amount of time to complete an action plan or achieve a goal.

Key learning points 3

- Performances can be analysed by the performer themselves, their peers and observers such as coaches.
- Video capture and analysis is a very effective performance assessment tool, especially features like slow motion, freeze frame and video playback.
- SMART goals should be used to establish action points for the improvement of performance.

Student activity 8.3   ⏱ 90–120 mins   P4   P5   M3   M4   D1   D2

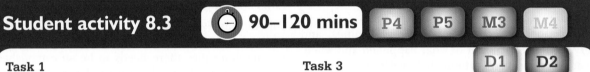

Task 1

Select two different methods of self-analysis, then carry out this self-analysis for two different individual or team sports of your choice.

Task 2

Write a report based on your self-analysis that identifies, explains and analyses identified strengths and areas for improvement. Where possible, try to make justified suggestions on your own personal development.

Task 3

Select two different methods of performance analysis, then carry out this analysis for an individual who is taking part in either two team or two individual sports.

Task 4

Write a report based on your performance analyses that identifies, explains and analyses identified strengths and areas for improvement. Where possible, try to make justified suggestions on the individual's personal development.

Further reading

Crisfield, P. (2001) *Analysing your Coaching*, Coachwise.

Galligan, F., Crawford, D. and Maskery, C. (2002) *Advanced PE for Edexcel, Teacher's Resource File*, Heinemann.

Miles, A. (2004) *Coaching Practice*, Coachwise.

Stafford-Brown, J., Rea, S., Janaway, L. and Manley, C. (2006) *BTEC First Sport*, Hodder Arnold.

Useful websites

www.efds.co.uk

Official site of the English Federation of Disability Sport, giving access to information about activities for people with disabilities

www.sportscoachuk.org

Excellent site full of jobs, tips, advice and framework for sports coaches.

12: Current Issues in Sport

12.1 Introduction

The state of current sport and the issues prevalent in sport today can be understood and interpreted only if we examine the society they are played in and how sports have developed. Sport in some way affects the lives of most people in our society, whether it is through playing or watching sport, getting caught up in the excitement of a tournament or supporting the activities of others. Sport in Britain has developed as a result of the development of our society, and the values and features prevalent in sport are also reflected in the values and features of our society. Sport has also been used to address some of the problems in society and to improve the quality of the society in which we live.

By the end of this unit you should:

- know how sport has developed in the UK
- know how media and technology influence modern sport
- know how contemporary issues affect sport
- understand the cultural influences and barriers that affect participation in sports activities.

Assessment and grading criteria

To achieve a PASS grade the evidence must show that the learner is able to:	To achieve a MERIT grade the evidence must show that, in addition to the pass criteria, the learner is able to:	To achieve a DISTINCTION grade the evidence must show that, in addition to the pass and merit criteria, the learner is able to:
P1 describe the development and organisation of a selected sport in the UK	**M1** explain the development and organisation of a selected sport in the UK	
P2 describe the influence of the media on a selected sport in the UK	**M2** explain the influence of the media on a selected sport in the UK	
P3 describe the effect that technology has on a selected sport	**M3** explain the effect that technology has on a selected sport	
P4 describe the effects of four contemporary issues on a selected sport	**M4** explain the effects of four contemporary issues on a selected sport	**D1** evaluate the effects of four contemporary issues on a selected sport
P5 explain the barriers to sports participation		
P6 explain three cultural influences on sports participation		
P7 describe three strategies or initiatives which relate to sports participation.	**M5** explain three strategies or initiatives which relate to sports participation.	**D2** evaluate three strategies or initiatives which relate to sports participation.

12.2 How Sport has Developed in the UK

Pre-Industrial Sports

There are two distinct periods in Britain: sport before the Industrial Revolution and sport after it. The Industrial Revolution covers a specific period of time from 1780 to 1850. In 1800, only one in five people lived in towns, but by 1851 for the first time over 50 per cent of the population lived in urban environments. By the 1880s, this had risen to 75 per cent of the population.

This was a period of major development in society because the ways people lived and worked were changing. Rather than being a country where people lived predominantly in the countryside and farmed areas of land, Britain became a society of city dwellers who worked for a wage in factories. This had a profound effect on leisure time and the form that sports took. It led to rapid changes in sports, with sports taking on the features we recognise in these activities today. Prior to the Industrial Revolution, Britain was described as being an agricultural society where people lived in the countryside and farmed the land.

The pre-industrial sports that people played were crude forms of sports we would recognise today. For example, folk football was a sport that was played between teams from different villages with the aim being to get the ball, which was an inflated pig's bladder, between the opposition village's church gates. There were no regulations regarding the numbers of players, boundaries of the pitch, time or conduct of the players. The game would go on over the period of a bank holiday weekend and was characterised by violence and unruly behaviour. Pre-industrial sports required large amounts of land and were totally unsuitable for the urban environment that the industrial revolution created.

The Industrial Revolution (1780–1850)

From around the mid-eighteenth century, the English economy underwent a vast transformation. It had been based on agriculture, with particularly busy periods of work for planting and harvesting. Working hours varied and there were long periods of free time available for workers to enjoy leisure activities.

The Industrial Revolution saw the development of factories producing a wide range of consumer goods.

Factory owners required their workers to accept longer hours and less free time. Typically, a worker would have a six-day week, working from 7.00 in the morning to 7.00 at night. There may also have been a night shift; this was to maximise the output of factories and reduce the unit costs. Overhead costs were high and could be reduced only if machinery was being worked for as many hours as possible. The second issue was that there was a shortage of people living in the towns and cities where these factories were based, so they had to attract workers from their countryside homes. This was done by offering better wages and the lure of consumer goods to raise standards of living.

The reality was a little different from the promise because these workers traded increased wages for longer working hours and less leisure time. Also, the standards of housing were much worse than in the countryside where they enjoyed plenty of space. The perceived rise in spending and standard of living never occurred because it was more expensive to live in cities. In the cities, families and workers were herded into 'slum' accommodation with little space.

Leisure activities became a problem because violent sports could result in serious injuries, and its associated excessive drinking led to hangovers and absenteeism, and gambling undermined the work ethic. Leisure cost the factory owners money and affected output. Factory owners supported the middle-class efforts to clean up society and impose a new form of morality. Campaigns were mounted against excessive drinking, idleness, sexual promiscuity, gambling, violent sports and the excessive holidays. The aim of the middle classes was to impose a work ethic on the population and make behaviour more polite and respectable.

The agricultural industry also underwent a parallel revolution with the scope and quantity of production increasing. This meant that the population of England became better fed, healthier and had more energy for work.

The economic forces contributed to changes in traditional sports because the employees had to bow to their employers' demands and, moreover, they had little time or energy to play aggressive contact sports. These demands were supplemented by the efforts of religious reformers, who believed violent sports led to moral corruption, and sport on the Sabbath was eventually banned. The Royal Society for the Protection of Animals (RSPCA) put pressure on the authorities to ban sports involving cruelty to animals. The Industrial Revolution led to a growth in the size of towns and cities and a reduction in the amount of space available for recreation. Folk football, which was played across vast swathes of countryside, was completely inappropriate for the urban setting. The result of all these changes was that sports activities slowly disappeared.

Sports, such as fox hunting, for the leisured upper classes and middle classes were still popular and carried on in pre-industrialised forms.

The 1830s and 1840s started to see an upturn in fortune for the workers, because the development of the railways led to an increased mobility. The sports of cricket and horse racing benefited from the easier access to the countryside, allowing the workers to go and watch meetings and matches. The 1840s saw a genuine improvement in real wages (meaning an increased spending power), improving diets and standards of living. There was also money available to spend on entrance fees into sports events.

The 1860s saw the development of nationally agreed rules, known as the codification of sport, and a changing attitude of the middle-class factory owners to their employees' sports activities. Two groups promoted the benefits of sport. First, the industrialists, who saw sport as promoting values which would make their workers more productive, such as teamwork and loyalty. Second, a group called the Muscular Christians took team sports to working-class communities to teach the Bible through sport and promote the value of a healthy mind in a healthy body.

Figures from the time suggest sport was still a minority activity, but spectating was growing, as was professionalism in the sports of football, cricket and horse racing. Social change included the urban population growing from 50.2 per cent in 1851 to 77 per cent in 1900. Working-class wages rose by 70 per cent and a half-day holiday was granted on Saturdays. This meant sport could be played and watched on Saturday afternoons and is the origin of the three o'clock kick-off in football matches.

Rationalisation and Regulation

'Rational recreation' is the term given to the introduction of leisure activities which were seen as being productive and moral. Up until the 1860s and 1870s the workers had relied on their public houses for amusement and entertainment, which were often socially destructive. Rational recreations were brought in by various philanthropic groups, such as the Muscular Christians and other middle-class groups who introduced new alternatives. Thus, societies such as the Mechanics Society, the Boys Brigade and the Young Men's Christian Association developed, and facilities such as libraries, public baths and sports grounds offered more purposeful activities.

This is an example of using sport and leisure as a means of social control, whereby people are persuaded to take part in positive, socially acceptable activities to prevent them from participating in otherwise socially destructive activities such as drinking, gambling and fighting. The middle-class philanthropists wanted to provide better activities for the working class to improve their standard of living, but their ulterior motive was to make sure they were healthier, fitter and more productive workers.

Twentieth-Century Development

Globalisation of Sport

The forms of sport that were established in England in the late nineteenth century quickly spread around the world, particularly through the influence of the British Empire. Officers and soldiers brought the new codified forms of sport to the countries in which they were stationed, and the sports in turn were adopted by the natives. By the end of the nineteenth century, the Olympic movement, under the influence of the French, was finding its feet and starting to involve more and more nations.

The influence of sport by the end of the twentieth century can be seen by the fact that three of the four largest international organisations were sporting organisations:

- The IAAF (International Amateur Athletic Federation) with 184 member countries
- FIFA (Fédération Internationale de Football Association) with 178 members
- The IOC (International Olympic Committee) with 171 members.

The non-sporting organisation was the United Nations, with 180 member countries.

Professionalism

The increasing playing demands of the sports of rugby, football and cricket mean that players have had to devote increasing amounts of time and energy to their sports. By the end of the nineteenth century, these three sports had all embraced professionalism. As the standards of the sports rose, payments had to be made to players to compensate for the wages they would otherwise have earned. Professionalism was initially looked down upon because the upper classes thought that sport should be played purely for the enjoyment derived from the activity. A class distinction arose between the upper-class amateurs and the working-class professionals, which remained until the latter part of the twentieth century. By the end of the twentieth century, professionalism was an accepted part of all sports and necessary to uphold the high standards of play demanded by the sophisticated audiences.

The Development of Sport as a Profitable Industry

As sports have increasingly embraced professionalism, their expenditure has increased. As a result, they have had to increase the amount of money coming into the sport to pay these expenses. Sports and their clubs have increasingly sought sponsorship as a source of income, along with trying to make the sport more attractive and increase the number of spectators coming to matches. As sports have become more popular and widely watched, they have increasingly drawn the attention of the media. This has opened up new sources of revenue to sports and has led to increased profits.

There is also an expanding industry in sport for non-competitive participants, and this has created a variety of opportunities for private companies to invest their money and make profits. It has also resulted in a growing industry with new, exciting employment opportunities.

The Development of Sport in Education

The key element in the expansion of sport in the education system was the 1944 Education Act, which made it policy for local authorities to provide adequate facilities for the teaching of physical education. Sport and physical education became compulsory elements of children's education and are now key features in the National Curriculum. Added to that, there are now many more opportunities to study sport at GCSE, AS and A2 level, National Diploma and degree level.

The Influence of War

The two world wars had a major effect on the development of sport. During World War I, in which the Allies (Britain, France, Russia, Italy and the USA) defeated the central powers (Germany, Austria, Hungary and Turkey), all sports stopped at national and international level as young people were recruited for the war and many were then killed during the fighting. The Olympic Games scheduled for 1916 had to be cancelled.

Between the wars, the upper classes returned to their leisure activities, playing tennis, golf and cricket, and also indulged in overseas holidays and nights of partying. The development of the railways allowed them to visit the seaside in the summer months. The working classes returned to watching football on Saturday afternoons and the first dog-racing meeting was held in 1926 at Belle Vue in Manchester.

During the 1930s, Great Britain experienced a series of financial and economic problems as a result of strikes and industrial unrest. Unemployment rose to three million and the development of Nazism and Fascism led the country to feel insecure, with a negative effect on national morale.

World War II again saw the cessation of sporting activities as all energy went into the war effort and training the young troops for war. The training used by the troops started to appear in schools, forming an integral part of physical education lessons.

The Organisation of Sport in Britain

The government in Britain still plays a key role in influencing the direction sport takes and the opportunities for participation in sport. Rather than directly being involved in sport, the government has developed agencies to influence policy for sport and this is backed up by the provision of funding. In this way, the government can keep sport 'at arm's length' but still maintain some control over it. The current government's major success has been to attract the Olympic Games to London in 2012.

Central Government Control of Sport

Sport in central government is administered through the Department for Culture, Media and Sport (DCMS) under the control of a Secretary of State for Culture, Media and Sport and a Minister for Sport. The DCMS looks after the interests of world-class sports people and also ensures that everyone has an opportunity to take part in sport. The roles of the DCMS in relation to sport are to:

● Widen access to sport for all citizens and offer Sport for All
● Promote the achievement of excellence in national and international competition
● Promote physical education and sport for young people and work with the Department for Children, Schools and Families (DCSF) to promote children's play through education
● Attract major sporting events to Britain, such as the successful bid for the 2012 Olympic Games
● Manage schemes to support the training of athletes, such as TASS (Talented Athletes Scholarship Scheme), which supports athletes in full-time education, and funding of athletes through lottery money.

The DCMS is not the only department representing the interests of people playing sport in Britain. Sport in schools and developing the physical education syllabus is under the control of the DCSF. Sports development departments are under the control of the local authorities within the Department for Communities and Local Government.

227

- **The CCPR (Central Council for Physical Recreation)**: represents the interests of national governing bodies (NGBs).
- **NGBs (national governing bodies):** all sports clubs are members of the NGB, which runs the leagues, and provides officials and disciplinary measures. For example, the Football Association (FA) is football's NGB.
- **ISFs (International Sports Federations):** in order to be involved in international competition the NGB needs to be affiliated to a relevant ISF.
- **The BOA (British Olympic Association):** selects, funds and manages the team to represent Great Britain and Northern Ireland at the Olympic Games.
- **The IOC (International Olympic Committee):** organises and manages each Olympiad.

Central Council for Physical Recreation

The Central Council for Physical Recreation (CCPR) (www.ccpr.org.uk) was set up against the bleak backdrop of 1930s Britain, which was experiencing economic unrest and high levels of unemployment. The school leaving age was 14 and, with the exception of students in private education, this was when education stopped. There was little opportunity after school to play sport and even in state schools sport was limited.

The CCPR was the first attempt to provide government influence in sport and aimed to promote the benefits of sport. Initially, the CCPR supported the work of the National Fitness Council to provide training for physical education teachers. In 1946, it was offered the use of Bisham Abbey at a low rent to be used as the national Physical Recreation Centre. Lilleshall was acquired in 1947 and Plas y Brenin in 1955; Crystal Palace was built in 1964 and Holme Pierrepont in 1973. These national sports centres were the central facilities to provide high-quality, residential training facilities and venues for national and international competition.

The CCPR worked to gain the support of the national governing bodies and within six months of its inception 82 NGBs were signed-up members. The CCPR prepared an influential report into sport in Britain, called the Woolfenden Report, which was published in 1960. Among its main recommendations was the formation of a sports council to promote sport in Britain. The Sports Council was formed in 1965 in an advisory capacity and became an executive body in 1972 when it was decided that the CCPR should be taken over by the Sports Council and transfer all its staff and assets. This was not agreed and the CCPR still exists today, representing the members of the NGBs.

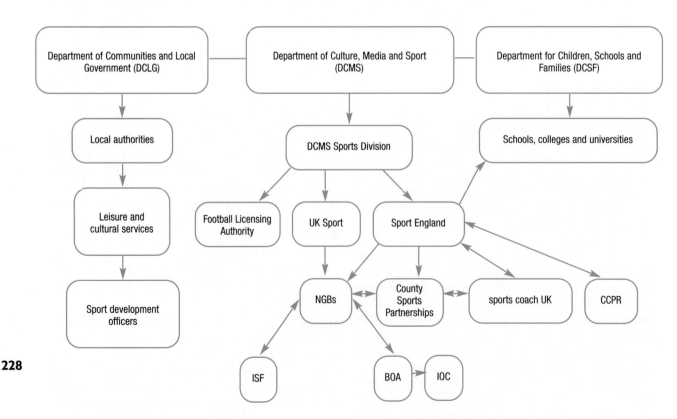

Fig 12.1 Bodies governing sport in England

UK Sport

UK Sport (www.uksport.gov.uk) was established in 1997 through a Royal Charter as the twin roles of the Sports Council were separated. The Sports Council had two remits: first, to promote excellence in sports achievements and, second, to promote participation in sport. These were seen as being radically different and it was decided to let the Sports Council (now Sport England) continue to promote participation in sport but to give the role of developing excellence to a new body with responsibility across the UK.

UK Sport directs the development of sporting excellence within the home countries; it supports athletes to become world-class performers through its World Class Performance Programme. Between 1997 and 2008, UK Sport invested £235 million into supporting athletes in summer Olympic sports. UK Sport's World Class Events Programme supported around 120 events between 1997 and 2009 of World, European or Commonwealth status and has £20 million to invest in events between 2006 and 2012. It used to be responsible for drug control in British sport; however, since December 2009, this responsibility has been taken on by UK Anti-Doping (UKAD).

Sport England

Sport England was formed from the old Sports Council by Royal Charter in 1997 and is responsible to the Secretary of State for the Department for Culture, Media and Sport. Sport England also operates nine regional offices across England (see Fig. 12.2).

It has responsibility for promoting and investing in sport and helping the government to implement its sporting objectives through the distribution of lottery funds. The vision of Sport England is 'to make England an active and successful sporting nation'. The business objectives of Sport England are to allocate its resources to:

- **Grow:** to get one million people taking part in more sport and to get school children taking part in five hours of PE a week
- **Sustain:** to ensure more people are satisfied with their sporting experience and reduce the number of 16–18 year olds dropping out from nine targeted sports (badminton, basketball, football, hockey, gymnastics, netball, rugby league, rugby union and tennis)
- **Excel:** to improve the development of talent in at least 25 sports.

Regional offices

There are nine regional offices, which administer the regional policies of Sport England and deliver local initiatives (see Figure 12.2):

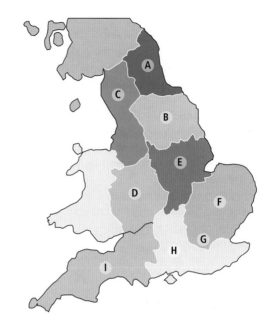

Fig 12.2 The regional offices of Sport England

- North East (A)
- North West (C)
- East Midlands (E)
- London (G)
- Yorkshire (B)
- West Midlands (D)
- East (F)
- South East (H)
- South West (I).

There are also regional offices for the other three countries of the United Kingdom, as outlined below.

Sport Scotland

Sport Scotland distributes lottery funding to help people in Scotland discover and develop their own sporting experiences, to help increase participation rates and to support the development of excellence.

The Sports Council for Wales

The Sports Council for Wales (www.sports-council-wales.co.uk) has been in action since 1972 and has its head office at the Welsh Institute of Sport in Cardiff. It has several programmes to encourage young people, adults and communities to become more active and achieve excellence:

1. Active Young People
   This includes a variety of schemes:
   (a) Dragon Sport – this involves getting primary schools to sign up for out of school sports activities
   (b) 5 × 60 – this is designed to get secondary

229

school pupils taking 60 minutes of physical activity five times a week

(c) PE and School Sports Scheme (PESS) □ a scheme managed by the Sports Council of Wales to improve standards of PE lessons in Welsh Schools

(d) Free swimming – this is a scheme funded by the Welsh Assembly Government to offer free swimming sessions to people aged 16 and under during school holidays.

2 Active Adults

Schemes, such as Community Chest, Development Grant and Sportsmatch Cymru encourage adults to be more physically active.

3 Developing People

This scheme is aimed at developing sporting opportunities for disabled people in the community. It is delivered by a network of Development Officers in every local authority in Wales.

4 Delivering Performance

Elite Cymru is a lottery-funded project that provides financial, medical and sport science support to elite and aspiring athletes to allow them to develop their full potential.

Sport Northern Ireland

The aims of Sport Northern Ireland are to work with partners to:

- Increase and sustain committed participation, especially among young people
- Raise the standards of sporting excellence and promote the good reputation and efficient administration of sport
- Develop the competencies of its staff, who are dedicated to optimising the use of its resources.

National Governing Bodies

To be recognised as a sport there must be a national governing body (NGB) to oversee the activities of the participants involved in that sport. Governing bodies are found at a county, regional, national and international level. If we look at football, for example, we find the structure shown in Figure 12.3.

Football has an international governing body (FIFA), a European governing body (UEFA), a national governing body (English FA) and county governing bodies (e.g. Herts FA), each of which has different responsibilities. You will find similar structures in all sports, although some sports, such as boxing, have more than one body governing the sport. When looking at a governing body, it is useful to look at features such as its membership, funding and policies as this will help to explain what its aims are and what the body is able or not able to do.

The regulation of the sport by a governing body involves setting and implementing the rules for the sport and organising events, such as leagues and tournaments.

- Key Learning Points
- The effects of the Industrial Revolution led to an increase in working hours and a decline in leisure time. Many activities were banned because they became costly in terms of working hours and productivity being lost.
- The workers had a low spending power in reality.
- The urban setting provided an inappropriate environment for playing sports.
- The Department for Culture, Media and Sport is responsible for promoting excellence in sport.
- UK Sport is responsible for promoting excellence in sport.
- National Sports Councils are mainly responsible for increasing participation rates in sport.

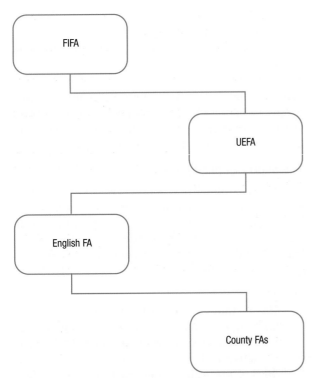

Fig 12.3 The structure of the governing bodies of football

Q Quick quiz 1

Using the following table, match the bodies involved in the administration of sport in Britain and Northern Ireland to a description of what they do.

Administrative body	Description of their responsibilities
Department for Culture, Media and Sport	Manages and organises each Olympic Games
Central Council of Physical Recreation	Selects, funds and manages team to represent GB and NI at the Olympic Games
National Governing Bodies	Represents the interests of NGBs
British Olympic Association	Responsible for administering sport in Central Government
International Olympic Committee	Runs leagues, provides officials and implements disciplinary measures in a sport

Student activity 12.1   ⏱ 90 minutes   P1   M1

Taking a sport of your choice, research and then describe how the sport has developed and been organised since the mid-nineteenth century. You could look at when the first rules were developed for the sport, when the first competitions took place and how these have developed up to the present day. To achieve M1, you need to explain these developments and show a deeper level of research.

12.3 How the Media and Technology Influence Modern Sport

It is interesting to compare how much we know about different sports and different sports performers. For example, we know a lot about footballers and their private lives; you could probably name the wives/girlfriends of five or six England footballers, even if you don't follow football. But could you name five or six of the current England women's football team? This is despite the England women's team being runners-up at the 2009 European Championships and the England men's failure to reach the finals of the 2008 European Championships. We have world champions as diverse as Beth Tweddle (gymnastics), Amir Khan (boxing), Tom Daley (diving) and Jessica Ennis (athletics), yet we know varying amounts about each of them. This leads to questions such as:

● Why does the media report extensively on football,

including off-the-field activities, but very little on gymnastics or trampolining?
● How does this media attention affect the sport and its participants?
● Are there issues of gender equality in media reporting?
● How do the media portray sports performers and why do they portray them in this way?

To answer these questions, we need to look at how sport is presented by the media and who reads and watches sports media.

Media

'The media' refers to the means of communication that reach large numbers of people. The happenings in sport are reported through a variety of media:

● Newspapers
● Television
● Radio
● Internet
● Films
● Books
● Magazines

231

- Teletext services
- Mobile phones.

Local and National Press

Each area in the UK has its own local newspaper. The local newspaper has a small circulation compared with the national newspaper and its aim is to provide local information only. It will therefore print only local sports stories. It will give reports on the best local teams and will cover national news only if there is a local angle, such as 'Local girl wins national judo championships'. In the same way, national newspapers report world events primarily if there is a UK angle,

such as 'England win 2006 Women's World Team Squash Championship'.

It is the editors who make decisions about what news we receive. They decide which news is most important and which news is most relevant. An editor will always have one eye on whether people will be interested in a particular story and if they can relate to it.

Television

Television is the most important aspect of the media in sport. Since the first televised World Cup in football in 1970 to the Sky deal with the Premiership

Channel	Average daily reach		Weekly reach		Average weekly viewing	Share
	Thousands	%	Thousands	%	Hrs/mins per person	%
ALL/ANY TV	32,101	72.9	40,913	92.9	23:37	100.0
BBC 1 (incl. Breakfast News)	20,232	46.0	35,294	80.2	4:33	19.2
BBC 2	10,338	23.5	26,967	61.2	1:31	6.4
TOTAL BBC1/BBC2	22,567	51.3	36,815	83.6	6:04	25.7
ITV (incl. GMTV)	17,131	38.9	32,695	74.3	4:21	18.4
CHANNEL4/S4C	11,037	25.1	28,137	63.9	1:39	7.0
CHANNEL 5	7,502	17.0	22,632	51.4	1:05	4.6
TOTAL/ANY COMMERCIAL TERRESTRIAL TV	22,534	51.2	37,056	84.2	7:05	30.0
Total terrestrial	27,764	63.1	39,195	89.0	13:09	55.7
Sky One	2,757	6.3	9,935	22.6	0:22	1.6
Sky Two	1,239	2.8	5,721	13.0	0.08	0.6
Sky Three	1,391	3.2	6,367	14.5	0.7	0.5
Sky News	1,367	3.1	4,591	10.4	0:07	0.5
Sky Sports 1	2,033	4.6	6,109	13.9	0:34	2.4
Sky Sports 2	1,752	4.0	5,795	13.2	0.18	1.3
Sky Sports 3	598	1.4	2,375	5.4	0:05	0.3
Sky Sports News	1,832	4.2	5,902	13.4	0:09	0.6
Sky Premiership Plus	82	0.2	523	1.2	0.:01	0.1
Sky Sports Extra	264	0.6	1,329	3.0	0:02	0.1
All Sky Sports	4,284	9.7	10,625	24.1	1:08	4.0

Table 12.1 Hours of viewing, share of audience and reach – multi-channel homes: including timeshift (week ending 24 September 2006) (*Source*: Broadcasters' Audience Research Board Ltd, 2006)

to pay £1.7 billion for three years from 2007/8, it has often been about money. TV companies are prepared to pay high prices for the rights to show the best sporting events. The largest events are the FIFA World Cup, the Olympics and the Superbowl. Some 800 million people worldwide watch the Superbowl each year. And the Superbowl viewing figures occupy nine out of the ten most watched sporting events on television in the USA. Only the women's figure skating from the 1994 Winter Olympics can make it into the list, at number 10! With these types of viewing figures, the TV networks are able to hike up their advertising rates and, at their peak in 2000, 30 seconds of airtime during the Superbowl could cost US$2.5 million!

In the UK, 20.4 million viewers tuned in to watch Italy win the 2006 World Cup final. During the match, this figure dropped to as low as 13.6 million. But for the penalty shootout, it rose back to the peak with 17 million watching BBC and 3.4 million watching ITV. In contrast, the Wimbledon men's tennis final, which was shown earlier, had an audience of 7.1 million on the BBC, watching Roger Federer take the title. The average Premiership football game shown on Sky TV in 2006 attracted audiences of 1.25 million. Pay-per-view games in 2006 attracted audiences of 215,000. The average crowd at a Premiership football match in 2006 was 34,000. In 2001, the Office for National Statistics reported that UK children aged between six and sixteen watch three hours of TV per day, compared with two hours elsewhere in Europe.

Table 12.1 shows the viewing figures for one week in September 2006. It shows how terrestrial channels (BBC1 and 2, ITV, Channel 4 and Five) still dominate overall viewing figures, but that channels like Sky Sports 1 have a relatively large share of viewers considering they show only sports programmes.

What is the effect of the media on sport? Table 12.2 lists some of the positive and negative effects.

Sport is presented on television in a 'mediated' form, meaning that television professionals have made decisions about how the sport is presented. It is usually done to make the sports event more attractive to the floating viewer. They know that the devoted sports fans will watch anyway, so they are seeking to attract the attention of viewers who are less committed to the sport, but may enjoy the sense of occasion. As a result, television changes sport to maximise its attractiveness and its number of viewers.

The effects of increasing television coverage of sport are as follows.

● **Money:** increased sums of money come into the sport from television companies who pay for the rights to broadcast the sports. Also, sponsors become more willing to spend more money on sponsoring sport as they know it will receive national attention. Hence, sports' finances receive a boost on two fronts, and this enables them to spend more money on players, players' wages and stadiums. The development of football in the 1990s was based on increased income from television companies and firms offering sponsorship. This extra income enabled the owners of the clubs to spend money on players from overseas, who were superstars of the sport. In turn this makes the sport more attractive to the viewers, who are willing to pay more to watch sport on television and at the grounds. For world events the risks

Positive	Negative
More participation may result from the desire to emulate the superstars	Less participation as people become couch potatoes, watching too much TV
Increased amount of money in the sport which can go to help grassroots	The majority of the money goes to players/clubs – very little goes to grassroots
Allows the players to be full-time professionals and so raises standards	Only certain sports get enough TV money to allow them to be professional
Clubs can provide better facilities/equipment/players	The popular/successful clubs get richer and the poor clubs remain poor
Positive role models can promote good behaviour	Negative role models can promote poor behaviour
Can bring different ethnic groups together – e.g. the multi-ethnic French World Cup squads in 1998 and 2006	Increased media hype may lead to nationalism and 'anti' feelings towards others<TT end>

Table 12.2 Positive and negative effects of the media on sport

233

can be great as evidenced by some Olympics that did not turn a profit, but the earnings can also be huge. The 2006 World Cup made profits of £741 million, with the cost of staging the event outstripped by sales of tickets, merchandising, sponsorship and media rights.

- **Changes in the rules of the game:** in order to make sports more attractive, the rules can be amended to make the action faster or to penalise negative play. In rugby union, the points for a try have risen from four to five, and bonus points are now given to teams scoring four or more tries or for losing by fewer than five points. One-day cricket has punished bowlers delivering no balls by offering batsmen a free hit on the next delivery from which they cannot be out. In hockey, the offside rule was changed and in netball players no longer have to wait for the umpire's whistle to restart play.

- **Changes in the presentation of the sport:** the introduction of Twenty20 cricket addressed the problem of low attendances by looking at a way to fit cricket into the lives of busy people. In England, a match will typically begin at 5.30pm and be over by 8.30pm, so this caters for people who are at work during the day but are keen to watch a match in the evening. The matches themselves have been organised as part of family entertainment, where the players are introduced by music, and there is additional entertainment such as firework displays, bouncy castles and barbecues on offer. To make the game look more spectacular, the players wear coloured clothing and use a white ball with black stumps. Such has been the popularity of Twenty20 cricket, it has spread quickly to other countries (e.g. Indian Premier League) and there is now a Twenty20 World Cup. It has changed the perception of cricket as being a dull, time-consuming sport and has introduced the sport to different types of spectators who would not attend county cricket. Also, it has brought increased finance into cricket and offered increased incentives to the players.

- **Changes in starting times:** the start times of matches are regularly changed to suit the needs of the television audience. Football games may kick off any time between 11.00am and 10.00pm, depending on where the game is played and when the audience is available. This is great for the television viewers, but comes at a high cost to the spectators at the game, who become much inconvenienced. Televised games on a Sunday are shown at 4.00pm and not 3.00pm after an enforced change one week attracted a much larger audience. The Monday-night games are an attempt

to generate the sort of audience loyalty seen in the USA where Monday-night football is watched religiously.

- **Sponsorship:** in the world of corporate sponsorship, how a brand performs off the pitch is just as important as how the players perform on the pitch. FIFA uses Sponsorship Intelligence, a company that researches the impact of events such as the 2006 World Cup. At this event it claims that Coca-Cola 'won the World Cup' in terms of successful promotion. Its research showed that out of the 15 World Cup sponsors, the best remembered was Coca-Cola, something it says might be attributed to that company's support of the World Cup since Mexico 1970.

Other Forms of Media Coverage

Radio is an increasingly popular medium and due to the wealth of radio stations on air, it is possible to devote stations entirely to sports coverage. BBC Radio Five Live is a current affairs and sports station that offers a viable alternative to television through its in-depth coverage.

Books are increasingly becoming an important source of media coverage, and they have the advantage of interpreting events we may not have fully understood at the time. Recently, Wayne Rooney signed a £5 million deal plus royalties to write five books over the next 12 years: a good example of how a player can make money off the field.

Visit any large newsagents and you will see the wide array of **sports magazines** available. The **internet** has also become a rich source of information for people following sports, and there is a vast number of websites dedicated to sport in general and to individual sports. The problem has been that much information has appeared in an unedited, unmediated format and often reflects the views of a minority.

Technology

As coverage of sport has increased and sport has attracted increased investment through television and sponsorship, so the demand for improved performance and exciting outcomes has increased. Technology has been in used in sport for several reasons:

- To improve the equipment and clothing of athletes/teams
- To make the viewing experience more enjoyable
- To help officials reach the correct decisions
- To inform the training programmes of athletes.

We will now examine these individually.

Clothing and Personal Equipment

The application of knowledge gained through biomechanics has led to changes in the design of the following:

● **Golf** the design of the shaft of the club to get the ideal amount of flex that will impart the greatest force on the golf ball (shafts can be graphite or iron)
● **Cricket bats** have to have a wooden face but technology has focused on the treatment of design of bats for maximum power and bat speed
● **Swimsuits** in the 2008 Olympic Games, swimmers started to wear polyurethane swimsuits that work by pushing the water away and helping the swimmers to stay afloat. The result is that there is less resistance on the swimmer from the water.

There have also been changes to the design of football and rugby strips, skis, speedskates, mountain bikes and tennis rackets to help improve performance.

The Viewing Experience

Although we take it for granted now, the viewing experience of watching sport on television has been revolutionised by the use of multiple cameras to give different views of the same events. When there is a controversial moment in cricket, football or rugby, it is often shown from at least four angles. The use of replays and freeze frames has resulted in increased ways to analyse and understand events. Sky Television has introduced computer-animated reconstructions to help their analysts make points to the viewers. These developments have helped to contribute to the enjoyment for the viewer; however, they can also increase pressure on the officials as all of their decisions come under great scrutiny.

Helping Officials Make the Correct Decisions

The use of the third umpire and the referral system in cricket has had a considerable effect on helping the umpires reach the right decision. Technology such as 'Hawk-Eye', 'snicko' and the 'hot spot' have helped umpires to come to the right decision, while the replay camera can be used to judge whether a batsman has been run out. Hawk-Eye technology and its associated referral system have been successfully implemented into tennis to judge the accuracy of the line calls from the umpire. In rugby union, a referee can refer a decision on whether a try has been scored to the video referee before awarding the try. Football is currently resistant to the use of technology in judging on decisions, such as whether the ball has crossed the touchline or to adjudicate on incidents where the referee has not had a full view. Preference is given to the human judgement of the referee and their assistant as it is felt that video replays will slow down the action and undermine the authority of the on-field officials.

Informing the training programmes of athletes

The introduction of science into sport has helped to develop a range of scientific techniques to test and analyse the fitness and skill levels of athletes. The ability to accurately carry out VO_2 max, lactate threshold, anaerobic power tests has enabled coaches to evaluate the effectiveness of their training programmes.

Key learning points 1

● Media refers to the means of communication used for reaching large numbers of people.
● Forms of media include television, newspapers and internet services.
● Television has impacted on sport by increasing the amount of money in sport, changing the presentation of sport and influencing when sports are played.
● Technology has influenced sport by contributing to the design of sports clothing and equipment, and by informing about the effectiveness of an athlete's training techniques. It has also influenced how sport is viewed and how it is officiated.

Q Quick quiz 2

1 List four effects that increased television coverage has on a sport.
2 List four effects technology has had on sport.

Student activity 12.2 ⏱ **90 minutes** | P2 | P3 | M2 | M3

Task 1

Using examples from televised coverage and newspaper (or online) reports, describe how a sports event is changed for presentation by media professionals and why this is done. To achieve M2, you need to explain and provide more detail about the changes.

Task 2

Choose a sport and describe the effect that technology has had on the sport over the last ten years and what these changes are aiming to achieve. To achieve M3, you need to explain these changes in more detail.

12.4 How Contemporary Issues Affect Sport

Deviance

Deviance is a form of behaviour which is considered to violate society's norms and therefore to be unacceptable. In sport, this manifests itself in a number of ways such as drugs, gamesmanship and violence. A sports person can exhibit positive and negative deviance.

Positive deviance equals over-commitment. For example, over-training or playing on through injury and pain and much of the 'no pain, no gain' philosophy supports this behaviour. In many sports, we applaud the images of athletes covered in blood but carrying on for their country.

Negative deviance equals either a desperate or calculated breaking of the rules or playing outside the spirit of a sport. This is the more recognisable side of deviance (e.g. using banned substances to win a race).

Drugs in Sport

The most notorious drug cheat in history was probably Canadian sprinter Ben Johnson, who tested positive at the 1988 Seoul Olympics for an anabolic steroid called stanozolol. Johnson had been beaten by his nearest rival, Carl Lewis, about a month before in an emphatic manner. When the Olympic 100 m final came around, Johnson led from gun to finish and won easily in a new world record time of 9.79 seconds. Two days later, he tested positive for drugs and was stripped of his medal and world record. It was common knowledge that Johnson had been using illicit drugs for years, but he maintains that the drug he was using was not stanozolol and that he had been set up.

But the problem hasn't gone away. Statistically speaking, Athens 2004 was twice as bad as the previous worst Olympic Games for doping offences. By the time the flame was extinguished in the Olympic Stadium, 24 doping violations had been uncovered. That is double the previous highest number of 12 at Los Angeles in 1984.

More recently we have seen sprinter Justin Gatlin, 100 m world record holder, testing positive for elevated levels of testosterone. And in 2003, Dwain Chambers, the former European 100 m champion became the first athlete in the world to be punished for taking tetrahydrogestrinone (THG), a previously undetectable steroid. Chambers' positive test caused his 4 × 100 m team to be stripped of their European gold in 2002 and silver in the World Championships in 2003. When he had served his ban and was reinstated in the 4 × 100 m team for the European Championships in 2006 and the team won gold again, Darren Campbell, who had lost both previous medals because of Dwain Chambers, refused to take part in the lap of honour. Under British Olympic Association rules, Dwain Chambers can never compete at the Olympics for Team GB as it has imposed its own life ban on anyone who fails a drug test.

The World Anti-Doping Agency

The World Anti-Doping Agency (WADA) (www.wada-ama.org) has the following mission statement:

> *'WADA is the international independent organization created in 1999 to promote, coordinate, and monitor the fight against doping in sport in all its forms. Composed and funded equally by the sports movement and governments of the world, WADA coordinated the development and implementation of the World Anti-Doping Code (Code), the document harmonizing anti-doping policies in all sports and all countries.'*

Gamesmanship

We often talk about sports performers playing fairly, but find it hard to define what playing fairly is. Is a player who appeals for every decision playing fairly or trying to influence the referee? Some definitions may help.

Key terms

Gamesmanship: not playing within the unwritten rules of the game and destroying the ethics, spirit, goodwill, fairness, etc.

Letter of the game: written rules of play.

Spirit of the game: playing fairly and abiding by unwritten rules, and expressing the correct attitudes and ethics of the game.

Sportsmanship: playing within both the written and unwritten rules.

As sport has become increasingly pressured with a 'win at all costs' approach taking over from the old ideals of athleticism (playing fairly as an amateur), so we have seen a rise in gamesmanship. Much sport is professional and the rewards for winning are great. There is pressure from fans, managers and, in world competitions, the nation, all desperate for a win. It is becoming less and less likely to find role models who will not compromise their ethical stance.

Sports Initiatives

Sport has often been used as a power for good. It has been argued that sport is good for society and has a positive influence. For example, those who believe it is functional claim it can increase participation, reduce crime and anti-social behaviour, and improve the nation's health. The government certainly subscribes to this view. It spends millions each year to provide sport and leisure opportunities for all and is particularly interested in deprived areas or those with high incidences of crime. There are a number of anti-crime initiatives the government has introduced which use sport as a vehicle for providing an alternative to committing crime. Sport England (which receives money from government funds) has a representative within the Home Office who has been working closely with the Community Cohesion Unit to show how sport can unite communities, especially in deprived areas.

Social Exclusion

To understand social exclusion it helps to look at occupations and income. Type of employment and income can be considered together as one is dependent on the other. This is addressed further in the next section.

Health Initiatives

Sport England also believes it can make an important contribution to improving health and reducing the estimated £8.2 billion cost of inactivity to the NHS. The 'Everyday Sport' physical activity campaign encourages even the most inactive people to incorporate a little more activity into their daily lives, taking small steps that can make a big difference – from taking the stairs instead of the lift or getting off the bus a stop early, to joining a sports club. Other initiatives include 'Sporting Champions', a scheme that takes sports stars into schools and communities to inspire young people about sport.

Racism

If we look at Britain as a whole, we can see that some sports are more popular in some areas and less popular in others. One of the major factors influencing the sports we play is where we are brought up. For example, rugby league is more prevalent in the north of England and rugby union in the south of England and Wales. Scotland has its own sports, such as skiing, curling and its Highland Games, and Ireland has sports such as hurling and Gaelic football.

Britain has developed into a multi-racial society. Many members of the population are from African-Caribbean or various Asian and European backgrounds. Their parents or grand-parents had been initially drawn to Britain by the need for jobs during the 1950s.

Some ethnic groups choose to retain separate cultural identities within British society, but black sports people participate successfully in most sports in Britain. However, racism does still occur in British sport, although it is not usually the overt racism that black footballers suffered in the 1980s and early 1990s.

Key terms

Race: the physical characteristics of a person.

Ethnicity: the cultural adherence of a person or group, characterised by their customs and habits (religious beliefs, diet, clothing, leisure activities and lifestyle).

Racism describes the oppression of a person or group by another person or group on the grounds of physical differences. Racism in British sport occurs in two ways, through racial stereotyping and stacking.

- **Stereotyping:** historically, racial discrimination has excluded black people from achieving in the workplace, so many black people entered sport as an arena where they could improve their life chances. Thus, many young black people spent more time improving their sporting ability at the cost of their academic abilities. This produced two stereotypes:

– black people are naturally good at sport
– black people are not intelligent.

- **Stacking:** black people tend to be guided into certain sports and certain positions within teams. They tend to predominate in sports such as track-and-field athletics, football, basketball and boxing. These sports tend to be inexpensive, requiring little specialist equipment, and can be practised relatively cheaply. Within these sports, black people tend to dominate in certain positions or events, usually those requiring physical rather than intellectual or decision-making qualities, such as wingers in rugby rather than positions of centrality.

This stacking comes from a stereotype that black people have a natural, genetic ability to be quick and powerful, but lack high intellectual abilities. This stereotype has in the past been perpetuated by teachers and coaches of sports who, when choosing teams, place black people in a position or an event because they believe all black people are fast and powerful.

More recently, black and Asian players have broken down these stereotypes. In football in the 1980s and 1990s, the majority of black players were forwards. That stereotype no longer exists, with players like Rio Ferdinand and Ashley Cole dominating in their defensive positions. However, an Asian football star is yet to emerge in the England football team.

Racism has been tackled on the football terraces under the Football Offences Act 1991, which makes it illegal to take part in racist chanting. An arrest can be made only if there are one or more people chanting and if the chants are causing distress to the person they are aimed at.

The 'Kick it Out' campaign to combat racism in British football has been fairly successful and it is now less of an issue. However, there are constant allegations of racism against black players in British teams when they are involved in international competitions.

This is a very difficult area of sport to debate. Many arguments can be made on each side. However, it is important to remember that social influences are as strong as other factors. Peer pressure, role models, historical success and society's norms all exert big pressures on young people looking for a sport and an identity. Concepts such as 'white flight' – the avoidance of seemingly black-dominated sports such as sprinting – may occur. In the same way, financial implications may simply be at the root of it all. There is no one answer and looking for a simple 'yes' or 'no' is not the way to answer this question.

Sexism

Before starting a discussion of the relationship between sex and sports participation, it is useful to examine the definitions of the terms we will use.

> ## Key terms
>
> **Sex:** the biological and therefore genetic differences between males and females.
>
> **Gender:** the learned social and cultural differences between males and females, in terms of their habits, personality and behaviour.
>
> **Sexism:** sexism means different things to different people. The following definition gives us a framework to work within:
>
> 'Sexism is a practice based on the ideology that men are superior to women. The ideology is expressed through a system of prejudice and discrimination that seeks to control and dominate women. It is systematically embodied in the structures and organisations of that society.' (Hargreaves, 1994)

Here is a comparison of men's and women's sport (General Household Survey figures, 1996):

- 71 per cent of men participate in sport, compared with 57 per cent of women
- 42 per cent of men participate in outdoor sports, compared with 24 per cent of women
- Twice as many men as women watch sport
- There are very few female professionals as compared with men
- There are few women in administrative positions in sport; IOC members for GBR are HRH The Princess Royal, Craig Reedie and Phil Craven
- The history and growth of sport is documented mainly in terms of the development of male sport
- Sport on television and in the written media is dominated by male sports.

Here are some possible reasons why women's participation rates are lower than men's.

- Historically, women in partnerships with men have taken on domestic responsibilities and thus any sport is fitted in between responsibilities of childcare, cooking, working, cleaning, washing, and so on. Sport can be time-consuming and costly, especially if childcare is needed.

- Class inequalities accentuate gender inequalities. Middle-class women have much higher participation rates than working-class women, as they typically have more money and access to private transport. The fitness boom has mostly benefited middle-class women.
- The major biological difference between men and women is that women can bear children and this has psychological and social repercussions. Women are allocated to reproductive, mothering and childcare roles, which limit the time and opportunity they have for sports activities. However, women are waiting longer now before having a family and this has improved their situation. Also, gender equality has meant that childcare and nurturing roles are more commonly shared between partners.
- Every society has a set of beliefs and values that dictate what is acceptable behaviour for women (and men) in all spheres of their lives, and sport is included in these values. Many people consider that some sporting activities can induce masculine traits in women, especially in competitive sports. Strong opinions are held as to what sports are acceptable or unacceptable for girls or women. Even strong peer pressure may prevent women from considering certain sports.

The conventional image of sport is based on chauvinistic values and male identity formation. Sport is the arena for the celebration of masculinity. To be successful at sport, you need to show skill, power, muscularity, competitiveness, aggression, assertiveness and courage. To be successful at sport is to be successful as a man, and to be uninterested or not talented is to be less of a man.

However, more recently body image has changed to accept a fitter, stronger female. Successful sportswomen have broken the old stereotypes and fashion has changed to support the image of a toned body as opposed to a flabby unfit one. Of course, there is also the argument that successful female athletes are a threat to the male-dominated world of sport. The reticence of males towards female sport could be simply viewed as a threat to male hegemony.

It could be argued that to be successful at sport a woman must show masculine traits that contrast with the so-called feminine traits of agility, balance, flexibility, coordination and gentleness. Successful sportswomen not only have to be exceptional athletes, they also have to retain their femininity.

Commercialisation of Sport

Commercialisation refers to the practice of applying business principles to sport. The advantages and disadvantages of commercialisation are outlined in Table 12.3.

Advertising

This is the way a company makes itself known to the public. In sport, this can be through using advertising boards around stadiums, placing an advert in the programme, TV commercials using sport stars, etc. Sponsorship, merchandising and endorsement all act as types of advertising.

Sponsorship

An agreement between a company and a team/governing body/stadium/competition. The company agrees to pay a certain amount to have its logo appear on kit or merchandising.

Advantages	Disadvantages
Sponsorship can help an event that would otherwise not happen without the money provided	The event becomes reliant on the sponsors and would not happen if they pulled out
Endorsements can help boost a performer's wages and sales of a product	The product may be unethical; the performer may not actually wish to use the product; the company may drop a performer who behaves badly or underperforms
Merchandising can help a club provide better facilities and buy better players	The fans could feel like they are being cheated, especially when shirts constantly change and prices are too high
Advertising can be a way for a performer to make extra income or back a worthy cause such as a charity	It can appear the performer has 'sold out' or it may seem like they are not taking their sport seriously enough

Table 12.3 The advantages and disadvantages of commercialisation

Merchandising

The sale of goods that are linked to the club, player or competition. Usually this is replica kits, flags, scarves, stickers, etc.

Endorsement

When a player promotes the use of a product. Companies pay well for a sports star to say their product is worth buying.

Commercialised sports do not work in all societies. They are predominantly found in developed societies where people have enough free time to be involved in watching sport, enough disposable income to spend on sport and the means of private transport to travel to the venues.

Education and Sport in Schools

Sport in schools has often been controversial. When working-class schools first started in the 1870s, children were drilled in military fashion so that they could be prepared for war. More recent controversy in the 1980s saw teacher strikes over pay lead to a withdrawal of teacher support for after-school sports fixtures when their pay demands were not met. When the National Curriculum started in the early 1990s, the suggestion was that all school children should receive two hours of PE per week, but in reality many schools provided less. Alongside this in the 1990s was the scandal of many schools selling off their playing fields for redevelopment.

The government response in the mid-1990s was a report called 'Raising the Game', which promised funding and increased status for schools that could persuade their teachers to provide more after-school activities and raise money for new facilities. The result was Sportsmark status for many schools and new specialist sports colleges with PE teachers taking on new roles such as school sports coordinators. The future for schools PE in the UK will no doubt centre on the 2012 London Olympics. The first response to this has been the proposal for school 'Olympics' to be held across the country each year in the run-up to 2012.

Other issues centre on how we do things in the UK. For example, countries like Australia have talent identification programmes in schools, which test students and assess their suitability for different sports. In this way they have encouraged a number of school children to take up events they would previously not have thought of, such as rowing. In the UK, we have been accused of having a laissez-faire approach to identifying talent. Although some might argue that this allows us to value all equally.

Child Protection

Following a number of high-profile child abuse cases involving sports coaches, new legislation has been put in place. All people working with children must be police-checked for any convictions involving children, and child protection training is now mandatory on most coaching courses.

Key learning points 2

- As sport becomes more important, the prevalence of gamesmanship activities increases.
- Racism in sport can be overt in terms of discrimination against certain racial groups and more covert in terms of stereotyping and stacking.
- Sexism is present in sport as female athletes are not provided with the opportunities on offer to male athletes.
- Commercialisation is the application of business principles to sport and includes advertising and sponsorship.

Q Quick quiz 3

Answer true or false to the following statements.

1 Deviance in sport is a label given to breaking the rules of a sport.

2 Gamesmanship is the deliberate breaking of rules of a sport.

3 Racism in sport occurs when different opportunities are offered to people of different racial groups.

4 Males and females have different rates of participation in sport.

5 Commercialisation always has positive effects on a sport.

Student activity 12.3 90 minutes P4 M4 D1

Choose four contemporary issues in sport and use a poster to present the issues in a visual form for the rest of your group to see. To achieve M4, you need to explain each of these issues on your poster. To achieve D1, in addition to your poster, you will need to write about each issue and evaluate its effect on contemporary sport.

12.5 Cultural Influences and Barriers that Affect Participation

 P5 P6 P7 M5 D2

Barriers to Sports Participation

As we will see later in this section, there is a clear relationship between gender, ethnicity, age and socio-economic group and sports participation; these could be perceived as barriers to participation. All these under-represented groups have something in common: they all have special requirements. Sport is predominantly marketed at young, white males and this group is well represented in sport. So arrangements have to be made to ensure that sports activities are accessible to all.

There are also other barriers which may have to be overcome:

- Time
- Resources
- Fitness levels
- Ability
- Lifestyle
- Medical conditions.

Time

Time is a major reason cited by people as a barrier. There are 24 hours in a day and we have to choose how to spend them. The management of time involves allocating time for work requirements, family responsibilities, activities for survival, such as eating and washing, sleep and time for relaxation. People need to find activities which fit in with their weekly schedule and put these times into their diary. They can then make arrangements for work and time to fit these activities in.

Resources

Resources include facilities, equipment and clothing. There is an uneven spread of facilities across the UK. Provision is dependent upon location (city or countryside), natural resources (such as water or mountains), the policy of the local authority on spending for sport and the demand from consumers. Equipment and clothing requirements can seriously deter people from sports – for example, the expense of going skiing or playing golf.

Fitness Levels

It is perceived that people who play sport or take exercise are fit and will look down on those who are not. This perception puts people off because they see their current situation as being miles away from where most people are or want to be. It needs to be explained to these people that there are many activities which can be performed at their own pace and as they get fitter they can increase the intensity they work at. Walking would provide adequate exercise for an unfit person and they can then move on to brisk walking, jogging or even running in their own time.

Ability

Not having the required skills and ability is a concern for some people as they do not want to look foolish or show themselves up. It is important that relevant coaching is provided to enable people to acquire the skills needed and to develop their ability. This is done through local sports development initiatives and government-sponsored schemes.

Lifestyle

Lifestyle issues, such as stress, smoking, alcohol and drug consumption, place barriers in front of people. All these activities will detract from attempts to do sport because smoking, alcohol and drug use all negatively affect health and make a person feel less likely to want to exercise. Stress and stressful situations mean a person is focusing on other issues and cannot contemplate playing a sport or taking exercise. These lifestyle issues need to be dealt with before a person can consider playing sport regularly and being successful.

Medical Conditions

These are a serious consideration for a person playing sport because if a person exercises inappropriately with a medical condition it can make the condition

241

worse; in the case of heart disease it may lead to their death. Having said that, there is virtually no medical condition which does not benefit or improve through regular exercise. Before a person plays sport or exercises they will be screened by a qualified person and then appropriate interventions need to be put in place to ensure the person takes part in the activity safely.

While we can see that sport benefits people and fulfils needs in their lives, it is important to point out that not all people have an equal access to sporting opportunities. These may be issues you take for granted, but in reality these differences exist because of the way our society is organised and how it has developed. A range of factors affect participation in sport, including:

● Gender
● Ethnic origin
● Age
● Socio-economic classification.

Gender

Statistics prepared by Sport England clearly show that women have lower participation rates than men (see Table 12.4).

With the odd exception, we can clearly see that men are more active than women. The figures show that, as a group, 65 per cent of men and 53 per cent of women had participated in at least one sporting activity in the four weeks before the interview. The only discrepancies were in sports such as keep fit and yoga, which traditionally attract more females.

Ethnic Origin

Recent statistics have shown a direct relationship between ethnic origin and participation in sport (see Table 12.5).

Table 12.5 and other research shows that:

● White ethnic groups have the highest participation rates

Sport	Men %	Women %
Walking	34.6	33.7
Swimming	12.3	15.2
Keep fit/yoga	7.1	16.5
Weight training	8.6	3.5
Running	7.1	3.1
Golf	8.3	1.3
Soccer	9.8	0.5
Tennis	2.2	1.6
Badminton	2.2	1.5
Fishing	3.1	0.2

Table 12.4 Percentage of men and women aged 16≤ participating in sport in the four weeks before interview (*Source*: Sport England, 2002)

Ethnic group	Participation excluding walking	Participation including walking
White	44.1	59.4
Any minority ethnic group	34.6	45.5
Indian	30.4	46.3
Pakistani/Bangladeshi	21.7	25.9
Black (Caribbean, African, other)	33.2	43.7
Other (Chinese, none of the above)	45.1	56.5

Table 12.5 Percentage of adults aged 16≤ participating in the four weeks before interview, by ethnic origin (*Source*: Sport England, 2002)

- People of Pakistani origin have the lowest participation rates
- Women of Pakistani origin have particularly low rates of participation
- Certain ethnic groups are well represented in some sports but very poorly represented in others.

Britain is now regarded as a multi-racial society and we must work to meet the needs of all groups. Sports development officers are working hard to offer opportunities to people from all ethnic groups and meet their specific needs – e.g. offering women-only swimming sessions for Muslim women.

Age

Age and also an individual's stage in the life cycle are key factors in influencing the level of participation and also the choice of sports. Younger people tend to choose more physical contact sports such as football and rugby, while older age groups will still be active but in more individual sports with less physical contact (see Table 12.6).

The relationship between participation and age is not always clear-cut, as swimming and keep fit have fairly stable levels of participation across the age groups. Fishing and golf increase slightly with age before falling off again, and soccer and running decline is related to age.

Socio-Economic Classification

Socio-economic classification is a system of classifying people based on their occupation and thus potential income (see Table 12.7).

Strategies and Initiatives

Sport England and local authorities are well aware of the problems faced by people from different cultures and the barriers faced by the general population. Since its inception in 1972, the Sports Council (now Sport England) has run a series of campaigns which started with 'Sport for All' and included 'Ever thought of sport?' and '50≤ and all to play for'. These campaigns were aimed at specific groups with low participation rates, such as women and older people.

Recent strategies have included:

- Game Plan
- Every Child Matters
- Sporting Equals
- Talented Athlete Support Scheme (TASS)
- Plan for Sport 2001
- Active Sports
- Sportsmark.

Game Plan

Game Plan was published in December 2002 to present the government's vision for sport up to 2020 and the strategy to deliver this vision. It includes strategies for developing excellence in performance and promoting mass participation.

Every Child Matters

Every Child Matters is a national policy which is to be achieved through local initiatives. The aim is for school provision to improve the children's attainment and life chances involving the actions of pupils, parents, teachers and governors. Sport and leisure

Sport	16–19	20–24	25–29	30–44	45–59	60–69	70≤
sWalking	40.7	47.1	42.3	50.5	52.0	46.1	26.8
Swimming	46.2	46.3	47.6	48.2	33.3	19.8	8.1
Keep fit/yoga	29.8	33.2	33.3	27.9	19.8	10.7	6.2
Snooker	42.5	41.3	30.3	19.4	10.7	6.2	3.5
Weight training	18.6	19.8	20.4	12.3	5.6	1.4	0.5
Running	19.7	18.1	18.0	13.9	4.6	1.0	0.2
Golf	14.6	17.4	17.1	14.5	10.9	8.1	4.0
Soccer	33.5	26.1	20.2	10.9	2.1	0.3	0.1
Tennis	24.0	14.7	10.1	8.7	4.8	2.1	0.5
Fishing	8.1	5.2	5.2	6.1	6.3	4.9	1.6
At least one activity	90.1	88.3	88.3	85.1	77.2	64.4	39.4

Table 12.6 Percentage of adults aged 16≤ participating in the four weeks before interview, by age (*Source*: Sport England, 2002)

243

Sport	Large employers/ higher managerial	Higher professional	Lower managerial & professional	Intermediate	Small employers	Lower supervisory & technical	Semi-routine	Routine	Long-term unemployed
Walking	47.1	46.2	41.7	32.7	30.0	29.4	28.5	23.5	19.5
Swimming	24.0	19.9	17.7	13.7	11.9	11.2	8.8	7.8	7.4
Snooker	9.9	9.2	9.6	10.2	9.4	9.1	8.5	7.0	5.5
Keep fit/yoga	20.8	18.3	15.3	14.8	11.1	9.4	7.1	6.3	4.6
Weight training	11.4	8.5	7.3	6.9	5.1	4.0	4.0	2.5	2.0
Running	10.1	8.1	6.6	5.2	3.3	3.4	2.2	2.3	3.2
Golf	9.5	8.4	6.1	4.2	4.8	4.7	3.3	3.8	4.2
Soccer	6.1	5.4	5.5	4.2	4.9	3.6	1.8	1.7	0.0
Tennis	3.1	4.0	2.7	1.8	1.7	0.5	0.8	0.5	1.0
Fishing	1.1	1.1	1.2	1.5	2.5	2.3	1.6	1.5	0.80

Table 12.7 Participation in sport, by socio-economic classification (*Source*: Sport England, 2002)

activities are a part of this scheme by using school facilities to deliver courses.

Sporting Equals

Sporting Equals is a strategy to promote racial equality in sport with the specific aims of developing a society where:

- People from minority ethnic groups can influence and participate equally in sport at all levels, as players, officials, coaches, administrators, volunteers and decision-makers, working with partners to develop awareness and understanding of racial equality issues that impact on sport
- Governors and providers of sport recognise and value a fully integrated and inclusive society
- A sporting environment is established where cultural diversity is recognised and celebrated.

Talented Athlete Support Scheme

The Talented Athlete Support Scheme (TASS) aims to provide funds for talented athletes at schools, colleges and universities to gain access to support for the development of their excellence. Money is provided for equipment, travel costs and sport science support, such as nutritional advice, sport psychology and physiological testing, and medical support such as physiotherapy and sports massage.

Plan for Sport 2001

This document was published in 2001 under the title 'A sporting future for all' and was an action plan setting out the vision and how it will be delivered. The action plan covers initiatives to develop sport in education and the community, and the modernisation of sporting organisations.

Active Sports

Active Sports is delivered on a local county basis and outlines the steps local authorities are taking to develop partnerships to deliver increased opportunities to participate in sport. For example, in Oxfordshire there is a network of partners working together to achieve the following aims:

- To increase participation in sport and active recreation
- To improve the levels of performance in sport
- To widen access to sport and active recreation
- To improve health and well-being.

Sportsmark

Sportsmark was introduced in 2004 as a partnership between the Departments for Education and Skills and for Culture, Media and Sport. It is an accreditation scheme for secondary schools to reward their commitment to developing out-of-hours sport provision as well as a well-designed PE curriculum. There are two levels of award: Sportsmark and Sportsmark Gold, at which a school can achieve a distinction award.

Key learning points 3

- Each individual may have barriers to prevent them from participating in sport.
- Time, facilities and cost are common barriers to participation.
- Gender, ethnic origin, age and socio-economic classification can all influence participation rates.

Q Quick quiz 4

Choosing from the list of words below, fill in the blanks to complete the following paragraph regarding the barriers to sports participation:

- Fitness
- Facilities
- Management
- Ability
- Equipment
- Schedule
- Clothing.

Time or the _____ of time is a major barrier to participation; however, if activities are fitted into their weekly _____ it will increase their chances of being active. Resources include the availability of _____ for sport but the expense of _____ and _____ can have a prohibitive effect. Also a person may not feel they have an appropriate _____ level or the _____ to play a sport or they may have a medical condition that they feel could be made worse.

Student activity 12.4 ⏱ **90 minutes** P5 P6 P7 M4 D2

Prepare a presentation to be carried out in front of the rest of the group that covers the following information:

- An explanation of four barriers to sports participation

- An explanation of three cultural influences on sports performance

- A description of three strategies or initiatives to increase sports performance.

To achieve M5 and D2, you will need to explain these initiatives in more detail and then evaluate the success of these strategies in improving sports performance.

References

Broadcasters' Audience Research Board (2006) 'Hours of viewing, share of audience and reach-multi-channel homes: including timeshift (w/e 24/09/06)', www.barb.co.uk (accessed 26 January 2010)

Hargreaves, J. (1994) *Sporting Females – Critical Issues in the History of Women's Sport,* Routledge.

Sport England (2002) 'Participation in Sport, 2002', www.sportengland.org/research (accessed 26 January 2010)

Further reading

Cashmore, E. (2010) *Making Sense of Sport,* Routledge.

Craig, P. and Beedie, P. (2008) *Sport Sociology,* Learning Matters.

Hargreaves, J. (1994) *Sporting Females – Critical Issues in the History of Women's Sport,* Routledge.

Polley, M. (1998) *Moving the Goalposts – A History of Sport and Society Since 1945,* Routledge.

Sport England (2001) *A Review of the Economic Importance of Sport.*

Tomlinson, A. (ed.) (2007) *The Sports Studies Reader,* Routledge.

Useful websites

www.bbc.co.uk/sport

Provides regularly updated reports and articles on sports-related topics

www.sportengland.org/support__advice/equality_and_diversity.aspx

Provides information about how participation in sport is being promoted in Britain by Sport England

14: Exercise, Health and Lifestyle

14.1 Introduction

A person's lifestyle can have a huge impact on their long-term health. Lifestyle plays a key role in the prevention of a large number of diseases, including coronary heart disease, cancer and obesity. This unit will give you the knowledge and skills to assess the lifestyle of an individual, provide advice on lifestyle improvement and plan a health-related physical activity programme.

By the end of this unit you should:

- know the importance of lifestyle factors in the maintenance of health and well-being
- be able to assess the lifestyle of a selected individual
- be able to provide advice on lifestyle improvement
- be able to plan a health-related physical activity programme for a selected individual.

Assessment and grading criteria

To achieve a PASS grade the evidence must show that the learner is able to:	To achieve a MERIT grade the evidence must show that, in addition to the pass criteria, the learner is able to:	To achieve a DISTINCTION grade the evidence must show that, in addition to the pass and merit criteria, the learner is able to:
P1 describe lifestyle factors that have an effect on health	**M1** explain the effects of identified lifestyle factors on health	
P2 design and use a lifestyle questionnaire to describe the strengths and areas for improvement in the lifestyle of a selected individual	**M2** explain the strengths and areas for improvement in the lifestyle of a selected individual	**D1** evaluate the lifestyle of a selected individual and prioritise areas for change
P3 provide lifestyle improvement strategies for a selected individual	**M3** explain recommendations made regarding lifestyle improvement strategies.	**D2** analyse a range of lifestyle improvement strategies.
P4 plan a six-week health-related physical activity programme for a selected individual.		

14.2 Lifestyle Factors

Physical Activity

Our lifestyle has become much more sedentary over the years. We now have methods of transport that require little physical exertion. Cars and buses have replaced walking and cycling. Recent studies have shown that 30 per cent of children go to school by car, and fewer than 50 per cent walk. This country has less time dedicated to PE lessons than any other country in the European Union. There are now relatively few manual occupations, and the majority of people's careers are spent in an office-based environment. Everyday tasks such as laundry, cleaning and cooking require little effort, as they are all aided by labour-saving devices. It is now even possible to go shopping by sitting in front of a computer and logging on to the internet.

For entertainment, the average person spends less time participating in active leisure pursuits and prefers to sit in front of the TV. The average adult watches over 26 hours of television each week, which is a virtually totally sedentary activity. Children also spend much less time pursuing activity-based play and choose computer games, videos or the TV to occupy their free time. All these factors have led to many people taking part in very low levels of physical activity.

Physical activity can increase a person's basal metabolic rate by around 10 per cent. This elevated basal metabolic rate can last for up to 48 hours after the completion of the activity. By taking part in physical activity kilocalories will be expended. The number of kilocalories used depends on the type and intensity of the activity. The more muscles that are used in the activity and the harder you work, the more kilocalories will be used up to perform the activity. For example, swimming the front crawl uses both the arms and the legs and will therefore use more calories to perform than walking, which mainly uses the leg muscles.

The body weight of the person will also have an impact on the number of kilocalories burnt while taking part in a physical activity. The heavier the person, the more kilocalories are required to move the heavier weight. So a heavier person will burn more calories than a lighter person when performing the same activity at the same intensity.

Key term

Physical activity: the state of being active.

National Recommended Guidelines

In order to gain the health benefits of physical activity, adults should aim to participate in physical activity for 30 minutes at least five times a week. Our national recommended guidelines for children state that they should participate in moderate-intensity exercise for 60 minutes per day, but the European Health Study 2006 found that they should be exercising for 90 minutes per day to gain the health benefits of physical activity.

Health Benefits of Physical Activity

Taking part in regular exercise has consistently been shown to have many benefits to a person's physical and mental health. Many types of disease can be alleviated or prevented by taking part in regular exercise.

Coronary heart disease and physical activity

Coronary heart disease (CHD) is the leading cause of death in the Western world. One-third of all deaths associated with CHD are due to not taking part in physical activity. Coronary heart disease is a narrowing of the coronary arteries, which are the blood vessels that pass over the surface of the heart and supply it with blood. CHD is usually a result of a build-up of fatty material and plaques within the coronary blood vessels. This is known as atherosclerosis.

Key terms

Coronary blood vessels: blood vessels that supply blood to the heart.

Atherosclerosis: build-up of fatty material in the coronary blood vessels, which makes their diameter smaller.

When a person with CHD takes part in a physically demanding task, the coronary arteries may not be able to supply the heart muscle with enough blood to keep up with the demand for oxygen. This will be felt as a pain in the chest (angina). If a coronary artery becomes completely blocked, the area of the heart muscle served by the artery will die, resulting in a heart attack.

Taking part in regular exercise appears to reduce the risk of heart disease directly and indirectly. Research has shown that exercise:

● Increases levels of HDL cholesterol
● Decreases the amount of triglycerides in the bloodstream.

Key terms

HDL cholesterol: the 'good' cholesterol that acts to clean the artery walls, which in turn reduces atherosclerosis.

Triglycerides: another type of fat; high levels in the bloodstream have been linked with increased risk of heart disease.

Hypertension: high blood pressure.

Fig 14.1 A normal lung (left) beside the lung of a smoker (right)

Hypertension and physical activity

A person is deemed to have hypertension if their blood pressure consistently reads at 140/90 or higher. Hypertension is a very common complaint, and around 15 to 25 per cent of adults in most Western countries have high blood pressure. If a person with hypertension does not reduce their blood pressure they are more at risk of suffering a stroke or a heart attack.

Psychological Benefits of Physical Activity

A number of studies have attempted to explore the effects of exercise on depression and found that exercise increases self-esteem, improves mood, reduces anxiety levels, increases the ability to handle stress and generally makes people happier than those who do not exercise. It is thought that one cause of depression may be a decreased production of certain chemicals in the brain, specifically adrenaline, dopamine and serotonin. Exercise has been shown to increase the levels of these substances, which may have the effect of improving a person's mood after taking part in exercise. For the last decade or so, exercise has been prescribed as a method of combating depression.

Smoking

You are probably aware that smoking is bad for you. It actually kills around 14,000 people in the UK each year, and 300 people die in the UK every day as a result of smoking. These deaths occur through a range of diseases caused by smoking and include a variety of cancers, cardiovascular disease and an array of chronic lung diseases.

The products in a cigarette that appear to do the most damage include tar, nicotine and carbon monoxide.

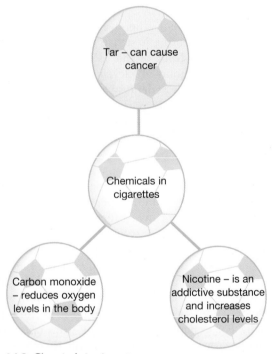

Fig 14.2 Chemicals in cigarettes

Smokers are making themselves much more likely to suffer from a range of cancers; 90 per cent of people suffering from lung cancer have the disease because they smoke or have smoked. You are also four times more likely to contract mouth cancer if you are a smoker. Other forms of cancer that have been linked to smoking include cancers of the bladder, oesophagus, kidneys and pancreas, and cervical cancer.

Cardiovascular Disease

Cardiovascular disease is the main cause of death in smokers. The excess cholesterol produced from smoking narrows the blood vessels.

When the blood vessels become narrower, blood clots are more likely to form, which can then block the coronary blood vessels. A blockage in these vessels can lead to a heart attack. It is estimated that 30 per cent of these heart attacks are due to smoking.

Alternatively, the blood clot may travel to the brain, which can lead to a stroke; or it could travel to the kidneys, which could result in kidney failure; or the block may occur in the legs, which can lead to gangrene, for which the main treatment is amputation.

Chronic Lung Disease

The following diseases are more prevalent in smokers:

- Emphysema – a disease that causes breathlessness due to damaged alveoli
- Bronchitis – makes the person cough excessively because of increased mucus production in the lungs.

Key term

Alveoli: air sacs in the lungs in which gaseous exchange takes place.

Smoking is responsible for 80 per cent of these conditions, which basically block air flow to and from the lungs, making breathing more difficult. These diseases tend to start between the ages of 35 and 45.

Other Smoking-Related Health Risks

Smoking can also damage health in a variety of other ways. A person who smokes may suffer from some of the following:

- High blood pressure
- Impotence
- Fertility problems
- Eye problems
- Discoloured teeth and gums
- Mouth ulcers
- Skin more prone to wrinkles.

Alcohol

Alcohol is a legal drug that may be consumed by people aged 18 or over – although by the age of 16, over 80 per cent of young people in the UK have tried alcohol. In fact, in the UK, people aged between 16 and 24 are the heaviest drinking group of the population. Studies reveal that one in two men and one in four women drink more than the recommended daily benchmarks, and over a quarter of males and females drink more than double the recommended daily amount.

The recommended daily benchmarks for alcohol consumption are based on adult drinking; there are no recommendations for children and young people as they should be refraining from alcohol consumption by law.

Recommended Daily Intake

The Health Education Authority recommends that women should drink no more than two units of alcohol per day and males should drink no more than three units per day. Both males and females should have at least two alcohol-free days per week.

It takes around an hour for the adult body to get rid of one unit of alcohol, and this may well be slower in young people.

Effects of Alcohol on the Body

Alcohol affects the brain so that it compromises our judgement and suppresses our inhibitions. It decreases our physical coordination and sense of balance, and makes our vision blurred and speech slurred. Excessive drinking can lead to alcohol poisoning, which can cause unconsciousness, coma and even death. Excessive alcohol consumption can often make a person vomit, and vomiting while unconscious can lead to death by suffocation, as the vomit can block the air flow to and from the lungs. The effects of alcohol have also been implicated in a large proportion of fatal road accidents, assaults and incidents of domestic violence.

Diseases Associated with Excess Alcohol Consumption

Alcohol consumption in excess of the recommended daily guidelines will often cause physical damage to the body and increase the likelihood of getting diseases such as cancer, cirrhosis, high blood pressure, strokes and depression.

Cirrhosis

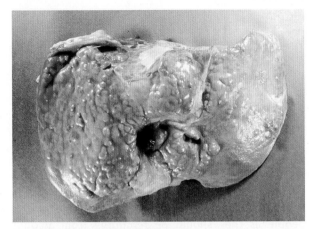

Fig 14.3 A liver affected by cirrhosis

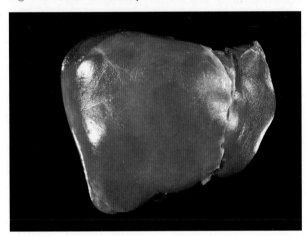

Fig 14.4 A healthy liver

Excessive alcohol consumption can result in cirrhosis of the liver. The liver is the largest organ in the body. It is responsible for getting rid of poisons from the blood, helps our immune system in fighting infection, makes proteins that help our blood to clot and produces bile, which helps with the breakdown of fats. The disease damages the liver and produces scar tissue. The scar tissue replaces the normal tissue and prevents it from working as it should. Cirrhosis is the twelfth leading cause of death by disease and causes 26,000 deaths per year.

Cancer
Around 6 per cent of deaths from cancer in the UK are caused by alcohol (*Oxford Textbook of Medicine*, 2003). A range of cancers have been linked with excess alcohol consumption; these include:

- Cancer of the mouth
- Cancer of the larynx
- Cancer of the oesophagus
- Liver cancer

- Breast cancer
- Bowel cancer.

Depression
Alcohol consumption has been linked with anxiety and depression. One in three young people who have committed suicide drank alcohol before they died, and more than two out of three people who attempt suicide have drunk excessively.

Stress

When we perceive ourselves to be in a situation that is dangerous, our stress response is activated. This has been developed as a means of ensuring our survival by making us respond to danger. For example, if you are walking home at night along a dark street and you hear noises behind you, your body will instigate physiological changes, called the 'fight-or-flight' response, as your body is preparing to turn and fight the danger or run away as fast as it can.

Adrenaline and cortisol are the main hormones released when we are stressed, which have the effect of:

- Increasing the heart rate
- Increasing the breathing rate
- Decreasing the rate of digestion.

It is not healthy for the body to be in a constant state of stress because of the excess production of adrenaline and cortisol. This results in excess cholesterol production that raises blood cholesterol levels and is a risk factor for CHD.

Stress and Cardiovascular Disease

If the excess hormones and chemicals released during stressful periods are not 'used up' through physical exertion, the increased heart rate and high blood pressure place excess strain on our blood vessels. This can lead to vascular damage. Damaged blood vessels are thicker than healthy blood vessels and have a reduced ability to stretch. This can have the effect of reducing the supply of blood and oxygen to the heart.

Stress and the Immune System

Stress can decrease our body's ability to fight infection, which makes us more susceptible to suffering from illnesses. This explains why we catch more colds when we are stressed.

Stress and Depression

Stress is also associated with mental health problems, and in particular with anxiety and depression. Here the relationship is fairly clear. The negative thinking that is associated with stress also contributes to these.

Diet

Our diets have changed significantly over the years. Today we have the largest range of foods available to us, but we are choosing to eat foods that are high in saturated fats and simple carbohydrates. Fast-food restaurants are flourishing because they are used so regularly by our society. Today, the nation's diet tends to be lacking in a number of important nutrients, including fibre, calcium, vitamins and iron. This is because a high proportion of the population relies on snacks and fast foods as their main source of nutritional intake. As a result, the Western diet is generally high in fat and sugars, resulting in a huge increase in obesity.

Estimates in 1990 suggested that 1 in 20 children aged 9 to 11 could be classified as clinically obese. If a person is obese they are much more likely to suffer from coronary heart disease, which is currently the biggest killer in Britain. As we are continuing to rely on foods that do not give us the right balance of vital nutrients, a number of people are suffering from poor nutrition. This not only impairs physical and mental functioning, but can also increase the risk of suffering from a range of diseases, including anaemia, diabetes and osteoporosis. A number of nutrition experts have also linked poor nutrition to emotional and behavioural problems that are seen to occur much more frequently among children today; these include hyperactivity and attention deficit disorders.

A healthy diet contains lots of fruit and vegetables. It is based on starchy foods, such as wholegrain bread, pasta and rice, and is low in fat (especially saturated fat), salt and sugar. Current recommendations for a healthy diet are shown in Table 14.1.

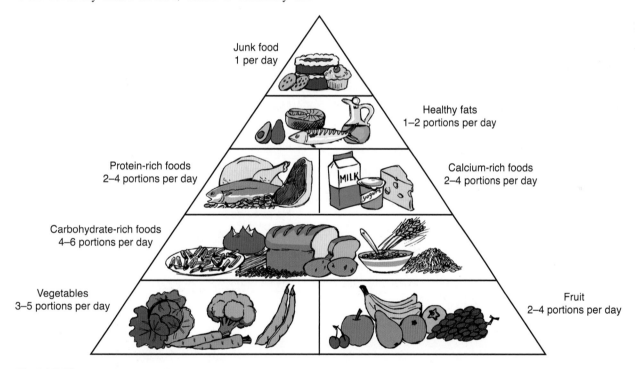

Fig 14.5 The nutrition pyramid

Food	Amount we should eat	Function	Example of food sources
Carbohydrates	50–60%	Provide energy for sports performance	
Sugars		Provide short bursts of energy	Jam, sweets, fruit, fizzy drinks, sports drinks
Starch		Provide energy for longer periods	Pasta, rice, bread, potatoes, breakfast cereals
Fat	25–30%	Provides energy for low-intensity exercise, e.g. walking	
Saturated fats		Insulate the body against the cold	Mainly animal sources: cream, lard, cheese, meat
Unsaturated fats		Help to protect internal organs	Mainly plant sources: nuts, soya, tofu
Protein	10–15%	For growth and repair	Meat, eggs, nuts, fish, poultry

Table 14.1 Recommendations for a healthy diet

Vitamin	Food sources	Function
A	Carrots, liver, dark green vegetables, mackerel	Maintains good vision, skin and hair
B group	Cereals, liver, yeast, eggs, beef, beans	Helps to break down food to produce energy
C	Most fresh fruits and vegetables, especially citrus fruits	Fights infection; maintains healthy skin and gums; helps with wound healing
D	Oily fish, eggs	Helps to build bones and teeth
E	Nuts, whole grains, dark green leafy vegetables	Antioxidant that prevents damage to cells
K	Leafy green vegetables, peas, milk, egg yolks	Helps to form blood clots

Table 14.2 Sources and functions of vitamins

Mineral	Food sources	Function
Iron	Liver, lean meats, eggs, dried fruits	Blood production
Calcium	Milk, fish bones, green leafy vegetables	Helps to build strong bones and teeth; helps to form blood clots
Sodium	Salt, seafood, processed foods, celery	Maintains fluid balance in cells; helps in muscle contraction
Potassium	Bananas	Works with sodium to maintain fluid balance, aids muscle contraction, maintains blood pressure
Zinc	Meats, fish	Tissue growth and repair

Table 14.3 Sources and functions of minerals

Key learning points 1

- People are much more sedentary today and many are not meeting national recommended guidelines.
- Children should be physically active for at least 60 to 90 minutes per day.
- Adults should be physically active for at least 30 minutes five times per week.
- People who take part in physical activity are less likely to suffer from CHD, hypertension, diabetes, obesity and depression.
- Smoking has been shown to cause cancer, chronic lung disease and cardiovascular disease in some people.
- Adult males should have no more than three units of alcohol per day and adult females should have no more than two. Males and females should both have at least two alcohol-free days per week.
- Excess alcohol consumption has been shown to cause cirrhosis, cancer and depression in some people.
- Stress can cause cardiovascular disease, decrease the immune system's response to infection and cause depression in some people.
- Today, many people are eating fast food and not taking in the right quantities of macronutrients, vitamins and minerals.
- A healthy diet contains lots of fruit and vegetables, is based on starchy foods such as wholegrain bread, pasta and rice, and is low in fat (especially saturated fat), salt and sugar.

Q Quick quiz 1

Match each description in the table below to the condition it describes, choosing from the following:

- Excess alcohol consumption
- CHD
- Hypertension
- Emphysema
- Cirrhosis.

Description	Condition
A disease that causes breathlessness due to damaged alveoli	
Damage and scarring to the liver	
A blood pressure reading of 140/90 or higher	
The build-up of fats in the coronary blood vessels	
This can lead to poisoning, unconsciousness and coma	

14.3 Assessing the Lifestyle of an Individual

When assessing the lifestyle of an individual, you will need to gather as much information on them as possible. This can be done effectively through a comprehensive questionnaire. It will be part of an initial consultation and must cover the following as a minimum requirement:

- Medical history
- Activity history
- Lifestyle factors
- Nutritional status
- Any other factors that will affect the person's health.

255

Lifestyle Questionnaire

Section 1: Personal Details

Name _____

Address _____

_____

_____

_____

Home telephone _____

Mobile telephone _____

Email _____

Occupation _____

Date of birth _____

Section 2: Physical Activity Levels

1   Does your occupation require you to take part in physical activity? If so, what?

_____

_____

2   What are your medium-term goals over the next three months?

_____

_____

_____

_____

3   What are your short-term goals over the next four weeks?

_____

_____

_____

_____

Section 3: Current Training Status

1   What are your main training requirements?

(a) Muscular strength.

(b) Muscular endurance.

(c) Speed.

(d) Flexibility.

(e) Aerobic fitness.

(f) Power.

(g) Weight loss or gain.

(h) Skill-related fitness.

(i) Other (please state)

_____

2   How would you describe your current fitness status?

_____

_____

3 How many times a week will you train?

_____

4 How long do you have for each training session?

_____

Section 4: Your Nutritional Status

1 On a scale of 1 to 10 (1 being very low quality and 10 being very high quality), how would you rate the quality of your diet?

_____

2 Do you follow any particular diet?
   (a) Vegetarian.
   (b) Vegan.
   (c) Vegetarian plus fish.
   (d) Gluten-free.
   (e) Dairy-free.

3 How often do you eat? Note down a typical day's intake.

_____
_____
_____
_____
_____

4 Do you take any supplements? If so, which ones?

_____
_____

Section 5: Your Lifestyle

1 How many units of alcohol do you drink in a typical week?_____

2 Do you smoke?_____ If yes, how many a day?_____

3 Do you experience stress on a daily basis?_____

4 If yes, what causes you stress (if you know)?

_____

5 What techniques do you use to deal with your stress?

_____

Section 6: Your Physical Health

1 Do you experience any of the following?
   (a) Back pain or injury.
   (b) Knee pain or injury.
   (c) Ankle pain or injury.
   (d) Swollen joints.
   (e) Shoulder pain or injury.
   (f) Hip or pelvic pain or injury.
   (g) Nerve damage.
   (h) Head injuries.

2 If yes, please give details.

_____

_____

_____

3 Are any of these injuries made worse by exercise?

_____

4 If yes, what movements in particular cause pain?

_____

5 Are you currently receiving any treatment for any injuries? If so, what?

_____

Section 7: Medical History

1 Do you have, or have you had, any of the following medical conditions?

(a) Asthma.

(b) Bronchitis.

(c) Heart problems.

(d) Chest pains.

(e) Diabetes.

(f) High blood pressure.

(g) Epilepsy.

(h) Other

_____

2 Are you taking any medication? (If yes, state what, how much and why.)

_____

Name

Signature   Date

One-to-one Consultation

It is always a good idea to follow up a lifestyle questionnaire with a consultation with the individual. The person running the consultation must know when to ask questions and prompt the client, and when to listen and take notes. The main rule of thumb is that the client should be doing most of the talking in a consultation; the consultant's role is to ensure that questions are answered accurately and fully. The client should be made aware that their lifestyle questionnaire and the follow-up consultation are confidential, and the questionnaire should be stored in a secure place.

Communication Skills

When conducting a consultation, you will need to use skills such as questioning and listening. One of the aims of the consultation is to develop rapport with your client, which means that they will start to trust you and accept the advice that you give to them.

Questioning

The consultation is a chance to gain information from your client so that you can use that information to help them improve their lifestyle; however, the quality of the information you gain will depend on the quality of the questions that you ask. There are different types of questions, such as:

● Closed questions
● Open questions
● Indirect questions.

Closed questions can be answered with a simple yes

or no, or by a short phrase. They are used to obtain facts or to clarify a certain point, for example:

● Where do you live?
● What is your occupation?
● Have you tried changing your diet?

Open questions will require a longer and more thoughtful response, as they are used to invite the client into a discussion or to explore an issue, for example:

● What activities do you enjoy doing?
● How are you getting on with your training?

Indirect questions are a softer introduction to a question and they may feel less intrusive, so are good for gaining sensitive information, for example:

● Do you mind me asking what you are trying to achieve?
● I was wondering whether you had thought about giving up smoking?

When you are choosing questions, you need to think about the information you are aiming to gather, as this will influence whether you ask a closed, open or indirect question. You should also think about the wording you use in your question and make sure that the client will understand it, rather than using wording that you think makes you look intelligent!

Listening

Listening is the second part of good communication and is vital in establishing rapport. If you are a good listener, people will like talking to you and you will gather all the information that you need. The following are guidelines on how to listen to people:

● Clear your mind of thoughts, as it is not easy to listen to listen and think at the same time.
● Avoid jumping to conclusions or prejudging a person by how the person looks or talks.
● Establish eye contact, but keep your eyes soft so the client does not feel you are staring at them.
● Once the client has answered your questions, summarise the main points of what they have said and even take notes.
● Give the client your full attention and avoid fidgeting.

As you are consulting, you also need to consider non-verbal communication, which is body language and facial expressions. It is best to keep your body language open, which means that you should not cross your arms or legs, as they look like a barrier, and you should sit in a posture that makes it look like you are interested – for example, leaning forward slightly, but not in a threatening way. You should keep your

expression relaxed and maintain eye contact when you are listening. Taken together, working on your questioning and listening skills and your non-verbal communication will help improve your consultation skills.

Key learning points 2

● A lifestyle questionnaire should address levels of activity, alcohol consumption, smoking, stress levels and diet. A one-to-one consultation should follow up a lifestyle questionnaire.

Q Quick quiz 2

Which of the following statements are true and which are false?

1 There should be an equal amount of talking between the trainer and the client during a consultation.
2 Once rapport has been created, the client will accept the advice that you offer.
3 Indirect questions can be used to put a client at ease.
4 'How do you feel your training is going?' is a closed question.
5 When you are listening, it is important to summarise what the client is telling you.

14.4 Lifestyle Improvement

P3 M3 P2

Physical Activity

When designing a physical activity programme, it is important to make the programme as personal as possible. It must meet the needs of the individual it is written for or it will result in the person being unhappy or unsuccessful. The key to this is gathering as much information as possible on the individual, by asking questions such as:

● What activities do you like to take part in?
● What have you done in the past that you enjoyed?
● Do you like to exercise alone or with other people?

You should take into account the facilities in the person's area. Do they live near a gym or leisure centre? One of the biggest factors to put people off going to a gym is if it is quite some distance away and takes them a while to get there. If the gym is close to where they live or work, this makes it a much more viable option. They could go to the gym in their lunch break or on the way to or from work.

Increasing Daily Activity

It is actually unnecessary to join a gym or go to a swimming pool to increase physical activity levels. There are lots of ways to attain the benefits of physical activity by just adapting everyday life. If a person takes the bus or train to work, they could get off one or two stops earlier and walk the remaining distance. If a person drives to work, they could park further away from their workplace and walk the remaining distance. If cycling to work is a viable option, it is not only good for you but is also cheaper and better for the environment. Many new cycle paths are being constructed to encourage people to cycle. Choosing options such as walking up a flight of stairs instead of taking a lift or escalator also help to increase a person's activity levels.

Fig 14.6 Gardening can increase heart rate and help tone muscles

Housework and gardening are productive ways of increasing daily activity levels. Vacuum cleaning and dusting the home, or digging the garden or mowing the lawn will increase heart rate and help tone muscles.

Reducing Alcohol Consumption

If a person is dependent on alcohol they must seek help to prevent the damage it does to their body and mind and to those around them.

In order to determine if a person is drinking more than the government recommended amounts of alcohol, it is a good idea to keep a 'drinking diary'. This involves noting what, how much and when that person drinks alcohol. If the person is just over the limit, simple changes could help them cut down. If they usually drink strong lager, they could opt for one that contains less alcohol. Or if they usually drink wine, they could have a spritzer instead, as this will make their drink last longer and help them to drink less. If they regularly meet up with friends in pubs, they could try to find alternative venues, such as a juice bar or coffee shop.

A GP can provide confidential advice and support. In order to help prevent the withdrawal symptoms of drinking, they may be prescribed antidepressants (e.g. Valium). Two drug treatments are also available to help a person stop drinking. A drug called Disulfiram makes the person feel very ill if they drink even a small amount of alcohol. Another drug called Acamprosate helps to reduce a person's craving for alcohol, but it does have many unpleasant side-effects. A person may attend organisations such as Alcohol Concern and Alcoholics Anonymous to help them stop drinking alcohol.

Stopping Smoking

Smokers have both a physical and a psychological addiction to smoking. The combination of these two factors makes cigarettes one of the most addictive drugs used today. Determining whether you are more physiologically than psychologically addicted to smoking will help to decide the best course of action in trying to stop smoking.

First of all, a person needs to think about why they smoke and identify the things they do that always make them want to light up. Once these triggers have been identified, the person can attempt to remove themselves from them. The next step is to decrease the person's dependence on nicotine. Either they can slowly decrease the amount of cigarettes they smoke over a set period or they could use a nicotine replacement therapy, such as a nicotine patch and/or nicotine gum. This process helps the person break the cigarette habit and also slowly reduces the amount of nicotine being taken into the body.

The NHS has set up a smoking helpline and runs clinics to help advise people on how to give up smoking. Each year there is a national no-smoking day, which has also been effective in making people think about giving up smoking and giving them a clear target day to attempt to stop.

Reducing Stress through Stress Management Techniques

The main methods of stress management are:

- Progressive muscular relaxation
- Mind-to-muscle relaxation
- Meditation/centring.

Progressive Muscular Relaxation

Progressive muscular relaxation (PMR) involves a person tensing and relaxing the muscle groups individually and sequentially to relax their whole body and mind. It is also called 'muscle-to-mind' relaxation, as muscles are tensed and relaxed to induce complete relaxation. Each muscle is tensed and relaxed to teach the person the difference between a tense muscle and a relaxed muscle. After a muscle is tensed, the relaxation effect is deepened, which also has an effect on the involuntary muscles.

The technique is practised using a series of taped instructions, or with the psychologist giving the instructions. It usually starts at the hands by making a tight fist and then relaxing. The tensing and relaxing carries on up the arms into the shoulders, face and neck, then down to the stomach and through the hips and legs.

These sessions last between 20 and 30 minutes, and need to be practised about five times a day to gain the maximum effect. Each time they are practised they have an increased effect and a person can relax more quickly and more deeply. The aim is that when the person needs to use the relaxation technique quickly, they can induce relaxation using a trigger, such as tensing the hand or the shoulders.

Mind-to-muscle Relaxation

Mind-to-muscle relaxation is also called imagery and involves the use of a mental room or a mental place. This is a place where a person can quickly picture themselves to produce feelings of relaxation when they need to relax.

Again, it involves the person using a taped script, or a psychologist giving instructions. Usually the psychologist asks a person to build a mental picture of a room. This is a room where they can feel relaxed and where there is somewhere to sit or lie down. It should be decorated in a pleasing manner. Alternatively, the person may imagine a relaxing place, such as somewhere they went on their holidays, or a beach or quiet place where they feel calm and relaxed. They are taught to imagine this place in detail and to feel the sensations associated with being there. They do this about five times, so that eventually they can go there when they need to and are able to relax more quickly and more deeply. As the person relaxes their mind, they feel the sensations transferring to their muscle groups and they can achieve overall body relaxation. It tends to work best for individuals who have good imagery skills. Other people may feel that PMR is more effective for them.

Meditation/Centring

Meditation/centring techniques involve the person focusing on one thing, such as their breathing (centring) or a mantra (meditation). By focusing their attention they become more and more relaxed. Again, these feelings of relaxation can eventually be produced when needed.

Diet

Food Preparation

The way food is prepared has a huge impact on its nutritional value. We should eat a fair amount of potatoes, but if you fry the potatoes to make chips, the food then belongs in the fats and oils food group, as it now has such a high concentration of fat.

You can prepare foods in certain ways to make them much healthier.

Breads and grains
- Use lots of wholemeal pasta and a small portion of sauce to prepare pasta dishes.
- Make sandwiches out of thick slices of wholemeal bread.
- Mash sweet potatoes and regular potatoes in larger than usual quantities for a shepherd's pie topping.

Fruits and vegetables
- Eat dried fruit, fresh fruit or vegetable sticks (e.g. carrot sticks) as snacks.
- A selection of vegetables or salads can accompany each main meal.
- Make fruit-based puddings, such as poached pears or apple and blackberry crumble.
- Add dried or fresh fruit to breakfast cereals.
- Include more vegetables in casserole dishes.

Meat, fish and vegetarian alternatives
- Use lean meat and remove skin and fat where possible.
- Grill meats wherever possible.
- Include pulses in meat dishes to reduce the fat

content and increase the fibre content, such as kidney beans in a chilli.

● Try to eat two portions of oily fish per week.

Milk and dairy foods

● Choose semi-skimmed or skimmed milk and low-fat or reduced-fat cheeses.
● Replace cream with fromage frais or yoghurt.
● Use strong-tasting cheese in cooking so that you require smaller amounts.

Foods containing fat and foods containing sugar

● Do not fry foods containing fat as it will just add more fat to them. Instead, grill or dry-bake them (without oil) in the oven.
● Use small amounts of plant-based cooking oils (e.g. olive oil or rapeseed) when frying foods.
● Make salad dressings with a balsamic vinegar base instead of oil.
● Sweeten puddings with dried or fresh fruits instead of sugar.
● Drink fresh water instead of fizzy drinks.

Timing of Food Intake

There is a saying that you should 'Eat breakfast like a king, lunch like a prince and dinner like a pauper.' This basically means that you should have your main meal at breakfast time, have a good-sized lunch and then eat your smallest meal at dinner time. The reasoning behind this saying is to have enough energy for the day and then to digest the food properly before going to bed. Heavy meals eaten before bedtime, such as a curry, take a long time to digest, which may disturb sleep. Any excess calories eaten during this meal will most probably be turned into body fat, as very few people actually take any form of exercise after a late heavy meal.

Key learning points 3

● Physical activity levels can be increased by adapting an individual's daily activities.
● A drinking diary can make a person aware of how much alcohol they are consuming.
● Nicotine replacement therapy and NHS support can help people stop smoking.
● Relaxation techniques, such as PMR and mind-to-muscle relaxation, can help reduce stress.
● The way foods are prepared and the timing of their intake can have an impact on an individual's health.

Q Quick quiz 3

Fill in the blank spaces to complete the following sentences.

In order to help a person improve their lifestyle it is important to increase their _____ _____. It would be beneficial to _____ or _____ to work rather than take the car. When at home, gardening and housework can be used to raise the _____ _____. It would improve health if alcohol consumption was reduced by keeping a _____ _____, or, if a person smokes, by using _____ _____ _____. Stress can cause people to smoke or drink more alcohol, but it can be reduced by using _____ techniques or using _____ to take them to a mental place or room. Also, diet can be improved by eating less _____ and more _____ and _____.

14.5 Planning a Health-related Physical Activity Programme

Collecting Information

When a trainer sits down to design a physical activity programme, they need to consider a range of factors to ensure that the programme is appropriate and that it will benefit the person rather than harm them. They will need to consider the following factors:

● PAR-Q responses – have any contraindications to exercise been identified?
● Medical history – does the client have any conditions which may affect the training programme and choice of exercises?
● Current and previous exercise history – this will give an idea about the current fitness level of the client.
● Barriers to exercise – does the client have constraints such as time, cost, family responsibilities or work commitments?
● Motives and goals – what is the client aiming to achieve and what is their time-scale?

- Occupation – what hours does the client work, and is their work manual or office-based?
- Activity levels – what amount of movement does the client do on a daily basis?
- Leisure-time activities – are these active or inactive?
- Diet – what, how much and when does the client eat?
- Stress levels – how does the client deal with stress, either through work or in their home life?
- Alcohol intake – how much does the client consume and how often?
- Smoking – is the client a smoker or ex-smoker, and how much do they smoke?
- Time available – the client needs to fit the training into their schedule and the trainer needs to be realistic when planning the programme.

Goal Setting

Short-term goals are set over a brief period of time, usually from one day to one month. A short-term goal may relate to what you want to achieve in one training session or where you want to be by the end of the month.

Long-term goals run from three months to a period of several years. You may even set some lifetime goals, which run until you retire from your sport. In sport, we set long-term goals to cover a season or a sporting year. The period between one and three months would be called medium-term goals.

Usually, short-term goals are set to help achieve the long-term goals. It is important to set both short- and long-term goals, but particularly short-term goals, because they will give a person more motivation to act immediately.

When goals are set, you need to use the SMART principle to make them workable. SMART stands for:

- **S**pecific
- **M**easurable
- **A**chievable
- **R**ealistic
- **T**ime-constrained.

Specific
The goal must be specific to what you want to achieve. It is not enough to say, 'I want to get fitter'. You need to say, 'I want to improve strength/speed/stamina.'

Measurable
Goals must be stated in a way that is measurable, so a goal needs to state figures, for example, 'I want to cut down my alcohol intake to five units per week.'

Achievable
It must be possible to actually achieve the goal.

Realistic
We need to be realistic in our setting of goals and look at what factors may stop us achieving them.

Time-constrained
There must be a time-scale or deadline for the goal. This allows you to review your success. It is best to set a date by which you wish to achieve the goal.

Strategies to Achieve Goals

Some commonly used and effective strategies are as follows:

- **Using a decision balance sheet**: an individual writes down all the gains they will make by exercising and all the things they may lose through taking up exercise. Hopefully, the gains will outweigh the losses and this list will help to motivate them at difficult times.
- **Prompts**: an individual puts up posters or reminders around the house that will keep giving them reminders to exercise. This could also be done with little coloured dots on mirrors or other places where they look regularly.
- **Rewards for attendance/completing goals**: the individual is provided with an extrinsic reward for completing the goal or attending the gym regularly. This may be something to pamper themselves, such as a massage, and should not be something that conflicts with the goal – such as a slap-up meal!
- **Social support approaches**: you can help people to exercise regularly by developing a social support group of like-minded people with similar fitness goals, so that they can arrange to meet at the gym at certain times. This makes it more difficult for people to miss their exercise session. Also, try to gain the backing of the people they live with, to support them rather than teasing or criticising them.

Principles of Training

In order to develop a safe and effective training programme, you will need to consider the principles of training. These principles are a set of guidelines to help you understand the requirements of programme design. They are:

- Frequency
- Intensity
- Time
- Type
- Overload
- Reversibility
- Specificity.

263

- **Frequency:** this is how often the person will train per week.
- **Intensity:** this is how hard the person will work. It is usually expressed as a percentage of maximum intensity.
- **Time:** this indicates how long the person will train for in each session.
- **Type:** this shows the type of training the person will perform and needs to be individual to each person.
- **Overload:** this shows that to make an improvement, a muscle or system must work slightly harder than it is used to. This may be as simple as getting a sedentary person to walk for ten minutes or getting an athlete to squat more weight than have done previously.
- **Reversibility:** this principle states that if a fitness gain is not used regularly, the body will reverse it and go back to its previous fitness level. It is commonly known as 'use it or lose it'.
- **Specificity:** this principle states that any fitness gain will be specific to the muscles or system to which the overload is applied. Put simply, this says that different types of training will produce different results. To make a programme specific, you need to look at the needs of the person and then train them accordingly. For example, a person who was overweight would need to take part in lots of low-intensity cardiovascular training in order to burn fat.

Appropriate Activities

When you are devising your training programme you need to be sure that you are including activities that are appropriate to your client. If your client is obese, a training programme that includes jogging would probably not be appropriate. This kind of exercise is a high-impact exercise which places a lot of stress on the joints. If a person is obese, they will be stressing their joints to a greater degree, which means they would be much more likely to injure or damage their joints. Therefore, walking or swimming would be much more appropriate, as these activities place much less stress on the joints.

You should also try to include activities that you know your client enjoys. That way, they will be much more likely to continue their exercise programme.

Exercise Intensity

The intensity of exercise can be monitored by expressing it as a percentage of maximum heart rate. Your maximum heart rate is the maximum number of times your heart could beat. To find this out, you would have to work to your maximum intensity, which

for most people would clearly be unsafe. Therefore, we estimate the maximum heart rate by using the following formula:

$$\text{Maximum heart rate} = 220 - \text{age}$$

So, for a 17-year-old, their maximum heart rate would be $220 - 17 = 203$ beats per minute (b.p.m.).

To work out the heart rate training zone, we take percentages of heart rate maximum. If we work between 60 and 90 per cent, we would be working in the aerobic training zone, where the exercise we are performing is effective in improving aerobic fitness without being dangerous. However, it is still a wide range for a heart rate to be within, so we change the zone depending on the fitness level of the participant.

Rate of perceived exertion (RPE) is another measure used to monitor exercise. RPE is scale that can be used by the participant to rate how hard they feel they are working between two extremes. Rather than monitoring heart rate, the participant is introduced to the scale and then asked during the aerobic session where they feel they are. Below is Borg's modified RPE scale.

1 Extremely light.
2 Very light.
3 Moderate.
4
5 Somewhat hard.
6
7 Hard.
8 Very hard.
9 Extremely hard.
10 Maximal exertion.

To achieve aerobic fitness gains, the participant needs to be working at around 6 to 7 on the modified scale.

Key learning points 4

- Ensure you collect all relevant information from your client to assess their lifestyle and determine any contraindications.
- Ensure you set short-term and long-term goals.
- Apply the principles of training to your training programme.
- Ensure your training programme incorporates appropriate activities.
- Ensure your client exercises at the appropriate intensity.
- Effective zones for different groups as a percentage of maximum heart rate (MHR) are: beginners – 60 to 70 per cent of MHR; intermediate – 70 to 80 per cent of MHR; advanced – 80 to 90 per cent of MHR.

Student activity 14.1 3 hours

Read through the following case study and then complete the tasks that follow.

Eddie is a full-time student who is studying a demanding course at university; he attends lectures from 9 a.m. to 5 p.m. every day. He also loves playing sport and plays football and cricket for the university; he also enjoys golf. Although he enjoys playing sport, he does not enjoy the training and feels that it gets in the way of his social life. He enjoys socialising and spends most evenings in the pub, even sometimes the night before a match. He worked out his alcohol consumption as 35 units per week, but he thinks it could be higher, and he has been smoking on what he sees as being a 'social basis', consisting of three to four cigarettes a day.

Eddie does not really have a weight issue and he is able to get good food from the canteen. He knows he needs to eat fruit and vegetables, so he makes sure that he eats as much fresh food as he can and only occasionally eats takeaways. However, he hardly ever eats breakfast as he prefers to spend the time in bed.

In terms of his current activity, Eddie plays football at the weekend and he does have a bike, but he chooses to get the university bus each day and occasionally goes training with the football team, which is mainly circuit training.

Task 1

Choose three lifestyle factors from the case study and describe the effect each one has on Eddie's health and well-being. To achieve a merit you need to explain the effects that each of the three lifestyle factors may have on Eddie's health and well-being.

Task 2

1 Design a lifestyle questionnaire that could be used describe the strengths and weaknesses of Eddie's lifestyle.

2 Use a role-playing exercise with a fellow student; you should play the role of the consultant and your fellow student should play the role of Eddie. In this role play, use the questionnaire to gain as much information about Eddie as you can.

To achieve **P2** you need to describe the strengths and areas for improvement of Eddie's lifestyle. To achieve **M2** you need to explain these strengths and areas for improvement. To achieve **D1** you need to evaluate Eddie's lifestyle and make a list of priorities for changing and improving it.

Task 3

Now that you have analysed the areas that Eddie has to improve, you need to decide the strategies you are going to use to help him to do this (**P3**). To achieve **M3** you need to explain why you have made these recommendations to improve Eddie's lifestyle. To achieve **D2** you need to analyse the effectiveness of these chosen methods.

Task 4

Now that you have looked at Eddie's lifestyle you need to focus on his physical activity and produce a six-week physical activity plan to help improve his health. Be sure to incorporate his current activity into the plan. You can use the following template to help him.

	Week 1	Week 2	Week 3	Week 4	Week 5	Week 6
Monday						
Tuesday						
Wednesday						
Thursday						
Friday						
Saturday						
Sunday						

Further reading

Baechle, T. and Earle, R. (2008) *Essentials of Strength Training and Conditioning*, Human Kinetics.

Dalgleish, J. and Dollery, S. (2001) *The Health and Fitness Handbook*, Longman.

Sharkey, B.J. and Gaskill, S.E. (2006). *Fitness and Health*, Human Kinetics.

Useful websites

www.bhf.org.uk

Tips on how to keep your heart healthy

www.nutrition.org.uk/healthyliving/lifestyle/how-much-physical-activity-do-i-need

Nutrition tips relating to physical activity from the British Nutrition Foundation

15: Instructing Physical Activity & Exercise

15.1 Introduction

The fitness industry continues to expand in a rapid manner and so does the demand for fitness trainers and instructors. The increasing competition has meant that customers are also looking for quality instructors who are knowledgeable and professional in their approach. This unit looks at the knowledge and technical skills that are required to become an effective instructor of physical activity and exercise.

By the end of this unit you should:

- know the principles of safe and effective exercise sessions
- be able to design an exercise programme
- be able to plan and lead an exercise session
- be able to review the design of an exercise programme and leading of an exercise session.

Assessment and grading criteria		
To achieve a PASS grade the evidence must show that the learner is able to:	To achieve a MERIT grade the evidence must show that, in addition to the pass criteria, the learner is able to:	To achieve a DISTINCTION grade the evidence must show that, in addition to the pass and merit criteria, the learner is able to:
P1 describe the principles of fitness training	**M1** explain the health and safety considerations associated with exercise programmes and sessions	
P2 describe the health and safety considerations associated with exercise programmes and sessions		
P3 describe the importance of warm-up and cool-down in exercise programmes and sessions		
P4 design a six-week exercise programme for two selected contrasting clients	**M2** explain choice of activities for exercise programmes for selected clients	**D1** justify choice of activities for exercise programmes for selected clients, suggesting alternative activities
P5 plan a safe and effective exercise session	**M3** explain choice of activities for the planned exercise session	**D2** justify choice of activities for the planned exercise session and suggest alternative activities.
P6 deliver a safe and effective exercise session, with tutor support	**M4** independently deliver a safe and effective exercise session.	
P7 review own performance in the designing of exercise programmes and the planning and delivery of the exercise session, identifying strengths and areas for improvement.		

15.2 Principles of Safe and Effective Exercise Sessions

Components of Fitness

Fitness is a wide-reaching concept and the instructor needs to be able to answer one of the following questions: 'What does this client need to be fit for?' or 'What daily functions do they need to able to perform?'

Any of the following answers may apply:

- Lose a bit of weight to look and feel better
- Improve my endurance so I can play with my children
- Put on some muscle so I can do more tasks
- Improve my golf
- Stop feeling this back pain
- Be more effective at work
- Have more energy on a daily basis
- Be able to run a marathon.

Fig 15.1 Playing with children

Each of these activities will involve a range of the components of fitness, which are the different aspects of fitness.

Aerobic Endurance

Also called cardiovascular fitness, this is the ability of the body to take in, transport and use oxygen. It depends upon the efficiency of the lungs in taking in oxygen, the heart in transporting oxygen and the working muscles in using oxygen. Examples of activities needing aerobic endurance fitness include long-distance running, swimming and cycling.

Flexibility

This is the range of movement available at a joint

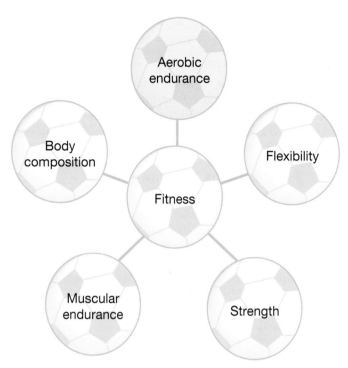

Fig 15.2 Components of fitness

or group of joints. Examples of activities needing flexibility include dancing, gymnastics, running and most everyday functions.

Strength

This is the maximum force that a muscle or group of muscles can produce. Examples of activities needing strength include weightlifting and scrummaging in rugby.

Muscular Endurance

This is the ability of a muscles or group of muscles to produce low-intensity forces repeatedly for long periods of time. Examples of activities needing

Fig 15.3 Running

269

muscular endurance include running, aerobics and carrying bags of shopping.

Body Composition

This is the make-up of the body in terms of how much of the body weight is fat and how much is not fat, which we call lean body weight (LBW). Many people would like to lose excess body fat and/or gain muscle bulk as they feel that this will make them look better.

Adaptations to Training

Our participant will start training because they are unhappy with their current position and they want to change something. They will be looking for 'training adaptations' or for their body's systems to adapt to the stimulus of training. Cardiovascular and resistance training will cause slightly different changes to occur.

Adaptations to Aerobic Endurance Training

Lungs:
- Respiratory muscles become stronger
- Lungs become more efficient
- Lungs are able to extract more oxygen from the air.

Heart:
- Heart muscle becomes larger
- Increase in the amount of blood pumped in each beat (stroke volume)
- Increase in amount of blood pumped per minute (cardiac output)
- Fall in resting heart rate.

Blood and blood vessels:
- Increase in number of capillaries (capillarisation)
- Increase in size of blood vessels
- Decrease in blood pressure
- Increase in blood volume and red blood cell count.

Muscles:
- Increase in number and size of mitochondria (energy-producing parts of cells)
- Increased tolerance to lactic acid
- Increased aerobic enzyme production (muscles will become better at producing energy using oxygen)
- Muscular endurance increases.

Bones:
- Bone density increases (if activity is weight bearing, like running).

Adaptations to Resistance Training

- Increase in muscle size (hypertrophy)
- Increase in strength of ligaments and tendons
- Increase in bone density
- Improved nervous system function
- Decreased body fat

- Improved body composition (ratio of muscle to fat)
- Increased resting metabolic rate
- Improved posture
- Less risk of injury.

Principles of Training

When designing an effective training programme you must take into account a range of factors to make sure that the programme is effective. These are called the 'principles of training'. When designing a training programme, these principles of training must always be applied.

Frequency: this means how often the participant will train. This may be three times a week.

Intensity: this means how hard the participant will be training. Intensity is usually stated in terms of what percentage of their maximum heart rate they will work at or by using the rate of perceived exertion.

Time: this means the length of each training session.

Type: this refers to the type of training they will be performing. For example, cardiovascular or resistance training.

Overload: this means applying intensity to the participant's training which is slightly higher than they are used to. The exact intensity of overload depends upon the individual's level of fitness and it can be produced by changing time, intensity or type.

Reversibility: this means that any adaptation which can be gained can also be lost if the training stops. It is commonly known as the 'use it or lose it' principle because if you don't use the fitness gain, you will quickly lose it.

Specificity: this means that any adaptations that occur will be specific to the training that has been performed. When designing a training programme every exercise must be specific to the needs of the individual, whether they are a golfer, a runner or want to lose some fat. If a programme is not specific the individual will not get the gains they require.

The principles of training spell the acronym FITTORS:

- **F**requency
- **I**ntensity
- **T**ime
- **T**ype
- **O**verload
- **R**eversibility
- **S**pecificity.

Health and Safety for Exercise Sessions

The health and safety of the individuals we are instructing in exercise environments is of paramount importance to a gym instructor. This is to ensure that they work within the law of the country and to ensure the safety of participants, themselves, colleagues, employers and employees. We are living in an increasingly litigious society where there is always blame to be apportioned.

Health and Safety at Work Act 1974

This Act is the basis of the British health and safety legislation and it clearly sets out the duties of employers and employees in implementing safety for themselves and the public. The Act says that employers must do everything that is 'reasonably practical' to ensure safety. This includes:

- Providing a safe working environment
- The safe use, storage and handling of dangerous substances
- Production of a written health and safety policy
- Maintaining a safe working environment, and appropriate health and safety equipment and facilities.

The Act also covers employees in the following ways:

- To take reasonable care of their own health and safety, and use the safety equipment provided
- To inform the employer of any potential risks to health
- To report any accidents and incidents.

Therefore, we need to minimise this risk by doing several things before training our participant.

- Fill out a detailed medical questionnaire and lifestyle form. This is called a PAR-Q or participation questionnaire and identifies any medical conditions and injuries a person may have; it helps us in our programme design.
- Fill out an informed consent form where the client is made to understand the risks of exercise and sign that they are willing to accept these risks.
- Check the training environment before every session to ensure all equipment is working properly and that there are no injury risks.
- Ensure the trainer is appropriately qualified and insured against personal injury.
- Check the client before every session to ensure they have no injuries and are dressed properly.
- Conduct a full warm-up and cool-down with the client.

Physical Activity Readiness Questionnaire (PAR-Q)
There is a range of questionnaires available but they all ask similar questions. An example is shown below.

The Exercise and Fitness Code of Ethics

The Exercise and Fitness Code of Ethics is a document produced by an organisation called the Register of Exercise Professionals (REPs). The code ensures that we deal with our clients in an appropriate manner and that we make their safety our priority. The code of ethics covers four main areas.

	Yes	No
1 Do you have a bone or joint problem which could be made worse by exercise?		
2 Has your doctor ever said that you have a heart condition?		
3 Do you experience chest pains on physical exertion?		
4 Do you experience light-headedness or dizziness on exertion?		
5 Do you experience shortness of breath on light exertion?		
6 Has your doctor ever said that you have a raised cholesterol level?		
7 Are you currently taking any prescription medication?		
8 Is there a history of coronary heart disease in your family?		
9 Do you smoke, and if so, how many?		
10 Do you drink more than 21 units of alcohol per week for a male, and 14 units for a female?		
11 Are you diabetic?		
12 Do you take physical activity less than three times a week?		
13 Are you pregnant?		
14 Are you asthmatic?		
15 Do you know of any other reason why you should not exercise?		

Fig 15.4 An example of a PAR-Q

Physical Activity Readiness Questionnaire (PAR-Q)

If you have answered yes to any questions, please give more details

_____

_____

If you have answered yes to one or more questions, you will have to consult with your doctor before taking part in a programme of physical exercise.

If you have answered no to all questions, you are ready to start a suitable exercise programme.

I have read, understood and answered all questions honestly and confirm that I am willing to engage in a programme of exercise that has been prescribed to me.

Name _____ Signature _____

Trainer's name _____ Trainer's signature _____ Date _____

Fig 15.4 *contd*

Principle 1 – Rights:

- Promote the rights of every individual to participate in exercise, and recognise that people should be treated as individuals
- Not condone or allow to go unchallenged any form of discrimination, nor to publicly criticise in demeaning descriptions of others.

Principle 2 – Relationships:

- Develop a relationship with customers based on openness, honesty, mutual trust and respect
- Ensure that physical contact is appropriate and necessary and is carried out within the recommended guidelines and with the participant's full consent and approval.

Principle 3 – Personal responsibilities:

- Demonstrate proper personal behaviour and conduct at all times
- Project an image of health, cleanliness and functional efficiency, and display high standards in use of language, manner, punctuality, preparation and presentation.

Principle 4 – Professional standards:

- Work towards attaining a high level of competence through qualifications and a commitment to ongoing training that ensures safe and correct practice, which will maximise benefits and minimise risks to the participant
- Promote the execution of safe and effective practice and plan all sessions so that they meet the needs of participants and are progressive and appropriate.

(Adapted from *The Code of Ethical Practice* (2005), produced by the Register of Exercise Professionals)

Contraindications

A contraindication is any factor which will prevent a person from exercising or make an exercise unsafe. The aim of the PAR-Q and the initial consultation is to identify any potential contraindications and then decide what needs to be done about them to minimise their chances of being a risk.

Common contraindications to exercise are:

- Blood pressure higher than 160/100
- Body fat higher than 30 per cent for a male and 40 per cent for a female
- Diabetes mellitus
- Resting heart rate higher than 100
- Lung disorders
- Blood pressure medications and blood thinners
- Coronary heart disease
- Angina pectoris
- Joint conditions.

There are many more contraindications and the rule to follow is that if you are in doubt then refer the participant to a doctor prior to training.

Warm-Up

A warm-up is performed to make sure that the heart, lungs, muscles and joints are prepared for the activities which will follow. The warm-up also helps to activate the nervous system. A warm-up can be specific to the training session which is being performed or it can be more general.

A warm-up involves general body movements of the large muscle groups in a rhythmical, continuous manner. For example, you may use running or cycling to warm up the muscles for a weight training session. The limitation of this is that it does not prepare for the movements which are to follow and the neuromuscular pathways would not have been activated. This would be particularly dangerous for an athlete.

A specific warm-up involves the rehearsal of the exercises which are to follow. This may be through replicating the movement with dynamic stretches or using low-intensity resistance training exercises to prepare for the heavier weights to follow.

A warm-up can be summarised as having three main objectives:

- To raise the heart rate
- To increase the temperature of the body
- To mobilise the major joints of the body.

By gradually raising the temperature it will give the heart time to increase stroke volume and thus cardiac output. As the warm-up continues we start to experience a widening of the blood vessels within the muscles (vasodilation). The capillary beds within the muscles will open up and allow more oxygen and nutrients to flow through the muscles. Also, the warm-up should involve some of the movements that the person will perform in their main session. This gives the warm-up 'specificity' and acts as a rehearsal for the exercises to come.

A typical warm-up will involve the following components:

- A pulse raiser
- Joint mobility
- Dynamic stretching for muscles.

The **pulse raiser** involves rhythmical movements of the large muscle groups in a continuous manner. This would involve CV-type activity such as running, rowing or cycling. The pulse raiser should gradually increase in intensity as time goes on. A pulse raiser would typically last for around five minutes but may go on for ten minutes. At the end of the warm-up, the heart rate should be just below the rate that will be achieved during the main session. A person who is fitter is able to warm up more quickly as their body is used to it, while an unfit person will take longer and needs to warm up more gradually.

A warm-up for a run may involve one minute of walking, one minute of brisk walking, one minute of jogging, one minute of running and then one minute of fast running. An advanced performer could progress to running very quickly.

Joint mobility is used to enable the joints to become lubricated by releasing more synovial fluid on to the joints and then warming it up so it becomes more efficient. This means moving joints through their full range of movement. The movements will start off through a small range and slowly move through a larger range until the full range of movement is achieved. The joints that need to be mobilised are shoulders, elbows, spine, hips, knees and ankles. If a trainer is clever, they can use the pulse-raising movements to also mobilise the joints. For example, rowing will have the effect of raising the pulse and mobilising all the joints.

Dynamic stretching is a relatively recent introduction but is very important for the specific preparation of the muscles for the movements that are due to follow.

Static stretching, where a muscle is stretched and held, has been proved to be of limited value in a warm-up. The reasons being that static stretching causes a fall in heart rate and tends to relax the muscles. It can also act to desensitise the muscle spindles, which protect the muscle against injury. Static stretching has a role to play in a warm-up because a short, tight muscle may prevent the participant from performing some of the exercises in their main session with perfect technique. For example, tight hamstrings make squatting and bent-over rows very difficult to perform well.

The benefits of dynamic stretching are that it:

- Keeps the heart rate raised
- Stretches muscles specifically through the range of movements they will be doing
- Activates the nervous system and improves synchronisation between the nerves and muscles.

To perform dynamic stretching you need to copy the movements in the session you will perform. These movements are repeated in a steady and controlled fashion. In performing a set of ten repetitions you slowly speed up the movement as the set progresses. Figures 15.5, 15.6 and 15.7 show dynamic stretches.

Fig 15.5 Squat and press

Key term

Dynamic stretching: stretching the muscles through their full range of movement in a controlled manner.

Fig 15.6 Rear lunge with arm swing

Fig 15.7 Chest stretch

Main Component

Content

The content of the main component can vary and is specific to the needs of the client. It may involve some of the following:

- CV training
- Resistance training
- Aerobic training
- Mixture of CV training and resistance training.

The main component will last around 40 minutes dependent on the length of the warm-up and main session (a training session generally will last an hour).

Resistance Training

The participant should aim for around eight to ten exercises covering all muscle groups at least once. The larger muscle groups may be worked more than once. The design of a resistance training programme is covered later in this unit.

Aerobic Training

An aerobic session may last between 20 and 60 minutes, although it is agreed that 35 minutes is a good target to aim for. Designing aerobic training programmes is also covered later in this unit.

Methods of monitoring exertion

When you are training aerobically, it is important that the intensity worked at is closely monitored. This can be done by a number of methods:

- Heart rate training zones
- Rate of perceived exertion
- Karvonen formula.

Heart rate training zones: the intensity of exercise can be monitored by expressing it as a percentage of maximum heart rate. Your maximum heart rate is the maximum number of times your heart could beat. To find this out, you would have to work to your maximum intensity, which for most people would clearly be unsafe. Therefore, we estimate the maximum heart rate by using the following formula:

Maximum heart rate = 220 − age

For a 20 year old, their maximum heart rate would be 220 − 20 = 200 b.p.m.

This is clearly a theoretical maximum heart rate because it is unlikely that every 20 year old in the country would have the same maximum heart rate. In reality, there will be a massive variation but it can be useful as a guideline.

To work out the heart rate training zone, we take percentages of heart rate maximum. If we work between 60 and 90 per cent, we would be working in the aerobic training zone, where the exercise we are performing is effective in improving aerobic fitness without being dangerous. It is still a wide range for a heart rate to be within, so we change the zone depending upon the fitness level of the participant.

Effective zones for different groups as percentage of maximum heart rate (MHR)	
Beginners	60–70% of MHR
Intermediate	70–80% of MHR
Advanced	80–90% of MHR

Rate of perceived exertion (RPE): this was developed by Gunnar Borg and is a scale which can be used by the participant to rate how hard they feel they are working between two extremes. Rather than monitoring heart rate, the participant is introduced to the scale and then asked during the aerobic session where they feel they are on the scale of 1–15 (see Table 15.1).

1	Rest
2	Extremely light
3	
4	Very light
5	
6	Light
7	
8	Somewhat hard
9	
10	Hard
11	
12	Very hard
13	
14	Very, very hard
15	Exhaustion

Table 15.1 Borg's 15-point scale

Borg's scale has been modified to a ten-point scale (see Table 15.2) because some participants have found working between 1 and 15 difficult.

1	Extremely light
2	Very light
3	Moderate
4	
5	Somewhat hard
6	
7	Hard
8	Very hard
9	Extremely hard
10	Maximal exertion

Table 15.2 Borg's modified RPE scale

To achieve aerobic fitness gains, the participant needs to be working around 12 to 15 on the 15-point scale and around 6 to 7 on the modified scale.

Karvonen formula: this is a more advanced way of working out a heart rate training zone. To find out the participant's heart rate training zone, you need to know the following information first:

- Age
- Resting heart rate
- Required exercise intensity (percentage of maximum intensity).

Age predicted maximum heart rate (APMHR) = 220 − age

Heart rate reserve (HRR) = APMHR − resting heart rate (RHR)

Target heart rate (THR) = HRR × exercise intensity + RHR

A participant, 20 years old, has a resting heart rate of 60 and wants to work at 70 to 80 per cent of their maximum intensity. They would have the following heart rate training zone:

APMHR = 220 − 20 = 200 b.p.m.

HRR = 200 − 60 = 140

Target heart rate reserve = 140 × 0.70 + 60 = 158 b.p.m.

Target heart rate reserve = 140 × 0.80 + 60 = 172 b.p.m.

We get a training zone of between 158 and 172 b.p.m. for this participant.

Cool-Down

A cool-down is performed to return the body to its pre-exercise state. Once you have finished training, your heart rate is still high and the blood is still being pumped to your working muscles, so you need to slowly bring the heart rate back to normal.

The cool-down has four main objectives:

- To return the heart to normal
- To get rid of any waste products built up during exercise
- To return muscles to their original pre-exercise length
- To prevent venous pooling.

The aim of the cool-down is opposite to the aim of the warm-up in that the pulse will lower slowly and waste products such as carbon dioxide and lactic acid are washed out of the muscles. Also, as the muscles work during the main session, they continually shorten to produce force and they end up in a shortened position. Therefore, they need to be stretched out so they do not remain shortened. Also, as the heart pumps blood around the body, circulation is assisted by the action of skeletal muscles. The skeletal muscles act as a 'muscle pump' to help return the blood to the heart against gravity. If the participant stops suddenly, the heart will keep pumping blood to the

275

legs, but because the muscle pump has stopped, the blood will pool in the legs. This causes the participant to become light-headed and they may pass out.

The cool-down consists of the following activities:

- Lowering the heart rate
- Maintenance stretching on muscles worked
- Developmental stretching on short muscles.

Lowering the Heart Rate

To lower the heart rate you need to do the reverse of the pulse raiser. First, choose a CV-type exercise involving rhythmical movements and the large muscle groups. This time the intensity starts high and slowly drops to cause a drop in heart rate. This part should last around five minutes and an exercise bike is a good choice because it enables the client to sit down and relax as well. The gradual lowering of the intensity allows the muscle pump to work and avoid venous pooling. You want to ensure the pulse rate is around 100 to 110 b.p.m. at the end of the pulse lowerer.

Stretching

Two types of stretching can be used in the cool-down: maintenance and developmental. A maintenance stretch is used to return the muscles worked to their pre-exercise state. During training they will be continuously shortened and they need to be stretched out to prevent shortening. Stretching will also help eliminate waste products from the muscles and also prevent soreness the next day. A maintenance stretch is one where the muscle is stretched to the point of discomfort and then is held for around ten seconds or until the muscle relaxes and the stretch goes off. All muscles worked in the main session will need at least a maintenance stretch.

Developmental stretching is used on muscles which have become short and tight. They may be short because they have been overtrained or due to the positions adopted on a daily basis. If a person is sitting down all day, either in front of a computer or driving, they may develop shortened pectorals, hamstrings, hip flexors and adductors.

Developmental stretching involves stretching a muscle and then holding it for around ten seconds until it relaxes. Once it has relaxed, the stretch is increased and held for ten seconds; this is repeated three times.

Key learning points 1

- The components of fitness are aerobic endurance, flexibility, strength, muscular endurance and body composition.
- Frequency, intensity, time, type, overload, reversibility and specificity are the principles of training.
- All participants in exercise sessions should complete a PAR-Q to identify any contraindications to exercise.
- A warm-up will raise heart rate, increase the temperature of the body and mobilise the joints.
- The main component of a training session will contain CV work and resistance training.
- The cool-down will return the heart rate to normal and stretch muscles to their original length.

Q Quick quiz 1

Fill in the blanks in the following sentences regarding the adaptations to aerobic endurance training.

1 _____ muscles become stronger.
2 Lungs are able to extract more _____ from the air.
3 Increase in the amount of blood pumped in each beat (_____ _____).
4 Increase in the amount of blood pumped per _____ (cardiac output).
5 Decrease in blood _____.
6 Increase in blood _____ and ___ blood cell count.
7 Increase in the number and size of _____ (energy producing parts of cells).
8 Increase in muscle size (_____).
9 Bone _____ increases (if activity is weight bearing).

Student activity 15.1 20 minutes P1

Match the descriptions to the principles of training in the table below.

Principle of training	Description
Frequency	How long the session lasts
Intensity	Working a system harder than it is used to
Time	How many times a week/month the participant will train
Type	Fitness gains can be lost as well as attained
Overload	Fitness gains will depend upon the type of training done
Reversibility	How hard a person works
Specificity	Description of the training performed

Student activity 15.2 45 minutes P2 M1

A training session involves a <u>trainer</u> instructing a <u>client</u> in a <u>training environment</u> – each of these variables (trainer, client, environment) can pose a health and safety threat. For each variable, identify two health and safety considerations.

1 For P2, describe the health and safety consideration.

2 For M1, explain the health and safety consideration.

For example, the trainer may not be qualified and may instruct exercises incorrectly.

Student activity 15.3 30 minutes P3

Complete the following table to show your understanding of the warm-up and cool-down.

Component	Content	Brief description of each part of the content	Describe its importance
Warm-up	Pulse raiser Mobiliser Dynamic stretches		
Cool-down	Pulse lowerer Developmental stretches Maintenance stretches		

15.3 Designing, Planning and Leading an Exercise Programme

To ensure that participants are happy with their progress and will keep training, it is important that the trainer is able to design exercise programmes and session plans which are relevant to the specific needs of the participant. This section looks at the process you need to go through in order to write an effective training session for the participant.

Stage 1 – Gathering Information

To enable the trainer to design a specific exercise programme you need to carry out a comprehensive initial consultation. This will involve the participant filling out a questionnaire about their health, medical conditions, goals and lifestyle. This is followed up by a face-to-face discussion to find out more information about the participant. The trainer will be building up a detailed picture of this participant and their life so that the exercises they choose and the programme they design will have the best chance of succeeding.

Factors to Consider

When the trainer sits down to design the programme, they need to consider a range of factors to ensure that the programme is appropriate and that it will benefit the participant rather than harm them. The trainer will need to consider the following.

- PAR-Q responses – have any contraindications to exercise been identified?
- Medical history – do they have any conditions which may affect the training programme and choice of exercises?
- Current and previous exercise history – this will give an idea about the current fitness level of the client.
- Barriers to exercise – do they have constraints such as time, cost, family responsibilities or work commitments?
- Motives and goals – what is the participant aiming to achieve and what is their timescale?
- Occupation – hours worked and whether work is manual or office-based.
- Activity levels – amount of movement they do on a daily basis.
- Leisure time activities – whether these are active or inactive.
- Diet – what, how much and when they eat.

- Stress levels – either through work or their home life, and how they deal with it.
- Alcohol intake – how much they consume and how often.
- Smoking – whether they are a smoker or ex-smoker and the amount they smoke.
- Time available – the client needs to fit the training into their schedule and the trainer needs to be realistic when planning the programme.

Client Groups

Clients are the central focus of the fitness industry and it is essential that we understand the individual needs and goals of each one. Each person needs to be treated as an individual to ensure they remain on their training programme. Clients will come from a range of backgrounds, ages, fitness levels, shapes and sizes. You may see the following groups of people as clients:

- Varied ability levels – beginners, intermediates, advanced
- Varied fitness levels – low, moderate or high
- Elderly
- Juniors
- Athletes
- People with specific goals, such as running a marathon or weight loss
- Pregnant women
- People with medical conditions such as asthma or diabetes.

When you meet a new client it is important that you consider what this person is feeling and thinking.

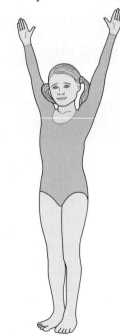

Fig 15.8 A young gymnast

You need to place yourself in their shoes to consider what it is they need. We call this 'walking a mile in their shoes'.

Activity Selection

When we have gathered information about the participant, we select an appropriate intervention in terms of the exercises we choose. You need to consider the following factors:

- Likes and dislikes – what is the participant comfortable doing? Why do they not like certain exercises?
- Accessibility – where can they get to for their training? This may be physical or limited by cost.
- Culture – are they limited by their culture in terms of expected roles and responsibilities, and also dress codes?
- Equipment available – are activities limited by the venue and what it has to offer? You may be training in a gym or maybe at the client's home or in a park.

Stage 2 – Establishing Objectives

To ensure the success of the programme it needs to be specific to the outcome a client wants. Therefore, it is important to find out exactly what this is. If you ask them what they want to achieve they will say that they want to get fit. You need to question them further and find out what this means to them. You may need to make suggestions as they may not know themselves. Their objectives could be any of the following:

- CV fitness
- Flexibility
- Weight loss
- Improved health
- Muscular strength
- Muscular size
- Muscle tone
- Power.

Once you have established the objectives, it is time to plan the programme.

Stage 3 – Planning the Programme

Programme design is an area of controversy, and different trainers have different ideas about what is right and wrong. Usually the programme will use the structure shown in Tables 15.3 and 15.4.

The training programme will usually last for one hour. The length of each component will depend upon the objectives of the client and the importance they place on each.

Warm-up	Raise pulse Mobilise joints Dynamic stretches	5–10 minutes
Resistance component	6–10 free weight or resistance machine exercises	30–45 minutes
CV component	Walking, running, cycling or rowing	20–60 minutes
Abdominal training	Abdominals and lower back	5 minutes
Cool-down	Lower the pulse Developmental stretches Maintenance stretches	5–15 minutes

Table 15.3 Programme structure

Objective:	Strength	Muscle size	Endurance	CV
Repetitions or duration	1–5	6–12	12–20	20 minutes +
Recovery period	3–5 minutes	1–2 minutes	30–60 seconds	N/A
Sets per exercise	2–6	3–6	2–3	1
Frequency per week	1–2 on each muscle group	1–2 on each muscle group	2–3 on each muscle group	3 sessions

Table 15.4 Meeting the objectives (adapted from Baechle and Earle, 2008)

Programme Design Rules

When designing the programme you need to follow rules and then check that you have done so.

Rule 1: Work muscles in pairs to keep them balanced

All muscles work in pairs and if they are not worked as pairs the body can become unbalanced. This means that joints will move out of their correct place, causing a change in posture and possibly pain. It also increases the chances of injury. The body works as a complete unit and it must be trained in this way too. Many gym programmes focus on a few muscle groups – usually the chest, arms and abdominals – as these are seen to make a person more attractive.

The main pairs of muscles are:

- Pectorals and trapezius
- Latissimus dorsi and deltoids
- Biceps and triceps
- Abdominals and erector spinae
- Quadriceps and hamstrings.

A check must be made to ensure that all muscle pairs have been worked equally.

Rule 2: Large muscle groups should be trained first

If you are training several muscles in one session it is important that the large muscle groups are trained first. The large muscles are the gluteus maximus, quadriceps and hamstrings, pectorals, latissimus dorsi and trapezius.

These muscles need to be worked first because they require the most effort to work and are best exercised when the client is feeling fresh. Second, if the smaller muscles become tired early on in the session it will be difficult to work the large muscles as hard.

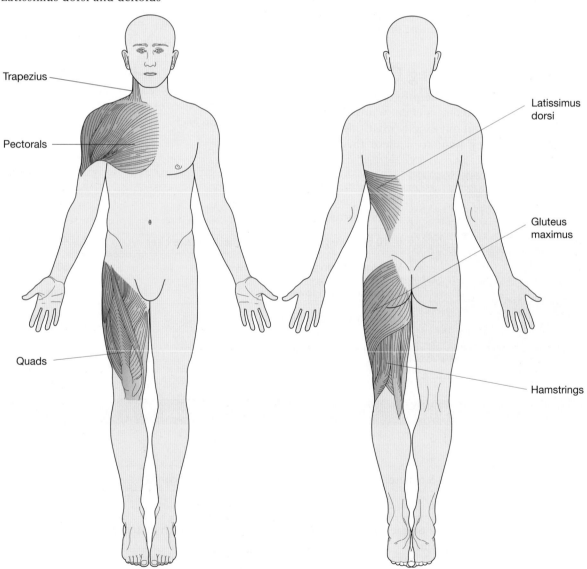

Fig 15.9 Large muscle groups

Rule 3: Do the difficult exercises first

Each exercise will have a difficulty rating and this depends upon two main issues: how many joints are moving and how much balance is needed. An exercise where only one joint moves can be seen as simple, while an exercise with two or more joints moving will be complex. Also, the more balance that is needed the more difficult an exercise becomes. The most difficult exercises need the most skill and should be done early on in the exercise session.

Rule 4: Work the abdominals and lower back at the end of the session

The abdominals and lower back are called the core muscles and these keep the body's posture correct. If they are tired out early on, it increases the risk of the spine becoming injured. They should be exercised after the resistance and CV work have been done.

Following these rules will make sure that the programme is performed in a safe and effective way.

Considerations for Aerobic Training

It is important to consider that not everyone will want to go to a gym to improve their fitness. You will need to be flexible in finding ways to make them more active in their daily lives. The Health Education Authority (HEA) has offered guidelines concerning health and fitness.

To improve cardiovascular fitness you need to train three times a week for between 20 and 60 minutes at 60 to 90 per cent of your maximum heart rate – jogging, running, swimming, cycling or rowing.

To improve health you need to be involved in an activity which makes you slightly warmer and slightly out of breath for 30 minutes between five and seven times a week.

This can involve activities such as brisk walking, gardening, mowing the lawn or recreational swimming. Also you can look at extra ways to increase activity levels, such as walking rather than taking the car, taking the stairs instead of the lift, getting off the bus at an earlier stop or parking the car in the furthest away parking spot!

Key learning points 2

There are a range of factors which will need to be considered when designing an exercise programme, including: medical history, exercise history, barriers, motives and goals, occupation, activity levels, leisure time activities, diet, stress levels, alcohol intake, smoking, time available, current and previous training history.

An exercise programme should have the following components:

● Warm-up
● Resistance component
● CV component
● Abdominal training
● Cool-down.

When designing an exercise programme you need to follow four rules.

Rule 1: Work muscles in pairs to keep muscles balanced.
Rule 2: Large muscle groups should be trained first.
Rule 3: Do the difficult exercises first.
Rule 4: Work the abdominals and lower back at the end of the session.

According to the HEA recommendations, to improve cardiovascular fitness you need to train three times a week for between 20 and 60 minutes at 60 to 90 per cent of your maximum heart rate. To improve health you need to be involved in an activity which makes you slightly warmer and slightly out of breath for 30 minutes between five and seven times a week.

Leading an Exercise Session

Preparation of the Session

When you take a participant through their exercise programme you need to follow a clear structure to ensure the training session is safe and that good customer care is applied.

Before the session starts you need to check the equipment and the environment:

● Availability of equipment
● Equipment is in working order
● All cables are strong
● Floor is clear of equipment and cables
● Temperature
● Ventilation.

Questions and Explanations

The session will start when you meet the participant. At this point you need to explain some safety issues and procedures. The following questions are appropriate to screen the participant prior to the session.

● Have you any illnesses or injuries I need to be aware of?
● Have you eaten today?
● Is your clothing appropriate and have you taken off your jewellery?

Then you need to explain some procedures:

● Fire exits and fire drill
● First-aid kit, first aider and nearest telephone
● Position of water.

Finally explain:

● The training programme and its demands
● The aims and objectives of the session
● The process of instruction.

Delivery of the Session

The aim of the exercise session is to get the participant working for as much time as possible in a safe and effective manner. It is important that the participant is supported and pushed to work as hard as they can within their limits.

The instructor will perform the following roles.

Communicate effectively

It is important that the client is able to understand you and respond in the way you would like them to. We communicate mainly through the words we use and also how we deliver these words and the body language we use. It is good practice to listen to your client and assess their level of knowledge before deciding how you will deliver your instructions. If a person is new to the gym you should keep things simple and use less technical language. The more experienced client will be able to communicate using more technical language.

Give instructions

An instruction is providing information on how to perform a technique. When providing instructions you must say what you want the client to do rather than what not to do. If you use the word 'don't' as in 'don't lock your knees', it increases the chances that they will actually do it!

Demonstrate

The instructor needs to give demonstrations to show the participant how to perform the technique. Once a demonstration has been give the instructor can explain the technique to the client and then let them practise to get the feel of the movement.

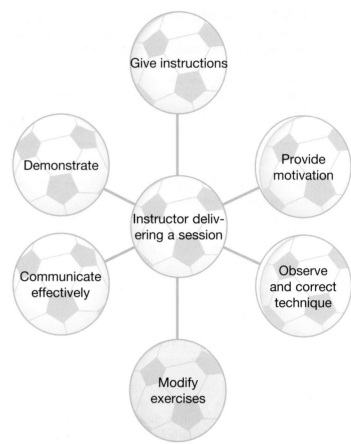

Fig 15.10 Instructor delivering a session

Provide motivation

The reason most people do not achieve the results they want is because their motivation is too low. They give up when the going gets tough. You will motivate them with what you say, how you say it and by using positive body language. This will push them to work as hard as they can within the limits of their fitness.

Observe and correct techniques

The instructor needs to observe the client's technique from a variety of positions by moving around the

Fig 15.11 Trainer and participant

282

client. Once they have observed for a short period, feedback needs to be given about what they are doing right and then what parts need to be corrected.

Modify exercises

If an exercise is too easy or too hard it can be modified in a variety of ways: changing the length of the lever used, getting them to stand up and resist the force of gravity, change the range of movement or the speed of movement (tempo).

End of Session

Once the session is finished you have two roles to perform.

● **Gain feedback**: it is important to ask the participant how they felt the session went and what they liked or did not like. Also, ask about the intensity of the session – whether it was too easy or too hard. This is vital when you reflect on your work and assess whether there are any changes that need to be made for next time to make your session even more effective.

● **Put equipment away and check for damage**: it is important to tidy up your equipment and leave the environment in a safe and acceptable state for the next person. Also, if any damage has occurred, it must be reported so that repairs can be made.

Key learning points 3

Before a session starts you need to check the environment, the client and tell them about the safety procedures.

During the session you need to be supporting the client in the following way:

● Communicate effectively
● Give instructions
● Demonstrate
● Provide motivation
● Observe and correct
● Respond to the client's needs.

At the end of the session ask your client for feedback about the session.

Q Quick quiz 2

Give short answers to the following questions:

1 Why should muscles be worked in pairs?

2 Why should the large muscles be worked first?

3 Why should the difficult exercises be done first?

4 Why should core muscles be worked at the end?

Match the main pairs of muscles that should be worked:

1 Pectorals and _____.

2 Latissimus dorsi and _____.

3 Biceps and _____.

4 Abdominals and _____.

5 Quadriceps and _____.

Choice of answers: triceps, hamstrings, deltoids, erector spinae and trapezius.

Student activity 15.4   ⏱ **120 minutes**   P4 P5 M2 M3 D1   D2

1 (a) For P5, use the following template to plan a safe and effective training session.

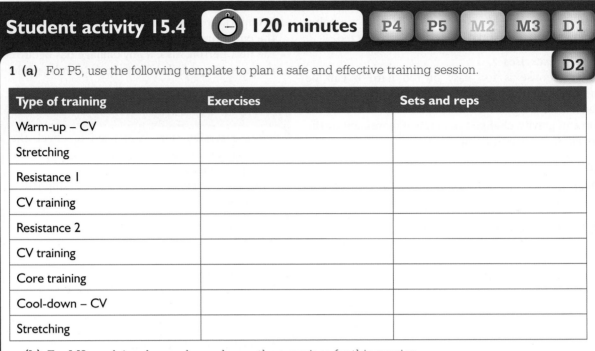

Type of training	Exercises	Sets and reps
Warm-up – CV		
Stretching		
Resistance 1		
CV training		
Resistance 2		
CV training		
Core training		
Cool-down – CV		
Stretching		

(b) For M3, explain why you have chosen the exercises for this session.

(c) For D2, justify your choices of exercises for the planned session.

2 (a) For P4, plan a six-week exercise programme for two contrasting clients, showing how they will progress over the six-week period. Use the following template to show the progression.

Type of training	Week 1	Week 2	Week 3	Week 4	Week 5	Week 6	Alternative activities (D1)
Resistance 1							
CV 1							
Resistance 2							
CV 2							
Core training							

(b) For M2, explain your choices of activity for the two contrasting clients.

(c) For D1, justify your choice of activities for the two selected clients, including alternative activities.

15.4 Reviewing the Design of an Exercise Session and Leading of an Exercise Session

P6 P7 M4

The Purpose of Reviewing Sessions

To improve as a trainer and a person it is vital to regularly review your performance and identify any changes that need to be made. We can receive feedback from a range of sources and it is all useful.

Feedback is information about performance. It is neither good nor bad; it is just information. It allows us to improve our performance in the following ways.

- **Track progression:** we can assess whether our training is having the desired effect on the participant. This can be done through fitness testing or from their own perspective.
- **Adapt sessions:** if we are not achieving our aim or an exercise has had a negative response we

can adapt the programme to achieve a different response.

- **Improve own performance**: we need to identify any weaknesses we may have as then we can improve how we work with our participants. Our strengths will always work for us but we will only improve if we address our weaknesses.

Codes of Practice

We must always be sure that what we do is ethical. Reflecting on how we act, talk and work with our clients will ensure we stay within accepted codes of behaviour.

Continued Professional Development

For a trainer to continue to improve their skills they need to be continually attending conferences and taking courses. This development should work on improving our weaknesses. It is also a requirement of the Register of Exercise Professionals (REPs) that each trainer who is a member of the Register must achieve 24 points for training per year.

Conducting a Review

The ideal time to conduct a review is as soon as you can after a session while the issues are still fresh in your own mind and your participant's. You may even be able to ask the participant some questions during the cool-down period, as the work is less intense and they will be starting to relax. You need to ask them specific questions regarding the session and its outcomes.

You could use a review form like the one shown below and cover the following detail.

Self-Evaluation

The client may not pick up things you see or feel yourself so you must ask yourself the same questions and answer them in an honest manner.

Particularly, you must assess yourself in terms of the safety of the session and then whether it was effective. Did it really meet the aims that you had set for your session?

The benefits of self-evaluation are as follows:

- You can plan future sessions to ensure they are enjoyable and effective
- Good evaluation is likely to increase the chances of the client sticking to their training programme
- The client will stay interested and motivated
- The client will keep progressing
- You are able to identify any training needs you may have
- You can set yourself goals for personal development and any training needs you may have.

Peer Evaluation

As part of your support group you may work with a colleague and observe each other's training sessions. This may give a third perspective on the training and highlight issues you would not have considered yourself.

Modifying an Exercise Programme

There are many ways to change a participant's training programme to ensure they continue to achieve overload and keep interested and motivated:

- Change a training principle
- Frequency – increase the number of times they train a week
- Intensity – make the programme harder by increasing speeds or resistance
- Time – make each session longer
- Type – change the training they do from aerobic to resistance training.

The body is expert at adapting and will only gain benefit from an exercise for a limited period. Therefore, if we change an exercise, we gain a new stimulus for the body to adapt to. So change from

Review Form

1 Did you think the programme was effective in meeting your aims?

_____

2 What did you enjoy and not enjoy about the training session?

_____

3 To what extent did you feel safe?

_____

4 Could the session be improved in any way?

_____

resistance machines to free weights or cable exercises and a change will occur.

You can also give the participant a new target each week to continue to push them – cycle 5 km in under ten minutes or run 5 km in 25 minutes.

SMART Targets

Regular evaluation can lead to improvements in performance. If you set yourself specific goals then you can monitor your actual performance. Achieving goals relies on effective goal setting using the SMART principle. This stands for:

- **Specific**
- **Measurable**
- **Achievable**
- **Realistic**
- **Time-constrained.**

As you continue to evaluate yourself and improve your training skills, communication skills and motivation skills, you will see yourself become a more professional and effective trainer.

Student activity 15.5 · 45 minutes · P6 · P7 · M4

1 Organise with your tutor a time when you can deliver your exercise session with a selected client. To achieve M4, you need to deliver the exercise session independently of tutor support.

2 Once you have delivered the session you need to review your own performance with regard to the design, planning and delivery of the session and then identify your strengths and weaknesses.

You could use the following template to help you think about areas you should be reviewing.

Categories to consider	Responses
Sources of feedback: 1. Your client 2. Your tutor 3. Yourself	
Design and planning: 1. Is it appropriate for the client? 2. Does it meet their goals and needs? 3. Is it varied and interesting?	

Delivery:
1 What did they enjoy about the session/not enjoy about the session?
2 What were your strengths and weaknesses with regard to:
  • your instructional skills
  • your motivational skills
  • your communication skills
  • your demonstrations
  • your explanations?	

Reference

Baechle, T. and Earle, R. (2008) *Essentials of Strength Training and Conditioning*, Champaign, IL: Human Kinetics.

Further reading

Ansell, M. (2008) *Personal Training*, Exeter: Learning Matters.

Baechle, T. and Earle, R. (2008) *Essentials of Strength Training and Conditioning*, Champaign, IL: Human Kinetics.

Coulson, M. (2007) *The Fitness Instructor's Handbook*, London: A&C Black.

Dalgleish, J. and Dollery, S. (2001) *The Health and Fitness Handbook*, Harlow: Longman.

Useful websites

www.netfit.co.uk/previous.htm
Extensive range of exercise and training techniques, some sports specific, others more general.

www.elitesoccerconditioning.com/FitnessTraining/FitnessTraining.htm
Drills, tips and ideas to help you maximise your footballing fitness and techniques.

www.sport-fitness-advisor.com/resistance-training.html
Excellent advice on how to design a resistance training programme for any sport in seven steps.

18: Sports Injuries

18.1 Introduction

While participation in sport and physical activity has a lot of positive aspects, such as improving fitness levels and being involved in a social group with common interests, it also has a negative aspect in the form of incurring physical injury. This unit will identify different types of sports injuries and how they can occur. It will consider both physiological and psychological responses to injury and then suggest some methods to prevent and treat sports injuries. Finally, this unit will outline a range of rehabilitation procedures that can be considered, together with important information on tracking and documenting injuries and their treatment.

By the end of this unit you should:

- know how common sports injuries can be prevented by the correct identification of risk factors
- know about a range of sports injuries and their symptoms
- know how to apply methods of treating sports injuries.

Assessment and grading criteria		
To achieve a PASS grade the evidence must show that the learner is able to:	**To achieve a MERIT grade the evidence must show that, in addition to the pass criteria, the learner is able to:**	**To achieve a DISTINCTION grade the evidence must show that, in addition to the pass and merit criteria, the learner is able to:**
P1 describe extrinsic and intrinsic risk factors in relation to sports injuries	**M1** explain how risk factors can be minimised by utilisation of preventative measures	
P2 describe preventative measures that can be taken in order to prevent sports injuries occurring		
P3 describe the physiological responses common to most sports injuries	**M2** explain the physiological and psychological responses common to most sports injuries	**D1** analyse the physiological and psychological responses common to most sports injuries
P4 describe the psychological responses common to sports injuries		
P5 describe first aid and common treatments used for four different types of sports injuries		
P6 design a safe and appropriate treatment and rehabilitation programme for two common sports injuries, with tutor support.	**M3** independently design a safe and appropriate treatment and rehabilitation programme for two common sports injuries.	**D2** evaluate the treatment and rehabilitation programme designed, justifying choices and suggesting alternatives where appropriate.

18.2 The Prevention of Sports Injuries by the Correct Identification of Risk Factors

  P1 **P2** **M1**

Taking part in sport can result in injury to any part of the body. These injuries can be caused by a variety of factors which can be grouped into two categories:

● Extrinsic risk factors
● Intrinsic risk factors.

Extrinsic Risk Factors

An extrinsic risk factor is something external to the body that can cause an injury. These include:

● Inappropriate coaching or instruction
● Incorrect advice on technique
● Environmental conditions
● Other sports players
● Equipment, clothing and footwear issues.

Inappropriate Coaching or Instruction

Inappropriate instruction given by a coach or a trainer is an obvious way in which sports participants can easily become injured. It is vital that all instruction is given by someone who has an up-to-date and in-depth knowledge about the sport and is also able to communicate this appropriately and effectively. It is essential that the rules and regulations for the sport, as laid down by the specific governing body, have been correctly interpreted and are appropriately enforced. Likewise, during training activities, it is important that the information given by the coach/trainer is reliable. For this reason, many governing bodies have coaching schemes that are constantly reviewed so that coaching qualifications can be maintained at the highest and safest of standards.

Incorrect Advice on Technique

The technique of performing an action or specific sport skill is usually dictated by the guidance that the sports participant has received from the PE teacher, coach, trainer or instructor. This being the case, the above is particularly relevant. But it is very easy for individuals to start to slip from these standards if they are not reinforced at the right time. If correction does not occur the participant can soon start to adopt bad habits in terms of skill level and performance. This incorrect performance of skill can in turn lead to injury problems. An obvious example is weightlifting, where back injuries particularly occur due to incorrect and bad or poor technique.

Environmental Conditions

The environment in which we perform sports can also have a big impact on the likelihood of sustaining an injury. The environment encompasses the area in which a sport is played, so if you were playing basketball the environment would consist of the sports hall, and include the playing surface, the lighting and the temperature. If the lighting was poor, a player may be more likely to misjudge attacking or defensive moves and injure themselves or another player. If the surface was wet, a player would be more likely to slip over because the surface becomes much more dangerous when it is wet.

Other Sports Players

Some sports are obviously more susceptible to incurring sports injuries as the rules of the sport allow for tackles, scrums, etc. These are called contact sports. For instance, after a rugby game players will often come away with at least a few bruises from tackling or being tackled by other players. In non-contact games, players can also sustain sports injuries from other players from foul tackles or accidental collisions.

Equipment, Clothing and Footwear Issues

It is important to remember to always use the equipment needed to play a particular sport correctly or this too can increase the chances of injury to either the player themselves or to other players. For example, if a javelin, shot-put or a discus are not held and thrown correctly any improper use could cause serious damage to an individual.

The use of appropriate clothing can also be an issue. Certain sports require, as stipulated by the respective governing body of the sport, certain pieces of protective clothing, such as shin pads for football, and pads, gloves and helmets for cricket and hockey.

Other sports, by their very nature, need to have clothing which is very flexible and allows a full range of movement. For example, gymnasts wear clothing which allows them to perform complex movements on the floor and on specialised equipment. If restrictive clothing was worn this could greatly reduce the range of movement allowed and therefore cause injury.

Correct footwear for the correct surface that the sport is to be played on is a must. There is a phenomenal array of specialised footwear for all sports, including running, basketball, tennis, squash, gymnastics, football and rugby. All these specialised pieces of footwear are made to be supportive to the player and totally suitable for the surface required for the sport. Football has grass, artificial turf and sports hall floors as its main playing areas and there are specialised shoes and boots for each surface.

However, although a sports person may be wearing the correct footwear, certain types of footwear make a person more susceptible to injury. For instance, the studs on a footballer's or rugby player's boot can make the wearer more susceptible to leg injuries because the studs plant the foot in the ground, so if the person is turning on a planted foot they are more likely to twist their knee.

Incorrect footwear can also be a factor in causing a person to injure themselves while playing sport. For example, a marathon runner needs a lot of cushioning in their trainers to absorb the repeated impact of running. If they were to wear trainers with little padding they would be much more likely to sustain an overuse sport injury.

Intrinsic Risk Factors

An intrinsic risk factor is a physical aspect of the athlete's body that can cause an injury.

These include:

- Inadequate warm-up
- Muscle imbalance
- Poor preparation
- Postural defects
- Poor technique
- Overuse
- Age.

Inadequate Warm-Up

This is a very common cause of sports injury. The warm-up prepares both the body and the mind for the exercise that is to come by gradually taking the body from its non-active state to being ready for the exercise. How long it takes to warm up will vary from person to person, and will depend on their level of fitness. The environment will also affect the length of the warm-up. In cold surroundings it will be necessary to carry out a longer warm-up than in hot surroundings.

A warm-up should consist of three components:

- A pulse raiser to get the blood flowing more quickly around the body and so help to warm up the muscle tissues and make them more pliable
- A mobiliser, in which the joints are taken through their range of movement, such as arm circles, to mobilise the shoulder joint
- The main muscles that are going to be used in the sport should be stretched.

Muscle Imbalance

A muscle imbalance means that one muscle in an antagonistic pair is stronger than the other. This is often seen in footballers who have strong quadriceps muscles from extending their knee to kick the ball, but their hamstring muscles are not as strong. This can result in knee injuries because the hamstring muscles are not strong enough to put a brake on the kicking action of the knee. As a result, when a striker goes to score a goal they can over-kick, so that their knee hyperextends and gets injured.

Poor Preparation

This includes a player's fitness levels specific to the sport they are going to take part in. If a person is not fit to take part in a sport they are more likely to injure themselves because they are so tired that they develop a poor sports technique. A sports person must also acclimatise to the environment in which they are going to play. For example, if a marathon runner living in England wants to take part in a race in Australia in the summer time, they will have to train in hot conditions to get their body used to the heat.

Postural Defects

Most people are born with a slight postural defect, such as having one leg slightly longer than the other. If there is a large difference between the two legs, this can affect the person's running technique, which may then place more strain on one side of the body, which would make the person more likely to sustain injuries after long periods of exercising.

Poor Technique

If a person is not using the correct methods for exercising, they are more likely to sustain a sports injury. For example, if a swimmer continues to perform the front crawl stroke incorrectly with their arms, they may be prone to shoulder or elbow injuries. Note how this differs from the description of incorrect advice on technique in the extrinsic factors section. Poor technique is related to the individual's performance without the use of equipment as opposed to incorrect techniques related to the misuse of equipment to perform a movement.

Overuse

An overuse injury is caused because a sports person does not take time to recover after exercise. Every time we exercise we place our body under strain, which means the body has to repair itself afterwards. If a person does not allow their body to repair itself it will become weaker until eventually parts of the body become injured. Also, if we continue to use specific parts of the body over a long period of time the repair is sometimes difficult to manage. A runner puts a lot of pressure and strain through their body and particularly through the knees. Injuries to the knee joint can start to be a problem if a runner has trained or competed for a long period of time, even allowing for rest periods within training.

Age

The type of injury that is most common varies with the age of the subject and also the level of competition. In young children most injuries are due to falling. In older children injuries that result from collisions and violence are more common. In older age groups and in top-level sportsmen and women there are fewer acute injuries and more overuse injuries and those that are due to intrinsic factors.

Preventative Measures

Besides maintaining fitness and doing a warm-up, an important way to prevent sports injuries is to wear protective clothing. As already noted, some sports' governing bodies stipulate the use of protective equipment in order to minimise injury. Some sports do not require these but an individual may still consider protecting themselves with the use of certain items such as a gum shield or knee pads.

Suitable clothing minimises the risk of sustaining an injury in any sport. At the very least, people should wear loose-fitting or stretchy clothing and appropriate footwear. Jewellery should always be removed.

Supervision by a suitably qualified coach will also help to prevent injuries. Supervision should ensure that the sports performer is using the correct techniques for their sport. They will also be able to design training programmes that can adapt with the performer's needs. For example, if the sports performer is not training to the best of their ability, the coach may include more rest during one week of the training programme to ensure the person has recovered suitably from their training. A coach will also ensure that the equipment and environment is appropriate for training and, if not, they would ensure that either protective clothing or equipment is used or an alternative safe training session is carried out.

Student activity 18.1   ⏱ **40 minutes**   P1 P2 M1

Fill in the following table to show your understanding of the extrinsic and intrinsic factors that can cause sports injuries, and the preventative measures that can be taken to protect against them.

Risk factor	Describe how this is a risk factor in relation to sports injuries (P1)	Describe preventative measures that can be taken to prevent this risk factor from causing a sports injury (P2)	Explain how preventative measures can prevent this risk factor from causing a sports injury (M1)
Poor coaching			
Incorrect advice on technique			
Environmental conditions			
Clothing/footwear			
Safety hazards			
Muscle imbalances			
Poor preparation			
Overuse			
Postural defects			

Key learning points 1

- Extrinsic injuries are caused by forces outside the body, such as the environment and contact with other athletes.
- Intrinsic injuries are caused by physical aspects of the athlete's body, such as postural issues or poor technique.

18.3 Sports Injuries and their Symptoms

The repair of injured soft tissue, such as muscle, actually commences within the first 24 hours following injury. One of the first signs that soft tissue is injured is the appearance of swelling. When the injured area starts to swell it will feel painful. This is due to the swelling creating pressure on the nerves surrounding the damaged tissue. The swelling occurs because the surrounding blood vessels are ruptured, allowing blood to bleed into the area and tissue fluid to gather around the injury site. The injured area will usually look red because the blood vessels surrounding the site dilate, which also has the effect of making the injured area feel hot. The injured area will show a reduced function or a total inability to function because of the pain and swelling.

The level of the above signs and symptoms will be directly related to the degree of the injury – the greater the degree of damage, the greater the effects of inflammation.

It is over a period of between 48 and 72 hours and up to 21 days that the repair is carried out with vigour by the body. The body's clotting mechanism seals the end of the torn blood vessels so that further blood plasma cannot escape into the surrounding tissues.

As the immediate effects of injury subside, the healing/repair process begins. This consists of:

- Absorption of swelling
- Removal of debris and blood clot
- Growth of new blood capillaries
- Development of initial fibrous scar tissue.

After 12 hours, and for the first four days, the cells become active and new capillary blood vessel buds form and gradually grow to establish a new circulation in the area. With the new blood supply the debris of dead cell tissues and the initial blood clot that was formed is cleared.

Q Quick quiz 1

Read the following descriptions of injuries and decide whether they were caused by extrinsic or intrinsic factors.

1 Kelly has sustained ligament damage to her knee after being tackled late by an opponent.
2 Malcolm has bought new training shoes but finds he gets shin pain when he runs.
3 Kelvin thinks he hurt his hamstring because he ran the 100 m without warming up thoroughly.
4 Tanya gets shoulder pain after training for the javelin.
5 Keisha slipped on a water puddle on the tennis court and sprained her ankle.

Scar Tissue

The damaged tissue is repaired by scar tissue. It is important to remember that scar tissue has 'plastic' properties.

Key term

Plastic properties: it can be stretched and 'moulded'.

Scar tissue is not elastic like muscle. It will form in a haphazard pattern of 'kinks and curls' and will contract or shorten if not carefully stretched daily for many months after the injury.

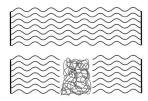

Fig 18.1 Scar tissue (bottom)

There is a great need for the new scar tissue to form in parallel 'lines' to give it strength. Correct 'stretching' causes the scar tissue to line up along the line of stress of the injured structure. Therefore, injured muscles or ligaments should be carefully mobilised and stretched daily (beginning five days after the initial injury).

The stretching will ensure that the scar is moulded to the desired length and improve the strength of the healed area (scar), and thus reduce a recurrence of damage to the scarred area and injured structure.

Muscular System

For a detailed discussion of skeletal muscular structure and function, read Chapter 1: Anatomy for Sport and Exercise.

Ligaments and Tendons

Other tissues that are frequently damaged during sport are ligaments and tendons. These are also soft tissue and are primarily made out of collagen. Ligaments connect bone to bone and tendons connect muscles to bone. Ligaments and tendons can adapt to changes in their mechanical environment due to injury, disease or exercise. A ligament or tendon is made up of fascicles.

Each fascicle contains the basic fibril of the ligament or tendon and the fibroblasts, the cells that make the ligament or tendon.

Unlike normal ligaments, healed ligaments are partly made up of a different type of collagen, which has fibrils with a smaller diameter, and are therefore a mechanically inferior structure. As a result, the healed ligament often fails to provide adequate joint stability, which can then lead to re-injury or a chronically lax (permanently slightly unstable) joint.

For additional information on ligaments and tendons see Chapter 1: Anatomy for Sport and Exercise.

Classification of Injuries

There are many ways in which we can classify the severity of an injury. One example is that there are three general stages of injury which can be applied to most sports injuries:

1 Acute stage (0 to 72 hours after injury).
2 Sub-acute stage (72 hours to 21 days after injury).
3 Chronic continuum (21 days after injury).

Note that the severity of the injury will dictate stages 2 and 3 of the above model – less severe will reach stage 3 some time before day 21; more severe may take longer than 21 days.

The following are examples of specific injuries and how they can be classified.

Haematomas

A haematoma is bleeding either into or around a muscle. If the bleeding is within the muscle, it is called an 'intramuscular' haematoma. This type of haematoma will lead to a pressure build-up within the muscle tissue as the blood is trapped within the muscle sheath. This will result in a marked decrease in strength of the injured muscle, a significant decrease in muscle stretch and a long recovery period.

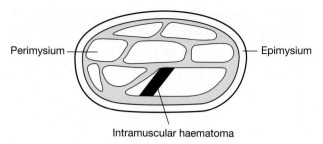

Fig 18.2 An intramuscular haematoma

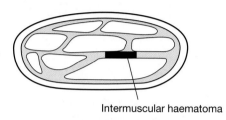

Fig 18.3 An intermuscular haematoma

Bleeding around the muscle tissue is called an intermuscular haematoma. This type of haematoma is much less severe than an intramuscular haematoma because the blood can escape from the damaged muscle and into the surrounding tissues, so there is less pressure in the area and the injury recovers much more quickly.

Sprained Ankle

Injuries to the ligaments of the ankle are usually graded into three categories.

- A first-degree sprain is the least severe. It is the result of some minor stretching of the ligaments, and is accompanied by mild pain, some swelling and joint stiffness. There is usually very little loss of joint stability.
- A second-degree sprain is the result of both stretching and some tearing of the ligaments. There is increased swelling and pain and a moderate loss of stability at the ankle joint.
- A third-degree sprain is the most severe of the three. It is the result of a complete tear or rupture of one or more of the ligaments that make up the ankle joint. A third-degree sprain will result in massive swelling, severe pain and gross instability. With a third-degree sprain, shortly after the injury most of the localised pain will disappear. This is a result of the nerve endings being severed, which causes a lack of feeling at the injury site.

From the explanations above, you can see that pain and swelling are the two most common symptoms associated with an ankle sprain. You can also expect some bruising to occur at the injury site. The associated swelling and bruising are the result of ruptured blood vessels and this in turn will produce heat or inflammation.

Psychological Responses to Injury

The response to injury varies from individual to individual. It may vary within an individual alone, dependent on when the injury occurs – at the start of a training session, middle of a season or during a major competition.

The reaction initially is negative in the main but positive attitudes can be formed. For example, it may give an individual more personal time to spend with family and friends, or time to develop new skills such as coaching, or to work on other aspects of their performance. Generally, though, the reaction is negative.

In reality, while some individuals struggle with the negative feelings that they experience, most cope without great difficulty, particularly if the injury is not so severe.

Various theoretical models have been proposed to explain the response to injury. These all include as early reactions:

- Shock
- Disbelief
- Denial.

These are followed by possible further responses:

- Anger
- Depression
- Tension
- Helplessness
- Acceptance
- Adaptation
- Reorganisation.

After the initial shock is over, many athletes tend to play down the significance of the injury. However, as the injury becomes more apparent, shock is often replaced by anger directed towards themselves or towards other people. The responses can vary in intensity depending on situational and personal factors but can be especially strong in individuals whose self-concept and personal identity are based on being 'an athlete/a player/a competitor'. The loss of this identity due to the inability to perform can cause much distress.

Following anger, the injured athlete might try bargaining or rationalising to avoid the reality of the situation. A runner may promise to train extra hard on return to training. By confronting reality, and realising and understanding the consequences of the injury, an individual can become depressed at the uncertainty of the future. An injured individual who belongs to a team may start to feel isolated from the 'group' and this in turn can lead to depression. It must be noted, however, that depression is not inevitable and has not always been observed during the grief reaction in research studies.

Tension and helplessness are then generated as the individual becomes frustrated at not being able to continue as normal with training or playing. Again, the isolation that injury causes, from a normal routine or from being with 'the team', can be difficult for some people to accept.

Finally, the individual starts to move towards an acceptance of the injury and adaptation of lifestyle while injured. The focus is then turned to rehabilitation and a return to sports activity. This stage tends to mark the transition from an emotional stage to a problem-coping stage as the individual realises what needs to be done to aid recovery. The timescale for progression through these stages can vary considerably depending on the individual and the severity of the injury, and setbacks during rehabilitation can lead to further emotional disturbance. In cases of very serious injury and ones in which the emotional reactions are prolonged, the skills of a clinical psychologist might be required.

It must be stressed that this process may not be a linear one for all individuals who experience some of these feelings.

Motivations and goal-setting strategies have been shown to help some people. It is possible as a coach, trainer or parent to help an injured individual recover sensibly, effectively and more positively by encouraging them to follow professional advice relating to physical rehabilitation. You can also reassure them that the feelings they are experiencing are not uncommon.

The channelling of a positive attitude can ease the rehabilitation for not just the injured player but also those around them!

Key learning points 2

- Physiological responses to injury – how the body reacts to an injury immediately after its occurrence and how it adapts over a period of time.
- Physical signs of injury may include swelling, bleeding, damaged tissue, discoloration and abnormal alignment of a limb or joint.
- Non-physical signs may include pain and heat (inflammation).
- Adaptation over time will include:
  - absorption of swelling
  - removal of debris and blood clots
  - growth of new blood capillaries
  - development of initial fibrous scar tissue.
- Psychological responses to injury – how the sports person mentally reacts and copes with the physical injury. This response can vary from individual to individual; can be determined by the severity of the injury; can be different dependent on when the injury occurs, e.g. start of the playing season; and can change within an individual during the course of rehabilitation.

Q Quick quiz 2

Fill the blanks in the following sentences.

1 A soft tissue injury, such as an injury to _____, will cause _____, which is painful due to increased pressure on _____.

2 There are three stages of injury: the _____ stage occurs 0 to 72 hours after the injury; then from 72 hours to 21 days comes the _____ stage, after which the _____ is entered.

3 A _____ is a description of bleeding into or around a muscle. The bleeding is called _____ if it is within the muscle, and _____ if it is around the muscle.

Student activity 18.2   60 minutes   P3   P4   M2   D1

Read the case study and then answer the questions below.

1 From your reading of the case study and knowledge of muscle injuries, what physiological responses will Carly be experiencing? (P3)

2 From your reading of the case study, describe the psychological responses Carly is experiencing. (P4)

3 Explain the physiological and psychological responses that Carly will be experiencing. (M2)

4 Analyse the physiological and psychological responses that Carly will be experiencing. (D1)

Carly is a talented 17-year-old long jumper who has just competed in the school's county championships. However, during her second jump, she felt a sharp pain down the back of her left hamstring. She thinks she may have heard a small 'pop' as well. She had to pull out of the jump and hobbled through the sand. She was not able to take any further part in the competition. When she goes to see a physiotherapist the next day, she feels pain and tenderness as he presses on the back of her left hamstring; there is also some bruising around the site of the injury. She finds that it is very painful when she bends her knee and also her hip. She is still a bit shaken up by the injury and feels very upset about getting injured, particularly as she has a national event coming up in a month's time in which she is desperate to compete. She asks the physiotherapist if she will be fit in time and he says he cannot answer that. She starts to get very worried and secretly thinks that she will rest for a couple of days and then start training again. But when she starts to think about jumping again, it makes her feel anxious.

18.4 Methods of Treating Sports Injuries

Injuries can be categorised into soft tissue and hard tissue injuries. Soft tissue refers to the muscles, tendons, ligaments and skin, whereas hard tissue refers to the skeleton, including joints, bones and cartilage.

Hard Tissue Injuries

Dislocation

Dislocation is the displacement of a joint from its normal location. It occurs when a joint is over-stressed, which makes the bones that meet at that joint disconnect. This usually causes the joint capsule to tear, together with the ligaments holding the joint in place. Most dislocations are caused by a blow or a fall. If a person has dislocated a joint then it will usually look out of place, discoloured and/or misshapen. Movement is limited, and there is usually swelling and intense pain.

Subluxation

A subluxation is when one or more of the bones of the spine moves out of position and creates pressure on, or irritates, the spinal nerves. This interferes with the signals travelling along these spinal nerves, which means some parts of the body will not be working properly.

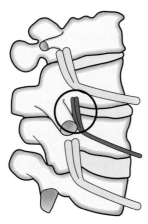

Fig 18.4 A subluxation

Cartilage Damage

Normal synovial joint function requires a smooth-gliding cartilage surface on the ends of the bones. This cartilage also acts to distribute force during repetitive pounding movements, such as running or jumping. Cartilage injury can result in locking, localised pain and swelling around the affected area. It appears as a hole in the cartilage surface. As cartilage has minimal ability to repair itself, it needs treatment in order to minimise the deterioration to the joint surface.

Haemarthrosis

Haemarthrosis is where there is bleeding into the joint. It is a serious injury, and swelling of the injury site occurs very rapidly. The swelling works to protect the joint structures by limiting or preventing movement of the injured joint.

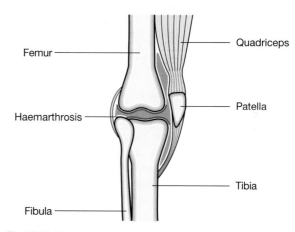

Fig 18.5 Haemarthrosis

Fractures

A fracture is the technical term for a broken bone. They result whenever a bone is hit with enough force to make it break, creating either a small crack or, in a serious fracture, a complete break. There are five main types of fracture.

- **Transverse fractures** are usually the result of a direct blow or force being applied at a sideways angle to the bone. The resultant shape of the bone ends helps transverse fractures stay in alignment more easily than those of other fractures, where the resultant ends do not line up so readily.

Fig 18.6 A transverse fracture

- **Spiral fractures** are also known as **oblique fractures**. They usually occur as a result of a twisting movement being applied about the long axis of the bone – for example, the foot being held trapped by football boot studs while the leg twists around it.

297

Fig 18.7 A spiral fracture

● A **comminuted fracture** is where there is splintering of the bone so that the bone is broken into a number of pieces. This type of fracture can take longer than others to heal, and is usually caused by direct trauma.

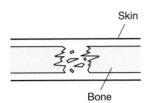

Fig 18.8 A comminuted fracture

● A **stress fracture** is an overuse injury. It occurs when muscles become fatigued and are unable to absorb added shock. Eventually, the fatigued muscle transfers the overload of stress to the bone, causing a tiny crack called a stress fracture. Stress fractures usually occur because of a rapid increase in the amount or intensity of training. The impact of an unfamiliar surface or incorrect trainers can also cause stress fractures.

Fig 18.9 A stress fracture

● An **open fracture** is also called a **compound fracture**. It is generally a more serious type of injury because the bone breaks through the skin. The break causes considerable damage to surrounding tissue and can cause serious bleeding if a large artery is ruptured. It also exposes the broken bone to the possibility of infection, which can interfere with healing.

Fig 18.10 An open fracture

Soft Tissue Injuries

Strains

A strain is a twist, pull and/or tear to a muscle or tendon, and is often caused by overuse, force

or over-stretching. If a tear in the muscle occurs, surgical repair may be necessary. Muscle strains can be classified into three categories.

First-degree strains commonly exhibit the following symptoms:

● Few muscle fibres are torn
● Mild pain
● Little swelling
● Some muscle stiffness.

Second-degree strains commonly exhibit the following symptoms:

● Minimal to moderate tearing of the muscle fibres
● Moderate to severe pain
● Swelling and stiffness.

Third-degree strains commonly exhibit the following symptoms:

● Total rupture of the muscle
● Severe pain
● Severe swelling.

Sprains

A sprain is a stretch and/or tear to a ligament and is often caused by a trauma that knocks a joint out of position, and over-stretches or ruptures the supporting ligaments. Sprains often affect the ankles, knees or wrists.

Muscle contusions or **haematomas** occur due to direct trauma, commonly a blow to the outer part of the thigh or back of the calf; this injury is commonly referred to as a 'dead leg' – it is a bruising of muscle tissue caused by the muscle being squashed between the object causing the impact and the underlying bone. The muscle fibres are squashed and associated capillaries are torn. This results in bleeding into the area with resultant haematoma formation. Usually the haematoma formed is fairly small. But in some circumstances the bleeding may be extensive and can cause a 'pressure problem'.

Oedema is swelling in the tissue due to trauma. The swelling may be a combination of tissue fluid and blood. The blood comes from local damage to capillaries at the injury site.

Bursitis is inflammation or irritation of a bursa. Bursae are small sacs of fluid that are located between bone and other moving structures such as muscles, skin or tendons. The bursa allows smooth gliding between these structures. If the bursa becomes inflamed it will feel painful and restrict movement within that area. Bursitis is an injury that usually results from overuse.

Tendonitis is inflammation or irritation of a tendon. It causes pain and stiffness around the inflamed tendon, which is made worse by movement.

Fig 18.11 Oedema (swelling)

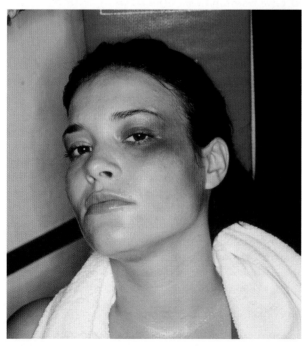

Fig 18.12 Contusion (bruising)

Almost any tendon can be affected with tendonitis, but those located around a joint tend to be more prone to inflammation. Tendonitis usually results from overuse.

A **contusion** is the technical term for a bruise. Contusions are often produced by a blunt force such as a kick, fall or blow. The result will be pain, swelling and discoloration.

An **abrasion** is when the surface of the skin is grazed so that the top layer is scraped off, leaving a raw, tender area. This type of injury often occurs as a result of a sliding fall.

First Aid

First aid is the immediate treatment given to an injured person. When a suitably qualified person arrives on the scene they then take over the care of the person. Anyone with some knowledge of first aid can have a huge impact on the health of an injured person, so it is always useful to know some basics. By completing a recognised first-aid qualification you will gain a very good basic knowledge of what to do in an emergency situation. It is not in the scope of this book to cover all aspects of first aid because practical work is required to complement the theoretical principles of first aid. Therefore, this section will cover only some very basic aspects of first aid.

Immediate Treatments

It is necessary to establish what is wrong with the person. If they are lying on the ground, you should follow the guidelines below.

1 Assess the situation – identify any risks to yourself and to the casualty.
2 Make the area safe, such as turning off an electric switch.
3 Assess the casualty and give first aid if appropriate. Establish if the person is conscious and then check their ABC. This would be thoroughly covered in a first-aid course:
  (a) **A**irway – they have an open airway
  (b) **B**reathing – they are breathing
  (c) **C**irculation – check their circulation by assessing if they have a pulse.
4 Try to get help as soon as possible.
5 Deal with the aftermath – complete an accident or incident report.

If you follow a first-aid course you will be taught how to:

● Check the ABC
● Open a person's airway
● Deal with them if they are not breathing by performing artificial resuscitation

299

- Check if a person has a pulse and how to administer cardiac compressions if they do not.

Calling for an Ambulance

If a person is injured and you believe the injury requires professional attention, you must ensure that someone calls for an ambulance. If you are dealing with a casualty by yourself, minimise the risk to them by taking any vital action first (check their airway, breathing and circulation), then make a short but accurate call.

- Dial 999 and ask for an ambulance.
- Give your exact location.
- Give clear details of the accident and the severity of the injuries your casualty has sustained.
- Give the telephone number you are calling from and the sex and approximate age of the casualty.

If you get someone else to make the call, always ask them to report back to you to confirm that the call has been made.

When the paramedics arrive, tell them as much as possible about how the casualty has behaved, such as if they are unconscious, if they needed artificial resuscitation, and so on.

Contents of a First-Aid Box

A first-aid box should contain a number of items in order for a person to effectively administer first aid. The contents of a first-aid box for a workplace or leisure centre must conform to legal requirements and must also be clearly marked and readily accessible. Below is a list of materials that *most* first-aid kits contain:

- Sterile adhesive dressings (plasters) – there should be a range of sizes for dressing minor wounds
- Sterile eye pads – a sterile pad with a bandage attached to it to cover the eye following eye injuries
- Triangular bandages – these can be used as a pad to stop bleeding, or to make slings, or used as a sterile covering for large injuries such as burns
- Large and medium wound dressings – a sterile, non-medicated dressing pad with a bandage attached to it
- Disposable gloves – these should be worn at all times when dealing with blood or body fluids
- Face shield for resuscitation – this may be used to prevent contamination by the casualty's vomit, blood or other body fluids.

Bleeding

A person may suffer from external bleeding, which is usually obvious to the first-aider as blood flows out from the site of injury. Internal bleeding, however, is not so obvious – it is not visible as the blood is flowing out of the injury site into the body. The first-aider should ensure they are adequately protected when dealing with a casualty who is bleeding to ensure that they do not expose themselves to any blood-borne viruses such as HIV.

External bleeding should be treated in the following manner:

- Lay casualty down
- Apply direct pressure with a gloved hand or finger to the site of bleeding and, as soon as possible, place a clean dressing over the wound
- Elevate and rest the injured part when possible
- Seek medical assistance.

Internal bleeding is difficult to diagnose, but some of the potential signs and symptoms are:

- Coughing up red frothy blood
- Vomiting blood
- Faintness or dizziness
- Weak, rapid pulse
- Cold, clammy skin
- Rapid, gasping breathing.

The treatment for a person you suspect has internal bleeding is as follows:

- Lay the casualty down
- Raise the legs or bend the knees
- Loosen tight clothing
- Urgently seek medical assistance
- Give nothing by mouth
- Reassure the casualty.

Shock

When a person is suffering from shock, there is not enough blood going to the major organs of the body. Shock can be caused by a number of things, including burns, electric shock, allergic shock or severe injuries. A person suffering from shock will usually have cool, moist skin, a weak, rapid pulse and shallow breathing. Other symptoms may include nausea, vomiting or trembling. The treatment for a conscious casualty suffering from shock is to reassure them, then try to find and treat the cause of shock, such as control any bleeding. Keep the casualty lying down and check for neck, spine, head or abdomen injuries. If none of these injuries is apparent then the casualty's feet should be raised so that they are higher than their head.

Unconscious Adult Casualty

If you see a person lying on the ground, talk to them first to see if they respond – they may just be asleep! If they do not respond, speak to them with a louder voice, asking them if they are all right. If you still receive no response, gently shake them. If the person is not injured but is unconscious, they should be placed in the recovery position (see Figure 18.13). This position helps a semi-conscious or unconscious person breathe and allows fluids to drain from the nose and throat so that they do not choke. The casualty should not be moved into the recovery position if you suspect that they have a major injury, such as a back or neck injury.

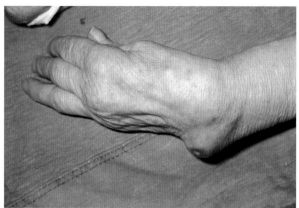

Fig 18.14 A fracture

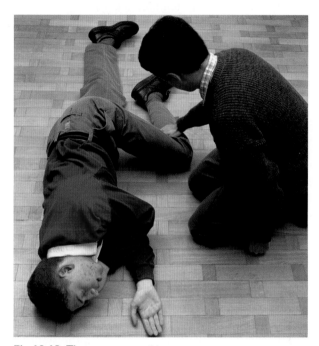

Fig 18.13 The recovery position

Fractures

There are five different types of fracture. All the closed fractures can be treated in a similar manner, but an open fracture needs special attention. A person can be diagnosed as having a fracture if the injured area looks deformed or is tender, if there is swelling in the area, if the casualty cannot move the injured part, or if there is a protruding bone, bleeding or discoloured skin at the injury site. A sharp pain when the individual attempts to move the injured body part is also a sign of a fracture. The casualty should be told firmly not to move the injured part, since such movement could cause further damage to surrounding tissues and make the casualty go into shock.

A fracture should be immobilised in order to prevent the sharp edges of the bone from moving and cutting tissue, muscle, blood vessels and nerves. The injured body part can be immobilised using splints or slings. If a casualty has an open fracture, the first-aider should never attempt to push the bones back under the skin. A dressing should be applied to the injury site to protect the area and pressure should be applied in order to try to limit the external bleeding. A splint can be applied, but should not be placed over the protruding bone.

SALTAPS

The sooner an injury is treated, the greater the chances of a complete recovery and the faster the rehabilitation. The immediate treatment can be summarised by the acronym SALTAPS:

- **S**ee the injury occur and the mechanism of injury
- **A**sk the casualty what is wrong and where they have pain
- **L**ook for signs of bleeding, deformity of limbs, inflammation, swelling and redness
- **T**ouch the injury or close to the injury for signs of heat, tenderness, loss or change of sensation and pain
- **A**ctive movement – ask the casualty to move the injured area; if they are able to, ask them to move it through its full range of movements
- **P**assive movement – try to move the injured site only if a good range of movement is available
- **S**trength – if the casualty has been taken through the steps above with no pain, use resisted movements to assess loss of function; for example, with an injured ankle you would assist the casualty to their feet, then ask them to stand unaided, then progress the test to walking and running.

This process will determine the extent and severity of the injury, although it may be obvious. Treatment at this stage should consist of protect, rest, ice, compression, elevation and diagnosis by a professional (PRICED), which is described below.

In minor injuries, all stages of SALTAPS can usually be completed. But if a person sustains a serious sports injury, such as a fracture or dislocation, the assessment should not be completed because further injury may occur.

301

PRICED

If a person has suffered from a soft tissue injury such as a strain or a sprain, ensuring that they follow the **PRICED** regime will help to limit the severity of their injury:

- **P**rotect the injured body part from further injury
- **R**est – as soon as a person has injured themselves they should be told to discontinue their activity; further activity could cause further injury, delay healing, increase pain and stimulate bleeding
- **I**ce – an ice pack or cold compress should be applied to the injured area; this will help to reduce the swelling and pain of the injury
- **C**ompression – gentle pressure should be applied to the injury site by surrounding the area with padding, a compressive bandage or a cloth; compressing the injured area will reduce blood flowing to the injury site and also help to control swelling by decreasing fluid seeping into the injured area from adjacent tissue; after applying a compression bandage, the casualty's circulation should be checked by squeezing the nail beds of the injured limb; if blood is seen to return to the nail bed on release, the compression bandage is not too tight; the compression bandage should be reapplied after 24 hours in order to maintain compression over the injury site
- **E**levation – the injured area should be supported in a raised position above the level of the heart in order to reduce the blood flow to the injury, which will further help to minimise swelling and bruising at the injury site
- **D**iagnosis by a professional – the injured person should be examined as soon as possible by a professional, such as a sports therapist or a physiotherapist, so that the injury can be accurately diagnosed.

Cold Application

Cooling an injured body part to minimise the swelling and bruising of an injured area and to reduce pain is essential. When a person sustains a soft tissue injury, blood vessels are torn and blood cells and fluid escape into the spaces among the muscle fibres. By cooling the injury site, the local blood vessels are constricted, so blood flow to the area is reduced. The application of something that is cold to the injured area not only has the effect of decreasing the flow of this fluid into the tissues but also helps to slow the release of chemicals that cause pain and inflammation. Cold also decreases the feeling of pain by reducing the ability of the nerve endings to conduct impulses.

Because cold reduces bleeding and swelling within injured tissue, it is best used immediately after injury

has occurred, and for up to 48 to 72 hours after an injury.

Ice bags (plastic bags with ice cubes in, a bag of frozen vegetables or chemical cold packs) can be used. Never apply ice directly on to the skin. The injured area should be covered with a cloth towel in order to prevent direct contact of the ice with the skin, which could cause a blister or 'ice burn'. The cold application should be applied to the injured area for no more than ten minutes. During this time, the person's skin will pass through four stages of sensation:

1 Cold.
2 Burning.
3 Aching.
4 Numbness – as soon as the skin feels numb the cold therapy should be stopped.

The cooling procedure should be repeated every two waking hours. There are a number of methods of cold treatments (cryotherapy) on the market, including ice and gel packs, ice bath immersion and cans of spray.

Heat Treatments

The application of heat to an injury site will act to dilate the local blood vessels, thus increasing the blood flow to the area. This type of treatment should only be given in the sub-acute stage in order to aid in the healing process. The increased blood supply will have the effect of absorbing the swelling and removing the dead cells from the injury site. It will also help to increase the growth of new blood vessels in the area and help scar tissue to form. The application of heat to muscles allows them to relax and aids in pain relief. Heat treatment would not be suitable during the early stages of injury, on an open wound or where tissues are very sensitive, such as the genital region.

Contrast Bathing

Contrast bathing is the process by which alternating treatments of both hot and cold therapy are applied to the injury site and should be used during the sub-acute phase. The application of a hot treatment will increase the blood flow to the area and, when this is followed by a cold treatment, the blood flow to the area will decrease and take with it the debris from the injury site. The injured site should be immersed in alternating hot and cold water for periods ranging from one to four minutes, with increased time initially in the cold water.

Support Mechanisms

In order to help protect and support some injuries,

it is possible to use a variety of products that are readily available at chemists, sports retailers and via the internet, including tubigrip, tape and neoprene support.

Bandaging and taping can be carried out in order to prevent injury, or to treat or rehabilitate an injured joint. Both are performed in order to increase the stability of a joint when there has been an injury to the ligaments that normally support it. They limit unwanted joint movement, support the injury site during strengthening exercises and protect the injury site from further damage.

Taping involves the use of adhesive tape (e.g. zinc oxide tape), whereas bandaging uses strips of cotton and/or specialised pressure bandages. Their purpose is to restrict the joint movement to within safe limits. Taping should not be carried out if the joint is swollen or painful, or if there are any lesions around the taping area. The person who applies the taping/bandaging should be careful to ensure that they do not bind the injury site too tightly so that circulation is affected.

It should also be noted that some individuals have an allergic reaction to some types of tape, such as zinc oxide. Ideally, they should be asked about this possibility before application of the tape. If there is any uncertainty, an underwrap can be applied to provide a protective barrier between the skin and the tape. Unfortunately, this can impair the tape's performance as tape also provides a proprioceptive response mechanism by having its contact directly with the skin. It reminds the individual that it is there to protect and maintain a joint within a range of movement.

The use of tape may well provide support and comfort for a sports person, but the benefits of use over approximately 20 minutes are diminished due to the material properties. This said, it is often used for time periods well beyond the 20-minute mark and its proprioceptive response declines after this amount of time. The psychological value of tape is valuable for a lot of players at all levels of competition, to the extent that it may even be applied to an injury that has fully recovered because the player still feels 'comforted' by the application of the tape!

Bandaging can be used to create pressure around the injury site in order to restrict swelling.

Key learning points 3

- Soft tissue injury – injury to muscles, tendons, ligaments and skin.
- Hard tissue injury – injury to the skeleton, i.e. bones, joints and cartilage.
- First aid – the immediate treatment given to an injured person, preferably by a qualified first-aider.
- SALTAPS – See, Ask, Look, Touch, Active movement, Passive movement, Strength.
- PRICED – Protect, Rest, Ice, Compression, Elevation, Diagnosis.

Q Quick quiz 3

Decide whether each of these statements is true or false.

1 Cartilage has the ability to heal itself quickly.
2 Haemarthrosis is defined as bleeding into a joint.
3 A second-degree strain is when a few muscle fibres are torn.
4 A sprain is an injury suffered by a ligament.
5 Oedema is a description of increased swelling in tissue.
6 Heat treatment is used to restrict the flow of blood to an injury site.

Student activity 18.3  40 minutes P5

Complete the following table to show your knowledge of first aid and other treatments for four different types of sports injury.

Type of sports injury	First-aid treatment	Other common treatments
Sports injury 1		
Sports injury 2		
Sports injury 3		
Sports injury 4		

You might choose from the following injuries: fractures, ligament injuries, muscle injuries, tendonitis, haematoma, burns.

18.5 Planning and Constructing Treatment and Rehabilitation Programmes

Rehabilitation is the restoration of the ability to function in a normal or near-normal manner following an injury. It usually involves reducing pain and swelling, restoring range of motion and increasing strength with the use of manual therapy (massage and manipulation), therapeutic methods such as ultrasound and an exercise programme.

If a sports person does not rehabilitate their injury effectively, they are much more likely to sustain another injury to the same area.

It should be taken into consideration that, as well as the physical rehabilitation of the player, the psychological rehabilitation may also need to be considered. The trauma of the injury itself and the resulting exclusion from training/coaching sessions, competitions, matches and after-competition social events can be very difficult for some individuals to come to terms with. In some cases, this alone can force injured players to try to start playing again much too soon.

Physical Rehabilitation Process

For rehabilitation to occur, an accurate and immediate diagnosis is needed to help establish effective treatment and rehabilitation management of an injury. Therefore, it is essential that an appropriately qualified person diagnoses the injury as early as possible. This may include a sports therapist, a physiotherapist, a doctor or some other suitably qualified person.

The diagnosis relies on accurate information given by either the injured person or someone who saw the injury happen. The smallest of details can make a difference to how accurate a diagnosis can be. So all information, including information regarding the environment, previous injury history, as well as the actual injury event is very important to communicate.

Post-Injury Treatment and Rehabilitation

There are numerous ways in which to classify injury and its management. The following is a commonly accepted role model. This is called the 'stepladder approach' to rehabilitation.

Phase 1

The aim of treatment at this stage is to:

- Prevent as much of the initial swelling as is possible (e.g. if you are dealing with a sprained ankle injury, do not remove footwear at this stage – it will help with compression)
- Protect the injured part from any further damage (e.g. remove from field of play)
- Control any bleeding (apply cover and add pressure)
- Help to relieve the pain (help support or position the injured part in a comfortable position – non-weight-bearing).

So the use of cold compression, elevation and rest are vital.

Phase 2

The aim of treatment at this stage is to:

- Control any bleeding and swelling (maintain sterile cover and cold compress, elevate)
- Relieve pain (cold compress and elevation)
- Protect from further damage (advise to refrain from using as much as possible)
- Give advice for home treatment (do not wear compression bandages throughout the night, correct use of ice, PRICED, etc.).

Phase 3

During this stage, the injury should be in the early stages of recovery:

- Absorption of swelling
- Removal of debris/dead cells from the area
- Growth of new blood vessels
- Development of scar tissue.

The use of treatments such as contrast bathing, elevation and massage, and passive exercises, such as non-weight-bearing exercises, will help to disperse the products of inflammation. The joint should be moved through its pain-free range in order to increase the range of movement, help to strengthen and lengthen the muscles around the injury, and also to help the scar tissue to form in alignment. Throughout these exercises, the person should feel no pain.

Contrast bathing as well as the use of heat packs may also aid the healing process. It may be necessary to use walking aids to protect from further injury or bandages for added support. The use of strengthening exercises specific to the injured area will help the tone of muscle and encourage stability around a joint. Attention to scar tissue development is essential during this stage.

Phase 4

Before starting active rehabilitation, it is important to make sure that the following applies to the injured part:

- There is no significant inflammation
- There is no significant swelling
- While there may be some joint stiffness, there is some range of movement free from pain
- There is the ability to undertake some weight-bearing.

Initially the range of movement needs to be improved as there may have been some weakening of muscles through injury. For every week of immobilisation, a person may lose up to 20 per cent of their muscle strength. Therefore, it is important to start to encourage movement first through non-weight-bearing exercises and then to progress to weight-bearing activities.

The use of supports may still be necessary in the early part of this stage. Prolonged immobilisation will lead to stiffness of the joints in the injured area and a decrease in ligament strength. However, if the injured area is mobilised early on in the rehabilitation process, regrowth of the damaged tissues is encouraged and sports ability and skills are maintained.

A selection of exercises used for the injured part should be encouraged on a regular basis as well as continuing to exercise the rest of the body without undue pressure on the injury. Care should be taken to avoid over-exercising, which may result in more damage and therefore a delay in rehabilitation.

The two main types of exercises that should be used throughout this stage are:

- Mobilisation activities to improve the range of movement and reduce joint stiffness
- Strengthening activities that will help stability of joints and strengthen the weakened muscles.

Phase 5

The aim of treatment at this stage is to:

- Improve balance and movement coordination
- Restore specific skills and movement patterns to pre-injury level
- Provide psychological reassurance of function.

Progression to a functional phase is dependent on the ability to repeatedly perform a task at the level below.

Here are some examples of exercises in the stepladder approach.

Phase 1: play/exercise should cease as soon as injury occurs. 'Playing on through the pain' is not the best advice. Immediate treatment should be given as specified earlier.

Phase 2: very little exercise should be performed during this stage as the aim of the treatment is to control the bleeding and swelling, and protect the injured body part from further damage. PRICED is recommended at this stage for up to 72 hours.

Phase 3: contrast bathing and massage are used during this phase along with stretching. Stretching the injured body part is very important in order to help ensure that the new tissue is laid down in the correct orientation. If there are any signs that the injured body part is not ready to commence this stage, such as heat or swelling around the injury, then stretching should not be started. When stretching, the person should have their injured body part made as warm as possible. This can be done through the use of a thermal heat pack or soaking in a hot bath. Stretches should be held (static stretches) to the onset of discomfort for 15 to 20 seconds. However, a person should never stretch to the extent that they are in pain. Stretching should be performed for short periods of time and frequently throughout the day.

Phase 4: the strengthening exercises that can be used start with isometric exercises. This is where the muscle contracts but no joint movement occurs. Once these have been carried out and no pain has been felt, concentric muscle contractions can be introduced. This is where the muscle shortens – for example, the biceps shortening in a biceps curl.

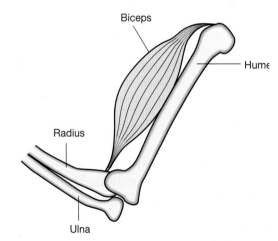

Fig 18.15 Concentric muscle contraction in a biceps curl

Once this type of muscle contraction can be carried out with no pain, eccentric muscle contractions can be performed. This involves the muscle lengthening under tension. An example of this is the quadriceps muscle lengthening as the knee flexes into the sitting position.

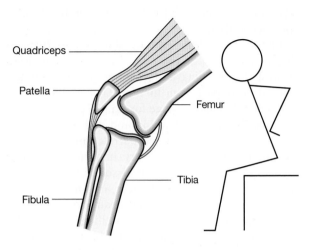

Fig 18.16 The quadriceps muscle demonstrates an eccentric muscle contraction when getting into a sitting position

If the person has injured their leg(s), initially all the strength-training exercises should be carried out in a non-weight-bearing position, so the injured body part should not take the weight of the body. Instead, the person should be sitting down, lying down or standing on their good leg. The next stage is partial weight-bearing, where the arms are used to help support the body weight. Lastly, the exercises can be carried out with the full body weight on the injured body part.

Phase 5: initially this stage should involve the very basic elements of the sports person's usual sport. For example, a footballer would start with running on the spot or in a straight line. Then they would progress to running up and down hills, then on a diagonal and changing direction. This would then progress to skill training. Once they are able to complete these exercises with no problems, they can commence full training and eventually be ready for competitive play.

Psychological Rehabilitation

Alongside the injured player's physical rehabilitation programme, there should run a psychological rehabilitation programme to deal with the feelings and emotions of the individual during the altering stages and phases of recovery to full fitness.

Frequently athletes react to injuries with a wide range of emotions, including denial, anger and even depression. An injury often seems unfair to anyone who has been physically active and otherwise healthy. Although these feelings are real, it is important to move beyond the negative and find more positive strategies to cope with this setback. In many cases, dealing positively with an injury will make for a more focused, flexible and resilient athlete/player.

The following are some suggestions that can help form a psychological coping strategy alongside the physical rehabilitation of an injury.

Learn about the Injury

The individual should learn as much as possible about the cause, treatment and prevention of their injury. Not fully understanding an injury can cause fear or anxiety. The professional treating the individual should be aware of this, but if the nature of the injury is not explained, there will be some uncertainty about the recovery as far as the injured player is concerned. Identification of the facts is a good starting point in the psychological rehabilitation process.

At the start of the physical rehabilitation process, diagnosis is key. If the individual knows *and* understands the answers to some of the following questions, a lot of uncertainty can be removed before the related feelings have time to develop.

- What is the diagnosis (what type of injury is it)?
- How long will recovery take?
- What type of treatment is available?
- What is the purpose of the treatment?
- What should be expected during rehabilitation?
- Can alternative exercise help?
- What are the warning signs that rehabilitation is not progressing?

By understanding the injury and knowing what to expect during the rehabilitation process, an individual will feel less anxious and may also feel that they have a greater sense of control over their recovery.

Responsibility for the Injury

This does not mean that the individual should blame themselves or anyone else for the injury that they have sustained. What it means is that they accept that they *have* an injury and that they can be in control of their own recovery. By taking on responsibility for the recovery process, individuals tend to find a greater sense of control and some go through the process quickly, rather than dwelling on the past or blaming the injury on an outside factor.

Monitor Attitude

Just as the person dealing with the physical rehabilitation will keep records on the progress of the individual, it is also important that the psychological aspects are considered and recorded. If an individual has accepted their injury and is positive at the start of rehabilitation, it does not mean that they will stay like this, feeling exactly the same over a period of time. Particularly if the recovery does not go as planned, it can be very easy for an individual to become disillusioned.

Using Support

A common response after an injury is to feel isolated and to withdraw from being around teammates, coaches and friends. It is important to maintain contact with others during recovery from an injury. Teammates, friends and coaches need to be good at listening when there is emotion to vent, or able to offer advice or encouragement. Simply realising that other people care and are willing to help so that the injury does not have to be faced alone can also be a tremendous comfort to an injured person. So, it might be that the injured player is encouraged to go along to training, to matches, remain around the gym and the weight room, or be visible and included by being an active member of the group – for example, scoring or compiling data, such as the number of tackles, etc.

Set Goals

When not injured, most sports people set themselves targets and goals to achieve, perhaps in training, or in a match, or by the end of a season. Injury does not mean that this should stop. Planning or setting goals can be a very positive focus. Rather than viewing the injury as a crisis, it can be seen as another training challenge. The goal is now focused on recovery rather than performance. This will help keep the individual motivated. By monitoring these goals, it becomes easier to notice small improvements in the rehabilitation of the injury. This in turn encourages confidence in the recovery process. It is important that realistic goals and targets are set so this should always be done in conjunction with the person in charge of the physical rehabilitation process. Most athletes have a tendency to try to speed up their recovery by doing too much too soon. It is important that the injury is accepted and that the individual takes professional advice and knows their own limits.

Training to Stay Fit

Depending upon the type of injury incurred, it may be possible to continue training to some extent and maintain cardiovascular conditioning or strength. This is vitally important to how quickly someone can go back to playing after the injury. If their overall fitness has dropped during the rehabilitation phase while the injury has been dealt with, the individual is not at an appropriate level of fitness to return to playing. A good alternative training programme should be devised between the coach/trainer, the therapist and the injured player to ensure appropriateness throughout.

With the right knowledge, support and patience, an injury can be overcome without it being a totally negative experience. By taking things slowly, setting realistic goals and maintaining a positive, focused approach, most athletes can overcome minor injuries quickly and major injuries in time.

Recording data

With any accident or incident resulting in a person being injured, it is important to keep accurate and up-to-date records to help prevent, where possible, the injury happening again.

This information will normally be maintained by a coach, a teacher or a sports centre, or wherever the injury took place. This information is necessary to protect individuals from being sued for malpractice but also helps to highlight issues which may prevent other similar injuries.

It may help to make sports environments safer, and more importantly, for the coach/trainer, it can help to log the process of injury–treatment–rehabilitation. This can become an accurate record to be used as a template for similar injuries on other players or to identify the recurrence in the same player, which may lead to taking into account why the injury is happening regularly. This could be down to inappropriate training regimes, inappropriate fitness levels and/or insufficient time to rehabilitate through the differing phases.

Key learning points 4

- Rehabilitation is the restoration of normal function following an injury.
- The stepladder approach to rehabilitation passes through five phases.
- It is important to offer support to address the psychological aspects of an injury.

Student activity 18.4   ⏱ **90 minutes**   P6   M3   D2

Use the following template to decide upon a treatment and rehabilitation programme for Carly, the long jumper from Student Activity 18.2, and another individual of your choice.

Name:
Description of injury:
Aims of rehabilitation:

	Range of motion methods	Strengthening methods	Coordination methods
Stage 1			
Stage 2			
Stage 3			

To achieve M3, this programme needs to be designed independently. To achieve D2, you need to evaluate your training programme, justify why you have chosen each method of treatment and suggest alternatives where it is appropriate.

Further reading

Cash, M. (1996) *Sport and Remedial Massage Therapy*, London: Ebury Press.

Crossman, J. (2001) *Coping with Sports Injuries: Psychological Strategies for Rehabilitation*, Oxford: OUP.

Peterson, L. and Renstrom, P. (2001) *Sports Injuries: Their Prevention & Treatment*, 3rd edn, London: Taylor and Francis.

Sports Coach UK (1999) *Sports Injury: Prevention and First Aid Management*, Leeds: Coachwise Solutions.

Useful websites

www.eorthopod.com
Provides patient guides, video & news on latest scientific literature for sports injuries and traumas

www.brianmac.co.uk/massage.htm
Provides information about the three main sports massage techniques and when to use these

19: Analysis of Sports Performance

19.1 Introduction

Every sportsperson is aiming to improve their performance in terms of their technical ability, physiological fitness, psychological strength and biomechanical efficiency. We tend to become even more reflective and ask more questions when things are not going well and we are losing competitions. In order to analyse our performances we need a structure or framework in which to work. This unit provides a structure for athletes to interpret their performances and their successes and failures.

By the end of this unit you should:

- know the performance profile of a sporting activity
- be able to analyse sporting performance
- be able to provide feedback to athletes regarding performance
- understand the purpose and resources required for analysing different levels of sporting performance.

Assessment and grading criteria

To achieve a PASS grade the evidence must show that the learner is able to:	To achieve a MERIT grade the evidence must show that, in addition to the pass criteria, the learner is able to:	To achieve a DISTINCTION grade the evidence must show that, in addition to the pass and merit criteria, the learner is able to:
P1 describe the performance profile of a selected sporting activity	**M1** explain the performance profile of a selected sporting activity	**D1** analyse the performance profile of a selected sporting activity
P2 describe five factors that may influence the performance of an athlete		
P3 perform an assessment of a selected athlete undertaking sporting activity using three components of their performance profile, with tutor support	**M2** explain the function of the cardiovascular system	**D2** analyse the performance of a selected athlete using three components of their performance profile.
P4 provide feedback to the athlete based on the assessment of their performance, with tutor support	**M3** independently perform an assessment of a selected athlete undertaking sporting activity using three components of their performance profile.	
P5 explain the purpose of, and the resources required for, analysis at two different levels of sports performance.		

19.2 The Performance Profile of a Sporting Activity

P1 **P2** **P3** **M1** **M2**

The performance profile is a visual method of looking at performance in a broad manner. It is used by the athlete and coach to pinpoint strengths and weaknesses and this information is then used to design future actions. When a coach works with an athlete the coach can make decisions on techniques and changes, with the methods being imposed on the athlete by the coach. In this method the success or failure of the training programme is viewed by the athlete as being dependent upon the effectiveness of the coach in meeting their needs.

However, the coach only has the 'outsider' view. Butler and Hardy (1992) identified that this was a major weakness as it affected an individual's intrinsic motivation. Bull (1991) agreed that an athlete's commitment to their training schedule and the accompanying educational work would be affected if the coach who had imposed the schedules was not always present. It would seem to be a more productive relationship if the expertise of two people was utilised. The coach is the expert in terms of 'the outsider' view of the athlete's performance, while the athlete is the expert in terms of 'the insider' view of their experiences and how they are feeling.

Butler (2000) described the athlete's role as follows:

'The athlete's assertions, discriminations and insights are not only valid but valuable. They make a significant contribution to the development of an effective training programme.'

The performance profile gives the coach and athlete a tool to provide a visual display of the areas of performance that are perceived to be important in working towards a top performance, and their assessment of the current position in relation to this.

Using a Performance Profile

First, you need to choose the sporting activity you want to examine and then you can look at any of the following:

- technical and tactical (shooting, passing, tackling)
- physiological fitness (strength, power, flexibility)
- psychological (motivation, arousal, confidence)
- biomechanical (speed, motion, momentum).

To construct a performance profile you would do the following:

- The athlete is asked to think about the qualities or skills that are shown by those athletes who perform at the top level of their sport in the same position, role or event as themselves.
- These qualities or skills are called the 'constructs', and they are placed on the performance profile.
- The athlete then describes their current position in terms of their competency by giving themselves a mark out of 10. This score of 10 is in comparison to an athlete they consider to be excellent in their chosen sport.
- The coach may do the same exercise to provide the 'outsider viewpoint'.

These scores can be filled in on the performance profile and used to:

- identify their current level of competence
- identify areas of strength and weakness
- monitor progress and any changes occurring
- monitor effectiveness of training programmes
- identify any differences in the viewpoints of athlete and coach
- provide a basis for designing a training programme.

Technical Analysis of a Sporting Activity

You can analyse a sporting activity in terms of the whole activity, an individual position or an individual aspect of the game.

Whole Activity

Snooker, for example, can be broken down into the following constructs:

- stance
- snookering
- cueing action
- back spin
- bridging
- top spin
- striking
- side spin
- long potting
- deep screw
- short potting
- follow through
- cushion shots.

311

Positional Activity

A midfielder in football would perform the following techniques:

- short passing
- blocking
- long passing
- long-range shooting
- crossing
- close-range shooting
- dead ball work
- defensive heading
- throwing in
- attacking heading
- tackling.

Individual Aspect of an Activity

A tennis player would perform the following backhand shots:

- smash
- lob
- volley
- flat drive
- half volley
- topspin drive
- drop volley
- slice.

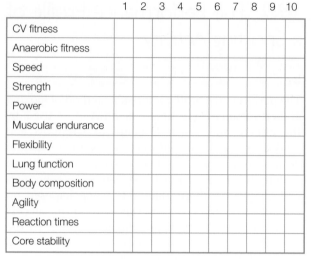

Fig 19.2 Physiological constructs for a tennis player

	1	2	3	4	5	6	7	8	9	10
CV fitness										
Anaerobic fitness										
Speed										
Strength										
Power										
Muscular endurance										
Flexibility										
Lung function										
Body composition										
Agility										
Reaction times										
Core stability										

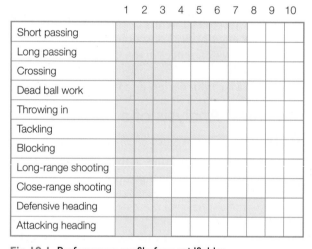

Fig 19.1 Performance profile for a midfielder

	1	2	3	4	5	6	7	8	9	10
Short passing										
Long passing										
Crossing										
Dead ball work										
Throwing in										
Tackling										
Blocking										
Long-range shooting										
Close-range shooting										
Defensive heading										
Attacking heading										

Physiological Analysis of a Sporting Activity

This is completed in the same manner as the technical analysis except the constructs will be different (see Figure 19.2).

Psychological Constructs

This is also completed in the same manner as the technical analysis, except the constructs will be different (see Figure 19.3).

Fig 19.3 Psychological constructs for a boxer

	1	2	3	4	5	6	7	8	9	10
Intrinsic motivation										
Extrinsic motivation										
Arousal control										
Anxiety levels										
Attentional focus										
Confidence										
Controlling agression										
State management										
Concentration skills										
Relaxation skills										
Emotional well-being										
Mental rehearsal										
Imagery skills										

Biomechanical Constructs

A fourth analysis can be completed of the biomechanical demands of a sporting activity (see Figure 19.4).

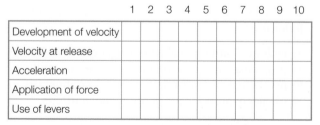

Fig 19.4 Biomechanical constructs for a javelin thrower

	1	2	3	4	5	6	7	8	9	10
Development of velocity										
Velocity at release										
Acceleration										
Application of force										
Use of levers										

Benefits of Performance Profiling

As a technique for analysing performance, profiling works very well because it can take into account a vast amount of information for analysis by coach and athlete. It also considers the roles of coach and athlete as equally important with their different viewpoints on performance. Crucially, it takes into account the opinion of the athlete and gives them an active role in the analysis process, allowing them to take ownership of their performance and outcomes. It also allows the coach and athlete to identify any areas of mismatch where there is a differing opinion, and provides a basis for discussion. It can act as a process of education for the athlete as they become self-aware of the varying demands on them as well as their relative importance.

Performance profiles can form the basis of a review of progress on a monthly basis as the athlete and coach track their progress. They can also inform the process of goal setting to set the way forward.

Key learning points I

- Performance profiling is a way of looking at performance in a broad sense.
  - It involves the opinion of the athlete as well as that of the coach.
  - It can be used to identify strengths and weaknesses.
- Performance profiling can be applied to technical, physiological, psychological and biomechanical components of performance.

The effectiveness of an individual's sporting performance comes down to a range of factors, which can be split into two categories:

- intrinsic – factors within the body
- extrinsic – factors outside the body.

Intrinsic factors would include:

- age
- health
- diet
- previous training
- motivation
- confidence
- ability level.

Extrinsic factors would include:

- group dynamics
- group cohesion
- temperature
- time of the day.

Intrinsic Factors

Age

It is generally accepted that performance declines after the age of 35. Up to the age of 35 the body is building up in terms of bone and muscle strength and cardiovascular fitness. After the age of 35 these structures of the body slowly start to lose their efficiency with a resulting performance decrement, although, having said that, training will slow down this decline and maintain strength, flexibility and cardiovascular fitness. We have seen many sports-people remain at the top level despite being over the age of 35. Martina Navratilova was winning tennis titles into her fifties. Ryan Giggs, Simon Shaw (Rugby Union), Ricky Ponting (cricket), Lee Westwood (golf) are all still able to perform at the top level in their sports despite their age.

Health

The health of an individual's organs and systems are all vital in gaining their adaptations from training and then producing top-level performances. The body functions as a whole organism made up of many systems and organs, and poor function in one area will affect the functioning of the whole organism.

Diet

There is a clear link between nutrition and health. When we eat we are ultimately feeding the cells of the body with nutrients to allow them to function and give them the basic building blocks to remain healthy. If we feed our cells with fresh, nutritious foods we will have healthy cells, contributing to our health. But if we feed our cells with poor-quality nutrients from processed or fast foods we will end up with unhealthy and ultimately diseased cells, contributing to illness.

Previous Training

Our current position is the result of all the activity we have or have not done in our lives. The performance the athlete is able to produce depends upon the quality of their training programme and the fine balance between training and rest periods.

Motivation

Motivation is the amount of drive and energy that we possess at any point in time. It influences our desire to win. If we have trained hard and looked after our nutrition and rest patterns, we will feel better and subsequently more motivated.

Confidence

Our confidence is the extent to which we feel we will be successful; it is affected by a range of factors.

313

These will include our previous experiences and our perception of these experiences as either successful or otherwise. In addition, there is our perception of our opponents and our ability to deal with the environment in which we are placed. For example, we may feel more confident when we compete on our home territory and slightly intimidated when we go away. Our confidence level is closely related to our anxiety levels and if we are anxious about our performance this will start to erode our confidence levels.

Ability Level

Our ability is the natural level of skills we possess and is the basis for developing further skills. Our performance is clearly the result of the ability and skills we possess.

Extrinsic Factors

Group Dynamics

Group dynamics refers to the sum of the processes occurring within the group that will influence its effectiveness. The most successful groups have a high level of attractiveness for the individual members, and the members will also share the same goals and work towards achieving these objectives.

Group Cohesion

Group cohesion is the extent to which the individual members of the group have an attraction to the group and keep the group together. Cohesion can be task-related or socially related. Task cohesion is the extent to which you are willing to work together in the sporting environment, and social cohesion is how well you get on away from the sporting field. Task cohesion is the most important factor but it can be boosted by social cohesion.

Temperature

Extremes of temperature can have a negative effect on performance due to the effect on the physiological systems of the body. Heat can cause excess sweating, dehydration and heat exhaustion, while cold can make it difficult for the cardiovascular and muscular systems to achieve the correct temperature for optimal functioning.

Time of Day

The time of day can influence performance in terms of nutritional and fatigue status. In the morning before a person has eaten they will be in a dehydrated state with low blood sugar and in a far from optimal state to perform effectively. Depending upon when they eat and drink they will fluctuate in terms of their nutritional status through the day. Other physical factors can change through the day. Mobility and flexibility will be lowest in the morning due to the inactivity of the joints and the lack of synovial fluid that has been excreted into the joint.

Q Quick quiz 1

Decide whether each of the following constructs for a netball player should be categorised as technical (T), physiological (Ph) or psychological (Ps)

- confidence
- passing
- speed
- aerobic fitness
- blocking
- arousal control
- aggression control
- movement
- power
- shooting.

Student activity 19.1 P1 P2 M1 D1

Example of a performance profile

CASE STUDY: WILLIAM

William is a 16-year-old rugby player who plays number 8 for his college U17 team. He is a very promising player, but has only been playing for about 18 months and is still learning about the game. To help him to improve his performances he has agreed to have a performance profile constructed. The results of the performance profile are shown below:

	1	2	3	4	5	6	7	8	9	10
Tackling							7			
Strength				4						
Power			3							
Rucking			3							
Aggression control		2								
Concentration			3							
Passing								8		
Aerobic endurance							7			
Arousal control		2								
Scrummaging					5					

Part 1

1 Describe the performance profile for William.

 P1

2 Explain the performance profile for William.

 M1

3 Analyse the performance profile for William.

 D1

Part 2

Describe how the following factors may influence performance:

P2

Factor	How it may affect performance
Diet	
Motivation	
Confidence	
Group dynamics	
Temperature	

19.3 Analysing Sporting Performance

Performance Profile Assessment

The performance profile relies on the respective viewpoints of the athlete and coach. It is also useful to gather information to be used in rating the score for each construct. The opinions of the athlete and coach would be qualitative data, while the information gathered from testing would be quantitative data.

The four aspects of the performance profile could be analysed using the following quantitative data

Technical constructs:

- notational analysis
- tally charts.

Physical constructs:

- multi-stage fitness test
- 40-m sprint

- 1 rep max
- 15 rep max
- sit and reach test
- peak flow test
- skinfold calipers
- T-test.

Psychological constructs:

- questionnaires
- interviews
- observation of behaviour.

Biomechanical analysis:

- video recording
- computer packages.

Notational analysis

Notational analysis is the tracking of the actions of an individual performer through the course of a game or match to see the frequency with which they perform a particular technique. It can be done through a computer package or by hand using tally charts.

A tally chart for football is reproduced in Figure 19.5:

Tally chart: football		
Skill	**Successful completion**	**Unsuccessful completion**
Short-range pass (< 5m)		
Medium-range pass (5–15m)		
Long-range pass (> 15m)		
Dribble		
Short-range shot (< 6m)		
Medium-range shot (7–18m)		
Long-range shot (> 18m)		
Tackle		
Block		
Defensive header		
Attacking header		
Throw-in		
Free kick		
Corner		
Penalty kick		

Fig 19.5 A tally chart for football

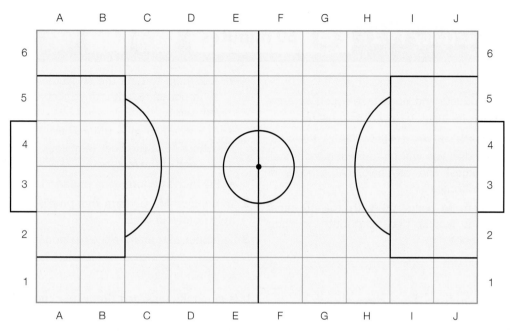

Fig 19.6 Football pitch sectionalised into areas

Passing record		
Skill	**Successful completion**	**Unsuccessful completion**
Short-range pass (< 5m)	G5–F5 D3–D2 I6–J5	F4–F3 C3–C4
Medium-range pass (5–15m)	G2–E4 C6–A6 H1–F3	D5–B4
Long-range pass (> 15m)	I4–E3 C1–B5	F6–D1 I5–D3 F1–C4

Fig 19.7 A passing record for football

This information is of limited value as you also need to look at where this action occurs. This can be done by sectionalising the area of play (see Figure 11.6) and giving each area a label. This will elicit more valuable information.

This can be done with a cricket pitch, tennis or netball court. You can then track where each type of skill occurs and its outcome.

An example of tracking the passing of a footballer is also reproduced in Figure 19.7.

The uses of notational analysis are to:

● identify individual strengths and weaknesses
● analyse all the actions of a player
● build up information to rate score on performance profile
● develop an action plan to improve performance.

317

Student activity 19.2   ⏱ 60 minutes   P3   M2   D2

Task

1 Select an athlete and undertake a performance profiling assessment in the following way:

- Introduce the process of performance profiling.

- Explain that you will be assessing technical, physiological and psychological aspects of their performance.

- Ask them to come up with the 10 most important factors that contribute to their performance.

- Ask them to rank the 10 factors in the order of importance with the most important at number 1.

- Ask them to give themselves a score of 10 (where 10 is the best they could possibly be) for each of the factors.

- Fill in the performance profile.

2 To achieve M2 perform this profile without any help from your tutor.

3 To achieve D2 analyse the performance profile.

19.4 Providing Feedback on Performance

It is impossible for anyone to improve or change unless they receive feedback.

Key term

Feedback: information about performance.

It has no value judgement attached to it as it is not positive or negative. It is simply information. The information is provided and the athlete has the choice of doing something about it or not.

Types of Feedback

There are different categories of feedback regarding its timing and the type of feedback given. They are:

- knowledge of performance and results
- immediate and delayed
- internal and external
- concurrent and terminal.

Knowledge of Performance and Results

Knowledge of performance (KP) is information regarding how well skills were performed in a technical sense and will involve qualitative judgements. Knowledge of results (KR) is information regarding the outcome of the skill – whether the action produced success or failure – this is a quantitative judgement. It is possible to perform a skill well (KP) and have a negative outcome (KR) or have a poor performance (KP) and a positive outcome (KR).

It is generally regarded that experienced performers are more interested in knowledge of performance, while novices are more interested in knowledge of results.

Immediate and Delayed

Immediate means that the feedback is given immediately after the skill has been performed, while delayed means feedback is provided at a time after the event – this could be a day or an hour later. The coach needs to consider the impact that the feedback will have on the athlete's motivation and how important it is for the athlete to receive it. Once they have considered those two questions they can decide when to give the feedback.

Internal and External

Internal feedback is generated within the body of the athlete. As you perform a skill you will feel whether you have performed it correctly or not due to the nervous pathways you have set down to produce the movement and judge its correctness. As we hit a tennis ball we feel whether we have struck it sweetly or not. External feedback is provided by an external party, who observes the performance. For example, the coach will observe the performance of the skill and offer feedback as to how it looked and how effective it was. External feedback may also be provided by using camcorders or other recording devices.

Concurrent and Terminal

Concurrent means literally 'running together'. This type of feedback is provided during the performance of the skill in terms of how it feels and often the outcome as well. Concurrent feedback is usually internal in nature and clearly immediate in when it is provided. Terminal means 'at the end'. This type of feedback is provided at the end of the performance. It is usually external and is always delayed.

Delivering the Feedback

Once the coach has decided on what feedback is necessary to address the individual's strengths and areas for improvement, they will need to decide when, where and how to deliver it. How the feedback is received depends upon how it is delivered.

Structure

When giving feedback you should use the sandwich technique. Feedback should have this structure:

● tell them what they are doing right
● tell them what they need to improve on
● tell them something else they did right.

This means that the feedback ends on a high note and the athlete understands what needs to be improved.

Non-verbal Communication

Feedback can be given visually and through gestures as well as verbally. The use of facial expressions, posture and hand gestures will convey more than the actual words used. The delivery of the message should match the message being given. This is called being 'congruent'. Also, gestures such as a pat on the back or a hand on the arm will convey information that cannot be imparted in words.

Avoiding Negative Approaches

Avoid any negative approaches or comments.

● Intimidation: 'If you don't improve you can find a new coach.'
● Sarcasm: 'My granny could have caught that!'
● Physical abuse: 'Unless you listen to what I say, you will be doing press-ups.'
● Guilt: 'You should be ashamed of yourselves the way you played out there. It was gutless and you let your supporters down.'

Private and Confidential

Ensure feedback is given in a private area as it may be sensitive and is not relevant for anyone else.

Focus on Behaviour

Focus on the behaviour rather than identity. This is the difference between a coach saying 'You are an aggressive person and this is not acceptable' and 'Your aggressive actions are not acceptable.' One addresses the behaviour, which can be changed, and the other addresses the identity of the person, which is long term and relatively stable.

Using the Feedback Provided

Once the feedback has been received and processed by the athlete, they have to decide how to use the information. It may be used in the following ways:

● to set SMART targets combining short-, medium- and long-term goals
● to develop or change a training programme to include technical, physiological and psychological components of performance
● to inform the process of performance profiling and assessment of scoring the individual constructs.

Key learning points 2

● Feedback is information about an individual's performance.
● Feedback can be categorised in two ways: knowledge of performance (KP) and knowledge of results (KR). KP is information about how well the skill was performed and KR is information about the outcome of the skill.
● Immediate feedback is given as soon as the skill has been performed, while delayed feedback is given at a period after the performance.
● Internal feedback is derived from sources inside the body and external feedback comes from sources inside the body.
● Concurrent feedback occurs as the skill is being performed and terminal feedback occurs after the completion of the skill.
● When providing feedback keep in mind the following:
  – using the sandwich approach of positive/negative/positive
  – providing it visually as well as verbally through body language
  – avoiding sarcasm, intimidation, abuse and guilt
  – ensuring it is delivered in a private area
  – focus on behaviour rather than identity.

319

Quick quiz 2

Match the type of feedback to its correct definition.

Type of feedback	Choice of definitions
Knowledge of results	Information given immediately after a skill has been performed
Knowledge of performance	Information generated from sources within the body
Immediate	Information about the outcome of the skill
Delayed	Information generated from sources outside the body
Internal	Information about how well skills are performed
External	Information provided at a period after the skill has been performed

Student activity 19.3 — 30 minutes — P4 M3

Task

Based on the performance profiling exercise that you conducted in Activity 19.2 provide feedback to your selected athlete in the following way:

- Make written notes about the strengths and areas for improvement for your selected athlete

- Conduct a feedback session with your selected athlete.

To achieve M3 this feedback should be provided independent of tutor support.

19.5 The Purpose and Resources Required for Analysing Different Levels of Sporting Performance

Sport England has identified four different levels of sporting performance, as follows.

Foundation Level

At foundation level focus is on the participants learning and understanding basic movement skills and developing a positive attitude to physical activity. This level is concerned with giving school children positive and meaningful experiences of sport.

Beginner or Participation Level

At participation or beginner levels the participants will be taking part in sport for a range of reasons, such as health, fitness and social. They may also be attracted by the competitive aspects of sport. This level of participation would involve out-of-school sports teams and Saturday league players.

Performance Level

At performance level the participants will be active in improving standards of performance through coaching, competition and training. This would involve the participants playing at county or national standard.

Elite or Excellence Level

Elite and excellence levels involve the participants reaching national standards of performance up to Olympic or world-class performances.

Purpose of Analysis and Resources Required

Foundation Level

At this level the emphasis is on fun and enjoyment, and learning the basic skills and techniques. Analysis will be limited to identifying the strengths and weaknesses of the children and giving them feedback to improve their enjoyment of the sports. The resources required are limited to support from teachers and parents.

Beginner Level

At beginner level there is an emphasis on developing techniques and improving weaknesses along with developing strengths. This is a point where talent may be assessed for further development through coaching and physical training. Analysis is again done in a fairly informal manner through recommendations or even talent scouting.

Performance Level

Analysis starts to become very important at this level as it is about achieving standards of performance to reach county or national level. Analysis will be conducted to:

- identify talent
- form the basis for squad selection at county and national level
- assess current level of performance
- identify strengths and weaknesses
- assess fitness level and health status
- inform the process of goal setting.

In terms of resources required there is a need to put in time and effort on behalf of personnel. This is a key stage in moving people towards becoming athletes and to ultimately developing elite potential. Equipment required will include fitness testing equipment, sport science facilities, expertise from sport scientists and time devoted to each individual.

Elite Level

At elite level every aspect of an athlete's performance is analysed to the smallest degree as they seek to gain all the advantages they possibly can to improve their chances of success. At this level, aspects of health, fitness and performance are analysed on a daily basis. Indeed, the athlete may be professional or training on a full-time basis. The purpose of analysis at this level is to:

- assess current health and fitness status
- identify strengths and weaknesses
- assess current level of performance
- inform the process of goal setting
- identify any future issues or problems.

As athletes at this level may have contact with their support team at facilities such as a national sports centre, they are heavily dependent on resources. These resources are human in terms of sport scientists with various expertise, and physical resources for assessing fitness levels and analysing skills and techniques.

Key learning points 3

- At foundation level focus is on the participant's learning and understanding basic movement skills and developing a positive attitude to physical activity. Analysis is provided at this level to help participants improve their skills.
- At participation or beginner levels the participants will be taking part in sport for a range of reasons, such as health, fitness and social and competitive reasons. Analysis is used at beginner level to improve performance and identify talent.
- At performance level the participants will be active in improving standards of performance through coaching, competition and training. Analysis is provided to assess current level of performance and how to improve it, as well as identify talent to move to a higher level.
- Elite and excellence levels involve the participants reaching national standards of performance up to Olympic or world-class performances. Analysis is done at elite level to identify any area where the athlete could improve so they can compete at the very highest level.

Student activity 19.4 ⊖ **30 minutes** P5

Task

Fill out the following table to explain the purpose and resources required for analysis at two different levels of sport.

	Participation level	Elite level
Purpose of analysis		
Resources needed		

References

Bull, S. J. (1991) *Sport Psychology: A Self-help Guide*, Crowood.

Butler, R. J. (2000) *Sport Psychology in Performance*, Arnold.

Butler, R. J. and Hardy, L. (1992) 'The performance profile: theory and application', *The Sport Psychologist*, 6, 253–264.

Further reading

Hughes, M. and Franks, I. (2004) *Notational Analysis of Sport*, Abingdon: Routledge.

Martens, R. (2004) *Successful Coaching*, Champaign, IL: Human Kinetics.

Weinberg, R.S. and Gould, D. (2007) *Foundations of Sport and Exercise Psychology*, Champaign, IL: Human Kinetics.

Useful websites

www.brianmac.co.uk/eval.htm

Provides details of how to evaluate and test sports performance

www.pponline.co.uk/encyc/sports-performance-analysis-coaching-and-training-39

Article detailing how sports analysis can help coaching and training

20: Talent identification & development of sport

20.1 Introduction

Talent identification (TID) is the process of recognising current participants with the potential to excel in a particular sport. Professional sports clubs and organisations invest heavily in talent identification and development. Potential talent may not be obvious at an early age, but there will normally be some indicators that enable trained individuals to identify it. The early indicators of talent cannot necessarily determine whether somebody will reach an elite level, but they will give an indication as to whether the individual could succeed.

The reliable identification of talent allows clubs and national governing bodies (NGBs) to target their resources on the individuals selected for systematic development, ensuring a more effective investment for the future.

Developing talented athletes is not simply about producing the next Olympic or world champion, it is also about developing athletes who can enjoy sports at different levels, and have experiences that make a lasting positive impact on their lives and those around them.

This unit is designed to help you understand the different predictors of talent and the ways of developing talent, and to devise programmes for the identification and development of talent in different sports.

> By the end of this unit you should:
>
> - know the key predictors of talent for performers in sport
> - be able to design a talent identification programme for a chosen sport
> - know key factors in talent development in sport
> - be able to design a talent development programme for a chosen sport.

Assessment and grading criteria		
To achieve a PASS grade the evidence must show that the learner is able to:	To achieve a MERIT grade the evidence must show that, in addition to the pass criteria, the learner is able to:	To achieve a DISTINCTION grade the evidence must show that, in addition to the pass and merit criteria, the learner is able to:
P1 describe the different types of talent		
P2 describe five different predictors of talent for performers in sport		
P3 describe one current talent identification programme in a selected sport	**M1** evaluate one current talent identification programme in a selected sport	
P4 using a standard structure, design a talent identification programme for a selected sport	**M2** explain the chosen activities for a talent identification programme for a selected sport	**D1** justify the choice of activities for a talent identification programme for a selected sport
P5 describe, using examples, five different key factors in talent development in sport		
P6 describe one current talent development programme in a selected sport	**M3** evaluate one current talent development programme in a selected sport	
P7 using a standard structure, design a talent development programme for a selected sport.	**M4** explain the chosen activities for a talent development programme for a selected sport.	**D2** justify the choice of activities for a talent development programme for a selected sport.

20.2 Key Predictors of Talent for Individuals in Sport

Types of Talent

Talent has several properties that are genetic – 'an athlete is born and not made'. However, talent is not always seen at an early age, but trained people may be able to identify someone's potential to succeed by using certain indicators. Who will be the next Chris Hoy, for example?

Within any sport that you watch and support, the players must have a high degree of talent. In unidimensional sports, only one type of talent is required – for example, the ability to run fast in a straight line over a given distance, or to complete a marathon.

Usain Bolt (Olympic Champion, World Champion and world record holder) and Paula Radcliffe (world record holder) are known throughout the world as talented athletes within their chosen events. As athletes, they represent the upper end of elite sporting talent, but in terms of their respective talents they are described as unidimensional. Sprinting from start to finish requires several ingredients, such as speed, balance, coordination, flexibility, strength and power. The marathon primarily requires massive levels of cardiovascular and muscular endurance, although there is only one goal – to be as fast as possible.

Playing half-back in rugby (e.g. Mike Phillips, Wales and the British and Irish Lions), Jonny Wilkinson (England and the British and Irish Lions) combines a variety of physical components and skills for the entire length of the game or session. As a player, a half-back is rarely seen running quickly at pace in a straight line. The role involves having to make multiple decisions, such as catching, passing, calling plays, handling, directional change and tackling. These are multiple outcomes in the broad sense, but there can be opportunities where unidimensional attributes are evident.

Sport is developed through schools, clubs, external organisations and play. There comes a point, however, when individual players choose to specialise. Tiger Woods was targeted at the age of four as a special talent. He may be an exception. In the modern world, Tiger Woods is known as the best golfer on the planet, but not as an all-round sports athlete; he would be classed as a 'uni-sport' talent. In comparison, Kelly Sotherton (Olympic heptathlete) or Jessica Ennis (2009 World Champion heptathlete) would be classed as multi-sport talent. They specialise in a wide range of events, with a high skill requirement to each.

Multi-sport Talent

Being a champion in one sport is an immense challenge, but achieving this in more than one sport is quite remarkable. This has been achieved in recent years by British sports performers Shelley Rudman and Rebecca Romero.

Shelley Rudman, a former athletics track hurdler, won a silver medal at the 2006 Winter Olympics in 'bob skeleton', less than four years after trying the sport for the first time, aged 21.

Rebecca Romero, aged 26, became 2008 track cycling Olympic gold medallist and champion, less than three years after taking up the sport. She was

Fig 20.1 Shelley Rudman

325

a former medal-winning Olympic rower, who transferred to the sport of cycling for new challenges.

1 What type of talent is required to participate in this sport?

2 Try to explain and justify why this type of talent is required.

Student activity 20.1 30–45 mins P1

The following examples of sports performers are all real people, and have all studied a BTEC National in sport or sport and exercise sciences at a college of further education.

1 A national-level swimmer who was ranked in the top ten English swimmers in two different strokes.

2 An individual who won the English Schools 200 m sprint final, and represented England U16s at both football and basketball.

3 A badminton player ranked second in England when playing in the relevant U16 and U18 age groups.

4 A golfer who competed in county, regional and national competitions successfully, with a scratch handicap (i.e. not allowed/given any shots on any course to help them).

Write a report that identifies and describes the different types of talent demonstrated by the individuals listed above, including:

- unidimensional
- multidimensional
- uni-sport talent
- multi-sport talent.

Predictors of Talent

Within the English language, 'talent' signifies some attribute that is either innate or learnt.

Key term

Innate: something that you are born with (e.g. having a natural talent in any striking activity, such as hockey, cricket, golf or tennis).

- T = technique
- A = athleticism
- L = leadership
- E = effective
- N = natural speed
- T = team player
- I = individual
- D = desire.

These are guidelines for sporting scouts who are looking for the next player. The selection process is split into categories of physical, technical, psychological and social ability. These are the four corners of learning (FA learning) on which players are assessed.

- physical – anthropometric measures, which relate to age groups and development

- technical – specific skill requirements at each development age group
- psychological – how do players seem – confident, social? What is their emotional state?
- social – interaction with family, friends and peers.

Physical

The main area to consider in relation to the physical parameters of the player is their individual make-up.

Players differ depending on their age and the development stage they are in. However, if a player is below a predictor height in relation to his chronological age, this suggests only that he is undersized, a little weaker than other players and therefore lacking in some of the physical fitness components such as speed and endurance. It does not mean that there is no talent. In contrast, some players develop and grow early; you might hear coaches talk about a 12-year-old who is physically better than those around him and who can run the length of the field at pace. This, however, leads to concerns about the 'what happens next' scenario. What happens when the underdeveloped yet talented player grows?

Talent identification is designed to help sports teams and coaches identify talented athletes and prepare them for participation in domestic, national and eventually international competition. Many sports programmes utilise information across all

Fig 20.2 A stadiometer is used to measure height

sports science disciplines, to identify young athletes with characteristics associated with elite performance. Athletes are then guided to sports that best suit their attributes and are provided with the opportunity to realise their potential in a high-quality talent development programme. There is, however, an important ingredient that is often overlooked. Talent is often the capture and development of 'accelerated expertise'. An individual may possess a certain quality, whether innate or learnt, but it is the ability to manage and develop this in the right manner that is important.

Growth, maturation and development are key components in any talent assessment criteria. Growth is a dominant biological activity that occurs during the first 20 years of life. It starts at conception and continues late into the teenage years. The term growth relates to the increase in size of the body, either as a whole or as individual body parts. Growth of the body is traditionally measured in a standing position, using various stadiometers. Individual limb lengths are measured using anthropometric techniques. This process allows the accurate measurement of each individual body part length.

Development is an interesting concept, taking in all areas of growth, maturation, learning and experience. Maturation refers to the instance of biological maturation, which can be seen through sexual maturity, skeletal maturity and physical maturity.

Weight relates to the individual body mass measured in kilograms. In simple terms, a person's body weight can be divided into two components: fat mass (FM) and fat-free mass (FFM). These components are the principles behind body composition and assessment. Fat mass includes both the internal and the external fat or adipose tissue, and fat-free mass includes muscle, bone and the vital internal organs.

A child's body make-up or shape can have a major influence on a scout or coach in all ages of the

development spectrum. Somatotyping relates to the make-up of the human body in terms of shape and its composition. There are three general components that relate to somatotyping:

1 Endomorph – this component refers to the degree of fatness on the body, wherever it may be

Fig 20.3a Ectomorph

Fig 20.3b Mesomorph

Fig 20.3c Endomorph

327

found. As a shape, an endomorph stature would be rounded in appearance.

2 Mesomorph – this component relates to the relative musculoskeletal development of the body. In its appearance, the body shape is muscular and toned.

3 Ectomorph – this component describes the slenderness of the body, with an absence of any muscular size and bulk.

Endomorphic body type:

- Soft body
- Underdeveloped muscles
- Round-shaped
- Overdeveloped digestive system.

Mesomorphic body type:

- Hard, muscular body
- Overly mature appearance
- Rectangular-shaped
- Thick skin
- Upright posture.

Ectomorphic body type:

- Thin
- Flat chest
- Delicate build
- Young appearance
- Tall
- Lightly muscled
- Stoop-shouldered
- Large brain.

Anthropometric measures are requisites that all medical teams will carry out on a regular basis with players who enter into a full-time development programme. All the components mentioned above are taken as part of the individual player profile. In addition, the medical teams will look at girth measurements. Girth relates to the maximal muscle circumference. It is measured at varied sites through flexion and extension. This is a valued tool, especially in relation to biological and skeletal age.

Physiological

Within some sports, the main criteria for assessing talent would be a player's fitness. We are aware that there are several components that can be targeted and assessed by eye. Aerobic endurance when measured in young children forms a pattern. Boys tend to continually improve with age, whereas girls can display a peak and drop-off in their late teens. At any age, it is easy to see how a player moves, with what tempo and intensity, and, most importantly, how quickly they recover. Without physically carrying out

performance tests, a lot of the fitness components are compared visually among talented players. If the sport requires testing to determine aerobic endurance, you would assess a player's aerobic capacity, aerobic power and, probably the most important in terms of player identification, their movement analysis. The physiological components play a vital part in continued assessment, but initial assessment relies on performance indicators such as how the player moves.

Different sports present different physiological demands and therefore require different combinations of physiological attributes and skill-related fitness. These attributes include:

- aerobic endurance
- anaerobic power
- strength
- flexibility
- coordination
- power
- agility.

Aerobic endurance

Aerobic endurance represents an athlete's maximal intake, transport and utilisation of oxygen. Most elite performers will require some aerobic endurance to sustain activity; however, it is particularly important to endurance athletes, such as long-distance runners, cyclists and cross-country skiers.

Anaerobic power

Anaerobic energy is produced without the use of oxygen. The anaerobic energy system can provide great amounts of energy, but fatigues quickly. Participation in sprinting, speed or power events, such as the long jump or sprint hurdles, will place greater stress on this energy system.

Strength

Strength can be defined as the muscle's ability to exert force and is influenced by somatotype (size and mass of the muscle). Events such as shot put require strength over a short period; however, events such as 400 m running require strength over an extended period and are described as muscle or strength endurance.

Flexibility

Flexibility describes an athlete's range of movement or motion. It is important for all athletes to support fluid movement and help prevent injury; however, it is essential to sports like high-board diving or gymnastics, to allow the range of motion necessary to present artistic movement.

Coordination

Coordination is important for all athletes in terms of efficient movement and motion, but it is essential to high-skill sports, such as racquet games (e.g. tennis, squash), ball sports (e.g. football, rugby) and acrobatic events (e.g. trampolining, pole vaulting). Coordination can be specific. Racquet sports place a high demand on the athlete's hand-to-eye coordination, while team games place a high demand on both hand-to-eye and foot-to-eye coordination.

Power

Power describes an athlete's ability to exert force quickly, combining both strength and speed. Power is illustrated by the high jumper combining strength and speed to produce the explosive muscle energy required to create lift and clear the bar.

Agility

Agility combines speed, strength, balance and coordination, and allows the athlete to change direction or body position quickly. Agility allows an athlete to move quickly and efficiently around a playing area (e.g. court, pitch) or their opposition, or to complete a sequence of complex movements (e.g. gymnastics).

Sociological

A child growing up in the world will see and experience new things every day, and there are a number of sociological aspects that will influence a performer's development and emergence of talent.

It is this social support that will allow an athlete to develop at the appropriate speed. When children play in sports teams, the referee will make decisions for or against a team as well as an individual. Any experience of success or failure will have an effect on the player. It is the role of parents, coaches and friends to recognise the stressors and strains that are being placed on the child. With parental and external support, the player has a security blanket that allows them to try new things and express themselves, knowing that they will have love and support regardless of the outcome. With this support, the child will accelerate and develop at a faster rate than a player who does not have the same supporting network. This is the same for a child's education. If a young player enjoys the sessions or lessons and takes positive experiences from them, they will learn and develop in an appropriate way. If the experiences they go through are negative in any way, this may well result in reduced performance.

Background

An athlete's background may have significant influence on their exposure to different sports and opportunities. Geography may influence exposure to different sporting opportunities – for example,

rugby league is predominantly played in the north of England, whereas rugby union is traditionally linked with the southern half of the country.

Socio-economic factors also have a role to play in the availability of sporting opportunities. Young people from low-income families often face greater barriers to participation in terms of access to facilities and coaching, specialised and expensive equipment, and transport to training or competitions.

Education

Like different families and communities, schools have their own traditions and may historically have placed emphasis on success in certain sports. The school's facilities and resources will further influence sports provision and offering.

Traditionally, private schools played rugby and hockey, while state schools played football; however, the introduction of the national curriculum has been significant in making the offering for both private- and state-educated children similar, although inequities still exist in the facilities and equipment available.

Parental involvement

Parental involvement obviously has significant influence on a child. There may be a 'family tradition' for a particular sport, which will likely create greater interest in that sport and therefore greater exposure for the young person, potentially to the exclusion of other sports.

Parental involvement changes at different stages of an athlete's participation in competitive sport. In the early years of a child's participation, positive parental involvement will require the parent to model a work ethic, be encouraging, supportive and positive. During the middle years, and likely stage at which talent is identified, positive parental involvement will require sacrifices and restrictions of the parents' own activities, and parents will be very child-centred. The absence of positive parental involvement may preclude a child's participation in sport and the emergence of talent.

Psychological

Psychological ability is probably one of the most important factors in relation to the complete player, but also the most overlooked. Psychological analysis in terms of performance is often difficult to quantify, but it defines what you would be looking for. When assessing players, psychology tends to refer to how the players train and play in relation to their sport. Within team sports, do the players make positive decisions at the right time, either through anticipation or through their individual game intelligence? In a sense, this relates to individual sportspeople as well, but the traits that scouts look for in a psychological analysis tend to focus mainly on the individual – their level of personal control, for example. Is the player composed and confident among his peers? Does he show good levels of concentration? Is there a player under nine years who has positive traits within his group, but would probably be defined as an accelerated player in terms of understanding and application?

Key learning points 1

- There are four types of talent:
    - unidimensional
    - multidimensional
    - uni-sport
    - multi-sport.
- A number of predictors can help to determine talent identification, including:
    - physical – height, weight, somatotype
    - physiological – aerobic endurance, anaerobic power, strength, flexibility, coordination, power, agility.
    - sociological – parental support, practice opportunities, education
    - psychological – confidence, concentration, decision-making skills
    - motor skills and technical and tactical skills.

Student activity 20.2 30 minutes P2

Imagine that you have been asked by your school sports coordinator (SSC) to go with them into the primary schools cluster group to talk to the teachers about five different predictors of talent (for a sport/activity of your choice). Prepare a short presentation for the SSC to deliver on their visits.

Quick quiz 1

1 Name a sportsperson who has demonstrated each of the following types of talent:
   - unidimensional
   - multidimensional
   - uni-sport
   - multi-sport.
2 Identify the main physical requirements for each of the following sports:
   - high jump
   - shot put
   - sprinting
   - basketball.
3 List the physiological requirements for each of the following sports:
   - marathon running
   - 100 m swimming
   - long jump
   - football
   - hockey.

20.3 Designing a Talent Identification Programme for a Chosen Sport

Identifying, developing and nurturing talented players are key priorities in a systematic long-term plan for success at elite level.

Talent identification has been described as 'the process of recognising current participants with the potential to excel and become elite players' (Reilly *et al.*, 2003). It means being able to predict performance over various periods of time by measuring the previously stated physical, physiological, psychological and sociological attributes of a performer, as well as their technical attributes. This means the system has to be smart enough to select individuals based on their future abilities and standards required to deliver medals in five years' time, not just their current performance abilities.

Talent identification (TID) is both an art and a science, involving a complex blend of scientific knowledge and assessment, alongside coaching art. It is designed to proactively seek out those who possess the raw material for world-class success, and who respond positively to an intense training and competition environment. The scientific approach of identifying talent involves a series of rigorous assessments and filters to detect individuals who have greater prospects for winning medals and success.

UK Sport has set the strategic lead and provides guidance on the field of talent identification, selection, confirmation and Olympic/Paralympic development.

Currently, the English Institute of Sport (EIS) acts as the support delivery agency, with specialist talent identification staff working in partnership with NGBs, implementing tailored programmes to detect and build greater stockpiles of world-class talent for the high-performance pipeline.

The potential to excel in sport depends on several factors. A combination of physical, environmental, mental and emotional factors will go a long way, but these do not guarantee elite success.

There are several identifications that many sports, sports academies and even governing bodies rely on to find, develop and nurture new talent. Within many sports, you often hear the phrase 'he/she looks and moves like a professional player'. Talent scouts use and adopt many different processes to assess players in games and sessions. Visual information, such as how someone moves, is the first real point of contact, but talent scouts will look for and consider other qualities and requirements of the modern game, including the following:

● Pace and mobility – does the player have it now or lack it due to age and strength?
● Game understanding and awareness – does the player know when, where and how to pass, run, receive, tackle or simply change the play?
● Attitude and application – do the players seem to be actually enjoying playing the game?
● Determination – will the player work hard to get the ball and work harder to get it back?
● Technical qualities – does the player have a good touch, passing range and ability, defending principles and attacking qualities?

You will no doubt see some of these attributes in very young players; however, a talent scout will look closer if the player is hoping to enter a talent development programme. There are several talent identification programmes that are used by many sports today. In reviewing and evaluating the processes that are in place, talent identification assessment is paramount in finding the right players.

Many of the current assessment programmes look at different specific components, but all cover the following three elements:

● technical
● physical
● mental.

Talent Programmes

TIPS

One of the most common talent programmes is TIPS (as introduced by Ajax FC, Amsterdam), which can be applied to all sports.

TIPS is broken down into four key areas, in which coaches and assessors will score and reflect a player's overall potential:

● talent – player's technical ability within their chosen sport
● intelligence – player and game understanding (this is often judged when the player has the ball and also when they do not have the ball)
● personality – this includes the player as a person, as a learner and in varied practices, how they react and learn as well as how they take on board specific and relevant information
● speed – this can be broken down into various components, but ultimately the players are considered in terms of reaction speed to and from the ball, including pure speed, both with and without the ball, and acceleration.

331

TIPS is a very common method and is a valuable tool for coaches, scouts and teachers within sport.

TABS

TABS examines the technical, the personal and the physical elements of the player:

● Technical
● Attitude
● Balance
● Speed.

Here, the emphasis is placed on the player's technical understanding and their ability. The next component relates to the player's attitude. Attitude can be assessed in training, in games, in the changing room and, to an extent, away from the sport. Balance is the first technical element that TABS looks at. In terms of player development, the work of Dr Istvan Balyi (2004) describes development as key learning stages and windows of opportunity. The first stage concentrates on the development of players aged between six and nine years, and focuses on the FUNdamentals of the game (for this age group, the 'fun' element should be included as part of the training programmes). It also includes ensuring the players understand the rules, as well as learning the ABCs.

The ABCs are the components in which players are trained:

● Agility
● Balance
● Coordination.

Even at this early stage of development, balance is vital in some development programmes. To an extent, as the players progress through the age groups and go through the training windows and opportunities, it is harder to train a specific movement pattern.

The final component is speed. Again through Balyi's work, the six- to nine-year age group offers a great opportunity not only to develop speed but to incorporate specific sessions into the player's development programme.

SUPS

The final development programme is SUPS:

● Speed
● Understanding
● Personality
● Skill.

Although they are in a different order to the previous two programmes, the key requirements follow the same trend.

Here the emphasis is placed on the physical pace of the player. If the player has pace, often the mindset

of the scouts is that he can develop technique and skill. Within these two criteria, the emphasis is placed on the understanding a player shows within small-sided games, along with their individuality and what they bring to the game.

Current Talent Identification Programmes

Systematic Talent Searches in the UK

British Cycling has been using a systematic approach for several years now, to assure a repeat of the record medal haul enjoyed by British cyclists at the Athens and Beijing Olympics. British Cycling has also developed a programme of testing in schools.

The British Cycling Talent Team Tests is a four-stage process:

Stage 1 – Opportunities for all
Delivered by trained Talent Team Testers through a network of secondary schools and Cycling Academies throughout England. Open to everyone of secondary school age using their own bikes or bikes supplied by their school.

Stage 2 – Identification of talent
The best riders from Stage 1 are invited to take part in Stage 2, which is delivered by a British Cycling Regional Talent Coach, who will visit the school or Cycling Academy during the summer. The tests are the same as Stage 1, but are performed on a standard mountain bike that is supplied by the Talent Team.

Stage 3 – Confirmation of talent
Invited riders will visit a local Cycling Academy to repeat the Talent Team Tests, only this time activities will be indoors, on special bikes equipped with power-measuring devices. This will enable the Talent Team to record an accurate measurement of the rider's abilities.

Stage 4 – Confirmation of commitment
Riders who performed exceptionally well at Stage 3 will be invited to attend the final stage. Stage 4 is a two-day event where the riders and their parents/guardians learn what support will be offered on the Talent Team's Tracking and Talent programmes. Riders will also learn about the GB Cycling Team, meet a member of the team and get to experience different disciplines of cycling.

(www.britishcycling.org.uk)

The Youth Sport Trust has worked in partnership with the Department for Children, Schools and Families (DCSF) and the Department for Culture, Media and

Sport (DCMS) to produce the PESSCL (Physical Education, School Sport and Club Links) strategy for implementation nationally in schools. It aims to support talented (and potentially talented) young people who are still involved in full-time compulsory education (under 16 years of age). The strategy has seen the development of the Gifted and Talented programme.

> The aim of the Gifted and Talented strand is: to improve the recognition of, and the support and provision for gifted and talented pupils in physical education and sport.
>
> There are three key areas of this work:
>
> A. High quality – raising the quality of PE for gifted and talented young people
>
> B. Support – ensuring appropriate personal development support for young talented performers in sport
>
> C. Raising the quality of coaching and competition for talented performers in sport.
>
> (http://gifted.youthsporttrust.org)

This has led to the development of a profile of gifted and talented pupils in PE and sport. Pupils are assessed by PE teachers using the checklist.

> Talented learners in PE and Sport are likely to:
>
> Think quickly and accurately
>
> • Work systematically
> • Generate creative working solutions
> • Work flexibly, processing in familiar information and applying knowledge, experience and insight to unfamiliar situations
> • Communicate their thoughts and ideas well
> • Be determined, diligent and interested in uncovering patterns
> • Achieve, or show potential, in a wide range of contexts
> • Be particularly creative
> • Demonstrate particular physical dexterity or skill
> • Make sound judgements
> • Be outstanding leaders or team members
> • Demonstrate high levels of attainment in PE or a particular sport.
>
> (www.youthsporttrust.org)

In addition to this profile, a talent identification framework has been developed to define attainment in PE or a particular sport. The framework is not sport-specific and is focused on the four strands to the national curriculum. Pupils are rated on their abilities in acquiring and developing skills, selecting and applying skills, tactics and compositional ideas, evaluating and improving performance and knowledge, and understanding of fitness and health.

The programme invests in the training of teachers to assess pupils against this profile. This talent identification method, while systematic, is reliant on subjective measures and assessment by teachers rather than objective testing.

World Class Performance Programme

The World Class Performance Programme is aimed at providing support for the UK's top athletes in Olympic sports. It is a lottery-funded programme administered by UK Sport, with funding currently in the region of £25 million per annum. UK Sport is a quango.

Key term

Quango: the term originated as a shortening of quasi-NGO, which is a non-governmental organisation that performs governmental functions, often with government funding or other support.

This programme is designed to support the identification and confirmation of athletes who have the potential to progress through the World Class Pathway, with the help of targeted investment. World Class Talent is managed by the NGBs, which are responsible for managing the programme and identifying the athletes.

UK Sport has had full responsibility for all Olympic and Paralympic performance-related support in England since 1 April 2006. This spans talent identification through to Olympic and Paralympic performance levels.

Non-Olympic sports have not been entirely left out. It will also provide consultancy for non-Olympic sports, to improve performance and develop future success.

The World Class Pathway aims are:

● to identify exceptionally talented young performers and give them a comprehensive basis on which to build future world-class success
● to select performers with world-class potential and develop their talents in order to give them the greatest chance of achieving major senior international success.

333

UK Sport currently operates the World Class Performance Programme at three key levels, as described below.

World Class Podium

This programme will support sports with realistic medal capabilities at the next Olympic/Paralympic Games.

World Class Development

This programme is designed to support the stage of the pathway immediately beneath the Podium pathway.

World Class Talent

This programme is designed to support the identification and confirmation of athletes who have the potential to progress through the World Class Pathway, with the help of targeted investment.

One example of this is the Amateur Rowing Association (ARA) World Class Start programme, which is aimed at the untrained athlete; the vision is to build the future of rowing in Great Britain by identifying and developing potential Olympians.

This talent identification programme is applied to local networks and delivered via clubs, universities and schools in partnership with the ARA. The selection procedure involves a proven battery of tests, designed to estimate the long-term (Olympic) ability to be successful in rowing. Tests are administered by the World Class Start team.

To take just two examples, Annie Vernon and Anna Bebington were rowing medallists at the 2008 Olympic Games, aged 20 and 19, respectively, five years after being selected through a talent identification scheme (ARA's World Class Start Programme, sponsored by Siemens).

TASS

The Talented Athlete Scholarship Scheme (TASS) is a government initiative aimed at providing support for talented athletes who may be in danger of dropping out of sport due to their commitment to both competitive sport and education. The initiative is operated through a partnership between sport and further/higher education institutions. Awards are granted to talented athletes to enable them to continue with their studies while training and competing at a high level.

TASS is specifically aimed at talented sportspeople aged 16–25, who want to remain in education. It helps them to fulfil their sporting potential by enabling them to develop and maintain a sensible balance between academic life, employment, training and competing as a performance athlete. Awards are distributed to performers who show a commitment to combine sport and education in a sensible manner. TASS aims to reduce the numbers who drop out of sport because of the financial demands of studying, training and competing.

NGBs are asked to nominate those athletes whom they would like to receive a TASS award. There are currently 50 sports that are eligible for TASS, of which 16 are disability sports.

You can visit the TASS website at www.tass.gov.uk.

UK Sport London 2012

The 'It could be you' initiative has a number of specific pathways:

- Girls4Gold
- Pitch2Podium
- Sporting Giants (Tall and Talented) – rowing, handball, volleyball
- Talent Transfer 10–4–12

Girls4Gold

In June 2008, UK Sport and the English Institute of Sport (EIS) began a search for highly competitive sportswomen with the potential to become Olympic champions in cycling and other targeted Olympic sports (bob skeleton, canoeing, modern pentathlon, rowing and sailing). Girls4Gold is the single most extensive female sporting talent recruitment drive ever undertaken in Great Britain.

Applicants had to be female, aged between 17 and 25 years, competing in any sport at county/regional level, fit, powerful and strong, mentally tough and competitive, and up for a once-in-a-lifetime opportunity to become part of Britain's sporting elite.

The ultimate aim of Girls4Gold is to unearth exceptional female talent capable of achieving medal success in London in 2012 and beyond. There are numerous British female World and Olympic medallists who have specialised in a new Olympic sport at a relatively late age, going on to achieve medal success in short time frames.

Phase 1 Talent Assessment events took place in July–October 2008, in partnership with the six Olympic programmes (cycling, bob skeleton, canoeing, modern pentathlon, rowing and sailing – windsurfing).

Each individual participant's Phase 1 testing results were systematically assessed alongside their athlete profile. Those meeting Phase 2 standards were invited to a sport-specific Phase 2 Olympic Talent Assessment event in one or potentially several sports between November 2008 and March 2009.

Pitch2Podium

Pitch2Podium is a programme created by UK Sport, the English and Scottish Institutes of Sport (EIS/SIS) and the football and rugby authorities (Football Association, Professional Footballers' Association, Premier League, Football League, League Football Education, Scottish PFA, Premier Rugby and the Rugby Football Union).

The aim of the programme is to provide young football and rugby players who have been unsuccessful in securing a professional contract, with a second chance to succeed in a new Olympic sport.

Sporting Giants

In February, 2007, UK Sport and the English Institute of Sport launched the first appeal of its kind in the UK – to find some potential giants of British sport.

The basic criteria were being tall (a minimum of 6'3" or 190 cm for men and 5'11" or 180 cm for women), young (between 16 and 25), with some sort of athletic background.

The TID was searching for talented people to become part of the performance programme in the Olympic sports of rowing, handball or volleyball.

The challenge was set by Britain's greatest ever Olympian, Sir Steve Redgrave. From an elite perspective, it is the chance to take Great Britain to new heights across more Olympic and Paralympic sports than ever before.

There were 4,800 applications, with just under 4,000 applications meeting all the basic criteria.

Handball, volleyball and rowing were the initial target sports, and some 'Sporting Giants' have now successfully joined Olympic development programmes. If an athlete did not meet all the specific criteria, they were guided into a different sport, where it appeared their talent characteristics might be better matched. For example, 35 males who did not reach the height criteria of rowing, but demonstrated immense upper body power and strength/endurance, were offered opportunities to trial in canoeing.

Talent transfer

Talent transfer looks specifically at already talented/elite performers in one area of sport who either may not be able to compete at the Olympics as the sport may not be included yet (e.g. karate, kickboxing or kung fu), or are retired or nearly retired athletes previously involved in UK Sports World Class Programmes, to investigate their suitability to switch sports and extend their athletic career – possibly contributing to the Olympic medal haul. An example of this sport-specific TID is Talent 2012: Fighting Chance.

The initiative offers high-level combat athletes from all kicking-orientated martial arts, including taekwondo, the opportunity to trial for a place in the elite Taekwondo Academy based at the National Taekwondo Performance Centre in Manchester.

The initial criteria are:

- aged 16+
- male or female
- all weight categories
- excellent skill level
- lightning reactions and decision-making
- current success at national level or above in a kicking-orientated combat sport
- desire and determination for success
- UK passport holder *or* eligible for a UK passport within next six months.

(www.uksport.gov.uk/pages/talent_id)

20–4–12

In 2006, a national grass-roots search for 20 potential Olympic champions in the build-up to the 2012 London Games was launched in support of Britain's ambitious plan to reach fourth place in the 2012 medals table.

The search saw £500,000 of public money invested in a UK-wide '20–4–12' talent search, targeting 11- to 16-year-olds who might have the raw talent to reach the Olympic podium.

The NGBs use a range of methods to identify talented performers, with most employing professional staff to manage the talent identification process.

Disability talent identification

The UK Sport-funded World Class Programmes for disabled athletes mirror those of the non-disabled programmes in providing funding and support services to athletes who are capable of or have the potential to win medals at the Paralympics.

Increases in participation for disabled athletes are championed by the English Federation of Disability Sport (EFDS), which supports NGBs in developing their disability programmes.

Identification of talented sportspeople with disabilities presents many parallels to non-disabled programmes; however, the classification of athletes brings an added dimension to identifying talent in disabled athletes. Classification is the method by which fair and equitable competition is achieved and it is based on disability and function.

Key learning points 2

- A development programme does not occur overnight. It is a systematic development plan that targets key components and areas through every development age.
- There are many development programmes that talent scouts use to assess potential players. In general terms, they look to identify physical, social, psychological and, most importantly, technical elements.
- There are many individual fitness components that are assessed through match practice. As well as the player's game understanding, they are considered for speed, acceleration, personality and skills.

Student activity 20.3   1–2 hours   P3   M1

Task 1

Select a talent identification programme for a sport of your choice. Write a report that describes and evaluates the talent identification programme you have selected.

Task 2

Working in small groups, produce a short presentation about talent transfer.

20.4 Structure of a Talent Identification Programme

Talent is an extremely complex concept that is hard to define, being a mixture of scientific knowledge and assessment, along with the skills of the observers/coaches. Each TID programme must have a clear set of aims, objectives, structure and format.

By using the programmes outlined above and scoring 'athletes' accordingly, you are left with a group of performers who have stood out in several aspects: speed, technique, personality and game intelligence/understanding.

Stages of a Programme

The TID aim is to find any individuals who possess and demonstrate the basic abilities to succeed in world-class sport, and who will respond positively to the intense environments of elite training and competition.

The objectives of TID are to provide the opportunity for athletes to develop to their full potential within a programme, and to offer funding and the opportunity for national and international sporting success.

TID programmes will vary in their structure and format, due to the different demands at different ages placed on the athletes (e.g. for swimming, dance and gymnastics the TID is earlier, as specialisation within the sport is earlier). Where athletes develop later (e.g. for rowing or cycling), the TID can find athletes later, such as the Tall and Talented programme's basic criteria of being tall (a minimum of 6'3" or 190 cm for men and 5'11" or 180 cm for women), young (between 16 and 25), with some sort of athletic background.

The time frames vary from sport to sport, depending on the demands of the sport, but it has been suggested that it takes roughly seven to ten years for an athlete to become world class. It is vital that athletes continue to take part in sport, otherwise 'late developers' can be overlooked.

From the TID programmes mentioned, it is clear that fitness testing/assessment and comparison to norm tables are crucial. The tests must apply to the sport, and will vary from sport to sport (i.e. the components of fitness necessary to be successful must be understood and tested appropriately). Performance standards represent a benchmark (compared with norm tables) against which talent is measured, and these are then used by NGBs to identify sport-specific talent.

Student activity 20.4 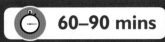 **60–90 mins** **P4** **M2** **D1**

Task 1

Choose a sport and design a talent identification programme for that sport. You will need to include:

- aims
- purpose
- structure and format
- phases and stages
- time-scales
- use of test batteries
- resources required.

Task 2

Explain and justify your chosen activities for your selected sport.

20.5 Key Factors in Talent Development in Sport

The purpose of identifying young talent is to predict with a high degree of probability whether or not a young athlete or player will be at the required level to successfully complete the sport training programme. It has also been suggested that it takes 8 to 12 years of training for a talented player/athlete to reach elite levels. Consequently, talent identification is only the first step in producing world-class athletes and Olympic medals. Talent development is a long-term commitment to practice and training.

Nowadays, highly developed systematic scientific research works are needed for spotting and determining the combination of talent factors and various parameters responsible for achieving the ultimate goal in different sports; scientists, knowledgeable coaches, trainers and physical educators have constructed a variety of test batteries to assist in the process.

> If something exists, it exists in some amount. If it exists in some amount, then it is capable of being measured.
>
> (Rene Descartes, *Principles of Philosophy*, 1644)

We have already discussed the physical, physiological, sociological and psychological factors that help to identify potential elite performers. Clearly these factors are also important when developing talent; however, there may be some obstacles along the way as well.

Physical factors

As mentioned earlier (see page 000), there are certain physical characteristics that all talented athletes need. These must be matched to their chosen sport/activity in order to make the most of the attributes.

Height

The Tall and Talented programme clearly shows this, with the targeted sports of handball, volleyball and rowing. Those athletes who were not as tall have been directed into other sports, such as canoeing.

Weight (body mass)

To be successful at the highest levels, athletes should be guided into sports where their body mass will be an advantage (e.g. heavier athletes might be more suited to rowing and bobsleigh rather than running and jumping sports).

Muscle girth (size)

The girth is a measure of a muscle's size, and therefore its possible strength. It makes sense that someone with a bigger muscle girth should be better in power/strength activities, while athletes with smaller muscle girths should be more agile. (We must always remember that the potential to be more skilful is crucial, and that size will not be the only criterion.)

Physiological factors

Different sports have different physiological demands; these include aerobic endurance and anaerobic power.

An athlete's physiological characteristics will affect their development. The following will help determine

337

the sports/activities and the positions within sports that people play:

- their muscle fibre type (fast or slow – i.e. their energy production)
- the efficiency of their cardiovascular system.

For example, why is Jermain Defoe a striker and Steven Gerrard a midfield player?

Our fibre-typing and ATP energy production pathways are generally genetic – 'athletes are born and not made'! Usain Bolt is a phenomenal example in sprinting.

Sociological

Parents

Parents are essential to the talented athlete's development, but it is important that this involvement is positive, and provides support and encouragement which is associated with greater enjoyment and increased self-esteem, rather than pressure and stress related to unfair or unrealistic parental expectation.

Parents can provide two types of support:

- tangible support – such as paying for equipment, training, travelling/transport and accommodation
- intangible support – always 'being there' for encouragement and emotional support.

Opportunities for Deliberate Practice

Parental and educational support are key aspects in the planning for deliberate, structured practice. The more opportunity young athletes have for quality practice, with more coach contact opportunities, the faster their game intelligence will develop, along with the tactical and strategic awareness/skills necessary to perform at higher levels. Any areas for development can be targeted to help develop their skills and performance.

Coach

The athlete will be spending long periods in the charge of the coach, so a positive relationship and good communication are essential. The coach needs to recognise the need to involve both parents and the school or university in the athlete's programme planning. Likewise, the athlete has a responsibility to communicate exam periods and important assignment due dates, as well as family commitments, to their coach.

The coach needs to be current and up to date in their coaching practice. They will need to read widely and continually seek out professional development opportunities to ensure they are providing their athlete with optimal training and support.

All coaches must adhere to a strict code of conduct, ensuring that the athlete is safeguarded correctly. This means that coaches always work in the best interests of their athlete, consulting and involving other professionals where appropriate.

Psychological

Psychological factors have been identified as part of talent identification; consequently, they must be a key factor in talent development.

At the top level, there is very little that separates athletes physically and physiologically; however, if one performer has better mental skills, they are more likely to be successful.

'Sporting attitude' could be a general overview. Sporting attitude is reflected in the talented athlete's behaviour towards their coach, parents, teammates, support staff and other competitors. Athletes should be guided in responding and thinking positively in all situations (particularly when things aren't going well), taking responsibility for their own performance and being respectful to others (coaches, officials, competitors and supporters).

A good sporting attitude will help the athlete to cope with success and failure, being gracious in defeat and magnanimous in victory – not always an easy task, depending on the situation. It requires respect for yourself and others and a recognition that defeat can bring with it as many, if not more, lessons for the future.

Exposure to positive role models from coaches, parents and older athletes will support the development of a good sporting attitude.

Confidence

Confidence can be developed by achieving challenging but realistic goals/targets during training and competition. Success developed in training, which is continued into competition, will help the athlete enjoy the sport and motivate the athlete to progress to greater challenges, with the knowledge and belief that they can be successful.

Motivation

Motivation and drive are paramount to success in elite sport and therefore it is important to establish what motivates the talented athlete to train, work hard and achieve. Motives can be performance motives or outcome motives.

Performance motives are directly related to mastery and fulfilment of potential and are in the control of the athlete. Examples include:

- beating a personal best
- landing a new move in a routine
- mastering a new technique.

338

The athlete has less control over outcome motives, as they do not have any influence over the performance of their opposition. Outcome goals could include:

● being world champion
● finishing in the top ten
● podium finish.

Outcome motivation alone may lead to the athlete becoming demotivated and developing an unhealthy mental profile, so it is important that athletes include performance motives, particularly young athletes.

Concentration and focus

The athlete will need to be equipped with techniques to support them in maintaining concentration and focus.

Anticipation and decision-making

Through practice and playing in different environments, athletes will be able to develop their situation awareness – that is, taking the appropriate action as soon as possible, based on the opposition's potential options.

Taking the correct option, or decision-making, can be developed through practice, but also through performance reviews, using a reflective approach, and watching recordings of performances.

Game (competition) intelligence

Successful athletes often know when to change what they are doing, such as working harder (up the performance tempo – stroke rate in rowing), applying more pressure (full court press in basketball) or, when it's possible, conserving energy when competing (slowing down in the 1500 m heats with a place secured).

This knowledge and understanding is again developed through training, practice, competition and discussion between performers and athletes.

Development of tactical skills is dependent on exposure to the competitive environment and the use of competition simulation and scenario-based activities in the athlete's training programme. Good mental preparation also supports the athlete's ability to make tactical decisions under pressure.

In team sports, rehearsal of set plays and set pieces will also be important in developing a player's tactical skills.

However, in sport as in life, not everything goes to plan, or as we would like it to, despite everything being in place!

Obstacles and barriers to success

Few, if any, elite athletes have had a smooth pathway to success, and most will have had to overcome a number of obstacles along the way. These might include:

● injury
● peer pressure
● parental pressure
● social isolation
● athlete role ambiguity
● gender
● age considerations
● family disruption
● poor grades
● lack of opportunity.

Injury

In all sports there is an inherent risk of injury; however, with a carefully planned programme, the risks can be kept as low as possible. For example, inappropriate volume and intensity of training are major contributors to injury in young athletes. Also, insufficient rest and recovery will increase the potential risk of injuries.

Peer pressure

Peers may be within the sport or outside the sport, and both are important to the sociological development of talented athletes. Peers within the sport are often more understanding of the demands and commitments required to be successful in sport and are frequently a source of support during periods of hardship and disappointment (e.g. disappointing performance or injury).

Relationships with peers outside sport can be just as significant, providing a break from sport and a change of focus, but it is important that these peers understand the athlete's commitment to sport and ambitions. While these relationships sometimes require more time and effort on the part of the athlete, they are very important to their social development.

Parental pressure

Parents frequently make significant personal and financial sacrifices to support their child's athletic career. This adds stress and pressure for the athlete, who may feel that they don't want to disappoint their parents. Some parents place unrealistic and unfair expectations on their children, adding further pressure on them to achieve.

Social isolation

This can be caused by the commitment and dedication required to become an elite athlete, which leaves limited time for relationships with peers. This can leave the young athlete excluded from their peer group.

339

Athlete role ambiguity

Elite athletes are often defined by their athletic ability, and their lives can become entirely about sports performance. This is frequently reinforced by parents, peers and teachers. Often elite athletes come to judge themselves by their performance, believing poor performance to make them a poor individual and, likewise, good performance making them a better person. It is important that elite athletes maintain some balance in their lives, so they grow up to be well-rounded and socially comfortable individuals.

Being in a squad where your role isn't clearly defined (e.g. being played in different positions) can have a negative effect on performance and development.

Gender

Gender may be a further barrier to success. Girls may face greater barriers to success in terms of social perceptions and cultural influences. Coaches will also have to take into consideration self-esteem and emotional differences between boys and girls, and adjust coaching practice accordingly.

Age considerations

The junior middle-distance runner who is an early developer, physically more developed and stronger than their peers, may experience success as a junior, but may struggle as the demands of certain sports may mean that an athlete doesn't make the transition from junior to senior competition as well as their later developing, taller, leaner peers, who catch them up.

Physical maturity occurs earlier in girls than in boys, and coaches will need to differentiate training in accordance with gender.

It is important that both the parents and the coach have a good understanding of the individual athlete and are sensitive to physical and emotional development at every phase of their development. An emotionally immature 15-year-old may need to constantly seek the coach's approval and recognition, and react negatively to criticism, while the emotionally mature 15-year-old may be comfortable with constructive criticism.

Key learning points 3

- Every player within any development age is special. What they see or hear or feel on a regular basis has an impact on their overall make-up, which at times runs alongside their actual playing ability.
- At every age and for any gender, the player is assessed as an individual and also against other players in the same development year or age group.
- Many young footballers display very good individual key factors; however, the football clubs will examine the application of these factors in specific sport-related situations, in order to assess their suitability for the club.

Student activity 20.5 **60–90 mins** **P5**

Prepare a presentation which describes the five key factors in talent development. Try to provide some realistic examples from your own knowledge and experiences to demonstrate these factors.

20.6 Talent Development Programmes

Before we can design a talent development programme, we need to look at some current programmes. There are a number of talent identification programmes and models in the UK. Among these are:

- World Class Performance Programme

- ECFA (English Colleges Football Association)
- Football Development Centres
- LTAD (Long Term Athlete Development) model (e.g. RFU)
- Premier Rugby – Elite Player Development Centres (EPDC)
- England Hockey – Single System Development Structure
- Badminton England Talent Development Programme.

World Class Performance Programme

UK Sport distributes lottery funding to develop talented and world-class performers through UK Sport's World Class Programmes.

World Class funding consists of:

● programme funding which supports the governing bodies' Performance Plans, assisting with training and competition, sports science and medicine
● coaching programmes and Athlete Personal Awards, which are paid directly to the athletes themselves.

The programme has three levels, representing a performance pathway managed by the NGBs:

● World Class Podium
● World Class Development.

World Class Podium

This programme will support sports with realistic medal capabilities at the next Olympic/Paralympic Games (i.e. a maximum of four years away from the podium).

World Class Development

This programme is designed to support the stage of the pathway immediately beneath the Podium. It will comprise sports that have demonstrated that they have realistic medal-winning capabilities for 2012, and now 2016. For sports already funded by the Podium programme, their continued success will be possible only if there is investment in the next wave of talented athletes coming through the system.

Talented Athlete Scholarship Scheme (TASS)

The Talented Athlete Scholarship Scheme (TASS), as explained earlier (see pages 000–000), represents a unique partnership between sport and higher and further education, and is a UK Sport-funded programme. The programme aims to bridge the gap between non-funded grass-roots sport and world-class sport.

The programme awards scholarships and bursaries to talented athletes who are in higher or further education. The programme objective is to reduce the drop-out of talented athletes from sport and maintain a pool of developing athletes at sub-world-class funded level. The athletes are identified by the NGB.

ECFA and Football Development Centres

The English Colleges Football Association (ECFA) was formed in 2002. ECFA developed the English Colleges Football League (sanctioned by the Football Association). It provides a competitive environment for young, talented footballers who have been recruited by Football Development Centres based in further education colleges around the country.

Each college must meet strict criteria before membership of the league is approved. These criteria ensure that an effective, planned programme is delivered. All coaches involved must be UEFA 'A' or 'B' licensed coaches, and players receive a minimum of six hours of coaching per week.

Long Term Athlete Development (LTAD)

This model (Balyi, 2004) is based on the principle of periodisation. In other words, a specific and well-planned practice, training, competition and recovery regime will ensure optimum development throughout an athlete's career. Ultimately, sustained success comes from training and performing well over the long term, rather than winning in the short term. There is no short-cut to success in athletic preparation. An overemphasis on competition in the early phases of training will usually cause shortcomings in athletic abilities later in an athlete's career. Child development is taken into consideration and care is taken in planning coaching. For example, optimal windows of trainability appear at various stages of the child's development and these are taken into consideration when planning coaching and training.

Balyi's model states that it takes 10,000 hours over 8 to 12 years of deliberate practice for a talented athlete to reach elite levels of performance.

Sports are classified as early or late specialisation. Sports such as gymnastics, figure skating, diving and table tennis require early sport-specific training and specialisation. Other sports, such as team sports, combat sports and cycling, require a generalised training regime in the early years.

The LTAD model has developed from five stages in 2001 to six stages in 2004, as shown in Table 20.1.

2001: Five-stage model (early specialisation)	2004: Six-stage model (late specialisation)
FUNdamental	FUNdamental
Learning to train	Learning to train
Training to train	Training to train
Training to compete	Training to compete
Training to win	Training to win
	Recruit, retain, retrain throughout life

Table 20.1 Stages of the LTAD

LTAD has been described as the golden thread that permeates the 2004 National Framework for Sport. It appeared as the preferred model (in fact, the only model) in the government's Game Plan National Sports Policy document (2002).

Many national federations and club teams, particularly in professional sports, continue to invest considerable resources in their attempts to identify exceptionally gifted youngsters, and LTAD is still being used by many NGBs in this country to remodel their talent development pathways.

An example of an NGB utilising LTAD is the RFU, which, together with Premier Rugby, has developed the Elite Premier Development Centres. An example programme is shown below.

ELITE PREMIER DEVELOPMENT CENTRES (PREMIER RUGBY) LONG TERM ATHLETE DEVELOPMENT

Newcastle Falcons Junior Academy adheres to the principles of Long Term Athlete Development (LTAD) throughout the Elite Player Development Centre (EPDC).

LTAD is a process that involves developing a planned training, competition and recovery regime that allows performers to fulfil their long-term sporting potential. Experts in the field believe that it takes 10,000 hours of extensive practice to excel in anything, which equates to about ten years' hard work.

Developing athletes should base their training around what is termed the **peak height velocity (PHV)**, or growth spurt. In boys, this usually occurs between the ages of 13 and 18, but everyone is different. Training should be specific to the individual and should be based on biological age, not chronological age. People mature and develop at different rates, and although missing a window of opportunity is not disastrous, it may mean that your genetic potential is never reached.

- The best time to develop skills is before your growth spurt
- The best time to develop your aerobic system is just after your growth spurt
- The best time to develop your strength is 12–18 months after your growth spurt.

FUNdamentals (age 6–9): school, club:

The emphasis is placed on enjoyment and participation in as many different sports as possible. This is a key time to develop basic running, jumping, throwing, kicking and catching skills, as well as agility, balance and coordination.

Learning to train (age 9–12): school, club:

This should involve learning general sports skills, as well as continuing to develop fundamental movement skills. Conditioning should be based around game play and body-weight exercises. Players can be introduced to the concept of training.

Training to train (age 12–16): school, club, school of rugby:

This should involve general conditioning and functional fitness for rugby. The growth spurt should be monitored, to allow for windows of opportunity to be maximised. Core skills can be developed and game sense and mental skills introduced.

Training to compete (age 16–18): school, club, county, academy:

Sport-specific technical skills can be practised under competitive conditions, and tactical preparation becomes more advanced. Conditioning programmes should be individualised around the growth spurt.

Training to win (age 18+): university, club, county, senior academy:

Players are introduced to adult programmes as their growth allows. It is important to optimise technical, tactical and skill performance in competition, with frequent physical and mental breaks to allow the training undertaken to take effect.

Key learning points 4

- There are a number of talent identification and development programmes in operation in the UK. Most are funded by the National Lottery and central government:
    - World Class Performance Programme
    - TASS (Talented Athlete Scholarship Scheme)
    - World Class Pathway programmes
    - Gifted and Talented
    - ECFA (English Colleges Football Association)
    - Football Development Centres
    - LTAD (Long Term Athlete Development) model.
- These programmes are mostly operated by government departments and quangos, and are delivered through NGBs and educational institutes.
- There is currently only one recognised talent development programme being widely used in the UK: the Long Term Athlete Development (LTAD) model.

Student activity 20.6   60 minutes   P6   M3

Task 1

Find a development programme that currently exists/operates for a sport of your choice. Describe the structure of your chosen talent development programme.

Task 2

Try to evaluate the programme. Consider whether the programme is similar to another programme you may have discussed, who the programme might target, and how the programme plans athletes' development.

20.7 Structure of a Talent Development Programme

Each talent development programme must have a clear set of aims, purpose, structure and format. This section will provide a framework by which to evaluate existing talent development programmes, and will support you in the design of your own programme.

Programme Aims and Purpose

Aim(s) of the Programme

Establishing clear aims will guide the whole process. The aims of the programme, for example, might be to:

- identify talented performers
- provide opportunities or funding for them.

Programmes can be non-sport-specific (e.g. TASS) or sport-specific (e.g. NGB talent development programmes). Aims of current talent development programmes include:

- investment in long-term, athlete-centred development

343

- winning Olympic medals
- bridging the gap between grass-roots/non-funded programmes and world class-funded programmes
- supporting talented performers in balancing sport and education.

Purpose of the Programme

Following on from the example above, the purpose of the programme might be to produce performers for a specific event such as the Olympics in 2012 and 2016, or the FIFA World Cup in 2014.

Measuring the Success of the Programme

This relates directly back to the aims and purposes of the programme. If these are met, then the programme is successful. Therefore, much care must be taken when deciding on the aims and purpose. For example, if the aim is to produce two gold medal performances at a particular championship and we achieve four silver medals, have we been successful?

Programme Format

The format of the programme will be partly determined by the aims and purpose of the programme, but it will also be determined by financial, political and geographical factors.

It might be that the programme concentrates solely on identifying potential medal hopefuls and providing financial support.

The development programme must provide a balance between multi-sport training and specialisation. If the sport requires early specialisation, then the athlete's potential options may become limited. If its purpose is to target a range of sports, it could be operated through NGBs or through a central body.

Programme Structure

Current talent development programmes deliver funding, training, coaching, support, mentoring and education to athletes, coaches and parents. Programmes are delivered in schools, academies, centres of excellence and high-performance centres.

Testing, Assessment, Evaluation and Review

Athletes benefiting from funded programmes are continually assessed, evaluated and reviewed to secure ongoing NGB and UK Sport support and funding.

Assessment methodologies will be many and varied, including objective physical and physiological tests, performance standards and results, and subjective athlete reviews and evaluations.

Testing and assessment need to be split into:

- comparing talented athletes to norm tables for general ability (generic testing)
- sport-specific testing to 'place' the athletes in the correct phase of the programme, focus their training and identify any areas for development
- monitoring and assessment throughout the programme.

Phases and Stages: Time-scales

The majority of sport-specific talent development programmes can be mapped against LTAD principles and recognise the LTAD model's stages. For example, England Hockey now has a model in place from U13s to U21s and full international level – that is, seven to ten years of talent development.

Resources

Talent development programmes need a wide range of resources to support them. The programme design and structure will influence the demand on the human, physical and fiscal (monetary) resources required.

Strategic approaches to the resourcing of talent development programmes are essential for the programme's sustainability.

Other Considerations

Communication

Good communication between the athlete, coaches, administrators, teachers, parents and NGBs is essential to ensure the athlete is guided through the programme clearly and effectively.

Effective talent development programmes give consideration to the key factors in the physical, physiological, social, psychological and skill development of athletes, and support them in attaining balance in their lives.

Goal/Target Setting

The athletes' development should be measured against the training programmes, and the coaching practice and the elite sports environment should be differentiated to meet the individual athlete's developmental needs.

The differences will be based on both long- and short-term goals, and will vary according to the age, gender and relative progression of the athlete.

Defining Success

Not all identified athletes will develop into high-performance/elite performers. It is important that participation, and not just winning, is reinforced at an early age. If athletes drop out, they clearly don't know how they will develop later.

The Value of Sport to Different Groups

Different ethnic and social groups have different opinions/values for sport, and this will impact on involvement and potential development. For example, how many parents actively encourage children into boxing, or have access to a horse and equestrian facilities?

Reasons for Participation in Sport

There are a number of reasons why sports participation is important:

- promoting healthy lifestyle
- improving self-esteem
- improving teamwork and cooperation
- risk taking/challenging yourself
- learning to set goals
- dealing with success and unsuccessful situations
- enjoyment and fun!

Self-perception and Impact on Athletes

There are two distinct poles here: some athletes feel better about themselves when they are performing better – their perceived athletic competence is higher. However, the athlete who places high value on winning and success (high expectations) can suffer if they are not performing as well as they want to.

Both of these can impact on the social aspects for children and adolescents: as their self-esteem develops, they can develop traits of confidence and independence, or become more sensitive to interpersonal differences. The commitment and dedication required to become an elite athlete leave limited time for relationships with peers; this can leave the young athlete excluded from their peer group.

Learning Environment

It is crucial to develop an environment where everyone feels they can contribute and have input at the appropriate time. This requires coaches to be knowledgeable, open-minded and flexible in their approach, and an athlete who trusts and feels able to talk to the coach. All parties have to be able to listen and receive constructive, honest feedback – whether it is positive or negative.

Key learning points 5

- Designing a talent-identification and development model is an extremely complex process and requires much planning.
- The aims and purposes of the programme must be well thought out, as they will determine the success of the programme and influence the format for delivery.

Student activity 20.7   ⏱ 60–90 mins   P7   M4   D2

You are working as part of the UK Sport talent development team and have been asked by an NGB to design a talent development programme. The age range they have asked you to include is 11–18 years. For each of the activities in your programme, explain and justify your choice of activities for the talent development programme. It might be a useful process to use a SWOT (strengths, weaknesses, opportunities, threats) analysis to help plan your programme.

STRENGTHS	WEAKNESSES
OPPORTUNITIES (What could you add to make the programme better?)	**THREATS** (What are the potential barriers to your programme's success?)

References

Balyi, I. (2004) *Long Term Athlete Development: Trainability in Childhood and Adolescence*, National Coaching Institute.

Brown, J. (2001) *Sports Talent: How to Identify and Develop Outstanding Athletes*, Human Kinetics.

Butler, R. (1998) Performance profiling: Assessing the way forward, in *Sports Psychology in Performance* (pp. 33–48), Butterworth-Heinemann.

Dick, F.W. (1997) *Sports Training Principles*, Black.

Fisher, R. and Bailey, R. (eds) (2008) *Perspectives: Volume 9. Talent Identification and Development: The Search for Sporting Excellence*, ICSSPE.

Gambetta, V. (2007) *Athletic Development: The Art and Science of Functional Sports Conditioning*, Human Kinetics.

Reilly, T., Williams, A.M. and Richardson, D. (2003) Identifying talented players, in *Science and Soccer* (Second Edition, pp. 307–26), Routledge.

Stafford, I. (2005) *Coaching for Long-Term Athlete Development: To Improve Participation and Performance in Sport*, Sports Coach UK.

Vaeyens, R., Lenoir, M., Williams, A.M. and Philippaerts, R.M. (2008) Talent identification and development programmes in sport: Current models and future directions, *Sports Medicine* 38 (9), 703–14.

Youth Sport Trust (2001) *The Young Athlete's Handbook*, Human Kinetics.

Useful websites

www.brianmac.co.uk/eval.htm

Provides details of how to evaluate and test sports performance

www.pponline.co.uk/encyc/sports-performance-analysis-coaching-and-training-39

Article detailing how sports analysis can help coaching and training

24: Physical Education & the Care of Children & Young People

24.1 Introduction

Physical education is a compulsory activity in the national curriculum. Children from the age of 5 to 16 will have PE lessons scheduled into their timetable. PE lessons include a variety of activities, such as games, gymnastics, athletics, swimming and racket sports. In these lessons, children work as both individuals and members of a team, and as such learn a variety of different skills as well as the importance of healthy, active lifestyles.

If you are thinking of working as a PE teacher, this unit will provide you with the basic theoretical knowledge and practical activities that are required for effective sports teaching as well as classroom management strategies.

The unit explores PE across the different Key Stages as well as the role and values of PE in a wider social context.

The importance of safeguarding the needs of children and young people in education is also examined, including the 'Every Child Matters: Change for Children' agenda, which will enable you to identify ways of safeguarding children and young people in the learning context.

By the end of this unit you should:

- know the structure of physical education within the curriculum
- understand the importance of physical education in society
- be able to structure a lesson of physical education
- know the responsibilities of those who work with children to safeguard and promote their welfare, and strategies for safeguarding children, young people and self.

Assessment and grading criteria

To achieve a PASS grade the evidence must show that the learner is able to:	To achieve a MERIT grade the evidence must show that, in addition to the pass criteria, the learner is able to:	To achieve a DISTINCTION grade the evidence must show that, in addition to the pass and merit criteria, the learner is able to:
P1 describe the structure of the physical education curriculum		
P2 describe the impact of stakeholder views on the development of the physical education curriculum		
P3 describe the ways in which the curriculum is implemented	**M1** explain the different ways that learning providers meet national curriculum requirements	
P4 explain the importance of physical education to children and young people's educational attainment		
P5 outline the importance of physical education to society in general		
P6 plan a lesson of physical education describing how learning is supported	**M2** plan a lesson of physical education explaining how learning is supported	**D1** plan a lesson of physical education analysing support for learning
P7 describe strategies for supporting the safety of children and young people		
P8 describe the legislation, policies and procedures that safeguard children and young people in a learning context	**M3** explain how procedures keep children, young people and those working with them safe.	**D2** evaluate procedures in terms of how they keep children, young people and those working with them safe.
P9 describe strategies to ensure own protection when working with children and young people.		

24.2 Physical Education and the National Curriculum

P1 **P2** **P3** **M1**

The national curriculum (NC) attempts to raise standards in education and sets out a range of learning experiences that the government has decided is essential for all young people in education.

The national curriculum is administered by the Qualifications and Curriculum Development Agency (QCDA), which is part of the Department for Children, Schools and Families (DCSF). The QCDA's main role and responsibility is to advise and support schools and colleges to deliver and develop the national curriculum, a variety of tests and a range of examinations.

Structure of the National Curriculum

Education in England, Wales and Northern Ireland is structured into Key Stages (see Table 20.1).

Physical education is a core subject at all Key Stages, which means it continues to be one of only five subjects that pupils of all abilities must pursue, from their entry into school at the age of five until the end of compulsory schooling at age 16.

Physical education: KS 1 ✓   KS 2 ✓   KS3 ✓   KS4 ✓

The education system in Scotland also makes physical education a compulsory subject at all stages. The structure of the Scottish curriculum runs from ages 3–18, and is organised into Early, First, Second, Third and Fourth stages.

Stakeholders in Education

The government and the QCDA make use of a large network of experts to advise them in educational matters and in the design of the national curriculum. These include people, groups and organisations with an interest in education, who are called 'stakeholders'.

Stakeholders might represent business, industry, commerce and universities, all areas into which young people may wish to progress when they leave compulsory education. These stakeholders are naturally keen to ensure that state education and the national curriculum provide all young people with the opportunities to develop the abilities and skills needed in modern life.

Sector Skills Councils (SSCs) are state-sponsored, employer-led organisations that cover specific economic sectors in the United Kingdom. They have four key goals:

- To reduce skills gaps and shortages
- To improve productivity
- To boost the skills of their sector workforces
- To improve learning supply.

Examples of stakeholders in physical education, sport and recreation include the following:

1 **SkillsActive**

This is an organisation that works across the UK to help the government achieve its key objective of developing a healthier, fitter nation.

'SkillsActive is committed to increasing the number of industry-recognised qualifications for the active leisure and learning sector. It aims to work with industry and higher education experts, partners and employers to develop tailor-made qualifications that will assist the growth of a highly committed and competent workforce. In doing so, SkillsActive aims to professionalise and upskill the sector in the run up to, and beyond, the London 2012 Olympic Games and Paralympic Games.'

Source: www.skillsactive.com

2 **National occupational standards**

Again led by employers, this is an example of an independent body that acts as a stakeholder in education. It states its main objectives as follows:

Key Stage	Year groups	Ages
Foundation Stage	Preschool—end of Reception Year	3–5
Key Stage 1	Years 1–2	5–7
Key Stage 2	Years 3–6	7–11
Key Stage 3	Years 7–9	11–14
Key Stage 4	Years 10–11	14–16

Table 24.1 Key Stages in education (England & Wales)

- Identify skills and knowledge needed for occupations
- Provide a reference to assess ability and training needs
- Identify and support career paths.

3   National governing bodies

National governing bodies (NGBs) are the organising bodies for individual sports. There are 130 national governing bodies of sport that are recognised by UK Sports Councils.

As sporting stakeholders, NGBs play a central part in the national drive to increase participation in sport. The opportunities and challenges of major forthcoming sporting events such as London 2012 and Glasgow 2014 are also a key focus for all sports.

Funded by Sport England, NGBs set the strategic direction for the development of their sport. These plans include Children and Young People plans (CYP) through which NGBs will deliver coaching courses for teachers and students.

NGBs also play an important role in supporting recent government initiatives, which influence curriculum design for PE.

4   Youth Sport Trust

The Youth Sport Trust is a charity that strives to improve the quality and quantity of PE and sport for young people. It operates throughout the UK and works closely with the UK Sports Councils.

Its core work can be divided into a number of key areas:

- Raising the standards of PE and school sport
- Improving educational standards through sport
- Getting more young people involved in sport
- Creating opportunities for young leaders and volunteers
- Supporting sporting talent in young people.

Fig 24.1 Children enjoying exercise

Physical Education in the National Curriculum

Children are required to demonstrate skills, knowledge and understanding in a variety of physical activity areas, which include games, dance, gymnastics, athletics, swimming and outdoor and adventurous activities.

The national curriculum sets out attainment targets, which describe expected levels of performance at the end of each Key Stage.

Pupil progress is measured by teachers, based on four strands of assessment:

- Acquiring and developing skills
- Selecting and applying skills, tactics and compositional ideas
- Evaluating and improving performance
- Knowledge and understanding of fitness and health.

CASE STUDY OF A GOVERNMENT INITIATIVE

PHYSICAL EDUCATION AND SPORT STRATEGY FOR YOUNG PEOPLE (PESSYP)

The Youth Sport Trust plays a central role in supporting the Department for Children, Schools and Families (DCSF) and the Department for Culture, Media and Sport (DCMS) in the delivery of the PE and Sport Strategy for Young People. The strategy sets out how the Olympic legacy aim to get more children and young people taking part in high-quality PE and sport will be reached, through the delivery of the 'five-hour offer'.

The Youth Sport Trust and Sport England are working with the DCSF and the DCMS on ways to help local delivery partners offer all young people aged 5 to 16 the opportunity to participate in five hours a week of PE and sport (three hours for 16 to 19-year-olds). The first outcome of this work is the new 'Guide to Delivering the Five-Hour Offer', a document which outlines the vision for the strategy and the five-hour offer in particular.

PESSYP has two main aims:

1   To improve the quality and quantity of curriculum PE in schools.

2   To improve the quality and quality of sport accessible and available to young people in schools, colleges and the wider community.

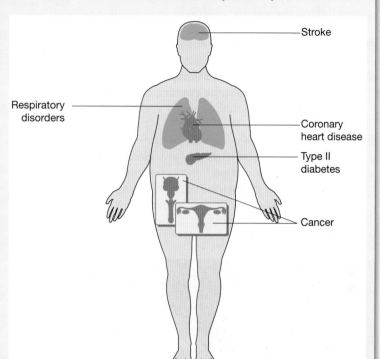

Fig 24.2 Medical conditions brought on by obesity

'All children and young people aged between 5–16 years should have the opportunity to participate in five hours of sport per week by 2011 (including two hours of high quality PE and sport at school).'

Source: www.youthsporttrust.org

The 'five-hour offer' is to be developed by School Sports Partnerships and local club links in the following way:

Two hours of curriculum PE + one hour of school sport + two hours of community sport = <u>five hours</u>

PE must provide support for whole school delivery of two key initiatives:

• Every Child Matters (ECM)

• Personal, Learning and Thinking Skills (PLTS).

Key Stage Implementation

Early Years Foundation Stage (ages 3–5)

Physical development is the main objective at this stage.

Very young children use play to develop physical skills and coordination, and to learn how to be creative and how to share and cooperate in social groupings.

Key Stages 1 and 2 (ages 5–11)

PE in primary schools aims for pupils to enjoy being active and to learn new skills as a foundation for 'physical literacy'.

At this stage, children will:

● Enjoy being active, showing what they can do

● Practise new skills across a range of activities that should include dance, gymnastics, games,

351

swimming, athletics and outdoor and adventurous activities

● Learn consistency by repeating their movements and linking their skills until their performance is clearer, more accurate and controlled over time

● Pace themselves in challenges in activities such as swimming and athletic activities

● Use their creativity in performing dances, making up their own games, planning gymnastic sequences, and responding to problem-solving and challenge activities

● Know how to improve aspects of the quality of their work, using information provided by the teacher and information and communication technology (ICT) opportunities, and increasingly help themselves and others perform effectively

● Know why activity is important to their health and well-being.

Fig 24.3 Exercising in water

Key Stages 3 and 4

At Key Stages 3 and 4, PE is currently undergoing changes brought about by the introduction of the revised national curriculum (2008–2011).

Greater Flexibility and Coherence

To give schools greater flexibility to tailor learning to their learners' needs, there is less prescribed subject content in the new programmes of study. Pupils will still be taught essential subject knowledge. However, the new curriculum balances subject knowledge with the key concepts and processes that underlie the discipline of each subject.

Key Concepts

There are a number of key concepts that now underpin the study of PE:

● Competence
● Performance
● Creativity
● Healthy and active lifestyles.

Key processes: these are the essential skills and processes in PE that pupils need to learn to make progress:

● Developing skills in physical activity
● Making and applying decisions
● Developing physical and mental capacity
● Evaluating and improving
● Making informed choices about healthy, active lifestyles.

Range and Content

The study of PE should include activities that cover at least four of the following:

1 Outwitting opponents, as in games activities.
2 Accurate replication of actions, phrases and sequences, as in gymnastic activities.
3 Exploring and communicating ideas, concepts and emotions, as in dance activities.
4 Performing at maximum levels in relation to speed, height, distance, strength or accuracy, as in athletic activities.
5 Identifying and solving problems to overcome challenges of an adventurous nature, as in life saving and personal survival in swimming and outdoor activities.
6 Exercising safely and effectively to improve health and well-being, as in fitness and health activities.

Curriculum Opportunities

The curriculum should provide opportunities for pupils to:

● Get involved in a broad range of different activities that, in combination, develop the whole body
● Experience a range of roles within a physical activity

- Specialise in specific activities and roles
- Follow pathways to other activities in and beyond school
- Perform as an individual, in a group or as part of a team in formal competitions or performances to audiences beyond the class
- Use ICT as an aid to improving performance and tracking progress
- Make links between PE and other subjects and areas of the curriculum.

Qualifications in PE at Key Stage 4

Most pupils now are able to gain some form of qualification or accreditation in Years 10 and 11. Some qualifications have an academic focus, while others take a more vocational approach. All provide the basis for future study and progression. The most popular routes to PE and sport qualifications at Key Stage 4 are:

- GCSE PE and Dance
- Short Course PE
- BTEC First Certificate in Sports Leadership
- BTEC First Diploma in Sports Science
- 14–19 Diploma in Sport and Active Leisure
- Level 1 Sports Leadership award
- OCR Nationals in Sport.

Criteria and Specifications

Examination specifications describe the syllabus content, aims, assessment methods and objectives and how the qualification is graded. Specifications are designed by examination boards rather than the QCA. Each examination board offers a slightly different specification, which gives schools and colleges a choice of qualification to best suit their learners.

Key learning points I

- Purpose and structure of the national curriculum.
- Stakeholders have a significant influence on curriculum design and content.
- Programme of study for PE at each Key Stage.
- PESSYP as a government initiative.
- There have been recent changes to PE at Key Stages 3 and 4.
- There is now a choice of qualification routes available at Key Stage 4.

Q Quick quiz I

1 What do the initials 'DCFS' and 'QCA' stand for?
2 Steve is 8 and Lucy is 15. Which Key Stages are they in?
3 Summarise the main objectives of 'SkillsActive'.
4 Describe the twin aims of the PESSYP strategy.
5 At Key Stages 3 and 4, 'games' has changed to 'outwitting opponents, as in games activities'. Explain possible reasons for this change.

Student activity 24.1 — 90–120 mins — P1 P2 P3 M1

Physical education plays an important part in every child's development and is a compulsory subject in the national curriculum.

Task 1

Prepare a leaflet that describes the structure of the physical education curriculum. You should include details of the Early Years Foundation Stage and Key Stages 1–4.

Task 2

- Draw a spider diagram to show the different stakeholders involved in the development of the physical education curriculum.
- Prepare a written report that describes the impact of these stakeholders on the development of physical education in the national curriculum.

Task 3

Prepare and deliver a PowerPoint presentation that describes and explains the different ways that the curriculum is implemented by different learning providers.

24.3 The Importance of Physical Education in Society

Importance of Curriculum PE

Physical education is a vital element in a comprehensive, well-balanced curriculum and can be a major contributing factor in the development of an individual in all aspects of life: physical, emotional, mental and social.

Through a high-quality physical education experience, an individual has the opportunity to:

● Understand the importance of obtaining and maintaining a high level of physical fitness
● Participate in a wide variety of physical activities, which helps to maintain an active and healthy lifestyle
● Become a skilful, intelligent and independent performer and leader
● Develop fair play, teamwork and socially desirable behaviour
● Gain in self-confidence and self-esteem.

Key term

Physical literacy: having the motivation, confidence, physical competence, knowledge and understanding to maintain physical activity throughout life. This definition reflects the learning outcomes of high-quality teaching and learning in PE.

Physical literacy and an active lifestyle remain the cornerstone of the PE objectives for all pupils, but so much more can be achieved with a broad and balanced curriculum.

Research findings show that pupils striving for academic success at school are far more likely to succeed if they take a full and active part in PE lessons.

● Regular participation in physical education, even if you are not naturally good at games, can make a big difference to academic results at all Key Stages.
● Research shows PE can improve literacy, numeracy and technology skills.
● PE sessions help youngsters improve their communication skills, which in turn helps in the classroom. Pupils are also using technology and IT to support and enhance their work in PE lessons.

Head teachers also report that there has been a noticeable improvement in pupils' key personal, social and learning skills.

Primary school head teachers speak enthusiastically about the positive impact PE can have on pupils' behaviour and their attitudes to work.

High-quality PE will support pupils' cognitive development so that they improve at:

● Creating conditions for personal success
● Taking more responsibility for own learning
● Thinking for themselves
● Solving problems.

Summary

High-quality and enjoyable physical education will enable children to develop a range of abilities:

● **Technical** ability, in a range of skills
● **Physiological** ability, in terms of fitness
● **Social skills,** in group and team settings
● **Cognitive** ability, in terms of thinking skills and problem solving.

Importance of Extracurricular PE and Sport

The PE and Sport Strategy for Young People (PESSYP) aims to offer children and young people in England at least five hours of high-quality PE and sport every week (for those aged 5–16 years). This begins in school with curriculum PE and by participating in after-school clubs.

By building on and improving the quality of existing PE and school sport opportunities available to young people, it is hoped that an increasing proportion of children will be guided into local sports, physical recreation and physical activity, both in school and in the local community. The strategy aims to promote a culture that enables and values the full involvement of every child and young person, whether as a competitor, volunteer, official or organiser. It is hoped that this will lead to a significant increase in the number of young people taking part in high-quality club sport on a regular basis.

The strategy is delivered on a local level through collaboration between schools, school sport partnerships, county sports partnerships (CSPs) and NGB-accredited sports clubs.

Extracurricular activities have been identified as a rich source of personal development for children and young people.

Benefits of regular involvement in physical activity and sport outside the curriculum can help young people to:

● Develop various sports skills

- Develop skills needed to socialise with their peers as well as adults
- Develop independence and confidence
- Develop a sense of achievement, which helps develop a positive self-image
- Develop leadership skills and qualities
- Learn how to cooperate and compete
- Develop agility, coordination, endurance, flexibility, speed and strength
- Develop the ability to make decisions and accept responsibilities
- Develop an interest in continuing sports participation as an adult.

However, the progression from school to club and community sport can be a daunting step for many young people. Traditionally, there has been a sharp decline in participation in sport and physical recreation in the 16–19 age group.

Crucial support is needed from schools, community sport and parents if this decline is to be arrested. Equally, this is an issue that both central and local government take very seriously and spend considerable time and money on.

Importance of PE and Sport in Society

The government believes that high-quality PE and sport:

- Raises standards
- Improves the health of the nation
- Helps ensure that the UK competes successfully on the world stage.

Sporting Benefits

Success in sport has a positive effect on the nation.

- We feel good when we win trophies and competitions. This 'feel good' factor is reputed to help us forget other problems, and can bring together different groups in society. This is known as 'social cohesion'.
- More people playing sport at foundation or 'grass roots' level means there is a larger pool of talent available for talent identification and future development.

Social Benefits

The social benefits of participation in sport are as follows:

- Safer communities with reduced crime rates
- Stronger social networks (social cohesion)
- Purposeful activity improves quality of life.

Economic Benefits

- Healthy and active population.
- Reduction in healthcare costs.
- Increased productivity at work.
- Productive use of leisure time stimulates economic demand.

Mass participation in sport and active leisure is an important aspect of government policy for the sporting, social and economic benefits shown above.

A healthy, active population will cost less, spend more on leisure, develop sporting and artistic interests, and generally cause far fewer problems.

Just what every government wants!

Key learning points 2

- PE promotes physical literacy.
- PE can promote higher attainment in a variety of abilities.
- PE and an active and healthy lifestyle provide a number of health benefits.
- The government values PE and sport for a variety of reasons.

Q Quick quiz 2

1 Explain the term 'physical literacy' in your own words.
2 Give examples of how PE and sport has helped you develop.
3 Describe how PE and sport can promote leadership.
4 Outline two reasons why the government believes in PE and sport.
5 Explain possible reasons for lower participation in the 16–19 age group.

Student activity 24.2 60–90 mins P4 P5

Physical education provides many health, education and social benefits and is encouraged by many different organisations.

Task 1

In pairs, discuss how physical education has benefited you in your:

• Educational attainment

• Role in society.

Task 2

Design a poster with illustrations and text that:

• Explains the importance of physical education to children and young people's educational attainment

• Outlines the importance of physical education to society in general.

24.4 Structure of a Physical Education Lesson

There is a saying: 'Fail to plan, plan to fail'. This is very true in teaching and very true in teaching physical education!

This section will take you through the process involved in planning a physical education lesson.

Key Terms in Lesson Planning

Teaching is the formal process and describes what the teacher says or does.

Learning takes place when the pupils can do, know or understand something that previously they could not achieve or did not know.

Learning outcomes are what it is intended that pupils will achieve, know and understand at the end of each lesson.

Assessment is the gathering of evidence to show pupil progress.

Normal Structure of Lessons

• A **lesson plan** sets out the objectives and content of one lesson.

• A **lesson** is a single part of a unit of work.

• A **unit of work** is part of a programme of study.

• **Programmes of study** make up each Key Stage of the national curriculum.

Each individual lesson contains key elements:

• **Purpose** – what are your intentions for this lesson?

• **Prior learning** – how can you build on learning in previous lessons?

• **Learning outcomes** – what do you want pupils to achieve, learn, and understand?

• **Pupil activities** – how pupils will achieve the learning outcomes.

• **Teaching points** – guidance, feedback and advice for pupils.

• **Assessment** – did most pupils achieve the learning outcomes?

• **Evaluation** – was the lesson successful? Why? Why not?

Every class is a group of individual children. Each pupil is an individual with different needs and learning preferences and each pupil will respond differently to learning situations. Successful teachers can vary their teaching styles and are able to adapt the activities and resources used in lessons to meet the needs of individual pupils or groups of pupils.

Successful lessons are normally introduced by teachers or adults, who guide the direction and pace of the lesson, while the activities and lesson content are based on child-centred principles and appropriate learning outcomes.

Successful lessons are characterised more by learning than by teaching. Skilled teachers will maximise pupils' learning potential by making use of a range of strategies such as:

• Inclusion

• Differentiation

• Questioning rather than telling

• Progression through structured learning situations

• Observation

• Individual feedback

• Praise and encouragement.

Key terms

Inclusion: this ensures equal opportunity for all pupils, irrespective of ability.

Differentiation: making use of a variety of teaching and learning styles and tasks to meet the needs of all pupils.

Lesson Planning in PE

Lesson planning in PE shares the same basic structure and characteristics as all other subjects in the school curriculum. However, on account of its practical nature, there are other considerations and safeguards that teachers of PE must include in all lesson plans.

- **Health & safety.** All schools are required to have 'risk assessment' policies in place – especially important in practical subjects like PE.
- **Special needs and medical conditions**.
- **Parental consent** is often required for lessons such as swimming, as well as after-school clubs and off-site activities.
- **First-aid resources.**
- **Appropriate kit and equipment.**

The structure of a PE lesson often follows a traditional pattern:

- **Warm-up** – teacher-directed or pupil-led
- **Specific focus** – skill-based or situation-based
- **Main activity** – appropriate event, game, etc.
- **Cool-down and conclusion.**

This structure concentrates on pupil activities, but there is far more to lesson planning than just the activities. Lesson planning takes time, especially for people new to teaching. You will find detailed examples of lesson planning templates with accompanying notes on below and on pages 358–359.

When you have the opportunity to teach a lesson or coach a session, try to make use of the **STEP** formula, which aims to manipulate four key factors to provide the best possible conditions for learners.

The STEP Formula

- **S** stands for **SPACE** – how can you make best use of space?
- **T** stands for **TASK** – are the tasks appropriate for pupils?
- **E** stands for **EQUIPMENT** – is the equipment suitable for pupils?
- **P** stands for **PUPILS** – how can pupils be best grouped?

Lesson Plan – Part One

SUBJECT:	CLASS:	DATE:

PURPOSE OF LESSON
These are your **teaching intentions** for this lesson,
e.g. to introduce a new topic or skills to consolidate previous learning.

PRIOR LEARNING (from previous lesson evaluations and pupil assessments)
How does information you have obtained about **pupils' learning** in previous lessons inform the planning of this lesson?
Teacher action (e.g. strategies for pupil and class management, choice of teaching and learning strategies)
How will this inform the planning of this lesson?

LEARNING OUTCOMES FOR THIS LESSON
State what you intend pupils to learn.
There might be one key learning objective or there might be a number of them.
You may need to identify different learning objectives for different pupils.
In addition to the main PE subject focus, there may be cross-curricular learning objectives, e.g. a maths learning objective or a social objective, such as teamwork and cooperation.

CLASSROOM OBJECTIVES
Learning objectives expressed in a form that **could be shared with pupils.**

SUCCESS CRITERIA
These relate to the learning objectives. They should provide evidence of learning.
Express them in a form that could be shared with children.

MONITORING AND ASSESSMENT
Tell pupils who, what, how and when you will be monitoring pupils' progress and assessing their learning during this lesson, e.g. 'I will assess your performance as a defender; I will question the whole class during the plenary'.

KEY VOCABULARY
Explain the **key subject-specific vocabulary** that the children will need or you intend to introduce/consolidate.

RESOURCES AND PREPARATION (including health and safety considerations)
List resources, including ICT, needed by (a) you, (b) the pupils, and (c) any other adults.
State how these will be organised.
State any safety precautions that are necessary.

Lesson Plan – Part Two

LESSON STRUCTURE			
PHASE TIMING	**TEACHER'S ACTIONS**	**PUPIL ACTIVITIES**	**RESOURCES**
Introduction Estimated time:	State how you will introduce the lesson, e.g. by referring to the lesson objectives. State how you will introduce activities that the pupils are going to carry out. Main teaching points/any questions you might ask. Giving instructions (state key ideas). Explain what comes next.	Explain how pupils (individuals, groups and/or whole class) will be involved. Identify opportunities for pupil contributions, discussion, questions and assessment. Indicate how teaching and learning will be assessed.	Identify resource needs.
Main Activities Estimated time:	This part of the lesson should normally take the greatest proportion of time. You may decide to work with small groups or the whole class. Show how you will: • Monitor their progress to ensure that all are learning • Ensure that all pupils are being challenged and that interest/pace is maintained • Ensure that all pupils understand what they are doing • Decide when to make whole-class interventions • Provide formative feedback • Set targets for individuals and groups for the remainder of this part of the lesson • Assess pupils' learning.	Show how pupils will be organised – individually, in pairs or in groups? Plan activities for pupils to facilitate the learning objectives. Show how these activities will permit inclusion and differentiation.	Identify resources needed for different activities.
Plenary or Conclusion Estimated time:	Time must be planned to allow every lesson to be brought to an appropriate conclusion: • To check and reinforce what has been learned (with reference to the learning objectives) • To question/assess the pupils about what they have learnt • To praise and give feedback • To preview next lesson • To allow time for tidying up and changing.	Indicate how pupils (individuals, groups and/or whole class) will be involved – targeting specific individuals where necessary. Give opportunities for pupil discussion, questions, and self-assessment.	

Lesson Plan – Part Three

LESSON OUTCOMES AND EVALUATION

PUPIL ASSESSMENT NOTES
Make brief notes about any significant pupil achievements or difficulties.
You may refer to the class as a whole or to individuals.

NEXT STEPS for support of pupils' learning (based on pupil assessment notes)
How might you need to change your planning for the whole class or for individuals?

(Show this in later lesson plans)

LESSON EVALUATION
This involves you analysing your performance as a teacher to identify how you can improve.
Evaluation should focus on the reasons for both successes and problems encountered in the lesson.
How well did children learn, and how effective were you as a teacher?
In order to improve, it is important that you analyse <u>why</u> some aspects were or were not successful, rather than simply describing what happened.
The key question is: **'How can I help children to learn more effectively?'**
Evaluate specific aspects of your teaching. For example:
• Introductions, use of resources
• Questioning skills, feedback to children
• Monitoring individuals' work
• Behaviour management, pupil attainment, etc.

NEXT STEPS for you as teacher (based on your lesson evaluation)
Evaluation is more than a purely descriptive process; it should include proposals for action in the immediate future.
What are you going to improve or adapt?
Changes should be evident in later lesson plans.

359

Key learning points 3

- Know the main terms used in lesson planning: purpose, prior learning, learning outcomes, pupil activities, teaching points, assessment and evaluation.
- Know the importance of inclusion and individual needs.
- Specific considerations in planning PE lessons include: health and safety, special needs and medical conditions, parental consent, first-aid resources, and appropriate kit and equipment.
- The structure of a PE lesson follows a traditional pattern: warm-up, specific focus, main activity and cool-down.

Q Quick quiz 3

1 Explain the difference between 'learning outcomes' and 'pupil activities'.
2 What does STEP stand for?
3 Outline three planning considerations specific to PE.
4 Explain the following forms of assessment: teacher assessment, peer assessment and self-assessment.

Student activity 24.3 60–90 mins P6 M2 D1

You have seen the outline plans for a physical education lesson and may one day be expected to plan your own lesson, either as a teacher or on work placement.

Task 1

Design and prepare a physical education lesson for a sport and Key Stage of your choice.

Task 2

Once your lesson plan is complete, write a report that describes, explains and analyses how learning is supported.

24.5 The Responsibilities of Those who Work with Children to Safeguard and Promote their Welfare

Safeguarding Children and Young People

Children have many needs to help ensure they grow up to be happy and well-balanced adults. School, family, and the community in which they grow up are the three major contexts in which children grow and develop. Children learn from all of these environments.

Children need to have some form of education throughout their childhood. This will usually start at home and then progress into pre-school playgroups and then into school. Both physical and social skills are learnt through teaching and through play. The ability to catch and throw a ball is a physical skill that takes time to learn. This is because children need to build 'motor programmes' of performing that activity. This means that a child's brain needs to be able to send the right signals to move the appropriate body parts in the right way in order to perform an action. The more a child practises the activity, the stronger the motor programme becomes and the more likely the child is to catch or throw the ball effectively.

Research has also shown that regular sports participation is strongly linked to improvements in pupil behaviour, school attendance and attainment. Sports participation has also been shown to help children to develop social skills, including teamwork and leadership skills.

Sporting activities allow children to mix with different children. Rather than always spending their time with their 'best friend', children will be placed into different sports teams and will 'mark' different players, which will help them to mix with and to meet new friends. This can help to break down barriers between individuals and groups of young people.

Sports participation can also help children to develop self-esteem and increase their self-confidence. This will help them to stand up for themselves and will therefore make them less likely to be bullied or feel pressured to take part in things they do not want to do – for example, some children may feel pressured to smoke because their friends smoke. Sports participation will also give children a place to go in their free time, which helps to combat anti-social behaviour. Taking part in sports can also help to increase the safety of children – for example, children who are taught how to swim will be less likely to drown.

Sports participation will also help children to remain healthy: it will help to strengthen the immune system, reduce the risk of the child becoming obese, and reduce the risk of coronary heart disease and cancers in later life. Taking part in high-quality and fun sports from an early age will motivate the child to develop good habits, which they will hopefully continue with into their adult life.

Social and Psychological Effects

Children's participation in sport is strongly believed to help them learn how to socialise with other people and it also introduces them to the values and beliefs of society. The basis for this belief is the fact that sport introduces children to other children, rules, social values and the desire to improve their own skills in order to stay in the game and enjoy it. Children will learn to respect other children through sports participation. Research has shown that children automatically admire others who have a greater sporting ability than themselves; however, a good teacher or coach will ensure that all participating children with differing abilities are accepted and respected.

Other valuable social skills can be learnt through sport – these include leadership, communication, cooperation, independence and confidence. There has also been a significant amount of research that implies sports participation can help children to perform better academically.

Sports participation will help children to deal with failure. In most sports, there are winners and losers, and a good coach or teacher will help to ensure children are placed on teams that will have their fair share of wins and losses. This will allow children to increase their confidence and self-esteem when on the wining team and then to accept failure and develop good sportsmanship skills when they are on the losing team.

Legislation, Policies and Procedures

All children, whatever their circumstances or abilities, should be able to participate in and enjoy physical education and sport. A number of laws and regulations are in place to help ensure all children have access to appropriately run sporting activities.

Every Child Matters

This is a government scheme devised to support children. Its main aims are to ensure that all children should have the support they need to:

- **Be healthy** – this includes physical health, sexual health, mental health, emotional health
- **Stay safe** – safe from abuse or neglect, accidental death, bullying, discrimination, anti-social behaviour
- **Enjoy and achieve** – attend and enjoy school, personal and social development, meet national standards or higher
- **Make a positive contribution** – support their community and environment, adopt positive behaviour in and out of school and develop self-confidence
- **Achieve economic well-being** – progress into further education, employment or training, and live in decent homes with access to transport and material goods.

(Adapted from www.everychildmatters.gov.uk, 30.11.06)

The UN Convention on the Rights of the Child

This is a set of legal instructions that promotes the rights of children. Although all humans have rights, children are more vulnerable than adults so they have this set of rights that takes into account their particular right for protection. It recognises the fact that children are human beings with their own rights and responsibilities that will develop as the child gets older. The convention promotes the fact that all children, regardless of race, gender, religion, ability or wealth, should be entitled to a basic quality of life, including shelter and food, and that children should all be encouraged to reach their full potential.

This convention means that any organisation working with children or providing services for children will be able to share information and work together to protect children. In 2005, a children's Commissioner for England was appointed, which means that children's views will be sought and considered in relation to the organisations that work with them.

United Nations Children's Fund (UNICEF)

This is an international charity that promotes the protection of children's rights, and campaigns to help all children receive their basic needs and reach their full potential.

Playing for Success

Another government initiative, from the Department for Children, Schools and Families, is called Playing for Success. This has helped to set up after-school clubs and weekend clubs held within top sports clubs. Through a sports medium, these clubs help to teach numeracy, literacy and ICT.

The Children Act 1989

This act puts the child first by promoting and safeguarding their welfare. It sets out rules and regulations for how a child should be treated, which any person working with children should adhere to.

The Child Protection in Sport Unit (CPSU)

This unit was founded in 2001 as a partnership between the NSPCC and Sport England. The unit was set up in response to evidence that sport can provide access for a person to abuse children. As coaches often work with children over a long period of time, trust develops between the coach and the child. Research indicates that the majority of abuse is committed by a person who the child knows and has come to trust. Therefore, the CPSU has been put in place to help create a safe sporting environment for children. This is done through the promotion of good practice and by encouraging people to confront practice that is harmful to children.

It is the responsibility of any person caring for or working with children, both parents and coaches, to ensure they are taking into account the child or children's rights and helping them to fulfil their potential. Some parents or coaches may push a child to compete and train when the child is either not interested or not physically able to cope with the regime. This would be considered a form of abuse as the adults are pushing the child into doing things that they do not want to do. It may also give the child a 'win at all costs' attitude, which could result in the child becoming aggressive and prone to foul play in their sport or even taking performance-enhancing drugs – all of which turn sports participation into a negative experience.

Safeguarding Self

Good Practice

In almost every sporting situation, children will look to their sports leader as their source of inspiration and knowledge. Children will frequently copy their instructor so it is imperative that the sports leader behaves in a suitable manner that would be appropriate for a child's role model. A sports leader should ensure that they encourage winning but do not encourage children to adopt a 'win at all costs' attitude. Children need to learn to lose with good grace and develop sportsmanship behaviour.

A person working with children should always follow these basic guidelines:

- Ensure they work within the bounds of applicable codes of practice
- Maintain safe and secure sporting environments
- Establish good working relationships with the children and their parents
- Control the behaviour of participants.

A sports leader should also be aware of the rights and needs of children; these are detailed in the section entitled 'The UN Convention on the Rights of the Child' (on page 361) and in the following pieces of information.

Good Practice Policy

A number of laws have been passed and agencies set up to promote the safety and welfare of children. Any person working with children should be aware of the relevant acts and agencies so that they can ensure they are working within the law and know how to get help and advice should they need it.

Recruitment

Any person recruited to work with children should have a CRB check prior to any contact with children. A CRB check will find out if a person has had any prior convictions, has been cautioned, has been given a reprimand or has been given a warning for a criminal offence.

In line with 'Child Protection: Preventing Unsuitable People from Working with Children in the Education Service' (2002), any person deemed inappropriate from the CRB check should not be employed to work with children.

Recognising Signs of Neglect and Abuse

Child abuse can take many different forms, but it can basically be defined as any form of physical, emotional or sexual mistreatment or lack of care that leads to injury, harm or distress. Most people responsible for abusing a child are in a position of trust and are known by the child and the family. Abusers can be male or female adults, or other young people. Any person under the age of 18 is considered to be a child; if they are suffering from any kind of abuse, you should have an awareness of the different types of abuse and the signs to look out for – very few children will admit to suffering from some form of abuse.

The main types of child abuse are:

● Physical abuse
● Sexual abuse
● Emotional abuse
● Neglect
● Bullying.

Physical Abuse

Physical abuse is where a person physically hurts or injures a child. A syndrome called Munchausen's syndrome by proxy is classed as physical abuse.

In sports, a coach may force a child to train or compete when they are physically not up to it, or give the child drugs to enhance their sporting ability; these are both forms of physical abuse.

Sexual Abuse

Sexual abuse is where a person uses children to meet their own sexual needs. This includes any form of sexual physical contact, showing children pornography or talking to them in a sexual manner. Many coaches will make physical contact with the children they are coaching in order to help them with their techniques or ensure their safety. It is imperative that coaches do their very best to ensure that the children are happy with this handling and that all contact is entirely appropriate.

Emotional Abuse

Emotional abuse is the consistent emotional ill-treatment of a child. This may involve telling the child that they are worthless, inadequate or unloved, or shouting and taunting the child, which may well result in severe and long-lasting adverse effects on the child's emotional development. Emotional abuse can also take the form of having greater expectations for a child than are appropriate for their age and ability. In sport, a coach could be guilty of emotional abuse if they constantly criticise the child, are sarcastic to the child or bully them.

Neglect

Neglect is when a parent or carer does not meet a child's basic physical and/or psychological needs so that it could result in the child suffering from ill-health or impaired development. Examples of neglect include inadequate provision of love, affection, food, shelter, clothing and medical care. Failing to protect a child from physical harm or danger is also a form of neglect. In sport, examples of how a coach could be guilty of neglect are if they do not ensure that the children are safe or if the environment is too hot or too cold.

Bullying

Younger people are often the perpetrators of bullying. Bullying can be verbal or physical and usually takes place over a period of time. This form of abuse can have a huge impact on a child's life and there have even been cases of children taking their own lives rather than face their bullies again.

A sports leader working with a group of children should make it explicit from the start that they will not tolerate any form of bullying and that it is the responsibility of every person to ensure that bullying does not happen. If any child is aware of any bullying, they must be instructed to tell the sports leader immediately. Some sports leaders discuss with the children what they think bullying is and then draw up some conclusions so that all the children know how they are expected to behave with one another.

If bullying has taken place, a sports leader must find out the facts and individually talk to the bully(ies) and the victim(s). They should then take appropriate action – this should be detailed in the facility's policies and guidelines. If the bullying was a one-off incident and there is more than one bully, it may then be appropriate to break up the group dynamics and split the bullies into different groups – many groups of bullies lose their confidence if they are not with their friends.

Bullying should always be dealt with swiftly and effectively, otherwise the bullies may gain confidence and it could become harder to put a stop to the bullying.

Effects of Abuse

Any child who has suffered abuse in the past or is currently suffering from abuse will usually experience long-term physical and/or emotional, sometimes life-changing, effects as a direct result of that abuse. Extreme cases of child abuse may result in the death of that child. All forms of abuse usually leave a child with psychological, health and/or developmental difficulties.

Many children are left with feelings of low self-esteem and may also wet the bed and have frequent bad dreams. Some children develop a range of anti-social and/or self-destructive behaviours in an attempt to try to cope with the abuse. They may be excessively aggressive to other children or bully them; alternatively, they may be very withdrawn and avoid communication and friendships with other children.

A child that is experiencing chronic abuse can experience behavioural changes. They may be easily startled and overreact to loud noises or a person shouting and sounding cross. Some children start to harm themselves as this somehow helps them to deal with the abuse they are receiving. Others may drink excessive amounts of alcohol or take drugs in an attempt to deal with the abuse they have received.

Signs of Abuse

A sports leader can help to keep children and young people safe by watching for unexpected changes in their appearance and behaviour. A child subjected to some form of abuse may show some of the following signs.

- A change in their behaviour. For example, a bubbly happy child may suddenly or gradually become quiet and withdrawn.
- Distrust of a particular person.
- A sudden inability to concentrate or performance declines for no apparent reason.
- Refusal to attend school or club.
- Has no close friends.
- Refusal to get changed in front of other people, or wants to keep covered up even in warm weather.
- Inappropriate sexual awareness or behaviour for their age.
- Some form of injury on parts of the body that are not usually injured. For example, it is common for children to have cuts and bruises on their knees from falling over; however, it is unusual to have injuries on other parts of the body such as the stomach, chest or back.
- An unsatisfactory explanation for an injury, e.g. the child has a black eye and bruising to the chest and they say they walked into a door.
- Significant weight gain or weight loss over a short period of time.
- Poor personal hygiene.
- Constant hunger.
- Extremely passive or extremely aggressive.
- Discomfort in or near the genital area – this could be observed from an inability to perform a sporting technique because of discomfort in the genital area.

However, if a child is exhibiting some or all of these signs it does not necessarily mean that they are being abused – there may be another explanation. Alternatively, a child that is being abused or who has been abused may not show any of these signs.

Course of Action

If you are working as a sports leader and you have any reason to believe a child is being abused, you must take action. The organisation you are working in should have clear policies and guidelines on how to deal with this situation.

If the child is keen to talk to you, the best thing that you can do is to follow these guidelines.

- Give them your full attention and listen carefully.
- Tell the child that you will not be able to keep what they have said to you secret but that you will only tell people who are going to make their situation better and, if appropriate, that these people will help to stop the 'bad' things happening to them.
- Ensure that you respond to what the child says with sensitivity.
- Encourage the child to talk, e.g. ask 'Do you want to tell me about this?' Do not put any pressure on the child to talk to you.
- Keep calm and try not to appear shocked. You may find what the child is saying upsetting but you should do your best to keep listening.
- Do not attempt to make any form of contact with the alleged abuser.
- If you believe the child's safety is in imminent danger, you should alert your sports facility's child welfare person and either they or you should contact the police or social services to take further action and help to ensure the health and welfare of the child.

When the child has finished talking to you, you should write a detailed account of what was said. If your centre has incident report forms, then this would be appropriate documentation to record the discussion on. If no incident report form is available, an example of an incident report form is shown in Figure 24.10; you could copy and use this.

The report should remain confidential and only the people who need to know this information should be given access to it in order to help protect the child.

Sports facility: _____

Your name: _____

Your position: _____

Contact number: _____

Child's name: _____

Child's address: _____

_____

Child's date of birth: _____

Parents'/carers' names and address: _____

_____

Date and time of any incident: _____

Your observations or details as reported to you: _____

_____

What the child said and what you said: _____

_____

If you are passing on someone else's concerns, record their name, address, position and contact number:

_____

_____

Action taken so far: _____

External agencies contacted (date and time):

Police – yes/no

If yes – which: _____

Name and contact number: _____

Details of advice received: _____

_____

Social services – yes/no

If yes – which: _____

Name and contact number: _____

Details of advice received: _____

Signature: _____

Print name: _____

Date: _____

Source: Adapted from www.nspcc.org.uk

Fig 24.4 A child protection incident report form

Key learning points 4

- The main types of child abuse are: physical abuse, sexual abuse, emotional abuse, neglect and bullying.
- People who abuse children are often people who the child and/or family trust.
- A child suffering from abuse may exhibit some or none of the typical signs of abuse.
- Any information a child discloses regarding abuse should be documented on an incident report form and reported to the appropriate people.
- If a child is deemed to be in imminent danger, immediate appropriate action should be carried out.
- Bullying should be dealt with swiftly and effectively.

Q Quick quiz 4

1 What are the basic needs of a child?
2 What are the rights of a child?
3 Which organisations promote the rights of a child?
4 How does sports participation develop a child's social and psychological skills?
5 What agencies have been set up to promote the health and safety of children in sport?
6 How should a person respond if an abused child confides in them?
7 What course of action should a person take if a child has told them that they are being abused?

Student activity 24.4 120–150mins P7 P8 P9 M3 D2

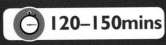

When working with children and young people, you will need to be aware of ways that you can safeguard and promote their welfare and behave in a manner that is appropriate to the age that you are working with.

Task 1

Write a report that describes different strategies that can be used by people working with children and young people to support their safety.

Task 2

Prepare a presentation that:

- Describes the different legislation, policies and procedures in place to safeguard children and young people.
- Explains and evaluates how procedures keep children and young people and those working with them safe.

Task 3

Write a leaflet that can be handed out to people working with children and young people that describes different strategies that can be used to ensure their own protection when working with children and young people.

Further reading

Lee, M. (1997) *Coaching Children in Sport, Principles and Practice*, Spon Press.

Useful websites

www.nspcc.org.uk/inform/cpsu/cpsu_wda57648.html
Videos and online articles the provide details of how to safeguard children in sport and how sports leaders can protect themselves while working with children

www.qcda.gov.uk
Information about the National Curriculum

41: Profiling Sports Performance

41.1 Introduction

Performance profiling is a straightforward method for individuals and teams to assess their physical, technical and mental strengths and weaknesses. Performance profiling involves the athlete deciding the physical, technical and psychological factors that they feel are most important to achieving their optimum performance. Then they rate their current position on each factor, in relation to what they consider to be their best possible performance.

It has become an important psychological tool in both sport and exercise environments. Performance profiling was devised by Butler (1989) and has developed through research in which he has been influential. Performance profiling is an application of personal construct theory (Kelly, 1955; Bannister and Fransella, 1986).

The key concept of personal construct theory is that each individual will 'perceive' the world and its events in different ways. The perception they make will involve them imposing a meaning on events and each individual has the freedom to choose whatever meaning they want. This theory proposes that people develop personal theories to make sense of themselves, other people and events in the world. The individual seeks to construct meaning by searching for repeated themes in the events before them and extracting the information they feel is important. Thus, personal interpretation provides meaning and understanding that may or may not reflect truth or reality.

Performance profiling gives the individual the opportunity to interpret their sporting performance in a way that provides meaning and reality for them.

By the end of this unit you should:

- understand the role and function of performance profiling in sport
- be able to determine the current sports performance of an individual
- be able to set targets for the future sports performance of an individual
- be able to review the sports performance action plan.

Assessment and grading criteria		
To achieve a PASS grade the evidence must show that the learner is able to:	To achieve a MERIT grade the evidence must show that, in addition to the pass criteria, the learner is able to:	To achieve a DISTINCTION grade the evidence must show that, in addition to the pass and merit criteria, the learner is able to:
P1 explain the role and function of performance profiling in sport		
P2 explain the different traits required for an individual to achieve excellence in their chosen sport		
P3 use performance profiling to assess the current sports performance of an individual, taking into account the performer's own profile of performance		
P4 describe the strengths of the performance and areas for improvement	**M1** explain the strengths of the performance and areas for improvement	**D1** critically analyse the strengths of the performance and areas for improvement
P5 assess the appropriateness of coaching techniques used during the profiling process, maintaining a coaching log		
P6 explain agreed targets with an individual to improve their future sports performance	**M2** justify the targets to improve future sports performance of an individual	
P7 devise an eight-week sports performance action plan for an individual, including contingency procedures for possible barriers to achievement		
P8 implement an eight-week sports performance action plan for an individual		
P9 use performance profiling to monitor and evaluate performance throughout the duration of the plan	**M3** adapt the plan to meet the changing needs of the performer	
P10 review progress and achievements, using evaluation criteria to describe the success of performance.	**M4** review progress and achievements, using evaluation criteria to explain the success of performance.	**D2** review progress and achievements, using evaluation criteria to analyse the success of performance.

41.2 Understanding the Role and Function of Performance Profiling in Sport

The Role of Performance Profiling in Sport

Developing Awareness

The main role of performance profiling is to enable the performer to develop awareness of what aspects of their performance are integral to their sport, and to prioritise which aspects should be regarded as the most important to their performance. These aspects can then be presented in an easy-to-understand visual format.

Promoting Opportunities

Due to the visual format of performance profiling, it presents the individual's perceived strengths and weaknesses, and thus clearly identifies which areas need to be worked on – opportunities to improve on these weaknesses can then be promoted.

Defining Goals

Although performance profiling is used as an alternative motivational technique to goal setting, it can also complement the process of goal setting, as goals are usually set to work on the weaknesses an individual perceives.

Building Relationships

Performance profiling is usually done in a collaborative manner, between the athlete and the coach or the athlete and the sport psychologist. This interactive process, which often involves open and honest discussion, can help the two parties come to a greater understanding of each other and what each thinks is important in performance.

Other Roles of Performance Profiling

Performance profiling can also be applied to achieve the following:

- Helping athletes to monitor changes in their performances and assess whether their training programme is achieving its desired outcomes
- Detecting any mismatch there may be between the individual and their trainer in terms of expectations and progress
- Helping the athlete to become actively involved in the process of assessing and evaluating their current performance level in their sport and their future expectations.

Functions of Performance Profiling

The main function of performance profiling is to provide a tool that helps athletes and teams to improve their sports performance, to motivate them and to direct their efforts at the appropriate activities to improve their performance. However, it also helps to quantify the perceptions that the coach and the athlete have about their level of performance and current standing on a range of the factors that contribute to successful performance. Training

Physical	Skill-related	Psychological
Aerobic fitness	Balance	Arousal control
Flexibility	Coordination	Anxiety/stress management
Muscular strength	Reaction time	Self-confidence
Muscular endurance	Agility	Concentration skills
Muscular size	Technique	Visualisation skills
Power		Positive self-talk
Speed		Mental toughness
Body composition		Aggression control
Stability		Competitiveness
Posture		Being a team player

Table 41.1 Physical, skill-related and technical factors that may contribute to individual performance

369

can be considered in a 'holistic' way because it is not just physical aspects of performance that are considered, but technical and psychological factors as well. This is where it can be more effective than goal setting, which tends to focus on two or three factors affecting performance, rather than looking at the whole picture.

Traits for Performance Excellence

Performance profiling can look at performance in its widest sense, and the individual athlete can then choose which factors influencing performance are most important to them. Table 41.1 looks at the possible physical, skill-related (technical) and psychological factors that could influence performance.

We need to add another category – that of technical and tactical, sport-specific skills needed to be successful in a sport (e.g. passing, tackling, heading

and shooting for a footballer). These technical factors are often presented separately to the physical, skill-related and psychological factors, as technical factors are underpinned by these factors.

Student activity 41.1 45 minutes P1 P2

Task 1

Explain the role and function of performance profiling in sport.

Task 2

Use the following table to choose five physical, skill-related, psychological and technical traits/factors that are important in achieving excellence in a sport of your choice. Then add an explanation of why these factors are important in your chosen sport.

Sport of your choice:

Physical	Skill-related	Psychological	Technical
1.	1.	1.	1.
2.	2.	2.	2.
3.	3.	3.	3.
4.	4.	4.	4.
5.	5.	5.	5.

Q Quick quiz 1

1 Summarise what is meant by 'performance profiling'.
2 Why is 'individual perception' central to performance profiling?
3 What benefits does performance profiling have over goal setting as a method of motivation?

41.3 Determining the Current Sports Performance of an Individual

Performance Profile

The performance profile is created by the following process, which is conducted between the coach and the athlete or the psychologist and the athlete. This will be done in the form of a consultation and will go through the stages set out below.

Stage 1 – Introducing the Idea

A period of time is spent introducing the process of performance profiling. The benefits and theory of performance profiling can be covered, and it is important to emphasise to the athlete that there are no right or wrong answers. What is important is what the athlete thinks and how they feel, and how this can improve their self-awareness of performance. It is often beneficial to show previous examples of performance profiles that have been constructed (although these should be anonymous to maintain confidentiality).

Stage 2 – Eliciting the Constructs

The process starts by asking the athlete what factors they think are important in their performance. They are asked to consider physical, skill-related, psychological and technical factors. This process may need some facilitation by the coach/psychologist, as the athlete may lack awareness of what is needed for an excellent performance in their sport. This is clearly dependent on their level of experience and knowledge of the sport. Table 41.1 could be used to help this process of eliciting the factors that we will now call 'constructs', as this is the term that Butler uses in his work.

The athlete should decide on around eight to ten constructs, which are then ranked from one to ten in the order that the athlete perceives their importance. They can be organised using the form provided in Table 41.2.

Stage 3 – Assessment

Once the ten constructs have been established, the athlete is asked to do three things:

1 Rate themselves on a scale of 10 per cent to 100 per cent, showing where their current level is on each construct in comparison to their best possible performance (100 per cent).
2 Rate from 10 per cent to 100 per cent to represent how far they would like to progress in each of the constructs.
3 Decide the order of each construct, from one to ten, where one is the construct most important to their performance and ten is the construct of least importance to their performance.

Trait/Construct	Percentage of current skill level compared to best possible performance	Importance of skill or attribute (rate in order 1–10)
	10 20 30 40 50 60 70 80 90 100	1 2 3 4 5 6 7 8 9 10
	10 20 30 40 50 60 70 80 90 100	1 2 3 4 5 6 7 8 9 10
	10 20 30 40 50 60 70 80 90 100	1 2 3 4 5 6 7 8 9 10
	10 20 30 40 50 60 70 80 90 100	1 2 3 4 5 6 7 8 9 10
	10 20 30 40 50 60 70 80 90 100	1 2 3 4 5 6 7 8 9 10
	10 20 30 40 50 60 70 80 90 100	1 2 3 4 5 6 7 8 9 10
	10 20 30 40 50 60 70 80 90 100	1 2 3 4 5 6 7 8 9 10
	10 20 30 40 50 60 70 80 90 100	1 2 3 4 5 6 7 8 9 10
	10 20 30 40 50 60 70 80 90 100	1 2 3 4 5 6 7 8 9 10
	10 20 30 40 50 60 70 80 90 100	1 2 3 4 5 6 7 8 9 10

Table 41.2 Performance profiling form (adapted from Burton and Raedeke, 2008)

Stage 4 – Utilising Results from the Performance Profile

Once the athlete has completed the performance profiling form (Table 41.2), the information can be transferred to the circular performance profile (Figure 41.1). This performance profile should have as many pie-shaped wedges as the athlete has constructs; the profile in Figure 41.1 has eight segments. The title of each construct (e.g. strength, speed, arousal control) and its number, to indicate its relative importance, should be written in the outer ring of the profile. Then, for each construct, the segments of the profile (each representing 10 per cent) should be shaded to show the current level (where the athlete is at). Then an arrow should be drawn to show the extent to which the athlete feels they need to improve (where the athlete wants to be). Figure 41.2 shows an example of a boxer's completed performance profile.

Once the results have been plotted, we are able to see the following:

● Their current rating
● The ideal level they would like to achieve.

From this circular performance profile, we are able to categorise the scores from each construct in the following way:

● Areas perceived to be strengths
● Areas perceived to be weaknesses
● Areas resistant to change.

If their current rating is above 5 and close to their ideal level, that is categorised as an area of perceived strength (e.g. reaction time); however, if their current rating and ideal rating are far apart, this is an area of perceived weakness (e.g. confidence). An area resistant to change is one where their perceived rating is low and their ideal rating is also low (e.g. aggression control). An area that is deemed 'resistant to change' needs to be investigated further, with the reasons for the resistance being investigated.

From this process, we are now able to discuss progress and develop options of how the athlete's scores can be improved. This process will inform the development of a coaching, physical training and psychological training programme. This performance profile may also help to inform the application of other techniques, such as performance profiling.

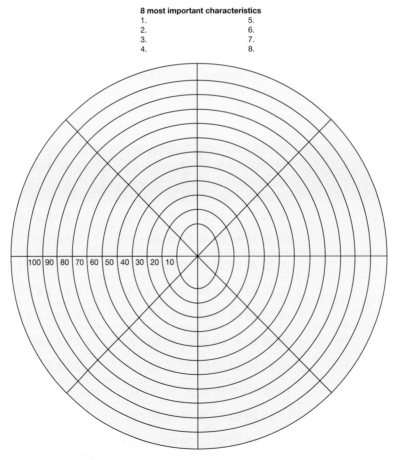

8 most important characteristics

1.	5.
2.	6.
3.	7.
4.	8.

100 90 80 70 60 50 40 30 20 10

Fig 41.1 Circular performance profile (from Burton and Raedeke, 2008)

8 most important characteristics

1. Strength   5. Confidence
2. Speed   6. Reaction time
3. Footwork   7. Aerobic fitness
4. Punches   8. Aggression control

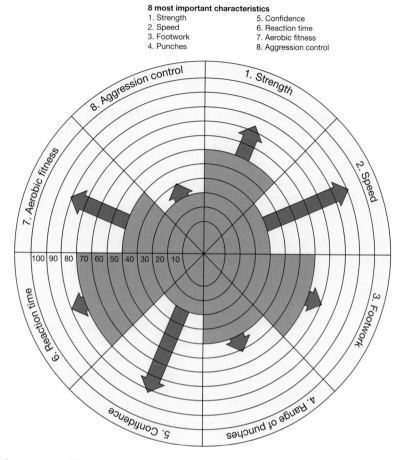

Fig 41.2 Circular performance profile of a boxer

Coaching Techniques

The interaction between the coach and the athlete as they work with performance profiles can be described as a form of 'coaching'. This coaching is different to the coaching that is done with regard to improving physical skills. This coaching is where one person helps and guides the other person towards making changes. This is described as a 'coaching alliance'. There are several facets to the coaching alliance, some of which are described below.

Support Mechanism

Performance profiling is used to support the work of a coach and to guide the development of the athlete by the coach. In this way, the development of the performance profile and subsequent analysis of improvements made using the performance profile act as a support mechanism between the coach and the athlete. Goals can be set that are directed at improving the areas of weakness. In particular, it would be beneficial if these goals were very short-term goals (e.g. weekly goals) that were set to enable the athlete take small steps towards improving the

areas of weakness on the profile. The setting of short-term goals, and their subsequent achievement or the failure to achieve them, can act as a basis for discussion between the coach and the athlete.

Recording Summaries

It is useful to make records of any meetings and discussions that are held between the athlete and the coach, as these will be useful in the review process that will occur later. These can provide proof that certain agreements have been reached and specific actions have been decided on in terms of how to improve the athlete's performance. The coach and the athlete may also become involved in 'reflective conversations', where the coach asks the athlete questions that trigger them to reflect on events that have happened in the past, what can be learnt from these events and how they can inform future action.

Communication

Effective communication between the coach and the athlete is vital in developing the effectiveness of the coaching alliance. Verbal communication can involve choosing the right words, which have the

373

same meaning to the coach and the athlete, using language that is of an appropriate level of technicality for the athlete, and presenting the language in the correct tone of voice to achieve the desired effect. Non-verbal communication involves the use of body language and gestures to back up the meaning of the message that is being presented.

Communication between the athlete and the coach may also be through the use of technology – email, text message and social networking sites. It is useful for the coach to adapt to the means of communication that the athlete feels most comfortable with, as that is likely to produce the most success.

Coaching Styles

The interactions between the athlete and the coach are open to different styles of coaching. The styles describe who makes the decisions in the process. At one extreme, the command style occurs when the coach decides what is to be done and then imposes their decision on the athlete. At the opposite end, the discovery style occurs when the athlete makes all the decisions. In between, the reciprocal style offers involvement from both parties. The process of performance profiling is based on the individual (in this case, the athlete) perceiving what they believe to be reality, and thus it is important to let the athlete have control over the decision-making process. In the process of goal setting, the most effective goals are those that are self-assigned (Erez and Kanfer 1983); the same applies to the process of performance profiling.

However, what happens if the performance profile that the athlete produces is unrealistic and bears no resemblance to reality? This is where the skill of the coach must be used to facilitate the process, using open questions to direct the athlete towards producing a more realistic picture.

Coaching Log

It is essential that the process of performance profiling is logged and recorded by both the coach and the athlete, although these may be separate documents. This can be done in several ways:

- Use of a diary to record the process
- Use of word-processing documents or an online storage system
- Development of a portfolio containing records of all relevant information.

Whichever method is used, it should contain the original performance profile and the subsequent profiles that have been developed at the review stages. Summaries of meetings and discussions, the actions that have arisen from meetings, the outcomes of the meetings and points for future discussion should all be noted.

The coach should make records of the different coaching techniques that are employed and their relative success or failure of each one. The success or failure can be judged by the outcomes that were produced. If the outcomes that arose were the ones that were intended, it may be concluded that that method of coaching/communication was successful.

Key learning points 2

- The performance profile is developed through a consultation.
- Eight to ten constructs are elicited by finding out what aspects of performance are most important to the athlete.
- Constructs are ranked according to their importance to the athlete.
- The athlete assesses each construct by giving a score for their current position and indicating their future position.
- Records of all meetings/interactions should be made so that they can be used in the review process.
- The coaching log can be a diary, portfolio or a collection of electronic documents.

Student activity 41.2   2 hours   P3 P4 P5 M2 D1

Task 1

Choose an athlete and then, using the four stages of the performance-profiling process, prepare a performance profile, using Table 41.2 and Figure 41.1.

Task 2

Describe (P4), explain (M1) and critically evaluate (D1) the strengths and the areas of performance as identified in the performance-profiling process.

Task 3

Assess the appropriateness of the coaching techniques that you used during the process of performance profiling and maintaining the coaching log. You will need to consider what coaching techniques you used and the success or failure of each of these techniques. Your response will include a discussion of coaching styles and methods of communication.

41.4 Setting Targets for Future Sports Performance of an Individual

Performance profiling and goal or target setting can be used as different techniques to influence motivation, or they can be used in conjunction with each other. In simple terms, performance profiling can provide the big picture of the athlete's current position and what he needs to improve on to achieve success; however, target setting can provide the smaller picture and fill in the detail that is needed for the athlete to improve. For example, our boxer in Figure 41.2 scored himself 40 per cent on the construct of aerobic fitness and indicated that he wanted to improve this to 80 per cent; however, there is no target to measure what 80 per cent would represent, nor is there any information on how the boxer will move from 40 to 80 per cent – we would call this the 'process' that is involved in progressing. Target setting can help to contribute further to the progress of the athlete by digging deeper into each construct and providing a clear target to achieve.

Outcome and Process Goals

Outcome goals are described as being the outcome that the individual would wish to achieve. For example, our boxer wants to improve his aerobic fitness, and the outcome that he may desire could be stated as follows: 'To not experience fatigue that will negatively affect performance during a fight'. This is not a perfect goal (we will examine the principles of goal setting later), but the outcome is clear. The outcome goal is often set over a long time period (long-term goal).

Process goals will reflect the processes that the athlete has to go through to achieve their outcome goal. For example, in order to improve their aerobic fitness, they may decide on the following process goals:

1 To run three times a week.
2 To complete a total of 20 km a week.
3 To attend two circuit training classes a week.
4 To undertake a nutritional consultation to help fuel aerobic activities.

These are the smaller steps that are taken to achieve the bigger outcome, and it is clear that process goals are usually set for the short term.

Short-term and Long-term Goals

These were alluded to in the previous section and are fairly self-explanatory. A short-term goal is usually a goal set to be achieved in a period of up to one month. Short-term goals could be set for as short a period as one session or one hour; they could be daily goals or weekly goals.

A long-term goal is therefore set for periods over one month, although sometimes goals between one and three months are called medium-term goals, up to lifetime goals. Long-term goals are often set for three or six months, season goals or one- to four-year goals (e.g. an Olympic athlete may set their goal to coincide with an Olympiad which is four years away).

SMART Principle of Goal Setting

In order to make goals effective, a series of principles have been drawn up; these are known by the acronym SMART. There are different descriptions of what SMART stands for, but for the purposes of this unit we will use the following terminology:

- Specific
- Measurable

- Achievable
- Realistic
- Time-constrained.

An 'S' is sometimes added to reflect the importance of goals being self-determined, as we commented on earlier in this unit. Also, we sometimes see SMARTER, with the 'E' standing for 'evaluated' or 'exciting' and the 'R' for 'recorded', which reflects the importance of using a log to record progress towards goals.

Now we can consider the outcome goal we set for the boxer in terms of the SMART principles: 'To not experience fatigue that will negatively affect performance during a fight'. The goal is specific in that we are clear about what the outcome would be. We can assume that it is achievable and realistic, but it is not clearly measurable – does the boxer expect to experience no fatigue or some fatigue, and how much fatigue would negatively affect his performance? We cannot truly measure whether the boxer has achieved their goal. Also, it is not time-constrained, as the boxer does not say when they would like to achieve this goal by. Finally, the goal is a negative one and aimed at avoiding something rather than achieving something, and this can add problems. Goals should be aimed at producing positive outcomes rather than avoiding negative ones, as the latter can promote negative thoughts.

This goal needs to be changed considerably to meet the SMART principles. The following questions need to be asked:

- What level of aerobic fitness is required to avoid fatigue that will affect performance?
- How can I measure aerobic fitness to show that I have achieved an appropriate fitness level to avoid fatigue that affects performance?

To measure performance, we need to put the outcome in terms of numbers. We could measure the boxer's aerobic fitness by either setting them a target to reach on the multi-stage fitness test or to achieve a certain time for a measured distance. Appropriate goals could include:

- To achieve level 14 on the multi-stage fitness test by 30 September 201_.
- To run 5 km in a time of 21 minutes by 30 September 201_.

Alternatively, a better measure of aerobic fitness for boxing could be developed that is specific to the sport of boxing.

Development of Attributes

Goals can be set to develop the performance of a range of attributes, or constructs as they are called in relation to performance profiling. Relevant attributes would include physical, skill-related, psychological and technical aspects of performance.

Barriers to Achievement of Goals

When setting goals, it is important to be realistic and realise that the road to achieving goals is not always smooth – there are often barriers in the way. With careful planning, the effect of these barriers can be minimised, but issues such as injury will lead to a rethink and reorganisation of goals.

Barriers that need to be considered will include:

- Occurrence of injury
- Illness
- Weather
- Shortage of equipment
- Availability of facilities
- Costs of training and travel
- Finance
- Changes in motivation level
- Anxiety and stress
- Lack of confidence
- Lack of social support
- Conflicting demands on time
- Factors outside of sport.

Periodisation

Periodisation is usually a term that is related to the athlete's physical training, whereby their training is divided up into blocks. These blocks of training are performed for a period of time to gain specific training adaptations. These blocks can be described as cycles, and the cycles are given different names to indicate their different lengths. A macro-cycle is the largest division of the training schedule and represents the overall training goal. The macro-cycle is broken down into smaller blocks called meso-cycles, which last between four and eight weeks. Within these meso-cycles there are smaller cycles lasting a day or a week, and these are called micro-cycles.

We can see that similar terminology could be applied to the setting of goals. The macro-cycle represents the long-term goal that the athlete is aiming to achieve. This is broken down into shorter-term goals, which represent the outcomes of each meso-cycle. In turn, the meso-cycle is broken down into smaller goals, the outcomes of which represent the purpose of each micro-cycle.

Sports Performance Action Plan

The sports performance action plan is the technique that is used to present the target setting in a clear, visual way, so that it is easily understood by the athlete. The action plan could look like the example shown in Figure 41.3.

Name of athlete: Sam Cox
Chosen sport: Boxing

Target/Goal: To be able to complete a 5 km run in 21 minutes by 30 September 201_.

Aims and objectives: The aim is to improve aerobic endurance to limit the effects of fatigue during a boxing match and to help improve recovery between rounds.

Process goals:
1 To run three times a week.
2 To complete a total of 20 km a week.
3 To attend two circuit training classes a week.
4 To undertake a nutritional consultation to help fuel aerobic activities.

Goal-related activity:
1 Record my progress in my training log.
2 Place my process goals on the wall of my gym.
3 Arrange to run with a training partner.

Training regime:
• 3 × runs a week
• 2 × circuit training sessions
• 6 × specific boxing training sessions.

Potential barriers to goal completion:
• Weather during the winter months
• Possibility of injury
• Time constraints due to family commitments.

Resources available:
• Support from my coach
• Financial support from the non-governmental body
• Access to alternative training facilities.

Methods of performance review:
• Changes to the performance profile
• Review of coaching log
• Monitor performance against short-term and long-term goals.

Fig 41.3 Sports performance action plan

Key learning points 3

● Outcome goals are related to the outcome that an individual wants to achieve, while process goals relate to the process of achieving outcome goals.
● Outcome goals are usually long-term goals, while process goals tend to be shorter-term goals.
● When setting goals, use the SMART principle to produce well-formed goals.
● There are many potential barriers to successful goal completion, including injury, illness, costs and time.
● A summary of the goal setting can be presented as a sports performance action plan.

Student activity 41.3   ⏱ **2 hours**   P6   M2   P7   P8

Task 1

Using the performance profile for the athlete that you prepared in Student Activity 41.2, set three targets for the athlete to achieve – these targets should be agreed with the athlete. To achieve P6, you need to explain each target, and to achieve M2, you need to justify your choices by giving reasons for the targets you have chosen. These targets are aimed at improving the future performance of the athlete.

Task 2

To achieve P7, you need to devise an eight-week sports performance plan for the athlete to address the targets that you set in Task 1. You also need to include any contingency procedures to help overcome any barriers that may be faced. In order to decide on the content of the training programme, you may need to look at Unit 4: Fitness Training & Programming and Unit 10: Sports Coaching. To achieve P8, you need to implement this eight-week training performance action plan with the athlete, and record the progress the athlete makes through performance profiling.

Q Quick quiz 2

1 How do performance profiling and goal setting complement each other?
2 Describe the principles that will contribute to the development of well-formed goals.

41.5 Reviewing the Sports Performance Action Plan

P9   P10   M3   M4   D1

Monitoring Performance

Using Performance Profiling to Monitor Performance Against Targets

The performance profile can be used to monitor the athlete's performance over any period of time. This monitoring can be done in different ways. The targets that have been set will improve the score on the constructs from the performance profile that have been identified as areas of weakness. Thus the athlete's performance on these constructs could be reviewed on a weekly basis, or they may choose two or three on which to focus on a daily basis, and give themselves a score reflecting how well they performed on a daily basis on those constructs. This daily focus can be compared to short-term goals, and focusing on something that is very short term can have a powerful effect, as the athlete has to do something about it immediately and would not be able to procrastinate.

Use of Assessments and Feedback

Feedback on progress can come from many sources. It can be provided immediately through discussions between the athlete and the coach, for example. However, quantitative assessments could be gained from other sources to see whether there is an actual change rather than one perceived by the athlete or coach. This may involve the implementation of fitness tests to see if there are any changes in the physical constructs, questionnaires to identify any changes in psychological changes or performance measures to quantify any technical changes.

Adapting the Action Plan and Adhering to the Action Plan

The main use of monitoring is to closely track the progress of the athlete and ensure that by the end of the eight weeks they have achieved their targets. If the feedback and assessments indicate that the athlete is not on track to achieve their targets, the action plan can be adapted appropriately. It may be that some of the barriers to achieving their targets are affecting progress, and thus the contingency measures suggested to overcome these barriers may need to be implemented. By making the athlete conscious that their progress is being monitored by the action plan, they will be more likely to adhere to it. This is mainly because they have someone that they are accountable to for their actions. For example, if they miss a session or eat poorly, there is someone there to pick them up for it rather than it going unnoticed. This accountability plays an important role in successful adherence.

Evaluation Criteria

Post-action-plan Performance Profile

The review of the success of the sports performance action plan is centred around the athlete filling in their new scores on the profile for each construct. The performance profile will now show their initial position, their desired position and their new position post-training. The athlete will also assess whether they have met the SMART targets that were set in conjunction with the process of performance profiling.

SWOT Analysis

Once the performance profile has been repeated, the coach and athlete can assess it using a SWOT analysis. In particular, they will look at their strengths and weaknesses post-training, but they will also look at the opportunities for the future and the threats to their future success.

Factors Affecting Performance

Once the performance profile has been reviewed, it is beneficial to have a period of brainstorming between the coach and the athlete to allow them to identify the factors that affected the athlete's performance over the eight weeks. This will provide an insight into the workings of the athlete, how they are motivated and what their likes and dislikes are. Above all, it can help inform future action through an analysis of past actions and outcomes.

Recommendations for Future Performance

Once the factors that affect performance over the eight-week period have been identified, the athlete and coach can start to look at preparing a development plan. They may ask the question: what is needed to improve performance over the next training period? Recommendations might include:

- Modification of the plan
- Development of skills and knowledge
- Future training courses.

In summary, the review process is vital to reflect on the successes or shortcomings of past performances and to inform the actions to take place in the future.

Key learning points 4

- The performance profile can be used to monitor the athlete's performance over a short-term and long-term period of time.
- When monitoring performance, physical and psychological assessments, as well as feedback from the athlete/coach, can be used as quantitative measures of change.
- Adherence to the action plan is improved due to the accountability that the performance-profiling process brings.
- The review of the performance profile can highlight the main factors that affect the athlete's performance.

Student activity 41.4 90 minutes P9 P10 M3 M4 D1

Task 1

Present your outcomes to show that you have reviewed the performance profile weekly and at the end of the eight-week period. Show how you have adapted the performance action plan to meet the changing needs of the performer.

Task 2

Review how the athlete has progressed, using the evaluation criteria that were developed in Task 1 to describe the success of the athlete's performance. To achieve M4, you need to explain why the athlete has been successful. To achieve D2, you need to analyse the factors that contributed to their success.

References

Bannister, D. and Fransella, F. (1986) *Inquiring Man: The Psychology of Personal Constructs*, Croom Helm.

Burton, D. and Raedeke, T.D. (2008) *Sport Psychology for Coaches*, Human Kinetics.

Butler, R.J. (1989) Psychological preparation of Olympic boxers, in Kremer, J. and Crawford, W. (eds), *The Psychology of Sport: Theory and Practice*, British Psychological Society.

Erez, M. and Kanfer, F.H. (1983) The role of goal acceptance in goal setting and task performance. *Academy of Management Review*, 8, 454–63.

Kelly, G.A. (1955) *The Psychology of Personal Constructs*, 2 vols, Norton.

Further reading

Burton, D. and Raedeke, T.D. (2008). *Sport Psychology for Coaches*. Human Kinetics.

Butler, R.J. (2000). *Sports Psychology in Performance*. Arnold.

Weinberg, R.S. and Gould, D. (2007). *Foundations of Sport and Exercise Psychology*. Human Kinetics.

Useful websites

www.teachpe.com

Extensive range of online resources that cover the major sports, their skills and techniques, coaching tips, and physiology and anatomy

www.instantanatomy.net

Free useful anatomy pictures and information, mainly from a medical viewpoint.

www.pponline.co.uk/encyc/sports-performance-analysis-coaching-and-training-39

Article detailing how sports analysis can help coaching and training

Index

383